_U. S. Grant_

For Doug,
with best regards,
Jean Raleigh
August 26, 2010

CIVIL WAR AMERICA

GARY W. GALLAGHER, EDITOR

THE UNIVERSITY OF NORTH CAROLINA PRESS

CHAPEL HILL

# U. S. Grant

AMERICAN HERO, AMERICAN MYTH

Joan Waugh

Designed by Kimberly Bryant

Set in Minion and Bickham Script by Tseng Information Systems, Inc.

Manufactured in the United States of America

The paper in this book meets the guidelines for permanence and
durability of the Committee on Production Guidelines for Book Longevity
of the Council on Library Resources.

*The University of North Carolina Press has been a member of
the Green Press Initiative since 2003.*

Library of Congress Cataloging-in-Publication Data

Waugh, Joan.

U. S. Grant : American hero, American myth / Joan Waugh.

p. cm. — (Civil War America)

Includes bibliographical references and index.

ISBN 978-0-8078-3317-9 (cloth : alk. paper)

1. Grant, Ulysses S. (Ulysses Simpson), 1822–1885.  2. Grant, Ulysses S. (Ulysses Simpson),
1822–1885 — Public opinion.  3. Grant, Ulysses S. (Ulysses Simpson), 1822–1885 — Influence.
4. Presidents — United States — Biography.  5. Generals — United States — Biography.  6. United
States. Army — Biography.  7. United States — History — Civil War, 1861–1865 — Public opinion.
8. Collective memory — United States.  9. Public opinion — United States.  I. Title.

E672.W38 2009

973.8′2092 — dc22

[B]

2009018550

Title page illustration: "Grant from West Point to Appomattox" (print) by Thure de Thulstrup
(Boston: L. Prang and Co., 1885). The commemorative portrait of Grant is surrounded by scenes
from his life (clockwise from lower left): West Point graduation, 1843; action at Chapultepec,
Mexico, 1847; drilling volunteers, 1861; directing action at Fort Donelson, 1862;
with Sherman at Shiloh, 1862; Vicksburg, 1863; Chattanooga, 1863; formal
acceptance as commander-in-chief, 1864; Appomattox surrender, 1865.

13 12 11 10 09    5 4 3 2 1

*for Caleb and Joshua*

# Contents

_U. S. Grant_

# Introduction

*U. S. Grant: American Hero, American Myth* is about a true hero, celebrated for his strength, his resolve, and his ability to overcome severe obstacles, banishing the possibility of failure. Grant once wrote, "One of my superstitions had always been when I started to go any where, or do anything, not to turn back, or stop until the thing intended was accomplished."[1] His feats attained mythic status and, like many national myths, contained elements of truth and exaggeration, accuracy and distortion. "As for Grant," a contemporary observed, "he was like Thor, the hammerer; striking blow after blow, intent on his purpose to beat his way through."[2] Grant's reputation is inevitably entwined with that of the Civil War, the tragic American epic. Like the president he served, Grant stood firm in his faith in a future beyond the terrible bloody battlefields of war. Unlike the president he served, Grant survived the war to implement their shared vision of reunion and emancipation, in a country still riven by dangerous crises. Inevitably, the hero stumbled, the myth was tarnished. Even heroes have flaws, and Grant's heroism lay not in his moral perfectionism but in his resolute determination to defeat those who would split the Union. This book traces the shifting legacy of general and president Ulysses S. Grant, who emerged from obscurity to claim victory as the North's greatest military leader.

Grant's meteoric rise between 1861 and 1865 was not necessarily predicted by his first thirty-nine years. An undistinguished student in the West Point class of 1843, Grant gathered honors in the Mexican War but later resigned from the regular army in 1854 under questionable circumstances. He took up farming in Missouri, failing to achieve success in that occupation and then in a number of others as well. When Lincoln asked for volunteers in 1861, Grant was clerking in his father's leather goods store in Galena, Illinois. He responded eagerly to his country's call and rapidly won fame in the Western Theater, scoring decisive and morale-raising victories at Fort Donelson, Shiloh, Vicksburg, and Chattanooga. Promoted to lieutenant general in early 1864, Grant assumed direction of the entire Union military effort in the last year and a half of the war. That spring, Grant and Confederate general Robert E. Lee waged titanic battles across the Virginia countryside, ending only when Grant crossed the James River and pinned Lee's army inside Petersburg. While Grant conducted the siege, his two principal lieutenants, Maj. Gens. William T. Sherman and Philip H. Sheridan took the war to Georgia and Virginia's Shenandoah Valley, conquering territory, defeating Rebel armies, and destroying large swaths of the southern countryside. Their combined victories vindicated Grant's strategic vision and guaranteed Lincoln's reelection.

The Union's greatest military hero was praised for the magnanimous terms of surrender he offered, and Lee accepted, at Appomattox Court House on April 9, 1865. Shortly afterward, he became the first four-star general in U.S. history, remaining as head of the army until 1868, when he was elected to the first of two terms as president on the Republican ticket. Grant's political career proved troublesome. Most Americans believed him to be honest and well meaning, but his administration was plagued by corruption and bungling, with the fragile promise of emancipation diminished by a white South redeemed. Immediately after leaving office, Grant embarked on a triumphal world tour that lasted for two years. Returning to live in New York City, he lost his entire savings in a disastrous business venture. To earn money, he agreed to write about his wartime experiences for *Century* magazine. Grant's articles proved so popular that he decided to write his memoirs, just as he was diagnosed with inoperable throat cancer. While sick with the cancer in 1884, he courageously completed *The Personal Memoirs of U. S. Grant*, which became a classic in American literature. Ulysses S. Grant died in 1885, the most famous of Americans both at home and abroad.

My project began with a question about Grant's life, and his death. Why did Grant's star shine so brightly for Americans of his own day, and why has it has been eclipsed so completely for Americans since at least the mid-twentieth century? Most Americans indisputably are ignorant of the *extent* of the once-powerful national legacy of Ulysses S. Grant. To recover that legacy, I advance two arguments. First, Ulysses S. Grant was a gigantic figure in the nineteenth century, and second, the memory of what he stood for—Union victory—was twisted, diminished, and then largely forgotten. Some may think that the first argument is axiomatic. It is not. The book explains how and why Ulysses S. Grant became the embodiment of the American nation in the decades after the Civil War, analyzing him as a symbol of national identity and memory, equal in stature to George Washington and Abraham Lincoln. More than a million and a half people watched his funeral procession in New York City on August 8, 1885, while the dedication of his massive tomb in Manhattan in 1897 drew a similar number. Even as the general was praised in lofty speeches at the end-of-the-century dedication, however, his reputation was subjected to a constant drumbeat of criticism from a small but influential group of ex-Confederate partisans; at the same time, eager reconciliationists from the North began to distort his legacy in pursuit of national unity.

Why is it important to recover the memory of Ulysses S. Grant as experienced by nineteenth-century Americans who forgave his transgressions in life and revered him in death? It is important because of the huge place that the Civil War still commands in American historical memory. Both a blessing and a curse, the war bequeathed a rich and riveting story of valor and idealism but also a distressing bequest of destruction, bitter recrimination, and racism. Grant had essential roles to play in the great national drama— his generalship was a major reason why the North won the Civil War, and his presidency determined in large part the success or failure of Reconstruction. Depending on one's point of view, he was either the brilliant leading U.S. military commander or the mediocre general who won by brutal attrition alone, either the stalwart and honest president trying to implement the northern vision of the war or the imposer of hated "Republican Rule" on a helpless, defeated region. In the long run, the image of the brutal general and inept president lingers most powerfully.

In his own era, the passage of time and memory softened Grant's image, so much so that by the 1880s and 1890s he symbolized national reconciliation as well as embodying Union victory. Grant was not a foe of sectional harmony—his famous 1868 campaign slogan summed up his sentiments, "Let Us Have Peace." But it was never peace at any price. In Grant's mind, reconciliation and the "Union Cause" had to be founded on southern acceptance of the victor's terms. The premier goal of the Civil War was to preserve the American republic and, after 1863, to fight for freedom and the destruction of slavery. To Grant, those were noble ideals worth fighting for, dying for, and remembering in distinctive ways. Thus, his "version" of sectional harmony rejected, indeed found repugnant, the increasingly popular idea that the Union and Confederate causes were "separate but equal," or even worse, that the two were somehow morally equivalent.

The book is divided into six chapters, with an interlude bridging the two halves of the text, and a brief epilogue. The first three chapters chronicle Grant's life and career, interweaving history, memory, and memorialization, introducing the man, the soldier, and the politician. Taken together, their purpose is to provide just enough of a background for understanding how and why Grant became a major American hero, and how and why Grant came to occupy such a huge place in American myth and memory. Reader, beware: my book employs the biographical method, but does not cover in depth Grant's military and presidential career. That is not its intent. For those who wish to pursue the details of Grant's life in full, I advise consulting one of the existing biographies or one or more of the specific, and numerous, studies of his career that have been published. Many of these works—indispensable to building my case for Grant's centrality in Civil War history and memory—are quoted in the text and cited in the footnotes.[3]

Chapter 1 covers the years from Grant's birth to the eve of the Civil War. Here I draw attention to competing myths regarding Grant's early life—the one of unrelieved failure that made his later success inexplicable, and the one showing that Grant experienced the ordinary struggles of life, which many Americans could relate to, that produced in him a strong character and resilience that boded well for his future and the future of the country. Chapter 2 surveys the war years, 1861–65, ending with Appomattox. Examining the most unmartial of military heroes, this chapter explains the origins and flowering of Grant's fame and mythic status. It chronicles his rise from an unknown officer in the war's distant Western Theater to lieutenant general commanding the United States armies (he was the first officer to receive that rank since George Washington). Unlike the aristocratic Washington, Grant demonstrated the potential of the common man in the democratic, free-labor North. Unprepossessing in appearance and deliberately eschewing military grandeur, Grant in 1865 enjoyed wild popularity and wielded immense power. Huge crowds greeted his every appearance, and Republicans and Democrats both sought his approval.

What did he do with that power? Chapter 3 picks up Grant's story from Lincoln's assassination and carries it up through 1877. As military commander overseeing Reconstruction policy, and as two-term president, soldier-statesman Grant struggled to define, defend, and preserve Union victory over an utterly defeated and embittered southern white population, as well as establish and protect freedom for ex-slaves. Grant admitted his lack of expertise in the humdrum but important world of national political machinations. "He had a true political sense, for he could see big things and big ideas," wrote one historian, "but he possessed no political cunning, he could not see the littleness of the little men who surrounded him."[4] His reputation suffered immense damage—some, but not all of it, deserved—from charges of policy failures, "cronyism," and abandonment of principle. An interlude offers a transition from Grant's life to his memorialization, focusing on his international tour, in which he symbolized for the world the powerful American nation that emerged from the Civil War. As a private citizen, Grant struggled to find a satisfactory place for himself and his family.

The three chapters that make up the second part of the text are the heart of the book, covering Grant's illness and death, the writing of his memoirs, his funeral, and the building of Grant's Tomb in New York City. Chapter 4 records the extraordinary national response to his agonizing death from throat cancer while struggling to complete his justly celebrated memoirs. *The Personal Memoirs of U. S. Grant* is a powerful example of an autobiography that swayed history, establishing its author as a principal architect in shaping the Civil War's historical memory. Chapter 5 reveals how both North and South seized on and singled out Grant's legacy as the magnanimous victor at Appomattox as *the* major theme of his commemoration. Here, Grant becomes a case study of the fascinating ways in which historical memory is shaped, and then reshaped, to suit current needs. Chapter 6 recounts the vigorous debate over Grant's monument and the proper way in which his memory should be honored. No Civil War monument was more spectacular or famous in 1897, and yet by the mid-twentieth century Grant's Tomb was a neglected site. A short epilogue sums up Grant's legacy in the twentieth century and the twenty-first.

This is the first scholarly work devoted to Grant's commemoration, adding a unique perspective to the existing literature. My primary research included reading scores of sermons, eulogies, memorial programs, newspapers, and pamphlets, in addition to letters, reports, diaries, memoirs, and scrapbooks; examining artifact collections and visual representations; and visiting Grant memorial sites. A few books and articles have focused on Grant's deathwatch, funeral, and monument, and will be cited accordingly. But those are pretty rare among Grant publications, virtually a cottage industry from the 1860s. As Grant emerged as a popular war hero, journalists scoured locales in Ohio, Kentucky, Missouri, Illinois (where he grew up and lived), and other states, interviewing family, friends, enemies, former teachers, soldiers, and current and former military colleagues. The insatiable search for Grant tidbits (fodder for friends and enemies, creating stories true and false) only intensified in the decades afterward, appearing in newspaper articles, forming the basis of campaign publications, providing color and content for hagiographies. More serious biographies by Hamlin Garland and Owen Wister appeared early in the twentieth century and were augmented later by scholarly studies published by Lloyd Lewis, Bruce Catton, William McFeely, and Brooks D. Simpson.[5] According to the 420-page *Ulysses S. Grant: A Bibliography*, books and journal articles about his overall military career, individual battles, or separate campaigns far outnumber biographies or political studies, confirming America's hunger for military history. Only a small part of the massive bibliography covers memory and memorialization, the major focus here.[6]

The recent rise of "memory studies" exploring the gap between history and memory, which expose a manipulated, "invented" past, has been nothing short of a phenomenon.[7] Cutting across disciplines, fields, centuries, and continents, scholars applying memory analysis have brought new insights to the ways in which the past has been used to justify present agendas, usually, but not always, servicing the needs of the nation-state. Traumatic events such as World Wars I and II, the Holocaust, Wounded Knee, and Gettysburg have been revisited using this method, illuminating the power of memory to create selective narratives that elevate some while leaving out others.[8] The work of Maurice Halbwachs, Jacques Le Goff, and Pierre Nora on collective memory versus individual memory, and on the tendentious relationship between history and memory, informs my discussion of Grant on several levels.[9] But I am even more indebted to scholars of American memory, such as Michael Kammen, John Bodnar, and David Blight, who have examined the different ways in which the American Civil War has been commemorated, and for whose benefit.[10] Long before memory studies became the vogue in academic circles, the story of the Civil War haunted generations of ordinary citizens, intellectuals, writers, and historians.

Remarkably, the literature on Confederate identity and memory, especially on the continuing power of the Lost Cause, flourished, while similar studies for the Union Cause lagged. Recent publications have begun to correct the imbalance, and my book will be added to the list. The end of the war brought forth a new nationalism, sanctified by death and embraced by a majority of northerners and southern freedpeople, that made the Union Cause just as much the subject of myth and reverence as the Lost Cause.[11] This has too often been overlooked in both recent academic literature (which finds fault with the powerful strain of American exceptionalism that characterized postwar nationalism) and in popular culture. Indeed, the moral seriousness and earnest patriotism that animated a sizeable portion of wartime northern society—soldiers and civilians alike—has seemingly been obliterated from current historical consciousness. So too has the immense prestige and respect once held by military heroes. "The generals stood as public symbols of the meaning of the conflict," wrote Philip S. Paludan. "They organized victory, shaping the choreography of the war, and no one more so than Grant."[12]

The record shows that ongoing debates about the war's causes, its prosecution, its leaders, and its consequences have captivated historians from several eras.[13] As a leading figure, Grant has been subjected to a great deal of scholarly scrutiny over the years, and rightly so. Some historians have questioned his laurels as a general, and others lament his failed Reconstruction policies. Grant's reputation is often determined by whether or not the historian in question believes that the Civil War was a "good war." A "good war" is defined as one that is entered into with just causes, one that is waged within agreed-upon rules, and one that does not violate the principle of "proportionality," that is, using only the force required to attain the goal. Generally, with notable and important exceptions, the Civil War, because of its outcome—preservation of the Union and emancipation—has been declared a good war, even among the generation of scholars that came of age during the protests against the Vietnam War.[14]

Nevertheless, in times of other wars, amid protests, historians are prompted to revisit the Civil War and its leaders and to find it lacking in moral righteousness.[15] They apply the standards of a "just" or good war to the Civil War and find that the conflict fails the test on every level. The causes were suspect, the rules violated by both sides, and proportionality flouted. A recent book singles out Grant's battle of Cold Harbor as one of the most egregious examples of the war's lawless brutality, leading not to glorious victory, but to "white supremacy and vengeful reconstruction."[16] For their active approval of waging relentless war on civilians, refusing prisoner exchanges, ignoring conditions in prison camps, and dismissing established rules of war when it suited them, Lincoln, Grant, Davis, Lee, and other leaders have been indicted by some scholars as war criminals. Harry Stout asserted, "The web of lies, suppression, and evasion that developed in the Civil War not only shock but also bear witness to the power of war to corrupt. . . . Nobody significant on either side was ever held to account. . . . They . . . created the environment in which unimaginable suffering and death took place."[17]

Some find it shocking that a devoutly Christian nation—ministers as well as their flocks—supported the war from beginning to end, justifying its worst excesses and glorifying its perpetrators. Most shocking, however, was the militarization of society. The leading generals of both sides became dangerously godlike in their prominence. "The North had a military icon of its own," Stout noted. "Grant was not only the army's greatest general but, more important, the people's great general. Only their religious-like faith in his leadership could have permitted the rivers of bloodshed to wash through their homes and towns. But they believed. Grant had a plan and now the fruits of that plan were evident."[18]

Can the messy business of any war be held to account by such impossibly high standards? Surely the question of intent must play a role in a moral judgment of the American Civil War. Grant did not intend for his assault at Cold Harbor to become a bloodbath, any more than Lee intended for Pickett's Charge to end in such a catastrophic manner. Grant believed that "to maintain peace in the future it is necessary to be prepared for war," yet he was no warmonger. He stated, "Although a soldier by education and profession, I have never felt any sort of fondness for war and I have never advocated it except as a means of peace."[19] Grant's bottom line was that the Civil War had to be fought, and won, by the United States: "The war was expensive to the South as well as to the North, both in blood and treasure, but it was worth all it cost."[20] Statements such as these, so seldom expressed by Americans now about our wars past or present, reflected the most common memory of the Civil War generation. It was a very different country then, and *U. S. Grant: American Hero, American Myth* seeks to illuminate that truth.

*chapter one*

# Youth

U. S. Grant sprang from humble, commonplace origins on the Ohio frontier. Huge statues and monuments in eastern and midwestern cities and scattered national military parks in Tennessee, Mississippi, and Virginia, most famously memorialize him, but serious students of the man should visit the obscure Ohio hamlets where he was born, reared, and educated in modest circumstances. The intrepid tourist visiting Point Pleasant can view Grant's birthplace, a twenty-square-foot wood structure. After his death, the house went "on tour" throughout the country before returning to its original location. Grant's boyhood home in Georgetown is also preserved, as is his father's tannery, and the two schoolhouses he attended.[1] Grant's memoirs highlight with pride his plain western "ordinariness," a trait that cemented a bond between himself and so many soldiers and citizens during his long public life. Countless contemporaries noted this characteristic of ordinariness, expressing it differently. A Herman Melville poem described Grant as "a quiet Man, and plain in garb," while Walt Whitman's Grant was "nothing heroic . . . and yet the greatest hero," and Mark Twain summed him up as "the simple soldier." For Union officer Theodore Lyman, the essential Grant "is the concentration of all that is American."[2]

The above descriptions flattered the Union hero, but they also contained a hard kernel of truth. Here, reality mirrored well-publicized myths spread by the earliest biographies but also vetted by later scholars.[3] Grant's family story echoed the experiences of a majority of his countrymen and -women who, like himself, grew up in rural small towns or on farms in the early national period of the nineteenth century. His experiences soon diverged from that majority when he left the Buckeye State and entered the United States Military Academy in New York in 1839. From that time, Grant gained an elite national perspective framed by his military education at West Point and his coming of age as a soldier in the Mexican War. Along the way, the shy youth from Ohio acquired strengths and developed talents that overcame his weaknesses of character and life challenges, setting the stage for his accomplishments. Grant's early failures perplexed many, and some prefer to ignore or disparage his first forty years, adding mystery to his myth. T. Harry Williams began an essay, "Grant's life is, in some ways, the most remarkable one in American history. There is no other like it." Williams added next, "His career, before the war is a complete failure."[4] Always, Grant retained his commonplace demeanor, puzzling even his closest friends who sought to understand his particular great genius. His great friend and comrade William T. Sherman said, "Grant's whole character was a mystery, even to himself."[5] Historian Bruce Catton remarked, "He looked so much like a

GENERAL GRANT'S LOG CABIN, FAIRMOUNT PARK, PHILA.

One of Grant's humble abodes on public display (author's collection)

completely ordinary man, and what he did was so definitely out of the ordinary, that it seemed that as if he must have profound depths that were never visible from the surface."[6] Is Grant really so much of a mystery? Surely, a glimmer of the "depths" of Grant's personality can be discerned through an examination of his youthful influences and, just as surely, provide the key to his later fame.

## Origins

Grant stated, "My family is American, and has been for generations, in all its branches, direct and collateral."[7] Matthew Grant, his earliest ancestor, came to Massachusetts in 1630; direct descendants went to Connecticut, then to Pennsylvania, and his immediate forebears ended up in the Western Reserve. The ability and desire to pack up and move somewhere else when failure struck or ambition beckoned was part and parcel of what ordinary white Americans considered their right. So too was the expectation and hope that one of those moves would result in an improvement from their previous lives. Many failed; but many succeeded. Character traits such as self-reliance, self-control, and thriftiness became associated with doing well in the country's burgeoning commercial economy. It was a time that afforded opportunities for poor, propertyless men to improve their condition. Jesse Root Grant was a shining example of such men.[8]

In the year of his son's birth, 1822, Jesse was already known as an ambitious and hard-working young man on the rough-hewn Ohio frontier. His own father, Noah, a captain in the Revolutionary War, was neither ambitious nor hard working. Instead he had a reputation for drifting and drinking. Noah left Connecticut, tried his luck in Pennsylvania, and ended up in 1799 living in Deerfield, Ohio, with his second wife, Rachel, and their seven children. Rachel's sudden death in 1805 broke up the family and eleven-year-old Jesse was alone in the world. Local families hired him to do chores and provided him with room and board. Then, Judge George Tod of the Ohio Supreme Court and his wife took pity on the loquacious teenager and included him in their family circle. From the Tods, a grateful Jesse received security, warmth, and encouragement for his future. By sixteen, Jesse had determined that the fastest route to independence was to master a trade. He chose wisely. He would be a tanner, someone who made leather from rawhides. A good living could be gained selling leather, providing a growing population with shoes and saddles and other desirable products.

Like most young men at the time, Jesse started at the bottom of his profession, first toiling in a local concern and then working as an apprentice at the tanning factory of his older half-brother, Peter, across the Ohio River, in Maysfield, Kentucky. Jesse was reunited with family members (Peter and his wife had taken in Noah and the two youngest Grant children) for the five years of his apprenticeship. Jesse had earlier received six months of schooling, "but his thirst for education was intense."[9] He loved to read, seizing the opportunity to do so in the evenings, after a hard day of labor. At twenty-one, he attained his full height of nearly six feet and was ready to go out on his own.

Slave-state Kentucky did not suit him, and he returned to Deerfield, and Ohio. His first real job was working in Owen Brown's tannery. He lived with the Browns, who reputedly operated a station on the Underground Railroad. They had a son named John, later the abolitionist comet whose 1850s bloody rampages in Kansas and at Harpers Ferry, Virginia, helped to start the Civil War. According to U. S. Grant, Jesse often ruminated about John Brown in later years. "Brown was a boy when they lived in the same house," his son wrote, "but he knew him afterwards, and regarded him as a man of great purity of character . . . but a fanatic and extremist in whatever he advocated."[10] Jesse's carefully accumulated savings were wiped out when he fell seriously ill from malaria. Fully recovered a year later, he started over in Point Pleasant, in Clermont County, Ohio, and soon impressed the small community with his steady industry. Anxious to start a family, Jesse courted a young woman whom he wanted to marry in the nearby town of Bantam.

Hannah Simpson was from a prosperous farming family with recent roots in Pennsylvania. Her parents, John and Sarah Simpson, had moved to Clermont County in 1819 with their four children. Quiet and plain, the twenty-three-year-old Hannah attracted her prospective suitor, who described her as an "unpretending country girl, handsome but not vain."[11] John and Sarah believed that twenty-seven-year-old Jesse would make a fine husband and a good provider. Although he was still an employee, he planned to own his own factory within a few years. Hannah and Jesse received her parents' consent, and they were married in June of 1821.

## Georgetown Days

Their first child was born on April 27, 1822, in a tiny rented two-room house high on a bluff above the Ohio River, beside the tannery where Jesse worked in Point Pleasant. The baby's rather odd name, Hiram Ulysses, was the result of a compromise forged between mother-in-law Sarah Simpson and Jesse (who both favored Ulysses, after the Greek military hero of mythic status) and Hannah and the rest of her family. Soon enough, Hiram was dropped and the little boy commonly called "Ulysses" (sometimes shortened to "Lyss"). Grant's own preference may have been for his original birth name. His schoolbooks revealed that he wrote "Hiram U. Grant" on the front pages.[12]

Jesse sought a livelier commercial venue and moved his family a short distance east to Georgetown, Ohio. Georgetown was a small village set back about ten miles from the river in Brown County. The village was surrounded by forests of oak, walnut, and maple trees and flanked on two sides by large creeks. The outer land was settled by farmers who grew corn and potatoes in the rich earth. To a large extent, both the farmers and townspeople came from the southern states of Kentucky and Virginia, distinguishing the Grants as proud "Yankees." Quickly, Jesse bought land, established his own tannery business, and built a modest but pretty two-story brick house. Over the years, the Grants had five more children: Samuel Simpson (1825), Clara Rachel (1828), Virginia Paine (1832), Orvil Lynch (1835), and Mary Frances (1839). The succession of babies guaranteed that Hannah would not have too much time to spend with Lyss. As a result, he enjoyed an unusual independence while growing up. "I had as many privileges as any boy in the village, and probably more than most of them," Grant recalled.[13]

Years afterward, reporters asked townspeople to assess Hannah's influence on her famous son. One observer commented: "Ulysses got his reticence, his patience, his equable temper, from his mother," while another put

Grant's birthplace in Point Pleasant, Ohio, as presented for young patriots. A large part of Grant's appeal, as general and as president, rested on his "common" roots, portrayed in countless representations such as this one from a children's book. (Elbridge S. Brooks, *The True Story of U. S. Grant* [Norwood, Mass.: Lothrop, 1897])

it more simply: "He got his *sense* from his mother."[14] A spare, undemonstrative, religious woman, Hannah rarely engaged in superfluous conversation. She preferred to stay within the confines of her domestic responsibilities, and there is no doubt that she took her maternal duties seriously. People noted that Ulysses was always clean and neatly dressed; the girls seemed to like him. He was described as nice and polite, and a good listener. Unlike many of his friends, he reputedly never swore. "He was more like a grown person than a boy," remarked a classmate.[15] Clearly, Ulysses imbibed well the values taught by Hannah. He admired her spirituality, although he declined to share it. She was pious, but not an "enthusiast." Ulysses was never baptized and felt no pressure to become a church member. His son, Jesse Root Grant, described his unchurched father as a "pure agnostic," adding that "I never [heard] him use a pious expression."[16] Hannah did make sure that the family attended services every Sunday at the town's Methodist church. In general, Ulysses's parents were fairly easygoing with their children. Although demonstrable tensions existed, particularly between Jesse and Ulysses, later a grateful son paid tribute. "There was never any scolding or punishing by my parents," he wrote, and there is much contemporary evidence confirming the accuracy of his statement.[17]

Jesse and Hannah prospered in Georgetown. The source of their prosperity was tanning, but Jesse added to his holdings by buying a farm. Children were expected to work, and Ulysses was no exception. He was a quick learner and eager helper, and at the tender age of five he already displayed the beginnings of his uncanny affinity with horses. By the time he was seven he was hauling wood for his father's shops and at age eleven was strong enough to plough by himself. Ulysses grew up hating the sight and smell of his father's factory, reeking of blood from slaughtered animals and the tannic acid used to cure the hides. One time, working beside Jesse, he said, "Father, this tanning is not the kind of work I like. I'll work at it though if you wish me to, until I'm twenty-one; but you may depend upon it, I'll never work a day at it after that."[18] He much preferred helping on the family's farm. Ulysses recounted those days with pleasure, and he especially enjoyed any and all work that involved managing horses, "such as breaking up the land, furrowing, plowing corn and potatoes, bringing in the crops when harvested, hauling all the wood, besides tending two or three horses, a cow or two, and saving wood for stoves, etc., while still attending school."[19]

Despite his family responsibilities, Ulysses was sent at age six to one town school and at age eight to another. Public education was not free, and day schools charged a modest "subscription" fee. Both parents valued education, particularly Jesse, who felt keenly his own lack in that area. He wanted his son to have all the advantages that had been denied to him. The Grant sitting room eventually boasted an impressive library of thirty volumes, and Jesse encouraged all his children to read often. At times a fidgety learner, Ulysses still remembered: "I never missed a quarter from school from the time I was old enough to attend till the time of leaving home."[20] One of his teachers assessed him as an average student but noted that his "standing in arithmetic was unusually good." At age twelve, his time in the village school ended when Jesse decided to act on his ever-growing conviction that Ulysses should obtain a better education and, with that education, a brighter future, elsewhere.

In 1834, Ulysses was a study in contrasts. He was clearly his father's favorite. That favoritism carried a burden for a boy who was small for his age and more like his reticent mother in personality. He also suffered from severe bouts of fever and ague, although he recovered his health fairly rapidly. Jesse's boasting about his son's limitless prospects brought forth many snickers among townspeople, who speculated openly that quiet shy Lyss was nothing special and might even be "slow." Some of their children joined in the taunting, calling him "Useless" and making life hard. "Boys enjoy the misery of their companions," Grant observed, "at least village boys in that day did."[21] Ulysses was no loner, however. How could he be? On the Grant side alone he had numerous cousins, many of whom he knew and played with growing up. He also had plenty of friends among the "village boys," enjoying with them the usual activities of the time—fishing and swimming in the summer and ice skating in the winter. His parents, Grant recalled, offered "no objection to rational enjoyments, such as fishing, going to the creek a mile away to swim in summer, taking a horse and visiting my grandparents in the adjoining county."[22] As also was the custom, he learned to handle a gun, winning praise for his marksmanship but refusing to kill animals for sport or food. Jesse's pride in the boy he called "My Ulysses" may have been exaggerated, but clearly his son exhibited unusual talents.

One example is the facility Ulysses exhibited in controlling the horses so indispensable to his father's business. His skills were soon admired outside of his family, and neighbors regularly hired him to break or train colts or tame a particularly troublesome horse. Often a crowd gathered to watch him work with horses in the courthouse square. He earned extra money in other ways, too, with Jesse's approval. Many times, Ulysses conveyed visitors by horse-drawn wagon or buggy to nearby as well as farther destinations, at least once making a trip of more than 200 miles to Toledo, Ohio. He saved his money and was able to buy a horse that he had his heart set on.

And then there is the famous horse-trading story recounted so vividly by the sixty-two-year-old dying man in his memoirs and repeated lovingly in so many works on Grant, usually called "The Horse Trade."[23] This is how it goes. Ulysses longed to possess a beautiful colt owned by a Mr. Ralston. Jesse offered him twenty dollars for the horse, but Ralston held out for twenty-five. "I was so anxious to have the colt, that after the owner left, I begged to be allowed to take him at the price demanded," wrote Grant. His father agreed, but with one stipulation. Ulysses should bargain first, just in case he could buy the colt for a lower price. "When I got to Mr. Ralston's house, I said to him, 'Papa says I may offer you twenty dollars for the colt, but if you won't take that, I am to offer you twenty-two-and a half, and if you won't take that, to give you twenty-five."[24]

A bemused Ralston collected his full price, much to Jesse's chagrin. "The story got out among the boys in the village, and it was a long time before I heard the last of it," Grant concluded ruefully.[25] His presentation elicited sympathy but invited a more complex reaction. True, his father shamed him,

Hannah and Jesse Grant (Library of Congress)

and the neighborhood boys teased him unmercifully. In Grant's retelling, however, the exchange was honorable and legitimate, even if it lost his father a few dollars. As Grant pointed out, the horse was worth the twenty-five dollars, and soon made even more valuable after rigorous and expert training. Thus, the consequences were temporarily hurtful, but in the long run the experience shaped the man who was respected far and wide for his personal honesty. Shortly after the incident, Jesse delighted his son by making Ulysses a "regular" wagon driver, responsible for a daily wood haul.[26]

Jesse also tutored his son about the world outside of Georgetown. He was not only a leading businessman in the community but also an outspoken commentator on current political issues. A former Jacksonian Democrat, Jesse embraced the Whig Party in the 1830s, liking its probusiness platform and commitment to free labor. When his close friend, the popular Democrat Thomas R. Hamer, ran for Congress, Jesse favored the Whig candidate. The two ended their friendship abruptly, with regrets on both sides. Jesse was a voracious reader of the *Georgetown Castigator*, the local newspaper, and contributed articles regularly. An avid public speaker, he joined several debate societies that flourished in the 1830s and 1840s. Jesse's loudly broadcast "Yankee" antislavery positions alienated many in the strongly Demo-

An idealized "Ulysses at Work." Through such images, the mythic story of the hard-working boy from Ohio who "saved the Union" was built, and then secured. (Rev. P. C. Headley, *Fight It Out on this Line: The Life and Deeds of Gen. U. S. Grant* [Boston: Lee and Shepard, 1885])

cratic, prosouthern town. Jesse faced opposition over his abolitionist positions among his numerous relatives in Kentucky and other southern states and even within Hannah's family, many of whom later supported the Confederate cause. Jesse must have enjoyed some respect, however, as voters elected him mayor of Georgetown in 1837.

Ulysses evidently did not share Jesse's political bent; nor did he wish to follow him in business. He did mention to Jesse that he had given some thought to being a farmer or river worker. Jesse brushed aside these suggestions as unrealistic. Instead he enrolled Ulysses in Richeson and Rand's Academy, a private school in Maysville, Kentucky. Ulysses boarded with his Uncle Peter's widow and enjoyed the experience of living in a bigger, more bustling town than his own. The dutiful boy attended the school, whose superior qualities were not always apparent. Instead he found himself "going over the same old arithmetic which I knew every word of before." His greatest achievement, Grant remembered, was in grammar, where he learned, "a noun is the name of a thing," until finally, "I had come to believe it."[27] Paying for Ulysses's education strained the growing Grant family's budget, and the bad effects of the financial panic of 1837 ended his brief period away from Georgetown. Happily, Ulysses returned home to his favorite haunts; unhappily his return was short-lived when, in the fall of 1838, he was packed off to school in Ripley, Ohio. There, the well-known abolitionist minister John Rankin had established a Presbyterian academy for the sons of ambitious fathers. It was during this time that Jesse hatched a new plan for Ulysses's future.

Georgetown resident Jake Ammen had recently graduated from West Point, the national military academy in New York. The Grant and Ammen families shared many things, including a deeply felt animus toward slavery. Jesse counted Jake's father, David Ammen, as a good friend. He was one of the few townsmen with whom Jesse agreed politically. The two socialized often, and their children played together. When Ulysses was seven, Jake's younger brother, Daniel, two years Ulysses's senior, saved him from drowning, cementing a lifelong friendship. Both boys looked up to Jake and admired his uniform. Upon Jake's return to Georgetown, Jesse consulted with him about the possibility of sending Ulysses to West Point, where a first-rate education was free to the students. He knew that the military academy curriculum emphasized engineering and mathematics, the mastery of which would guarantee his son a solid preparation for a useful profession. Best of all, Jesse found out that most West Pointers left the army after a few years of service to return to civilian life with no stigma attached. Jesse's mind was made up. Ulysses would go to West Point.

Two obstacles had to be overcome before Jesse's dream would become a reality. The first was the need to secure an appointment from Representative Thomas Hamer, his estranged friend. Jesse swallowed his pride and wrote a formal letter asking Hamer to recommend his son for a place at the U.S. Military Academy. To Jesse's great delight, Hamer responded positively, agreeing to the request. The procedure required that the sponsor fill out the application papers. Hamer did so expeditiously, hesitating only when asked to write out the candidate's full name. His first name certainly was Ulysses, Hamer thought, but what was his middle name? Hamer guessed that it must be Hannah's family name; hence the official West Point records showed that "Ulysses S. Grant" would be arriving with the class of 1839.

The second obstacle was Grant himself. Jesse claimed that Ulysses was initially enthusiastic. But that claim could not survive the light of day. Grant wrote down for posterity the shocking conversation with his father. "Well," Jesse proclaimed, "I believe you are going to receive the appointment." "What appointment?" a bewildered Ulysses asked. "To West Point. I have applied for it," was the response. "But I won't go!" replied his son. Shortly afterward, as Grant recalled, "He said he thought I would, and I thought so too, if he did."[28] Obviously, Lyss's protests fell on deaf ears. Jesse proved implacable in his firm belief that West Point was the best place for Ulysses to fulfill his destiny. Undoubtedly, he was right, although Grant later summed up his feelings by stating, "A military life had no charms for me."[29]

Early in the morning of May 15 Ulysses left his parents' house for the long trip to New York. Pictures reveal a clear-eyed seventeen-year-old who seemed more boy than budding man. Weighing 117 pounds and just barely surpassing the West Point minimum height of five feet (he would grow to his full height of five feet, eight inches while at the academy), Ulysses was slight, with attractive features almost feminine in repose. Looks were deceptive, as he was also sturdy and strong, befitting a youth who could work as hard as most men. On his way to Ripley via stagecoach to board a steamer to Pittsburg, he lugged his belongings in the standard trunk for traveling, a gift from Hannah and Jesse. Unknown to them, the brass tacks reversed Ulysses's initials, reading "U. H. G." instead of "H. U. G." He might be a country bumpkin in the eyes of his future West Point colleagues, but he knew enough to switch to Ulysses Hiram Grant, saving himself untold misery but further complicating the saga of his changing name.

"My life in Georgetown was uneventful," Grant observed many years later.[30] Perhaps it could be considered so. Yet Grant's own rich, if short, narrative of his early years suggests quite the opposite. From a small town in Ohio emerged a self-reliant, active, resolute, serious, determined young man. His family provided him with the freedom to succeed, and the freedom to fail. He did both, and his successes and failures strengthened and shaped his character and intelligence. The greatest gift he received was Jesse's imagining a vast and wonderful future for his son, however improbable, and and then scheming and sacrificing to make that future possible. Now it was up to Ulysses to prove himself worthy of his father's hopes.

### West Point Cadet

If in the spring of 1839 Ulysses was unhappy about the prospect of four years far away from home, he was nevertheless thrilled to be traveling across the country. The trip from Georgetown to West Point was no small undertaking in those days. Grant traveled the distance by every method of available transportation—stagecoach, steam and canal boats, and train—but was especially excited by the last, describing the eighteen-mile-per-hour speed as "annihilating space."[31] His itinerary included enjoyable visits to Philadelphia and New York City. In the former, Grant spent some time with a cousin, who characterized her younger relative as "a rather awkward country lad, wearing plain clothes and large, coarse shoes as broad at the toes as at the widest part of the soles."[32] He arrived at West Point on May 29, 1839, promptly passing his admission examinations.

At check-in, Grant was apprised that his official name was now "Ulysses S. Grant," and no protest on his part would alter that fact, although for a while he continued to sign documents "U. H. Grant."[33] Older cadets joked that the new cadet's initials really stood for Uncle Sam, after the popular patriotic symbol of the young country. From that time, his classmates called him Sam, adding one more name to the list. Much later, a fellow Ohio cadet, William T. Sherman, said (not unkindly) of his friend, "A more unpromising boy never entered the Military Academy."[34] It may have appeared that way to Grant as well. He immediately felt backward and clumsy next to the majority of cadets, most of whom hailed from the more "civilized" northeastern and, in lesser numbers, southern states.

In the year of Grant's arrival, the United States Military Academy was just thirty-seven years old. Its purpose was to train and educate an officer corps for the country's small army. Cadets would benefit from a rigorous *national* education intended to protect the security of the United States. They also forged professional and personal relationships based on patriotic and martial ideals that knitted the diverse land more closely together. Located above the Hudson River on a beautiful and isolated site about fifty miles north of New York City, West Point offered a demanding four-year curriculum that included the military arts, science, literature, art, and civil engineering.[35]

Examinations were held twice yearly and determined the ranking of each cadet, which in turn determined the students' postgraduate assignment. Highly ranked graduates, such as the Virginian Robert E. Lee (1829) and the Pennsylvanian George B. McClellan (1846), were assigned to the engineering corps, while the majority served in the infantry. The cadets' adherence to the strict regulations imposed on personal behavior also influenced ranking. Punishment for infractions was swift, ranging from demerits to dishonor and dismissal. Lee graduated with no demerits, but most students, including Grant, accumulated a hefty number. Unlike many of his classmates, however, Grant never received demerits for frequenting the local tavern; rather, he was known for his relative abstemiousness.[36]

The worst time for the new cadets was the first year, when a combination of hazing by upperclassmen and introduction to the Spartan regimen made life routinely miserable from the time they rose at 5:00 A.M. to lights-out at 10:00 P.M. Some students left, or were banished, but Grant survived, and adjusted. "There is much to dislike but more to like," he stated firmly. "I mean to study hard and stay if it be possible."[37] Despite his pledge, Grant proved to be a middling to poor student, although he earned top grades in mathematics. Never a particularly enthusiastic scholar of military strategy and tactics, he lacked reverence for the Napoleonic theory of warfare that so captivated his professors. "I did not take hold of my studies with avidity," Grant admitted. His biggest problem surfaced in drill, where his tone deafness made parades a painful experience. Listening to music was never agreeable for Grant, who joked about his "tin ear." He said, "I know two songs, one is 'Yankee Doodle' and the other is not!"[38]

There were also unexpected pleasures and a few achievements at West Point, "this prettiest of places," as he described it, expressing his unabashed delight at the beauty of the dramatic landscape.[39] Grant quickly discovered the school's excellent library and spent many hours alone reading novels, including those of Sir Walter Scott, James Fenimore Cooper, Washington Irving, and Frederick Marryat.[40] The art master Robert Walker Weir brought out in the young cadet a heretofore hidden talent for drawing. Grant's subjects — rendered in watercolor, oil, and sketches — were finely drawn copies of Italian landscapes, skillful and delicate depictions of local landmarks, and sympathetic portrayals of the local Native American tribes.[41]

"Sam" did not spend all his time reading books. The Academy's secluded setting fostered friendships as well as competition among its cadets. Grant enjoyed acquaintances with students (and future Civil War generals) such as the aforementioned Sherman, George H. Thomas, Richard S. Ewell, William S. Rosecrans, James "Pete" Longstreet, Lafayette McLaws, Don Carlos Buell, Daniel H. Hill, John Pope, and Winfield Scott Hancock. His close circle of friends included William B. Franklin of Pennsylvania, Frederick T. Dent of Missouri, and Rufus Ingalls of Maine. Within his first two years of college, Grant's experiences differentiated him dramatically from his family and friends back in Ohio. His cohorts were now a cosmopolitan group representing a diverse range of economic, educational, and regional backgrounds. West Point trained his mind and body, enabled him to indulge his love of literature, and gave him the opportunity to develop his artistic abilities. Still quiet and shy, Grant proved to himself and his family that he

One of two
glorious memories
of West Point
(Elbridge S. Brooks,
*The True Story of
U. S. Grant* [Norwood,
Mass.: Lothrop, 1897])

could measure up to the standards of one of the nation's best educational institutions.

A cadet's second summer allowed time for a ten-week visit home with family. Having achieved his full height, Grant eagerly looked forward to his homecoming in June 1841, which would take place at the family's new house in Bethel, Ohio, ten miles west of Georgetown. In 1839 Jesse's business interests had prospered and expanded to such an extent that he opened a new tannery in Bethel, which offered excellent water transportation. To sell his products, Jesse bought a leather goods store in the growing town of Galena, in northwestern Illinois. Everything seemed to be going well for the Grant family, and Ulysses thoroughly relished his hard-won vacation, basking in the warmth of his proud family. Jesse signaled his approval of his

Second Lieutenant "Sam" Grant (Library of Congress)

son's achievements with a gift of a handsome colt. Jesse and Ulysses agreed on a simple plan for the remaining two years and just beyond. Work hard, graduate with dignity, perform his service in the army, and then resign to pursue a financially rewarding career. Ulysses thought he might apply for a job as a college mathematics teacher.

### Graduation and Julia

By the spring of 1843, much of the plan had succeeded. Grant graduated twenty-first in his class of thirty-nine, not the highest ranking, but hardly the worst. As he looked back on his West Point years, for Grant two events elevated his experience above his modest expectations and his middling record. Early on, he witnessed a grand review of the cadets by General Winfield Scott, commander of the U.S. Army. A dazzled Grant pronounced the six-foot-five, handsome and elegant hero of the War of 1812 "the finest specimen of manhood my eyes had ever beheld."[42] He remembered feeling that one day he might occupy Scott's exalted position. Rightly fearing ridicule from his peers, Grant kept the presentiment to himself. The second occasion came just before graduation, when he put on a splendid riding exhibition in front of the entire student body. The cadet who was described as a "clumsy, slow gaited, heavy footed lad" on the parade ground regularly astounded fellow students with his displays of horsemanship. Longstreet called him "the most daring horseman in the Academy."[43] Grant was disappointed when his application for the Dragoons (the Cavalry) was denied due to lack of space. Still, the future seemed promising when Brevet Second Lieutenant Grant was assigned to the Fourth Infantry Regiment at Missouri's Jefferson Barracks in St. Louis County.

After a visit to his family in Ohio, Grant traveled to Jefferson Barracks to begin his military career. A good friend and former roommate, Fred Dent, lived only a few miles away, with his parents and seven siblings, and Grant quickly paid his respects. The lonely young man became a frequent guest at the spacious Dent residence, called White Haven. Fred was named after his father, Frederick F. Dent, a St. Louis merchant who preferred the title "Colonel" although he held no official military status. The Colonel, a slaveowner, despised all Whigs and abolitionists, a fact that did not prevent Grant from becoming a favorite with the family. Ulysses was especially fond of the eldest daughter, eighteen-year-old Julia, who had been educated at an elite boarding school in St. Louis. A romance was struck between the two. Grant expert John Y. Simon has written of Julia: "Noticeably cross-eyed and rarely considered beautiful, she was nonetheless a belle. Willful and charming, she captivated Lieutenant Grant."[44] Julia possessed a trim figure, a sparkling personality, and a warm heart, qualities that attracted her ardent suitor. Even more tantalizing was Grant's growing realization that marriage with Julia Dent offered a lifetime of an unconditional love that had so far been denied him.

When the Fourth Infantry received orders in May 1844 to leave for Louisiana, Grant "mustered up courage" and asked for Julia's hand in marriage. Julia agreed, but stipulated that their engagement be kept secret for a while.[45] Her mother, Ellen Dent, expressed warm feelings for her daughter's suitor, but Colonel Dent was unenthusiastic about the prospect of his daughter's marriage to a poorly paid junior-grade officer in the U.S. Army. Julia felt she needed time to win over her father before making a public declaration. Indeed, most of their five-year courtship and engagement would be conducted in the midst of Grant's long absences in army service. Grant suffered evident frustration with the state of affairs, as is shown in two of many sweetly plaintive letters to his intended. "Julia can we hope that you[r] pa will be induced to change his opinion of an army life?" he asked after hearing that Colonel Dent had once again refused to give his blessing to their marriage. A bit later he wrote, "My happiness would be complete if a return mail should bring me a letter setting the time—not far distant—when I might 'clasp that little hand and call it mine.'"[46] Grant's parting lines usually went something like this: "Your Devoted Lover"; "Most Truly and Devotedly Your Love, Ulysses"; or "I am most devotedly your Ulysses S. Grant." His letters to Julia revealed a tender, anxious lover unafraid to express his emotions freely. A relieved Grant finally secured Julia's father's approval of their engagement during a brief leave in the spring of 1845.[47]

## The Mexican War

Personal matters aside, Grant was troubled by his new assignment, which took him to "Camp Salubrity," outside of Natchitoches, Louisiana. During his earlier family visit, he had witnessed his father's passionate declamations over the 1844 presidential election, which pitted Tennessee Democrat James K. Polk against the venerable Kentucky Whig senator Henry Clay. The issue joined was expansionism. Whigs like Jesse opposed the United States' annexation of Texas on the grounds that it would only enlarge and benefit the slaveholding section of the country. The Democrats, on the other hand, urged war against Mexico unless America's rights—in Texas and along the border—were respected. Polk's election validated Whig fears: Texas was formally annexed in 1845. Mexico claimed that annexation was a declaration of war, sparking war fever in the United States as tensions rose higher and higher over the disputed land.

The advantages or disadvantages of American expansionism were hotly debated within the context of a popular doctrine called "Manifest Destiny." Its many enthusiasts contended that the United States was destined to rule over the entire North American continent. Commonly held assumptions of Anglo-Saxon superiority and the exceptionally beneficial nature of the country's democratic-republican institutions provided powerful justification for American domination from the Atlantic to the Pacific. The expansionists' cause was aided by Mexico's instability, corruption, and poverty—and by the fact that its vulnerable western provinces were lightly governed and even more lightly settled. Earlier, Polk had offered to buy the territory for $30 million, but Mexican leaders rejected his overture out of hand.

Grant's unit was part of a defensive force massed by the federal government, initially to prevent the Mexican government from interfering with Texas annexation. As 1844 turned into 1845, the dispute shifted to a tense debate over the precise boundary between the two countries. Mexicans argued that the Nueces River marked the border, while Americans contended that the Rio Grande, further south, was the proper demarcation. The latter, of course, would add more land for the United States. Whig critics continued their drumbeat of opposition against the blatantly expansionist policies of the Polk administration, charging that the prosouthern president was provoking a war over national boundaries to appease the "Slave Power."

Brushing aside critics' objections, and expressing concern that Mexico might attack Texas, Polk ordered General Zachary Taylor to lead the cleverly named U.S. Army of Observation from Louisiana to occupy the disputed land between the Rio Grande and the Nueces. In May 1846 a Mexican force attacked the U.S. troops, with fighting continuing for two days. Under Zachary Taylor's command, Grant and the Fourth Infantry saw action at Palo Alto on May 8 and Resaca de la Palma the day after. Soundly defeated by a smaller force, the Mexicans drew back south of the Rio Grande. "The victory for us has been a very great one," Grant declared.[48] In response to the outbreak of hostilities, an outraged Polk claimed that Mexico "has invaded our territory and shed American blood on American soil."[49] This was a pretext, as he had decided on war already. Polk asked for and received from Congress an official declaration of war on May 13, 1846.

From the beginning, Polk's war divided the nation along regional and political fault lines. Whigs remained skeptical of the administration's motives. As Grant later wrote, "We were sent to provoke a fight, but it was essential that Mexico should commence it."[50] Illinois congressman Abraham Lincoln, intending to cast doubt on Polk's motives for going to war, sarcastically asked the president to locate precisely *where* U.S. sovereignty had been violated. Southerners, on the other hand, exhibited strong support. That support came in the form of manpower. The regular army, with its few thousand professional soldiers, could not fight by itself against a much larger Mexican force. The administration called on male citizens to volunteer in regiments formed by states. By far the most enthusiastic response came from the slaveholding region. The states nearest to Texas contributed 49,000 citizen soldiers, while those along the eastern seaboard sent only 13,000.[51]

While in Mexico, Grant wrote many letters to family and friends, relating incidents and episodes that interested him, revealing his skills as "one of the most articulate of all American soldiers."[52] The missives show him to have been alternately excited, fascinated, and horrified by his first experience of warfare. How did he find the reality of battle? "Although the balls were whizing thick and fast about me I did not feel a sensation of fear until nearly the close of the firing a ball struck close by me killing one man instantly," he confided to Julia. In June 1848 he wrote to a friend, "You want to know what my feelings were on the field of battle! I do not know that I felt any peculiar sensation. War seems much less horrible to persons engaged in it than to those who read of the battles."[53] Grant rarely provided details of his own battlefield actions, but he remained cool and composed under fire. This ability enabled him to think and act decisively while others around him were rendered incapable of movement. For Grant, as for most of the West Point–trained officers, the Mexican War was truly a "school of battle." He passed the first test of soldierhood with flying colors.

A series of swift and decisive victories silenced political opposition and made the war, if not its origins and consequences, popular on the home front. New Mexico and California were conquered easily, but still the Mexican government refused to surrender. In the main theater of action Taylor readied his troops to subjugate central Mexico. In late September, his army captured the crucial city of Monterrey. Americans suffered a numerical disadvantage at Monterrey, just as they did in almost every clash between the two armies. But, as Grant explained, "There is no force in Mexico that can resist this army. . . . The Mexicans fight well for a while, but they do not hold out. They fight and simply quit."[54] At Buena Vista, in February 1847, Taylor's force of 6,000 men fought against General Antonio López de Santa Anna's 20,000 troops in a battle that the Americans won as a result of the Mexican general's hasty retreat. "Rough and Ready" Zachary Taylor was now a great hero in the eyes of the American public, winning the presidency on the Whig ticket in 1848. Lieutenant Grant much admired Taylor's informal manner and his gritty determination "to do the best he could with the means given him."[55]

Grant had ample opportunity to observe and analyze Taylor's applied military strategy from a safe position. Since the summer of 1846, Grant had served as regimental quartermaster. His duties included managing the regiment's horse and mule trains, keeping records, and ordering equipment as necessary. He quickly proved adept at managing logistics but protested "a duty which removes me from sharing in the dangers and honors of service with my company at the front."[56] At the battle of Monterrey in late September 1846, a frustrated Grant left camp to view his unit's action. His arrival coincided with an order to attack, and, as he later recalled, "lacking the moral courage to return to camp—where I had been ordered to stay—I charged with the regiment."[57]

During the fighting, the regimental adjutant was killed, and Grant replaced him temporarily, remaining at the front. The next day, hard fighting resumed. Ammunition was running low, and Grant volunteered to ride through the streets for help. To protect himself from heavy fire, Grant expertly flattened his body against the side of the horse, riding swiftly to deliver the message successfully. With victory secured, Grant received kudos for his act of bravery, including recommendation for promotion to brevet first lieutenant.[58] Shortly afterward, Grant's Fourth Infantry was transferred along with a substantial part of Taylor's army to join a naval operation converging in early March just below Veracruz. Winfield Scott was mounting a separate campaign to march up the National Road and capture Mexico City. Veracruz fell to heavy U.S. bombardment by late March. The port city was organized as a base for army operations, and Grant was extremely busy with his quartermaster and commissary duties. Although unglamorous, his firsthand experience and knowledge about logistics and supplies came in handy in later times. Still, he complained, and wrote glumly that "I had little to do except to see to having the Pork and Beans rolled about." By April 8, Scott and his army of 14,000 were marching inland. The commander was determined to move quickly to avoid the dreaded disease of yellow fever that sickened and killed many of his troops. Grant echoed Scott's concern to Julia: "We will all have to get out of this part of Mexico soon or we will be caught by the yellow fever which I am ten to one more affraid of than of the Mexicans."[59]

Justly celebrated, Scott's campaign was not without problems in execution. Delays in supplies and reinforcements and an army diminished as volunteers flocked home left Scott unable to protect his supplies at Veracruz. He boldly cut loose from his base, living off the land. He employed night marches and ordered a series of frontal attacks, pushing his men, who gained in morale and skills, to move swiftly. Following the Spanish conqueror Hernán Cortés's route, Scott's small army outflanked and outfought the beleaguered Mexicans during the spring and summer of 1847. Ably assisted by such West Point–trained officers as Robert E. Lee, P. G. T. Beauregard, and George B. McClellan, Scott was close to taking Mexico City by early September. Grant would remember his commanding general's adept movements and dashing generalship in another war.

Mexican forces scrambled to protect the capital and mounted a defense at Chapultepec. Scott stormed the formidable fortress on September 13. During the fighting that followed, Lt. Sam Grant demonstrated quick thinking under pressure. Noticing enemy fire behind a low wall, Grant ordered a few soldiers to assist him in dragging a howitzer up to a church belfry, from which they successfully shelled the line. Once again, his actions were noted and praised highly. Once again, he was recommended for promotion, this time to brevet captain. On September 14, 1847, the victorious North Americans entered Mexico City's beautiful plaza and established military rule. The war was over, and a relieved Ulysses wrote Julia, "Since my last letter to you four of the hardest fougt battles that the world ever witnessed have taken place, and the most astonishing victories have crowned the American arms." He added solemnly, "But dearly have they paid for it! The loss of officers and men killed and wounded is frightful."[60] Grant was accurate on the latter count both for Scott's campaign and for the war as a whole. Overall, a total 5,800 soldiers died on the battlefield, and 11,500 perished from disease. The price tag was equally startling. The United States spent more than $100 million, making the Mexican War the costliest to that point in American history.[61]

While representatives from the United States and Mexico discussed the terms of a peace treaty, Scott's army remained in Mexico City. Quartermaster Grant spent eight long months in the capital, enjoying the sights, sketching pictures, and doing some traveling as well. He even started a bakery, earning extra money for the needs of his regiment. The little business boomed, prompting him to brag, "In two months I made more money for the fund than my pay amounted to during the entire war."[62] Grant's time in Mexico ended when the Treaty of Guadalupe Hidalgo was ratified on May 30, 1848. The provisions of the treaty are well known. The Rio Grande was established as the boundary between Mexico and the United States. In addition Mexico ceded 529,000 square miles of new territory for $15 million in compensation, plus the assumption of 3.5 million in debts Mexico owed U.S. citizens. The new territory included California, New Mexico, and parts of modern-day Colorado, Utah, Nevada, Wyoming, and Arizona. It was official: Americans had won an imperial war with relative ease and expanded their power and influence at the expense of a weak southern neighbor. The United States Army demonstrated strength in leadership, in soldiers, and in technology. The last proved especially important in building the momentum toward victory, as railroads, steamboats and telegraphs were all used effectively to aid campaigns.

President Polk—whose legacy included the expansion of executive war powers—joined ordinary people in welcoming home soldiers with cheers and praise. The national consensus proved to be short-lived, as debates soon raged over whether the vast new lands would be open to settlement by slave-

owners or reserved for free labor. Grant personally never shared in the jubi-
lation that animated so many of his fellow Americans in regard to the war
effort. Later, he contended that the spoils did not justify the moral and political cost of the war. It is thus worthwhile to evaluate with some precision
Grant's early military experience.

Grant's remembered resistance to army life must not be accepted simply
at face value. In retrospect, Jesse's decision to send Lyss to West Point was
a wise one. During his four years at the U.S. Military Academy (1839–43),
Grant endured and matured. And in his early career, he flourished even if
he did not enjoy the "military life." A few years after graduation, Lieutenant
Grant fought in the Mexican War, where he showed courage, uncommon
common sense, and dash and skill, winning congratulations and promotion.
His first brush with war had a profound impact on him. The knowledge that
he was a good, maybe even a great soldier gave him a quiet self-confidence
that increased over the years. His physical strength was bolstered as well.
He marched along dusty roads, fought mosquitoes as well as men, endured
sweltering heat, and accepted stoically but with a heavy heart the terrible
loss of friends and comrades.

Grant not only demonstrated a talent and taste for fighting; he also gained
insight into the psychology of the officers whom he would later fight with,
or against, in the Civil War. In addition, the young officer analyzed carefully
the contrasting leadership styles of the two commanding officers, and great
heroes of the Mexican War, Winfield Scott and Zachary Taylor, finding the
latter's casual style more to his liking than the proper style of the former.
From both, he imbibed lessons on waging successful military campaigns
with a largely volunteer army, untrained, hard to discipline, and prone to
desertion. Most tellingly, Grant noted the aggressive role that slavery played
in the origins of the Democratic-led war, as well as its consequences. Grant
later stated, "The Southern rebellion was largely the outgrowth of the Mexican war."[63] The political fallout from the Mexican War triggered events in
the 1850s leading to secession, and to civil war in 1861. Grant's ultimate judgment was harsh. "I regard the [Mexican] war as one of the most unjust
ever waged by a stronger against a weaker nation." He continued, "It was
an instance of a republic . . . not considering justice in their desire to ac-
quire additional territory."[64] From Grant's vantage point, the Mexican War
opened up a Pandora's Box that would not be closed until Appomattox in
April of 1865. Notwithstanding his objections to the military and to the war,
from 1839 to 1848 Grant transformed from a physically immature boy into a
man and a professional soldier. His nascent character traits of tenacity, de-

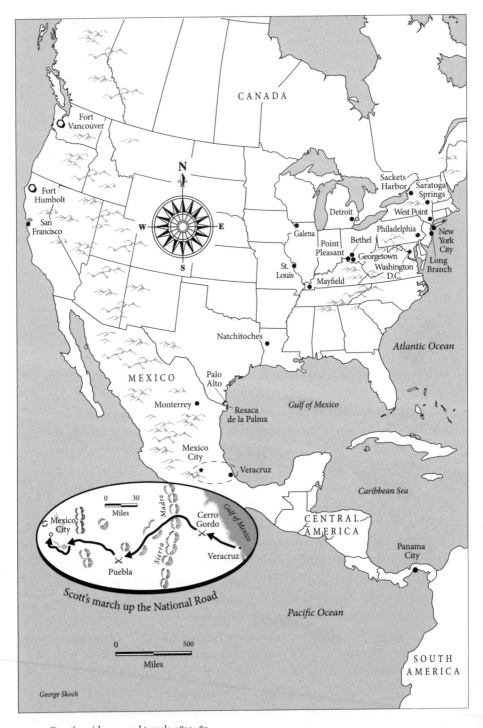

Grant's residences and travels, 1822–85

termination, and fortitude took firm root, predicting his remarkable ability to "triumph over adversity," an ability he summoned often in the future.[65]

## Marriage and Early Army Life

In June 1848 Grant stopped first at White Haven on his way home from the Mexican War. His primary goal was to marry his beloved Julia Dent, and signs were finally auspicious on all fronts. Finalizing the details of the wedding would have to wait until Grant saw his family in Ohio. Jesse followed his son's unit during the war and broadcast his battle exploits widely. During his visit, Grant was frustratingly reticent about his own role but pleased to be the center of the townspeople's attention. His personality became animated as he related with lucid and captivating detail the Mexican battlefield. He seemed to possess a gift for storytelling. "How clear-headed Sam Grant is in describing a battle! He seems to have the whole thing in his head," declared an admiring comrade.[66] Even Jesse's strongest detractors had to admit that his son was impressive.

Ulysses's future was undoubtedly a topic of conversation with his father. Ulysses weighed his options and, contrary to his father's preference, chose to remain in the peacetime army. The drawbacks were many. Low pay, frequent moves, and a slow pace of advancement led the list. Not yet apparent were other disadvantages. The federal government was planning to downsize the army to a number even lower than before the Mexican War. Headquartered in Detroit, Michigan, the Fourth Infantry would be stretched to the limit. Grant weighted the positive factors more heavily. The army offered monetary security and job stability. He needed both at that moment. Leaving the military and looking for another position could delay his marriage indefinitely, and that Grant could not bear. At least he and Julia would be together.

Ulysses and Julia were married in the Dent's St. Louis house on August 22, 1848, in a Methodist ceremony described as a "sweet, old-fashioned wedding."[67] James Longstreet, a close friend from West Point and the Mexican War, and a cousin of Julia's, was Grant's best man and, like two of the groomsmen (Cadmus M. Wilcox and Bernard Pratt) would fight for the Confederacy. The proslavery cast of the wedding party might have explained the absence of Ulysses's family from the event. For the couple, however, the union was a fortunate one. Julia and Ulysses remained deeply in love throughout their marriage. Their mutual attraction, both physical and emotional, was apparent for all to see. Of the two, historian Bruce Catton observed "that they shared one of the great, romantic, beautiful loves of all

American history."[68] Close family friend Adam Badeau remarked of the couple, "No more beautiful domestic life can ever be known."[69] The core of their love was their unstinting commitment to each other's happiness in good times and in bad. This commitment was based on loyalty and a genuine mutual admiration. No one can read Grant's letters to Julia without coming away impressed by his passionate need for her. Few doubt that her passion equaled his.

Yet, at first glance, their relationship seemed perilous. Raised in the slave state of Missouri, Julia took the labor of black house servants and nurses for granted, not giving up the few slaves she owned even during the war years. She was proud of her southern heritage and never publicly commented on the glaring contradiction between her belief that slavery was a benign institution and her husband's role in smashing that institution. In addition, Julia expected, and desired, a comfortable, genteel lifestyle. How would she fare married to an itinerant army officer from a family whose background and sensibilities were so different from her own? It helped that Julia possessed grit and gumption and an almost perverse optimism. It also helped that she thought her husband handsome and brilliant, and his future, and hers, very promising. If everyone else was surprised by Ulysses's rapid elevation to head of the northern army during the Civil War, the ever-loyal Julia was not. She basked in his reflected glory but, as always, served as his ballast and confidante. No other wife of a prominent general spent more time with her husband on campaigns, where he welcomed, and needed, her presence.[70]

Julia had ample preparation for the rigors of her later wartime role beginning in 1848 when she accompanied Ulysses to a remote army post in Madison Barracks, near Sackets Harbor, New York. The lot of an officer's wife was usually filled with uncertainty and loneliness. Many chose not to live with their husbands, preferring to stay with their parents or other family members.[71] Julia promised Ulysses that whenever possible she would go with him. She made their first little homes together happy ones, first in New York and then in Michigan. Their happiness increased many times when she became pregnant. For health reasons the post doctor advised Julia to return to the Dents' home in St. Louis to give birth, and that is where Frederick Dent Grant was born on May 30, 1850. "And no one," Julia recalled, "ever had such a fine, great boy." After her recovery, Julia wrote, "Ulys came to St. Louis for his family and took us back to Detroit, where we remained until next May."[72]

The family's domestic bliss lasted about two years and revolved around church, children, and friends. In 1851 Julia announced that she was expecting another baby. Time passed pleasantly. Ulysses worked as the regimental quartermaster—a task he found more tedious than demanding. Familiar work and domesticity abruptly ended in the spring of 1852, when a large portion of the Fourth infantry was ordered to the Pacific Coast, which required a larger military presence. Grant would act as the quartermaster. It was not the first, and would not be the last, time his fate was determined by events outside his control. The Treaty of Guadalupe Hidalgo had not yet been signed when gold was discovered in California. The Gold Rush of '48 drew many thousands of immigrants from the continental states and around the world. After a contentious debate, Congress admitted California as a free state as part of the Compromise of 1850. The compromise imposed limits on the expansion of slavery but protected the institution where it existed. It pleased no one, inflamed sectional grievances, and set the stage for the dissolution of the Whig Party and the rise of the Republican Party by the mid-1850s.[73]

## Alone on the Pacific Coast

Grant's immediate concerns were personal. The trip to the West Coast— by boat—was long, arduous, and dangerous. Julia's condition prevented her from accompanying him; she returned to St. Louis indefinitely. It was unclear when they would see each other again. Just before his departure Grant wrote: "Dear Dear Julia, We sail directly for the Isthmus. I never knew how much it was to part from you and Fred. until it came to the time for leaving."[74] Sailing from New York Harbor on July 5, 1852, on the overcrowded steamer *Ohio*, Grant prepared for an extremely hot and uncomfortable trip to the tropics. His duties assuaged temporarily his intense homesickness. The *Ohio* was sailing toward the Isthmus of Panama, the most expeditious route between America's East and West Coasts. Briefly, the plan was to cross the isthmus by train, by boat, on mules, and on foot, arriving at Panama City and the Pacific Ocean, and then board another ship for San Francisco. Under the best of circumstances, the trip was a difficult one.

Shortly after landing, Grant's commanding officer, Colonel Benjamin Bonneville, was informed of a serious outbreak of cholera. A significant number of the *Ohio* passengers were already stricken. The colonel decided that he would lead the healthy majority of the regiment across the isthmus and ordered Grant to follow with the regiment's baggage and with the remaining passengers—soldiers and civilians—men, women, and children, many of them sick with cholera. No doctor, little food, and no other officer accompanied them. Grant recalled, "I was left alone with the sick and the

A hero in Panama (Elbridge S. Brooks, *The True Story of U. S. Grant*
[Norwood, Mass.: Lothrop, 1897])

soldiers who had families." His travails included failure of transportation,
problems with supplies, navigating through tropical rainstorms, mud-filled
roads, and frequent stops to bury the dead. "July is at the height of the
wet season, on the Isthmus," Grant explained. "At intervals the rain would
pour down in streams, followed in not many minutes by a blazing, tropical
summer's sun." But he persisted, finally securing the needed travel arrangements, pushing his pathetic group and its baggage on toward Panama City.
Finally, they arrived, only to be told that they were in quarantine until the
disease abated. An old ship served as hospital, and Grant tirelessly tended
to the sick. "He was like a ministering angel to us all," one grateful patient
recalled.[75]

In September, Grant and the surviving members of the Fourth Infantry
sailed to San Francisco, arriving in early September. Grant never forgot the
searing trauma of this trip. "About one-seventh of those who left New York
harbor with the 4th infantry on the 5th of July," he said, "now lie buried on
the Isthmus of Panama or on Flamingo island in Panama Bay."[76] Enduring
death, disease, and daunting obstacles, Grant showed the same gritty deter-

mination and intelligent leadership that first surfaced in the Mexican War. While Grant struggled in the jungles of Panama, Julia had given birth to their second son, Ulysses S. Grant Jr., in July. She was staying temporarily with Jesse and Hannah at the Grant family home in Ohio, and the baby's place of birth in the Buckeye State gave rise to his nickname, "Buck." Grant did not find out about the birth of his second child until two months after his arrival at Fort Vancouver in Oregon Territory (now Washington State). Staying at the fort for one year, he shared quarters with former West Point roommate Rufus Ingalls. His duties as post quartermaster were light and included fitting out the expeditions that regularly sallied forth from the fort. Military records indicate that his work was performed satisfactorily, but his homesickness returned with full force. From the fall of 1853 to the summer of 1854 Grant was miserable, lonely, and increasingly desperate for his family. He knew the cure for what ailed him. He needed to bring Julia and his sons to live with him. But his paltry salary was hardly enough to sustain his own needs in the overpriced economy, with just a few dollars left over to send home.

Grant turned his energies to solving this problem. He lived in a part of the country where men were making fortunes, not in gold, but in selling goods and services to those who flocked to California. Grant could easily engage in some extracurricular activities in his off time, and the possibility of earning extra money made him optimistic. He was impressed with the bounty of the Oregon Territory: "So far as I have seen it it [sic] opens the richest chances for poor persons who are willing, and able, to work . . . of any place I have ever seen." His letters to Julia cheerfully detailed various enterprises. "I am doing all I can to put up a penny not only to enable you and our dear little boys to get here comfortably," he wrote to her, "but to enable you to be comfortable after you do get here."[77]

With business partners, mostly fellow officers, Grant embarked on a number of moneymaking schemes. The ideas were good, the outcomes bad. San Franciscans were desperate for ice. He and his associates shipped 100 tons and were anticipating the profits when they heard that their shipment had been delayed, allowing others to benefit from the scarcity but not them. Other ventures included growing and harvesting different crops, raising hogs, and operating a boardinghouse. "I have been quite unfortunate lately," he reported to Julia. "The Columbia is now far over its banks, and has destroyed all the grain, onions, corn, and about half the potatoes upon which I had expended so much money and labor."[78] A possible success amid the failures was thwarted when one of his partners absconded with the funds. Grant proved to himself and to everyone else that he lacked Jesse's moneymaking talents. Two lifelong traits emerged in compelling relief—impetuousness and impecuniousness. Unable to budget his income, Grant proved an easy mark to friends in need, often loaning them his last few dollars. Credulous to a fault, he found it hard sometimes to distinguish between honest and dishonest ventures. In short shrift, Grant found himself owing money, and being owed money that he never collected. No matter how hard he tried, the goal of reuniting with Julia remained achingly out of reach. "I am almost crazy sometimes to see Fred. I cannot be separated from him and his Ma for a long time."[79] As the months turned into years, Grant applied for leave and transfers; all were denied.

In 1853 he was promoted to full captain. The higher pay grade made little difference to his circumstances. "A cook could not be hired for the pay of a captain," he observed ruefully. "The cook could do better."[80] The promotion brought another posting. Grant reported to Fort Humboldt, California, on a freezing day in early January 1854. He was the new commander of the F Company of the Fourth Infantry. It would be hard to imagine a worst set of circumstances than the ones that greeted him at the tiny remote outpost. "My dear Wife," he cried out to Julia, "You do not know how forsaken I feel here!" His new duties left him with too much time on his hands. "I do nothing here but set in my room and read and occationally take a short ride on one of the public horses."[81] He despised his commanding officer, Major Robert Buchanan, whose petty cruelties made his life more miserable every day. So miserable in fact that, according to the familiar story, Grant took to drinking regularly, and one day neglected to attend to his work. Buchanan allegedly seized on the opportunity to get rid of his least favorite officer. He told Grant to resign or face a court-martial. Although friends allegedly advised him to fight the injustice, Captain Grant officially resigned in a letter to Major Buchanan dated April 11, 1854.

## Was U. S. Grant a Drunk?

As John Simon remarked, "much that happened in the period 1852–54 remains obscure, including the combination of factors impelling Grant's resignation from the army."[82] Buchanan never filed an official report suggesting that he actually threatened Grant with a court-martial; other evidence was inconclusive. For most of his time on the Pacific Coast, Grant's work was praised and his drinking unremarkable in a profession where alcohol was consumed in astonishing amounts. The scholar Charles G. Ellington produced a substantial investigation into Grant's drinking.[83] Ellington noted that although previously Grant consumed alcohol, there was no evidence to suggest that he overindulged. What drove him to drink to excess in his two years on the West Coast? Despair at his circumstances is the major factor. Biographer William McFeely contended that "Grant did not leave the army because he was a drunk. He drank and left the army because he was profoundly depressed."[84]

Ellington documented other reasons as well, drawing from many contemporary sources. Grant could not physically tolerate more than one or two glasses of whiskey, consistently displaying an inability to "hold his liquor." He also sought to cure his blinding migraine headaches and other ailments with drink. After carefully reviewing conflicting testimonies and separating myth and rumors from fact, Ellington argued, "The only valid conclusion that can be drawn about Grant's drinking is that he drank—like most soldiers of his time. But he was not a drunkard. Grant did not consume large quantities of liquor because his body did not require much to achieve the inevitable results. Some of Grant's contemporaries recorded that he went on 'sprees,' but none accused him of failing in his duty because he was under the influence."[85] This distinction is vital because after Grant resigned, he controlled and limited his drinking, with help from his wife and friends such as his military aide, John A. Rawlins. "He did not drink when Julia was around," wrote Simon, "but also abstained when she was not with him."[86] Author Jean Edward Smith declared, "Grant was a binge drinker. . . . He could go for months without a drink, but once he started it was difficult for him to stop." Smith, however, concluded "for the most part Grant remained sober." Indeed, recent Grant scholars agree with Ellington that as a Civil War soldier, as president, and in retirement, Grant rarely imbibed and never when it counted.[87]

Grant never admitted in his memoirs or anywhere else that drinking might have played a role in his retirement from the army. For Grant, as for most nineteenth-century people, losing control in such a way was a shameful and private moral failing. As historian James McPherson commented, "If Grant was an alcoholic, he should have felt pride rather than shame because he overcame his illness to achieve success and fame without the support system of modern medicine and organizations like Alcoholics Anonymous."[88] Whatever really happened, Grant's career was harmed significantly by the 1853 episode. Rumors of uncontrolled drunkenness—greatly exaggerated and largely unsubstantiated—haunted him throughout his public life. After Shiloh, many newspapers published rumors that Grant was drunk before the battle and demanded his removal. Wounded by the charges, he preferred to let his record speak for itself, and let his supporters defend his character. Quietly he reassured Julia that he was "sober as a deacon no matter what is said to the contrary." A friendly biographer and former Union brigadier general, James Grant Wilson, admitted: "It is difficult to ascertain the precise truth with regard to the private personal habits of men who have become distinguished in public affairs. The tongue of slander is busy against them, and, on the other hand, a zealous partisanship is always ready to magnify their virtues and to cover or deny their faults." Still, Wilson insisted that the origins of "this hue and cry against Grant was chiefly the work of newspaper correspondents and the adherents of less successful soldiers or political leaders who wished to aid their friends by defaming Grant."[89]

Grant's alleged alcoholism has tarnished his historical reputation. College and high school textbooks, popular and academic histories often portray him as a drunk, insisting also that he won the war through the force of overwhelming numbers combined with a brutal disregard for human life.[90] Popular culture perpetuates the stereotype. James Thurber's famous piece published in 1930 comes to mind; in "If Grant Had Been Drinking at Appomattox," Thurber imagined a bizarrely confused and hung-over General Grant unexpectedly surrendering his army to General Lee at their famous meeting. Some Civil War movies, such as John Ford's *The Horse Soldiers* (1959), feature the general with a glass of whiskey glued to his side. Television has also provided fodder for Grant the drunk: in an episode of the highly rated series *The Beverly Hillbillies* called "The South Rises Again" (November 29, 1967), Granny spies actors from a Civil War movie, including one portraying an inebriated General Grant.[91] The cover of a recent novel about Grant had his likeness plastered on a bottle of liquor, while a "how to" book entitled *Cigars, Whiskey and Winning: Leadership Lessons from Ulysses S. Grant* put a more positive spin on his drinking.[92] And, as almost every Civil War history professor can testify, one of the most commonly asked questions from students and public alike is, "Was Ulysses S. Grant a drunk?"

### The Family Man

If Grant was silent on his drinking, he did not shy away from describing his inner turmoil. For that, his missives to Julia are vividly instructive. Bruce Catton observed rightly, "These letters show a Grant who is not at all like the man who became a legend—hard, self-contained, unimaginative, stolid. On the contrary they present an intensely warm, deeply emotional man who poured out his heart."[93] Ulysses was suffering a grave emotional crisis.

It had been so long since he had seen Julia. He barely knew his first son, and he had never met his second son. He had only just tasted the delights of domesticity before they were snatched away from him. Even Fort Humboldt would be bearable if his wife and sons could join him, but that could not happen. From there he wrote Julia, "I do not feel as if it was possible to endure this separation much longer."[94] His thoughts turned increasingly to resignation. In a letter dated March 6, 1854, Grant broached the subject of leaving the army with Julia. "I sometimes get so anxious to see you, and our little boys, that I am almost tempted to resign and trust to Providence, and my own exertions, for a living where I can have you and them with me." He then admitted that the prospect of failure haunted him: "Poverty, poverty begins to stare me in the face, and then I think what would I do if you and our little ones should want for the necessaries of life."[95] Grant's agony ended with his decision to leave the army. He chose his family over his career, and uncertainty over security. In the short term, his resignation proved an exhilarating liberation. His exhilaration was tempered, however, by the cold reality of his financial situation. He literally found himself without money. Funds were raised locally to get him from San Francisco to New York. The last leg of his trip was facilitated by money raised in New York by an acquaintance, Captain Simon Bolivar Buckner, who in 1862 would surrender the Confederate stronghold at Fort Donelson to Grant. One can only speculate about the humiliation that Grant endured during this period. He had enjoyed an elite education, proved himself an able and brave soldier in a major war, and compiled a solid record in the peacetime army, at least until the end. Now, at age thirty-two, he returned home in the eyes of many a poverty-stricken failure.[96]

Grant did not travel directly to Julia but stopped first in Ohio in hopes of obtaining some funds from Jesse. The painful contrast between this reunion and the one that took place after the Mexican War must have devastated Grant; it surely strained relations between father and son. Jesse's opinion was predictable. At sacrifice to himself and the rest of the family, Jesse provided his son with the opportunity of a lifetime. Ulysses had not only failed to wring anything substantial from that opportunity, but left the army under a cloud of suspicion. "West Point spoiled one of my boys for business," he said. "I guess that's about so," replied a wounded Ulysses.[97] Jesse had long since turned to his younger sons Simpson and Orvil to help him run his various business enterprises. He seemed to write his eldest old son off like a bad investment, refusing to loan him enough money to start a new life with Julia and the children near the family home. Still, father and son communicated on a regular basis, and Ulysses found encouragement and affectionate support from his mother and sisters.

## The Farmer

Grant returned to White Haven, where the Colonel and his wife offered him a home, if not enthusiastically. Grant decided to become a farmer. "Whoever hears of me in ten years, will hear of a well-to-do old Missouri farmer," he told an acquaintance.[98] His choice made sense. He loved working the land, and he was good at it. Opportunity to farm beckoned close at hand. Colonel Dent deeded Julia around 100 acres of land on the family estate. The gently rolling Missouri farmland was very similar to Brown County's, which pleased him greatly. At first, Ulysses, Julia, and their two sons lived at White Haven, but soon they moved into "Wish-ton-wish," a house surrounded by beautiful oak trees that was owned by Julia's brother. Within three years, the birth of two more children, Ellen, who was called Nellie (1855), and Jesse Root (1858), completed the family circle.

Meanwhile, the switch from soldier to farmer was not easy. Grant lacked the money to buy the seed and the equipment he needed to make farming a good livelihood; his dependence on the Dent family was galling. He garnered a modest income from cutting and selling cordwood in St. Louis. Daily he loaded a huge wagon with wood and drove it into town. When the wagon was empty, he returned home for more. Appropriately roughly dressed in his old army clothes, Grant looked distinctly shabby in the eyes of some of his old comrades, such as Pete Longstreet and Rufus Ingalls. Grant was embarrassed by their obvious pity but nevertheless happy to talk over old times and catch up on the news in St. Louis taverns. Mostly, he was consumed by work. Grant performed much of the hardest field labor with his own hands. From dawn to dusk, he "cut props, hauled wood, plowed, sowed, reaped, raised hogs, grubbed out stumps, and built fences."[99] The local people considered Ulysses to be a competent farmer, who kept his fields and tools in good shape. They respected his military service and were impressed by his evident mastery of, and interest in, local and national political issues. Gossipy neighbors wondered why Captain Grant, as they called him, did not put Colonel Dent's slaves to work in his fields. Rather, when extra labor was needed, he hired free blacks and paid them more than the average wage. He could have benefited from selling the one slave that he owned (courtesy of Colonel Dent) but instead freed him.[100]

A northerner alone and silenced in a world of slaveowners, Grant nursed a contempt for slavery and observed closely the habits of southern white

Julia Grant and her father, Colonel Fredrick F. Dent, with Julia and Ulysses's son Jesse and daughter, Nellie, ca. 1865–70 (Library of Congress)

families in his part of Missouri. He had always known, and lived among, pro-southern, proslavery Democrats—in Ohio, in Kentucky, and at West Point. Like so many Americans, he watched uneasily as the divisions and contro-versies deepened between the sections as the 1850s unfolded. His adult life in a border state gave him a solid perspective on both sides. When a north-ern friend expressed doubt that southerners would fight for their indepen-dence, Grant replied that, to the contrary, "they will make a strong fight." He observed that "each side under-estimates the other and over-estimates itself."[101] Undoubtedly his actions spoke more loudly than his words to his in-laws. A former Dent slave described Grant as "a very kind man to those who worked for him and he always said he wanted to give his wife's slaves their freedom as soon as he was able."[102] The Grants did not socialize very

Hardscrabble: the house Grant built (Library of Congress)

much, but Julia was well liked and her husband tolerated kindly by their neighbors. By the summer of 1856 Grant had completed the building of the two-story, four-room log cabin for his family that he and Julia named "Hardscrabble." Life was indeed hard, but thanks largely to low expenses, he managed to keep his family fed, sheltered, and clothed, if plainly. Julia, who hated the idea of moving into a log house, proved to be adept at budgeting and good naturedly endured her extremely modest standard of living. Several times, Ulysses broached the subject of moving north, but Julia always talked him out of it, preferring to stay with her own people.[103]

Financially things went from bad to worse. Another appeal to Jesse for money was denied. With Grant barely hanging on, his farming years ended when he suffered three blows: the financial panic of 1857, an unusually cold winter, and the collapse of his health. Farming had aged him. Friends described him as looking old and bent, with a full beard, his shoulders permanently hunched. He gave up his dream of becoming a "well-off farmer," not because he minded the grinding labor but because the future looked so grim. What was the point of an educated man like himself working so hard if no improvement was forthcoming? When Julia's mother died, Colonel Dent moved to St. Louis, offering his son-in-law his home again. Grant sold his equipment; he traded Hardscrabble for a house in St. Louis, where he sought work. Once again, he had to rely on the Colonel. Dent secured Grant a partnership in a real estate office. Unsuited for the business, Grant quit in late summer of 1859 and applied for a newly opened position of county engineer, a job for which he was eminently qualified. Grant's candidacy was rejected by the county commissioners. He explained to his father the reason: "The two Democratic Commissioners voted for me, and the freesoilers against me. . . . You may judge from the result . . . that I am strongly identified with the Democratic party! Such is not the case. I never voted an out and out Democratic ticket in my life. I voted for Buch. for President to defeat Freemont [sic] but not because he was my first choice."[104]

As a soldier, Grant had avoided active involvement in politics, never voting in a presidential election. That changed when he became a civilian. In 1856 he cast his first vote for James Buchanan, a prosouthern Pennsylvania Democrat, over Republican candidate John C. Frémont. When friends asked why, he claimed he believed that the Democrats would best preserve the Union. Later, a more precise quote was attributed to him: "I voted for Buchanan because I didn't know him and voted against Fremont because I did know him."[105] An ardent Union man, Grant viewed with mixed feelings the growing popularity of the Republican Party, embraced by his father and brothers. "When I was in St. Louis the year before Lincoln's election," he said, "it made my blood run cold to hear friends of mine, Southern men—as many of my friends were—deliberately discuss the dissolution of the union as though it were a tariff bill. I could not endure it. The very thought of it was a pain."[106] As the election of 1860 drew nearer, he considered himself a Stephen Douglas supporter, but he waxed increasingly enthusiastic about the prospect of a Republican victory. Author and journalist Alfred D. Richardson, one of Grant's earliest biographers, described his political awakening as, "Grant is a Douglas Democrat, But is Converted to Republicanism."[107]

## Galena, Illinois

When Grant lost his job in St. Louis, Jesse came through for his son, finally. At his prompting, Ulysses moved his family to pretty and prosperous Galena, Illinois, although he and Julia continued to own land in White Haven, eventually accumulating 1,100 acres of property.[108] In Galena, he worked as a clerk in his father's leather store (managed by Orvil) for eleven months and earned a decent living, with prospects of becoming a part owner. There, he rented a nice little brick house on High Street overlooking the riverside town and attended the Methodist Church with his family. There, he regained a measure of his composure and self-confidence, now leavened with humility and with an empathy for others' pain that is often a result of failure. There, he lavished attention on his four children, becoming the loving family man he had dreamed of being earlier. There, he made friends with Elihu Washburne and John Rawlins, the former a powerful Republican congressman who supported his military career, the latter a Democratic lawyer who served as Grant's chief-of-staff. And there, in April of 1861, along with the other stunned citizens of Galena, he heard about the fall of Fort Sumter in South Carolina to Confederate forces.

If Grant's childhood homes in Point Pleasant and Georgetown speak to the promise of the "American Dream," his log cabin dubbed Hardscrabble embodies the darker side of that dream. Tourists to "Grant's Farm," a privately operated park can visit the only home (largely reconstructed) hand-built by a president of the United States.[109] The log cabin carried a powerful symbolism in nineteenth-century political contests. Presidential candidates from Whig aristocrat William Henry Harrison in 1840 to homespun Republican Abraham Lincoln in 1860 pointed with pride to their origins in such a humble dwelling and reaped the electoral benefits. Like Lincoln, Grant was an uncommon common "western" man who had known both hard times and hard labor. Unlike Lincoln, Grant endured a decade in his middle years soured with abject public failure. His life did not fit the neat "pull yourself up by your own bootstraps" story that celebrated upward personal individual success and scorned losers. After the Mexican War, Grant was positioned for advancement and prosperity. Instead, for nearly a decade he experienced a stunning series of setbacks that left him at times nearly destitute.

Grant's experience was routine in an economy subject to panics and depressions in the midst of overall growth and prosperity. A man's failure was feared as much as his achievement was embraced. Cultural historian Scott Sandage studied "men who failed in a nation that worships success," concluding that by the mid-nineteenth century the meaning of failure had expanded from one that was purely financial to one that emphasized a defect in character. The 1857 edition of *Webster's Dictionary* proved Sandage's point. Failure no longer meant only bankruptcy, insolvency, or bust, but also "some weakness in a man's character, disposition of habit."[110] By the 1850s, log cabins were fine for hardy pioneers, but any man of ambition would have a more suitable dwelling by the time he reached his thirties. Hardscrabble encapsulated a low point in Grant's life, when he farmed on his wife's family's land just southwest of St. Louis, making regular forays to that city to sell his products. Hitting bottom, Grant's life took an upward tick in 1858 and 1859, and shortly afterward his Civil War accomplishments skyrocketed him to lasting fame and success, if never to great fortune.

Temporarily down and out, Grant mastered his demons, and emerged the better for the struggle. Historians and biographers have not always agreed that the seeds of success were planted in failure. Two prominent examples from different time periods will frame the point. William B. Hesseltine's 1935 Grant biography featured a chapter titled: "Forty Years of Failure," explaining that "the forty years of adversity had no uses. They did not give rise to the twenty succeeding years of accomplishment, nor did they serve as an adequate preparation for glory." Hesseltine portrayed Grant as "essentially colorless" and "devoid of dramatic characteristics," and argued that only such an individual could "emerge from years of adversity and as inertly proceed to years of success." William S. McFeely's 1981 Pulitzer Prize–winning *Grant* offered a similar explanation. "I am convinced," McFeely declared in the introduction, "that Ulysses Grant had no organic, artistic, or intellectual specialness. He did have limited though by no means inconsequential talents to apply to whatever truly engaged his attention. The only problem was that until he was nearly forty, no job he liked had come his way—and so he became general and president because he could find nothing better to do." Both authors found Grant an unexplainable phenomenon, for which his early life offers no guide.[111]

A much more persuasive analysis is that Grant's painful experience with financial and personal failure accounted for his unusually strong character displayed under the stresses of wartime. A man was judged by the quality of his character in the nineteenth century. Character was the culmination of estimable qualities possessed by an individual but also implied "the estimate attached to the individual by the community."[112] Allan Nevins claimed Grant "gained his place in the American pantheon not by intellectual power. . . . He gained it by character." Much later, Brooks D. Simpson echoed Nevins, arguing, "Grant's generalship was shaped as much by character as it was by intellect."[113] Simpson's assessment does not denigrate Grant's intelligence but rather highlights qualities attributed to him by many contemporaries, such as tenacity, aggressiveness, modesty, integrity, simplicity, resoluteness, and imperturbability. The sum of those qualities created the mythic Grant symbolizing the endurance and power of the United States. The testing of those qualities under incredibly stressful conditions bore fruit in his Civil War career.

## chapter two

# The Magnanimous General

There is a vast trove of Civil War histories assessing the wartime reputation of Ulysses S. Grant.[1] The story of a humble, loyal, patriotic soldier rising from obscurity to eminence as the relentless military commander who became the hero of the Union remains one of the most compelling in American history. Historian Allan Nevins noted, "The war, which had made the fortunes of a multitude of men while ruining another multitude, had created no career quite so spectacular as Grant's." By the end of four years, Nevins wrote, he was "the head of the greatest army in the world, acclaimed the most famous of living soldiers, the hero of a nation ready to give him any honor within its power." What were the qualities that elevated him above his supposedly more intelligent, educated and successful peers? Alternatively, was he simply mediocre at best, an incompetent butcher at worst, beneficiary of superior northern manpower and resources? In his study of Union generalship, T. Harry Williams estimated Grant: "He won battles and campaigns, and he struck the blow that won the war. No general could do what he did because of accident or luck or preponderance of numbers and weapons. He was a success because he was a complete general and a complete character. He was so complete that his countrymen have never been able to believe he was real."[2]

From 1862 to 1865 Grant's generalship dominated the war and shaped the peace. Indisputable is his wartime legacy of preserving the Union and bringing emancipation to a country unprepared for freedom's consequences. U. S. Grant and President Abraham Lincoln's impressive partnership—forged in the heat of military campaigns won, lost, won again—secured Union victory and allowed for generous peace terms at Appomattox. From April 9, 1865, Grant emerged as the top military victor, but importantly a *magnanimous* warrior of mythic status to whom the people of the re-United States turned for leadership time and again in the years after Lincoln's assassination.

The mythic warrior is on display astride his favorite horse, Cincinnati, at the Ulysses S. Grant Memorial in Washington D.C. Situated directly west of the Capitol dome, the monument was dedicated on April 27, 1922, the hundredth anniversary of Grant's birthday. Commemorative activities marking the centenary took place throughout the country.[3] In Ohio, President Warren G. Harding offered stirring remarks to a crowd assembled at Grant's birthplace in Point Pleasant, while in New York City, Marshal Joseph Joffre (French general-in-chief during World War I) praised Grant before a huge throng gathered at his tomb. The elaborate ceremonies in Washington featured Vice President Calvin Coolidge speaking in front of the huge eques-

Central pedestal of the Grant Memorial, Washington, D.C. (*The Grant Memorial in Washington* [Washington, D.C.: Government Printing Office, 1924])

trian statue (the second largest in the world) set upon a 272-foot marble platform.[4] Flanking the bronze general, statuary groups representing "Artillery" and "Cavalry" evoke the action and chaos of war. Impressive bronze lions on pedestals guard each of the four corners and guide the eye back toward the central figure of Grant on horseback facing the Washington Monument and beyond it, the Lincoln Memorial. In finely wrought and accurate detail, the sculptor, Henry Merwin Shrady, captured the steely determination, fortitude, and calm of the Union commander. In the twenty-first century, the sculpture is virtually invisible in the city of ever-growing massive monuments. Parking lots, heavy traffic, an ugly reflecting pool all impede access, and decades of rust diminish its former grandeur. Plans are afoot for a restoration, but so far, the emphasis is on creating an "urban civic square," not on restoring Grant's memorial. Tourists who somehow find their way to the monument wonder aloud about the identity of the man on the horse. One word, "Grant," carved on the supporting marble pedestal, is the only identifying mark.[5] In 1922, no other information was needed. The statue confirms in bronze the enormous esteem the nation held for Grant almost fifty years after his death when the simple, silent western man stood as the symbol of the victorious Union Cause and a powerful reunited nation.

### "Traitors and Patriots"

Because of Illinois residency requirements, Ulysses S. Grant could not vote in the momentous 1860 presidential contest that brought victory to the Prairie State's favorite son, Abraham Lincoln. The Republican triumph was short-lived when a secession crisis erupted. The party's pledge to protect slavery where it existed but prevent its extension elsewhere was rejected by seven Deep South states. By February of 1861 the Confederate States of America established a provisional government led by the former U.S. senator from Mississippi, Jefferson Davis. In the tense months before President Lincoln's March inauguration, various compromises were proposed, and rejected. The United States demanded reunion, while the new Confederate States of America boldly proclaimed independence. Before dawn on April 12, 1861, rebel cannons opened fire on federal troops stationed at Fort Sumter, South Carolina. Their defeat and subsequent surrender brought forth a declaration of war from President Lincoln on April 15. In response, four more slave states joined the rebellion, completing the dissolution of the old United States of America.

Both North and South mobilized on a huge scale. Galena rushed to respond to Lincoln's call for 75,000 volunteers. A rally was held, with speakers urging the young men to enlist in a company raised from Galena and other communities in Jo Daviess County. The town fathers asked Ulysses Grant to preside over the formation and training of the unit. He agreed; he felt a powerful patriotic duty to assist his country in fighting to keep the American republic whole in the face of secession's threat. He wrote: "Whatever may have been my political opinions before I have but one sentiment now. That is we have a Government, and laws and a flag and they must all be sustained. There are but two parties now, Traitors and Patriots and I want hereafter to be ranked with the latter, and I trust, the stronger party."[6] Despite some pressure by Galena officials, Grant refused to serve as company commander, believing his experience entitled him to a higher rank with commensurate responsibility. He said a tearful goodbye to Julia at Galena's little train station as he traveled to Illinois's training camp and offered his services to Governor Richard Yates, who promptly appointed Grant his aide.

When pleas to the War Department for a fighting command in May of 1861 went unheard, Grant applied himself to the deskwork at hand, and made an excellent impression. The governor placed Grant in charge of the 21st Illinois Infantry Regiment, where he enforced needed discipline and earned the respect of his men. His first battle test came in July at Salt River in Missouri when he pursued a Confederate force spotted nearby. Apprehensive, he approached the site only to discover that the Rebels had fled. That one minor action gave him a deep insight into the enemy's psyche, and his own. "I never forgot," he wrote, "that he had as much reason to fear my forces as I had his. The lesson was valuable."[7]

## Unconditional Surrender

Rising to brigadier general in August 1861, Grant next found himself assigned to running the big Union supply and training camp at Cairo, Illinois. Republican congressman Elihu Washburne of Illinois, Grant's patron and a friend of President Lincoln, recommended him for the position. "Mr. Washburn," he wrote, "allow me to thank you for the part you have taken in giving me my present position. . . . I can assure you . . . my whole heart is in the cause which we are fighting for and I pledge myself that if equal to the task before me you shall never have cause to regret the part you have taken."[8] Grant was anxious to get to the battlefield and demonstrate his skills in managing men instead of papers. Emboldened by his Salt River success, Grant decided to occupy Paducah, Kentucky, with the goal of thwarting Confederate control of the Tennessee River. Engaging in his first serious battle, on November 7, 1861, he led 3,000 troops, largely men from Iowa and Illinois, down the Mississippi River to roust the southerners from their encampments at Belmont, Missouri. The outcome was inconclusive, but Grant's efforts garnered him favorable attention from superiors and the nation's press. Amid a floundering Union war effort, here was a rare general willing to fight aggressively using the resources at hand. The *Cincinnati Gazette* described Belmont as a success, while the *Chicago Journal* reported that the "general opinion prevails that the rebels suffered far greater losses than we."[9]

First at Belmont, and then in almost every subsequent operation, Grant combined strategic and tactical maneuvers, employing both the navy and the infantry to gain control of crucial rivers—the Cumberland, the Ohio, the Tennessee, and especially the Mississippi—that provided watery routes to invading the southern heartland. Plans for the Western Theater were formulated by President Lincoln and his first general-in-chief, Winfield Scott. They aimed to dominate the Mississippi River from Illinois to the Gulf of Mexico, closing off the trade in men and supplies that succored the Confederate nation. In response, the southerners concentrated on defense, fortifying critical points to protect against Federal attacks. Grant's next campaign helped to secure the upper Mississippi River as he moved inexorably south, executing the Union's strategy.

In early 1862, using naval gunboats and 15,000 foot soldiers, Grant captured strategically important Fort Henry on the Tennessee River (February 6) and then the more imposing Fort Donelson on the Cumberland River (February 15). Donelson's two senior commanders fled ignominiously, leaving Brigadier General Simon B. Buckner in charge. Buckner sent a note asking Grant to discuss terms of surrender for the Rebel army of approximately 15,000 men, and "twenty-thousand stand of arms, forty-eight pieces of artillery, seventeen heavy guns, and from two to four thousand horses." Buckner received a terse reply:

Hd Qrs, Army in the Field
Camp near Donelson, Feb.y 16th 1862

Gen. S. B. Buckner,

Confed. Army,

Sir;

Yours of this date proposing Armistice, and appointment of commissioners, to settle terms of capitulation is just received. No terms except an unconditional and immediate surrender can be accepted.

I propose to move immediately upon your works.

I am sir; very respectfully
Your obt. Servt.
U. S. Grant
Brig. Gen.[10]

For the first, but not the last, time, Grant accepted the surrender of an entire Confederate force. And for the first, but not the last, time, Grant showed magnanimity toward the enemy. When asked if he was going to observe the traditional ceremonies that attended surrender, Grant responded in the negative. He explained, "The surrender is now a fact. We have the fort, the men, the guns. Why should we go through vain forms and mortify and injure the spirit of brave men, who, after all, are our own countrymen."[11] After the fall of Fort Donelson "Unconditional Surrender" Grant acquired a new nickname, a promotion to brevet major general of volunteers, and fame, with its pitiless gaze and enticing perquisites. When a newspaper printed an erroneous rumor that the general liked cigars, grateful citizens sent him boxes upon boxes of them, prompting him to switch from the pipe to a lifelong addiction to cigars. His oldest son remembered, "The cigars began to

Vol. VI.—No. 271.]    NEW YORK, SATURDAY, MARCH 8, 1862.    [SINGLE COPIES SIX CENTS.
[$3.00 PER YEAR IN ADVANCE.

MAJOR-GENERAL ULYSSES S. GRANT, U.S.A., THE HERO OF FORT DONELSON.—FROM A PHOTOGRAPH.—[SEE PAGE 152.]

They got the hero's name right, but *Harper's* and other popular periodicals mistakenly used incorrect photographs as a model for Grant illustrations as late as 1864. The face above is said to belong to William Grant, a beef contractor from Illinois. (*Harper's Weekly*, March 8, 1862)

come in from all over the Union. He had eleven thousand cigars on hand in a very short time."[12]

After the stinging defeats in the summer and autumn of 1861 at Bull Run and Ball's Bluff, northern spirits rose dramatically in response the first major Union victories of the war at Forts Henry and Donelson. Celebrations broke out across the country. Governor Yates of Illinois reported on the scenes in his state: "People by thousands [*sic*] on the roads and at the stations, with shoutings and with flags. Thank God that our Union is safe now and for-ever."[13] In this campaign, Grant demonstrated flexibility and determination, taking advantage of favorable circumstances to act promptly. Responding to critics who worried that he was not following proscribed military regula-tions and West Point textbook maneuvers, Grant retorted, "I felt that 15,000 men on the 8th would be more effective then 50,000 a month later."[14] The conquests forced Confederate retreat from Kentucky and middle Tennessee, bringing Nashville under Federal control and pushing the main body of the western Confederate army back to the key railroad junction of Corinth, Mississippi, close to the Tennessee border. Each step forward brought controversy and headaches. Grant took a quick trip to Nashville without consulting the top western commander, General Henry W. Halleck. Angry at his inferior's "insubordination," and concerned about rumors that Grant had been drinking, Halleck unceremoniously removed him from field command. The popular hero was quickly restored after worries were assuaged, and rumors proved false. Eager to press his advantage after Fort Donelson, Grant planned an attack on the Confederates at their new stronghold in Corinth.

### "I was worse scared than I was at Shiloh"

In preparation, Grant concentrated his troops at Pittsburg Landing on the west bank of the Tennessee River. Early in the morning on April 6, 1862, Confederate general Albert Sidney Johnston launched a surprise attack on sleeping Union camps near Shiloh Methodist Church, after which the battle is named. Both sides fought a desperate, bloody battle; as darkness descended, the Yankees fell back perilously close to the river, but the lines held. Grant later wrote: "Shiloh was the severest battle fought at the West during the war. . . . I saw an open field, in our possession on the second day, over which the Confederates had made repeated charges the day before, so covered with dead that it would have been possible to walk across the clearing, in any direction, stepping on dead bodies, without a foot touching the ground."[15]

Some expected defeat, including one of Grant's division commanders, William T. Sherman, who was also surprised by Johnston's assault. As Sherman recalled, late that rainy evening he found Grant standing under a tree, soaked to the skin. Intending to offer a plan for retreat, something in Grant's face stopped him. Instead, Sherman said, "Well, Grant, we've had the devil's own day of it, haven't we?" "Yes," Grant replied, "Lick 'em tomorrow though."[16] On April 7, Grant personally directed the counterattack that drove the enemy off the field, aided by Sherman, and the timely arrival of fresh troops supplied by General Don Carlos Buell's Army of the Ohio.[17] Grant commended his soldiers for a great victory, making "special notice of the brave wounded and those killed upon the field. Whilst they leave friends and relatives to mourn their loss they have won a nations gratitude and undying laurels not to be forgotten by future generations who will enjoy the blessings of the best government the sun ever shone upon preserved by their Valor."[18] When news of the victory reached Washington, D.C., Congress officially stopped all business and President Lincoln proclaimed a national day of worship. On April 9, both the *New York Times* and the *New York Herald* printed news of a magnificent Union conquest in the Western Theater, portraying U. S. Grant as the hero of the battle. Shiloh placed a victory in the northern column, but the details were hard to bear. The battle was the bloodiest engagement (23,000 casualties) in American military history up to the time. On the Union side, 1,754 died, and on the Confederate, 1,723. On both sides, thousands of poorly trained soldiers ran from the first shots, deserting or straggling. The "Hurrahs Changed to Hisses" when public opinion turned against Grant as the long casualty lists brought sorrow and dismay to the northern population.[19]

The press demanded a scapegoat, and they found one in the battle's commander. In a series of damming articles, journalist Whitelaw Reid of the *Cincinnati Gazette* accused Grant of being callously unprepared and brutally incompetent.[20] His charges were denied vigorously by Grant and Sherman, then and later, and historians have found them largely without support. The most credible assertion is that by not fortifying Pittsburg Landing, Grant exposed his largely green troops to grave peril. Overconfidence led him to assume that the enemy would await the Union attack at Cornith. His critics charged Grant with gross miscalculation and bad generalship causing the needless deaths of northern soldiers. *Chicago Tribune* editor Joseph Medill called Shiloh "a most reprehensive surprise followed by an awful slaughter." The *New York Tribune* urged "that an investigation should be made of the utter inefficiency and incompetency, if not the downright treachery, of the generals."[21] The popular judgments against Grant brought harsh consequences. Responding to the heavy criticism, Halleck again removed him from field duty. Deeply hurt, Grant considered resignation, "but General Sherman happened to call on me as I was about starting and urged me so strongly not to think of going, that I concluded to remain."[22] In the end, as John Keegan pointed out, "Shiloh was . . . incontestably a victory, won at a time when Northern victories were few. He [Grant] would survive the attacks on his reputation."[23]

Just before, during, and after the battle of Shiloh, Grant and Sherman formed an extraordinary relationship that boded well for the future of the Union Cause. Military historian Joseph T. Glatthaar studied the "partners in command," and concluded that their friendship, based on mutual trust, created "an unyielding bond through selfless collaboration, devising and implementing a fresh concept of warfare that utilized manpower and resources with maximum effectiveness and culminated in Union victory."[24] A contrast in temperaments, the taciturn Grant and the quick-tempered Sherman complemented each other well. In the fall of 1861, unfriendly newspaper reporters pronounced Sherman's view that the war was going to last much longer than predicted "insane." Sherman suffered a collapse and retired from active duty. Returning in February of 1862, he worked under Grant's command, and his career took an upward trajectory. Writing from Paducah, Kentucky, Sherman assessed his new commander's performance at Fort Donelson as "most extraordinary and brilliant." Reassured by Grant's calm, steadfast demeanor and purposeful leadership style, the tall, red-haired, and talkative Sherman found a boss who appreciated his brilliant talents and protected him from his own worst traits. In 1864, Sherman told Grant, "I knew wherever I was that you thought of me, and if I got in a tight place you would come—if alive." After the war, he jokingly summed up their relationship, "He stood by me when I was crazy and I stood by him when he was drunk; and now sir, we stand by each other always."[25]

Shiloh matured Grant and his men. Importantly, it proved the making of one of the greatest armies of the Civil War, the Army of the Tennessee. "It fell to my good fortune to be the commander of what composed the main body of men constituting the Army of the Tennessee," Grant said later.[26] He knew that esprit de corps could be created in the ranks with strict training; battle experience; confident, dedicated leadership; and a winning record. The Army of the Tennessee was a product of all those elements, despite suffering casualties and setbacks. Immediately after Shiloh, a reporter wrote a dispatch claiming that among Grant's soldiers "no respect is felt for him, and no confidence is felt in him." But others took immediate pride in their performance. "We had a famous battle yesterday, and entirely routed the enemy after a desperate fight, lasting from 7 A.M. until 6 P.M.," wrote one soldier. "Everyone expresses themselves quite satisfied with the fighting," he continued. "Gen. [Ulysses S.] Grant told our major that the Fort Donelson fight was, as compared to this, as the morning dew to a heavy rain."[27] From then on, western Union soldiers employed a saying about any particularly terrible battle experience, "I was worse scared than I was at Shiloh."[28] Like Zachary Taylor's army in Mexico, the volunteers who composed the Army of the Tennessee boasted about their lack of "spit and polish" but made up for their generally slovenly appearance by earning a reputation for rapid marching; hard, disciplined fighting; and endurance, reflecting their top leader's predilection for offensively styled, aggressive warfare. The men who fought

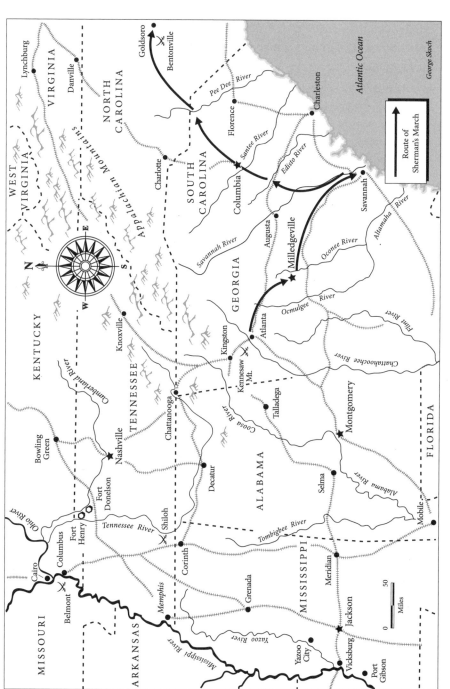

The Western Theater in the Civil War

under Grant, and later under Sherman, at Shiloh, Vicksburg, Chattanooga, Atlanta, and Columbia claimed Grant's full admiration. In his memoirs he paid tribute: "Our armies were composed of men who were able to read, men who knew what they were fighting for, and could not be induced to serve as soldiers, except in an emergency when the safety of the nation was involved, and so necessarily must have been more than equal to men who fought merely because they were brave and because they were thoroughly drilled and inured to hardships."[29] The western soldiers and later veterans returned that respect in full.

The bloody victory in Tennessee also provided Grant with a bracing wake-up call. After Shiloh, he realized that he had underestimated Confederate resolve. In 1861, each side expected the other would give up after suffering terrible losses. Union battlefield defeats at Bull Run and other setbacks dampened northern morale but did not lead to a peace conference to discuss Confederate independence. Likewise, the Western Theater victories at Forts Henry and Donelson, followed shortly by Union capture of the important cities of Nashville, Memphis, and New Orleans produced widespread depression among Confederates but failed to end their experiment in nation-building. Additionally, pacification policy in 1862 demonstrated the strains of forced reunion, offering a disturbing preview of Reconstruction. Grant and Sherman in Memphis and western Tennessee, and General Benjamin F. Butler in New Orleans, reasserted Federal authority amid an extremely difficult atmosphere created by hostile, unrepentant white people unwilling to foreswear loyalty to the Confederacy. Outside of heavy Union security, soldiers and military property were often targets for guerrilla actions clearly supported by the local population. In response, Grant ordered that for every U.S. property loss "a sufficient amount of personal property" would be seized from Confederate sympathizers. Grant declared that "persons acting as Guerillas without organization, and without uniform to distinguish them from private citizens, are not entitled to the treatment of prisoners of War when caught, and will not receive such treatment."[30] Later in his military career, Grant wielded even greater influence over Union policy toward the southern civilian population.

A harsher kind of war beckoned. Grant recalled, "Up to the battle of Shiloh, I, as well as thousands of other citizens, believed that the rebellion against the Government would collapse suddenly and soon, if a decisive victory could be gained over any of its armies. . . . [After Shiloh] I gave up all idea of saving the Union except by complete conquest."[31] In a letter to his brother, Ohio's senator John Sherman, General Sherman provided his own analysis: "The South has an united People, and as many men as she can arm, and though our armies pass across & through the land, the war closes in behind and leaves the Same enmity behind. We attempt to occupy places, and the People rise up & make the Detachments prisoners."[32] In the summer and fall of 1862, Grant and Sherman hammered out ideas about a "raiding strategy" that would target and destroy Confederate property—railroads, farms, factories, and plantations. They agreed that unless and until the southern home front felt the "hard hand of war" the conflict could continue indefinitely. "We cannot change the hearts of those people in the South," Sherman wrote to Grant in October 1862, "but we can make war so terrible that they will realize the fact that however brave and gallant and devoted to their country, still they are mortal and should exhaust all peaceful remedies before they fly to war."[33] In order to launch the contemplated overland assaults on the southern heartland, Grant needed to secure the entire length of the Mississippi River, executing the next phase of Lincoln's strategy for the Western Theater.

## "Vicksburg is the key"

Restored to command over the District of Tennessee in June of 1862, followed shortly by Lincoln's summons of Halleck to Washington as his general-in-chief, Grant set as his next goal the seizure of the "Gibraltar of the West," Vicksburg, Mississippi. A bustling commercial and transportation center for the region's planter class, Vicksburg was a critical link between the eastern and western halves of the Confederacy. Situated on cliffs high above the Mississippi River, Vicksburg enjoyed formidable natural protections—both land and water—from enemy invasion. Numerous bayous, swamps, and rivers surrounded the city, making the land difficult to traverse by infantry. Vicksburg was vulnerable to invasion from the east, but in 1862 most of middle Mississippi was under southern control. Wartime fortifications enhanced nature, creating a virtually impregnable fortress. "Vicksburg is the key," Lincoln argued, "This war can never be brought to a close until that key is in our pocket."[34] Jefferson Davis agreed, although he hoped to keep the key in the Confederacy's pocket. To that end, in November 1862, he appointed Pennsylvania-born Lieutenant General John C. Pemberton commander of Mississippi and eastern Louisiana and gave him an army of 30,000 to protect Vicksburg from capture.

History records the capture of Vicksburg as one of the greatest American military campaigns, but Grant's early attempts ended in discouragement and a few notable disasters. On November 2, 1862, he moved his army south from Grand Junction, Tennessee, along the lines of the Mississippi Central Railroad. His immediate destination for the 30,000-strong Army of the Tennessee was Holly Springs, Mississippi, after which he would assail Vicksburg from the south. At the same time, he ordered Sherman to detach a part of his force and attack Vicksburg from the north. The forces would converge on Vicksburg simultaneously from different directions. It was a good idea that failed miserably. Confederate cavalry destroyed Grant's supply base at Holly Springs on December 20, and he lost contact with Sherman. A week later, Sherman's 32,000 men sustained a heavy loss at the battle of Chickasaw Bayou.

In January 1863, Grant retreated back to Memphis to reconceptualize his campaign. He went downriver again and put his soldiers to work on building canals and other river projects. He sought a water route that would allow his army to avoid the killing fire of the Vicksburg cannons and get on dry ground either south or east of the city. These efforts to bypass Vicksburg's formidable defenses also ended badly, fueling rampant speculation that Grant's days were numbered. "Grant is getting along at Vicksburg with such rapidity," complained the *Indianapolis Daily Journal*, "that, in the course of fifteen or twenty years, he will be ready to send up a gunboat to find out whether the enemy hasn't died of old age."[35] Prominent Wisconsin Republican and Union general Cadwallader Washburn fumed, "Grant has no plan for taking Vicksburg, he is frittering away time and strength to no purpose." The *New York World*'s sources revealed that "neither the generals in command of our land forces there nor their superiors at Washington expect or hope to take Vicksburg this year."[36] The editor of the *Cincinnati Commercial* wrote to Lincoln's secretary of the treasury, Salmon P. Chase, reviving rumors of Grant as "a poor drunken imbecile. He is a poor stick sober, and he is most of the time more than half drunk, and much of the time idiotically drunk." The president heard the reports of Grant's drinking and commented, "I think Grant has hardly a friend left, except myself." More tellingly the supportive but wary Lincoln said, "What I want, and what the people want, is generals who will fight battles and win victories. Grant has done this and I propose to stand by him."[37] In a prudent measure, Lincoln and Edwin M. Stanton appointed Charles A. Dana, a former journalist serving in the War Department, as a special agent. His mission? To spy on Grant's headquarters. Grant, fully aware of Dana's brief, welcomed him into his inner circle, making the former journalist an ally instead of an enemy. Dana's reports back to Stanton and Lincoln were positive, vindicating his later judgment that "General Grant's seasons of intoxication were not only infrequent . . . but he always chose a time when the gratification of his appetite for drink would not interfere with any important movement that had to be directed or attended to by him."[38]

Grant came up with a successful blueprint to capture Vicksburg in March and April 1863. His plan was simple, bold, and ingenious. With the help of David Dixon Porter, commander of the Union naval forces in the region, Grant marched his army down the west side of the Mississippi below Vicksburg. Porter's boats and transports, having earlier steamed past the Vicksburg batteries, transported two of Grant's three corps safely across the river. Sherman was ordered to stay behind and make a false attack on Vicksburg to confuse Pemberton—and Pemberton's commanding general, Joseph E. Johnston, headquartered in the state capital, Jackson—as to Grant's real intentions. As soon as all of Grant's army was across the river, Sherman rejoined the main force.

On May 1, the majority of the Union army was east of the Mississippi. Grant was on the march and cut off from his supply base. Ironically, Sherman fretted, but Grant's instructions to him were clear: "The enemy is badly beaten, greatly demoralized and exhausted of ammunition. The road to Vicksburg is open; all we want now are men, ammunition and hard bread— we can subsist our horses on the country, and obtain considerable supplies for our troops."[39] The next two and a half weeks saw Grant's army (smaller in number than the enemy's) moving swiftly west and then east again, engaging and defeating two Confederate armies (Pemberton's and Johnston's) at Port Gibson, Raymond, Jackson, Champion Hill, and Big Black River. After the victories, a soldier in the 165th New York commented, "As a strategist, Gen. Grant is the superior of many of our army commanders."[40] Morale soared; in seventeen days Grant's army had marched 180 miles and won five battles. Their casualty rate, at 4,300, was lower than the Confederates' at 7,200, highlighting the point that except for Shiloh, Grant's overall losses in the Western Theater to the winter of 1863 were fewer than those of his eastern Union counterparts, and many fewer than Lee's.[41] The defeat at Big Black sent Pemberton and his weary men scurrying back to the safety of Vicksburg. By noon of May 19, Grant arrived at Vicksburg and immediately ordered the first of two frontal assaults. Both were unsuccessful, and "I now determined upon a regular siege," Grant wrote in April, "to 'out-camp the enemy', as it were, and to incur no more losses."[42]

Grant put his men to work digging trenches until the nine miles of Confederate fortifications behind Vicksburg were encircled by twelve miles of Union earthworks. By June the Federal army was not only well entrenched but also enlarged greatly. No longer numerically disadvantaged, Grant now had roughly 75,000 men to deploy, with more arriving daily. An iron wall of rifles and cannons ringed the beleaguered city. With supply lines cut, Pemberton never received Johnston's message to escape with his army intact. In Washington, D.C., politicians and pundits were frustrated at the lack of news coming from Mississippi. Cutting off all communications and supplies, Grant's siege brought great suffering to Vicksburg's 3,000 civilians and 30,000 soldiers. The constant rain of Union artillery shells drove terrified families out of their homes and into caves dug in the hillsides. A soldier approved of the siege, reflecting a common sentiment, "I think General Grant's plan of starving them out is a very good one, and saves the slaughter of a number of lives, which would inevitably happen were he to charge the Rebel intrenchments."[43] After forty-seven days, General Pemberton admitted defeat, met with Grant to discuss terms, and agreed to surrender his army on July 4, 1863.

The stars and stripes were flying over Vicksburg on that day as Grant and his aides rode into town to meet with Pemberton and his officers in a local house. The general received a chilly reception, to say the least. Asking for a drink of water, he was told to get it himself; expecting a chair, he was offered none. Taking the slights graciously, Grant ordered rations to be distributed generously to the hungry Confederate soldiers and townspeople. His troops, ordered to suppress their cheers at the time of the signing of the surrender, were nonetheless jubilant. "This was the most Glorious Fourth I ever spent," remembered Private Isaac Jackson with the 83rd Ohio Regiment. A volunteer of the 118th Illinois declared, "We have been completely victorious and I cannot believe that the bold plan of Gen. Grant's could have been so completely carried out without some disaster if every man, from the humblest private up to the major-generals, had not done his duty in soldierlike style." Union captain Ira Miltmore wrote his wife: "The backbone of the Rebellion is this day broken. The Confederacy is divided. . . . Vicksburg is ours. The Mississippi River is opened, and Gen. Grant is to be our next President."[44] Indeed, good news for the United States in the first week of July was widely celebrated, and not just for the surrender of Vicksburg, but also for the Federals' win on the distant fields of Gettysburg, Pennsylvania, on July 1–3.

### "Grant is my man, and I am his"

Grant's surrender terms were generous. "Men who have shown much endurance and courage as those now in Vicksburg," he wrote to Pemberton, "will always challenge the respect of an adversary, and I can assure you will be treated with all the respect due to prisoners of war."[45] The Confederates—27,230 enlisted men and 2,166 officers—were given "paroles," pieces of paper signed by soldiers that allowed them to go home if they promised not to take up arms again, thus sparing them from incarceration in a northern prison camp. Sherman, congratulating Grant on the great victory, wrote, "To me the delicacy with which you have treated a brave but deluded enemy is more eloquent than the most gorgeous oratory of an Everett."[46] Grant heard some criticism for his decision. How many soldiers would return to take up arms against the United States? Many did in fact violate parole, causing bitterness in some quarters. A sizable number, however, never returned to the battlefield, depriving the South of much-needed manpower. Claimed Grant, "I knew many of them were tired of the war and would get home just as soon as they could." He further elaborated the ideas behind his surrender policy: "The men had behaved so well that I did not want to humiliate them. I believed that consideration for their feelings would make them less dangerous foes during the continuance of hostilities, and better citizens after the war was over."[47] Besides the surrender of the army, the Federals captured 172 cannon and 60,000 long arms, a hard loss for southern forces. Grant established Union control of the entire southern portion of the Mississippi River and cut the Confederacy between its eastern and western halves. Southern trade in the trans-Mississippi west was now plugged. The loss of Vicksburg provided a body blow to southern morale. Davis described it as the "darkest hour of our political existence."[48] Vicksburg checked Confederate momentum, and while the major eastern armies remained locked in stalemate, the western forces were freed up to move elsewhere as needed.

Grant accorded great importance to the campaign. "The fate of the Confederacy was sealed when Vicksburg fell. Much hard fighting was to be done afterwards and many precious lives were to be sacrificed; but the *morale* was with the supporters of the Union ever after."[49] Today, Gettysburg, not Vicksburg, is designated the "turning point" of the Civil War. Many more visitors flock to Pennsylvania than to Mississippi to walk the battlefield and to learn about Civil War history, just as more tourists go to Antietam than to Shiloh.[50] Historians debate the relative importance of the Eastern versus the Western Theater, with some urging less attention to Virginia and more to Mississippi to provide balance. A scholar of Vicksburg agreed with Grant's assessment. "The campaign's effect on the outcome of the war was profound, arguably more so than that of any other military event," declared Michael B. Ballard. "The impact of the surrender on Southern morale was considerably greater than that of Lee's withdrawal from Pennsylvania."[51] William McFeely asserted that "the excitement in Washington and all across the North when the twin Forth of July victories of Gettysburg and Vicksburg were announced was enormous. General Grant, of Vicksburg, and not General Meade, of Gettysburg, emerged as the hero of the day."[52]

Vicksburg's most important outcome was Grant's elevation to the top rank of generals. Bruce Catton argued, "Superior force had been put in his hands, and it was to be used not so much to win strategic victories as to destroy a nation."[53] When Lincoln heard of the fall of Vicksburg on July 7, he proclaimed momentously, "Grant is my man, and I am his, the rest of the war."[54] A week later Grant opened a letter from the president that must have given him gratification. "I do not remember that you and I ever met personally," Lincoln began. "I write this now as a grateful acknowledgment for the almost inestimable service you have done the country." Lincoln admitted to Grant that at times he had little faith in the general's strategy, "but I now wish to make the personal acknowledgement that you were right, and I was wrong."[55] In short order Grant was promoted to major general in the regular army and appointed head of the Military Division of Mississippi. The reorganization united under Grant's command the three western armies—the Army of the Tennessee, the Army of the Cumberland, and the Army of the Ohio—with the goal of removing the Confederate presence in eastern Tennessee. Sherman, at Grant's request, assumed Grant's former position as commander of the Department of the Tennessee.

### A Manifold Victory

In October, Grant took charge of the campaign for control of the strategically important city of Chattanooga, Tennessee. After suffering a disastrous defeat in northwest Georgia at the battle of Chickamauga on September 20, General William S. Rosecrans and his Army of the Cumberland retreated to Chattanooga. Confederate occupation of Missionary Ridge and Lookout Mountain effectively cut off supply lines to Chattanooga. This presented a potentially dire scenario, threatening starvation for the Federal soldiers trapped in the city and greatly endangering the Union effort to control eastern Tennessee. Grant studied the situation carefully and wrote out orders for victory. The scene was recorded for posterity: "At this time, as throughout his later career, he wrote nearly all his documents with his own hand, and seldom dictated to any one even the most unimportant despatch. His work was performed swiftly and uninterruptedly, but without any marked display of nervous energy."[56] Winning the approval of Lincoln and Stanton, Grant fired the hapless Rosecrans and replaced him with Major General George Henry Thomas, known as the "Rock of Chickamauga" for his courageous role in saving the army from destruction in that battle. Soon to be appointed to Grant's staff, Horace Porter was serving as chief of ordnance for the Army of the Cumberland when he met his future boss. He later offered a vivid description of Grant's appearance on October 23, 1863:

> Many of us were not a little surprised to find in him a man of slim figure, slightly stooped, five feet eight inches in height, weighing only a hundred and thirty-five pounds, and of a modesty of mien and gentleness of manner which seemed to fit him more for the court than for the camp. His eyes were dark-gray, and were the most expressive of his features. Like nearly all men who speak little, he was a good listener; but his face gave little indication of his thoughts, and it was the expression of his eyes which furnished about the only response to the speaker who conversed with him. . . . The firmness with which the general's square-shaped jaws were set when his features were in repose was highly expressive of his force of character and the strength of his will-power. His hair and beard were of a chestnut-brown color. The beard was worn full, no part of the face being shaved, but, like the hair, was always kept closely and neatly trimmed. . . . His voice was exceedingly musical, and one of the clearest in sound and most distinct in utterance that I have ever heard. . . . He was civil to all who came in contact with him, and never attempted to snub any one, or treat anybody with less consideration on account of his inferiority in rank.[57]

Corps commander General O. O. Howard watched with admiration as Grant asserted control over his new command with "a quiet firmness."[58] Along with Thomas's troops, the corps of Maj. Gens. Joseph Hooker and William T. Sherman brought the Union total to 70,000, as opposed to 40,000 for the enemy, although the latter enjoyed superior position high on the ridges. With no time to spare, Grant reopened the supply line relieving his desperate troops and prepared for battle. On November 24, Hooker's troops captured the Confederate position on Lookout Mountain; the next day, 20,000 Union soldiers stormed up Missionary Ridge and overwhelmed the Rebels.

Grant unleashed a devastating blow to Confederate fortunes, and the Union assault on Missionary Ridge was never forgotten by the men who made it. A veteran recalled, "The plain unvarnished facts of the storming of Mission Ridge are more like romance to me now than any I have ever read in Dumas, Scott or Cooper." Charles Dana reported to Secretary of War Stanton that "the storming of the ridge by our troops was one of the greatest miracles in military history." An officer enthusiastically proclaimed, "It is unexampled—another laurel leaf added to Grant's crown."[59] The taking of Chattanooga prompted the *New York Herald* to declare, "General Grant is one of the great soldiers of the age . . . without an equal in the list of generals now alive."[60] "It would have been a victory for us to have got our army away from Chattanooga safely," Grant wrote. "It was a manifold greater victory to drive away the besieging army; a still greater one to defeat that army in his chosen ground and nearly annihilate it."[61]

Grant secured Chattanooga, Knoxville, and eastern Tennessee for the Federals, and left the Confederate western military command in ruins. Victory at Chattanooga also established control over important railroad networks, boding well for future campaigns such as Sherman's drive to capture Atlanta. "If Vicksburg made Grant a public hero," McFeeley stated, "his conversion of defeat into victory at Chattanooga proclaimed his military greatness."[62] Sherman said: "You are now Washington's legitimate successor, and occupy a position of almost dangerous elevation; but if you can continue as heretofore to be yourself, simple, honest, and unpretending, you will enjoy through life the respect and love of friends, and the homage of millions of human beings who will award to you a large share for securing to them and their descendants a government of law and stability." More plainly, a soldier wrote home a line published in a newspaper, "This victory crowns Grant as the hero of the war."[63] President Lincoln once again sent a warm message of congratulations to Grant: "I wish to tender you, and all under your command, my more than thanks, my profoundest gratitude, for the skill, courage and perseverance with which you, and they, over so great difficulties, have effected that important object. God bless you all."[64] Lincoln also proclaimed a national day of thanksgiving, and the U.S. Congress joined in, passing a joint resolution paying tribute to General Grant and ordering a medal to be struck in honor of his achievements.

## The Soldier-Statesman

In November 1863, Grant stood as the most successful Union general of the Civil War. "General Grant, out of a maze of tactics more wondrous than ever before puzzled the brains of observers afar off, has evolved a victory for our arms the importance of which it is impossible to estimate," declared an admiring *New York World*. The victor at Fort Donelson, at Shiloh, at Vicksburg, and at Chattanooga had demonstrated strategic brilliance and tactical success. "The art of war is simple enough," Grant is reported to have said. "Find out where your enemy is, get him as soon as you can, and strike him as hard as you can, and keep moving on."[65] Unlike his timid eastern Union counterparts, Grant was aggressive in battle and secured conquered territory to such an extent that no western Confederate general or army remained unscathed. Outwardly quiet and unpretentious, inwardly confident, Grant's style of command was practical, flexible, and, above all, decisive. Grant emerged a celebrated warrior-chieftain whose likeness was plastered on innumerable northern patriotic posters, illustrations, and postcards. Unprepossessing in real life, his visual representation spoke of power, of strength, of courage, and of a country that would remain united. A thriving prewar commercial market for newspapers, journals, magazines, and portraiture swelled to greater heights as it collided with a public hungry for war news and striking visual representations of famous battles and leading generals. "In Civil War military portraiture Ulysses S. Grant . . . reigned supreme," observed Mark E. Neely Jr. and Harold Holzer in *The Union Image*.[66] The February 6, 1864, cover of *Harper's Weekly* featured an elaborately patriotic Thomas Nast illustration showing Columbia pinning a gold medal on General Grant's chest, with the simple title "Thanks to Grant."[67]

Northerners eagerly followed his exploits with the aid of newspaper columns, and journals, filled with the details of his battlefield victories in Mississippi and Tennessee. The author of an admiring book rushed into print in March of 1864 previewed its content:

The best introduction to this volume that can be written, is to state that the subject of it is but forty-one years of age; has participated in two great wars; has captured during the present struggle five hundred guns, one hundred thousand prisoners, and a quarter of a million of small arms; has redeemed from rebel rule over fifty thousand square miles of territory; has reopened to the commerce of the world the mightiest highway on the globe; has stubbornly pursued his settled path in spite of all obstacles, and has never been beaten. All this has been realized . . . for the sole and patriotic purpose of securing the restoration of the Union.[68]

In Nashville, a soldier captured Grant's growing celebrity: "Gen. Grant passed through on the train and the soldiers who have never seen him lined the track and gazed at him as they would a caged animal, crowding as close as they can to the car, sticking their heads in the windows and gawking at him."[69] Lincoln wanted to appoint Grant the commander-in-chief of the Union armies. With Grant's ascension in mind, Elihu Washburne was push-

"Thanks to Grant," by Thomas Nast. Columbia pins the Congressional Gold Medal on Maj. Gen. U. S. Grant. A proliferation of artifacts, paintings, and printed images made Grant into an iconic figure symbolizing and mobilizing nationalistic sentiment in the Civil War and Reconstruction era, as well as for later generations. (*Harper's Weekly*, February 6, 1864)

ing a bill through Congress to revive the rank of lieutenant general, not again bestowed since it had been given to George Washington. Hearing the rumors, the *New York Tribune* offered its approval, "Gen. Grant has fought more successful battles than any of our Generals. . . . His Vicksburg campaign last Summer is the most brilliant series of successes achieved during the war, while his later victory at Missionary Ridge argues that blending of audacity in conception with energy in execution which argues a decided Military genius. . . . Success and renown to Lieutenant-General Grant!"[70]

Lincoln hesitated for a short time before promoting Grant, whose immense popularity had prompted some of the president's opponents to think about him as a possible candidate in 1864. The pro-Democrat *New York Herald* proclaimed, "The next president must be a military man." *Herald* editor James Gordon Bennett was pushing hard for Grant to run in the election on the Democratic ticket, replacing the hated Lincoln. A *Herald* editorial gushed: "The whole country looks up to him as the great genius who is to end this war, restore the Union and save us from the dangers which the end of the war may bring upon us."[71] Although Grant was in agreement with Republican policy by 1864, his political inclinations were unknown, and both parties courted him. Lincoln feared appointing another general-in-chief like George B. McClellan, a prominent Democrat and harsh administration critic who was also being touted as a candidate. Lincoln needed reassurance, as he put it, that Grant did not have the "presidential grub" gnawing at him.[72] Grant eased Lincoln's concerns through Elihu Washburne and others. In a letter responding to a prominent Democrat's request that his name be forwarded as a candidate, Grant expressed astonishment and declared: "Nothing likely to happen would pain me so much as to see my name used in connection with a political office. I am not a candidate for any office nor for favors from any party."[73] Writing to his father, Grant vented his frustration at politicians who were pressuring him to run for office: "All I want is to be left alone to fight this war out, fight all rebel . . . oposition, and restore a happy Union, in the shortest possible time."[74] Lincoln was pleased by what he heard and never again worried about political competition from his top general.

Grant's lack of interest in *running* for political office did not mean he was ignorant about the role of politics in the war. Lincoln's statement in his second inaugural address, "The progress of our arms, upon which all else chiefly depends," illuminates how little separation existed between politics and military in the war.[75] To a greater or lesser extent, every Civil War general played two roles: soldier and statesman. Many fell by the wayside. The best struggled to meet the challenge. A few were very successful. U. S. Grant emerged as the leading Union general of the Civil War because he developed political skills that complimented his military abilities. "He understood," observed T. Harry Williams, "as did no other general on either side, that there was a relation between society and war, that sometimes in war generals had to act in response to popular or political considerations."[76] And because of his deep understanding of politics, soldier-statesman Grant knew the president's role as commander-in-chief of the war was unquestioned.

One excellent example of Grant's political sagacity was his unstinting support for emancipation. In 1861, the "Union as it was" (i.e., with slavery) provided the justification for waging war. In 1863, the Union Cause was enlarged to include emancipation. Grant successfully set up a refugee camp in Grand Junction, Mississippi, intending it to serve as a prototype for a humane transition from slavery to freedom.[77] The Emancipation Proclamation brought northern resources and manpower to bear in the destruction of the South's economy and society, and contained within it a provision for the recruitment and arming of black soldiers in the United States Army. Now, black men, mostly ex-slaves, would wear the blue Union army uniform, and the Union army would become the instrument of liberation for millions of black people. Emancipation was unpopular among northern Democrats and contributed to the rise of a strident antiwar opposition; it was detested by southern whites of all backgrounds, complicating greatly the conduct of the war and its aftermath.[78]

Thus, the Federal army was placed in a position of responsibility for carrying out the political as well as military aims of the war. Military leaders were expected to recruit, train, and lead largely volunteer forces; win on the battlefield; establish the rule of law over occupied areas; work to restore loyalty to the Union; and devise and implement an economic and social plan for the huge number of ex-slaves occupying contraband camps. The U.S. government made the voluntary enlistment of black soldiers in the United States Colored Troops one of its primary objectives, and, writing through Halleck, Grant assured the president of his active support in this critical endeavor: "You may rely upon it I will give him all the aid in my power. I would do all this whether the arming of the Negro seemed to be a wise policy or not, because it is an order that I am bound to obey and I do not feel that in my position I have a right to question any policy of the Government."[79] Grant recognized that black freedom would give the Union army a huge advantage. He knew that neither the southern home front nor the army could operate without slave labor. Moreover, the formation of regiments filled with former slaves would provide a double blow to the Confederate cause. Despite the advantages to enrolling black soldiers, substantial opposition arose in the North, both on the home front and in the army, among officers and ordinary soldiers alike. Grant brushed aside objections and initiated an energetic and efficient recruiting effort in the western theater.[80]

For the remainder of the war, Grant consistently voiced his strong support for African American troops. After hearing that Confederates had committed atrocities against black soldiers captured at the battle of Milliken's Bend, Grant wrote to Confederate general Richard Taylor stating the Union's policy: "I can assure you that these colored troops are regularly mustered into the service of the United States. The Government and all Officers under the Government are bound to give the same protection to these troops that they do to any other troops." Later, Grant was quoted in the *New York Times* as saying that he was determined "to protect all persons received into the army of the United States, regardless of color or nationality."[81]

## Lieutenant General of the United States

In 1864, President Abraham Lincoln turned to U. S. Grant to defeat the Confederate rebellion. An early historian of the War, James Ford Rhodes, wrote of Grant that at this time "he was now without question the most popular man in the United States. Both parties and all factions vied with one another in his praise. . . . It happens to but few men of action to receive during their lifetime such plaudits as Grant received in the winter and early spring of 1864."[82] On March 3, Grant was ordered to Washington; on March 9, he received his commission as lieutenant general; and on March 10 he went to work. He then had roughly two months—until May 4, when he crossed the Rapidan River, commencing the Overland Campaign—to analyze and master the political and military situation in the East; to concentrate a large number of scattered troops; to organize those troops into strong fighting forces and place them according to his strategic vision; and to formulate his "winning plan" for all the Union military forces. He had to do all this under the intense scrutiny of northern politicians, the press, and the public, who expected, indeed demanded, a quick end to the war. A Republican senator expressed the typical sentiment about Grant: "He has organized victory from the beginning, and I want him in a position where he can organize *final* victory and bring it to our armies and put an end to the rebellion."[83]

As 1863 turned into 1864, the North celebrated the New Year with the expectation that the war could now be won quickly. Actually a careful observer would note that there were both hopeful and worrisome signs for the United States. Bitterness over the defeats suffered in the preceding winter and spring at Fredericksburg and Chancellorsville to Robert E. Lee and the Army of Northern Virginia was replaced with hope after morale-lifting summer and fall victories—surely, the end of the rebellion was near. The Union controlled the Mississippi River; U.S. armies held Tennessee, West Virginia, Virginia north of the Rapidan River, and most of Louisiana; Federals occupied the majority of the coastal forts along the Atlantic and the Gulf. The situation invited optimism. Yet, large parts of southern territory remained undisturbed. While the Confederate goal of independence could be achieved waging limited warfare, fulfillment of the Union Cause required unconditional military victory, which meant not only winning battles, but also occupying southern land and controlling the South's people, a daunting task. Confederate citizens endured privations that would have been unthinkable in 1861, and morale remained high—as long as Lee's army won battles.

Davis and Lee's national strategy was to inflict huge casualties on the North, wearing down the will to fight. It almost worked. Lee laid out the scenario in a letter written in 1863, predicting that there "will be a great change in public opinion at the North. The Republicans will be destroyed & I think the friends of peace will become so strong as that the next administration will go on that basis. We have only therefore to resist manfully."[84] Virginia's bountiful and strategically critical Shenandoah Valley remained in Confederate hands, and two experienced armies—Lee's in Virginia and Johnston's in northwestern Georgia—were preparing for battle. Smaller Confederate armies in the trans-Mississippi posed a threat to Union security. Finally, five Union commanders in the Eastern Theater had failed to defeat the Confederates. General George Gordon Meade, the sixth, vanquished Lee at Gettysburg, although not decisively. The contending forces were encamped about fifty miles southwest of their 1861 positions, locked in stalemate, a situation that favored the Confederacy. Grant summarized the situation aptly: "In the East the opposing forces stood in substantially the same relations towards each other as three years before. . . . They were both between the Federal and Confederate capitals."[85] Lincoln's previous field commanders had not taken the fight to the enemy. With the presidential election looming, this state of affairs had to be changed, and Lincoln bet his presidency that Grant was the man to do it.

*"The country herein trusts you"*

On the afternoon of March 8, 1864, forty-one-year-old Ulysses S. Grant came into the Willard Hotel in Washington, D.C., shaking off the rain that soaked the city's streets that day. The desk clerk, unimpressed by this rather modest looking man who asked for lodging, offered him one of the smaller rooms at the top of the establishment. Grant, lacking the retinue of many top officers and with his tired fourteen-year-old son, Fred, at his side, accepted the room and then signed in simply as "U. S. Grant and son, Galena, Ill." The clerk, immediately aware of his mistake in treating the conquering hero of the Western Theater like any ordinary general, recovered and offered him another room, "Parlor #6," one of the finest suites in the hotel. From that time on, crowds gathered everywhere Grant went, making even the simple act of dining in the hotel an ordeal.[86] Later that evening, Grant made an appearance at one of the Lincolns' regular receptions. The reception was heavily attended, as everybody wanted a chance to view the man whom the president had called upon to command all the armies of the United States, and to direct Union victory. This occasion marked the first time Lincoln and Grant met. Lincoln recognized Grant right away and with his usual warm manner made the general feel welcome by saying, "Why, here is General Grant! Well, this is a great pleasure."[87] Grant ended the evening in the midst of a cheering throng in the East Room, where he stood on a sofa so that he could see and be seen by prominent Washingtonians. So far, Grant had made an excellent impression.

The commission was officially bestowed the next morning, March 9, in a ceremony at the White House. Lincoln underscored the immense importance of the occasion: "With this high honor devolves upon you also, a corresponding responsibility. As the country herein trusts you, so, under God, it will sustain you." Grant's response was simple and heartfelt: "With the aid of the noble armies that have fought on so many fields for our common country, it will be my earnest endeavor not to disappoint your expectations. I feel the full weight of the responsibilities now devolving on me and know that if they are met it will be due to those armies, and above all to the favor of that Providence which leads both Nations and men." Lincoln's phrase is telling, "As the country herein trusts you, so, under God, it will sustain you."[88] "Trust" and "sustain" are the key words—the country trusted Grant to bring the war to its conclusion. Would it sustain him enough if the campaign encountered difficulties? Lincoln and Grant met after the ceremony for some plain talk. Lincoln explained that he had never wanted to interfere with his commanding generals, but their reluctance to fight, coupled with congressional pressure pushed him into the position of military commander. As Grant later related, "All he wanted or had ever wanted was someone who would take the responsibility and act, and call on him for all of the assistance needed." Grant took this opportunity to assure him, "I would do the best I could with the means at hand, and avoid as far as possible annoying him or the War Department."[89] Confirming this trait, Lincoln said Grant "doesn't worry and bother me. He isn't shrieking for reinforcements all the time. He takes what troops we can safely give him . . . and does the best he can with what he has got."[90] By so stating, Lincoln revealed an important element of Grant's military success.

## Grant, Meade, and the Army of the Potomac

Grant's meetings with President Lincoln and Secretary of War Stanton brought to his attention General Meade's position in the new plan. Lincoln and Stanton expressed their desire to keep Meade as commander of the Army of the Potomac but also voiced their willingness to replace him, if Grant wished. Grant pondered his options. The Army of the Potomac was the largest, best-known, best-equipped army in the country, and yet it had failed, time and time again, to aggressively pursue Lee. Would a change of leadership help, Grant wondered, or was the lack of aggression now so deeply ingrained that change at the top would make little or no difference? Months before Grant gained his new appointment he speculated on possible problems he might encounter in the Eastern Theater: "Here [Western Theater] I know the officers and men and what each Gen. is capable of as a separate commander. *There I would have all to learn.* Here I know the geography of the country and its resources. *There it would be a new study.* Besides more or less dissatisfaction would necessarily be produced by importing a General to command an Army already well supplied with those who have grown up, and been promoted, with it"[91] (Italics added).

Grant's speculation proved correct, as the Overland Campaign demonstrated all too well. Civil War armies, like all other institutions, developed cultural traits. The culture of the Army of the Tennessee was aggressive, embodying a "can do" attitude. The culture of the Army of the Potomac was cautious, timid, and contentious, embodying a "can't do" attitude. The army's culture reflected the strengths and weaknesses of George B. McClellan, its most famous commander. Well-trained, organized, disciplined, more spit-and-polish than other Union forces, the army suffered long-standing command problems. Grant decided to retain Meade but established his own "headquarters in the field" to oversee the army's operations. It would, of course, be very awkward, something Grant realized sooner than Meade. "He was commanding an army and, for nearly a year previous to my taking command of all the armies, was in supreme command of the Army of the Potomac," Grant explained. "All other general officers occupying similar positions were independent in their commands so far as any one present with them was concerned." To relieve the potential embarrassment, Grant's orders for the army's movement would be given to Meade to execute. Grant and Meade started off on a solid footing, although their relationship later became strained.[92]

Grant knew that the Army of the Potomac's history of nasty political infighting and troubled leadership was partly the price of operating in the shadow of Washington, D.C. Originally he desired to keep his headquarters in the Western Theater. "Don't stay in Washington," Sherman implored him. "Come out West, take to yourself the whole Mississippi Valley. . . . For Gods [sic] sake and for your Countrys [sic] sake come out of Washington." But the political stakes were far too high for him not to take on the Army of Northern Virginia directly. He remained in the East, but not in Washington. He had to find a way, as Sherman put it, to "resist the pressure that would be brought to bear upon him to desist from his own plans and pursue others."[93] His solution, as stated above, was to travel with Meade. Sherman would command the western armies, under Grant's direction. Another possible problem was resolved. Grant's promotion to lieutenant general elevated him above Henry Halleck, who was demoted to chief of staff. Halleck was not a great warrior, but he was an able politician and manager of logistics. Grant smoothed over an uncomfortable situation, and Halleck remained at his desk in Washington, fending off the politicians and supporting Grant and the armies in the field.[94]

In Nashville for a short trip, Grant held long discussions with Sherman and four other officers he had asked Sherman to bring with him: Maj. Gen. James B. McPherson (later killed during the Atlanta Campaign), Maj. Gen. John A. Logan, Maj. Gen. Philip H. Sheridan (selected to head the Cavalry Corps in the Army of the Potomac), and Brig. Gen. Grenville M. Dodge. Here, among the men he trusted, he laid out his strategy for the Western Theater under Sherman's command. The object was to capture the Confederacy's major railroad hub at Atlanta, destroy its railroad lines, cut off supply lines to the troops, and defeat Gen. Joseph E. Johnston's Army of Tennessee. Grant hoped that in tandem with the planned Virginia offensives, the western campaign would strangle the Confederate nation and force its surrender. Later, Sherman remarked of the strategy, "He was to go for Lee and I was to go for Joe Johnston. That was the plan."[95]

## The Press Reaction

Grant was a hit with the northern press. Horace Greeley, the eccentric editor of the *New York Tribune*, wrote: "Senators state with joy that he is not going to hire a house in Washington and make war ridiculous by attempting to maneuver battles from an arm-chair." Anti-Lincoln but pro-Grant and pro-war, the *New York Herald* put it more simply. "We Have Found Our Hero," a headline announced, and the story below added, "We are free to say that it materially strengthens our hopes that the great campaign about to open will substantially put an end to the rebellion."[96] The *Chicago Tribune*, strongly pro-Lincoln and proemancipation, wrote: "Gen. Grant has shown his signal military ability by determining at the very outset of commencing upon his new duties, to break up the scatteration policy which has characterized Halleck's administration, and to this end the armies in Louisiana and Texas are to be massed with the Mississippi armies for the 'smashing blow' this season. Grant means work."[97] A more cautious student of the war's history was a *Harper's Weekly* editorialist who reminded readers that Grant:

> will be opposed by a skillful and tried soldier; by a trained army swelled by a remorseless conscription, fighting upon ground familiar to it, and for a cause which it has ardently espoused. The battle will be desperate, as the issues are momentous. Let us, as sensible men, remember how uncertain the event of every battle is, and not take leave of our common sense by declaring that we must and shall win. . . . Three years of fierce civil war, as they have made us sadder men, should certainly make us wiser men."[98]

The Republican-leaning *New York Times* also provided a cautionary note. "As long as the armies of Lee and Johnston exist, we shall have a great deal of work to do; and even they, we fear, will have to be killed half a dozen times before they can be accounted dead."[99] But this type of comment was the exception, not the rule. The press praised Grant the military hero, approved his campaign strategy (or at least the bits made public), and predicted a climactic battle in which Grant would defeat Lee and end the war in short order. In truth, there was much reason to be suspicious of an easy victory, as President Lincoln and General Grant knew all too well. Superior numbers and overwhelming industrial power did not translate into winning the war without the kind of military leadership that would bring decisive victory on the battlefield. A few skeptics pointed out that as great a general as Grant appeared to be in the West, he had never faced Robert E. Lee. The *Philadelphia Daily Evening Bulletin* believed, "The people will have renewed hope of an early extinction of the rebellion, as soon as General Grant is made the head of all our armies," but also warned, "it must be remembered that the Army of the Potomac has been opposed to the best army of the South, led by the best general in the rebel service."[100] The *New York Times* quickly retorted: "That is true enough. But do these people ever think that, if it be true that Grant has never fought Lee, it is equally true that Lee has never met Grant."[101]

Grant was wary of such high expectations, as he explained to Julia: "I know the greatest anxiety is now felt in the North for the sucsess [*sic*] of this move, and that the anxiety will increase when it is once known that the Army is in motion."[102] He believed victory in the field and survival of the Union (and Lincoln's presidency) would be synonymous. The Democratic opposition, temporarily at bay due to recent Union victories, would resume their attacks on the Republican leadership if Grant became mired down in Virginia like all previous Federal commanders pitted against Lee. Democrats had enjoyed successes in the 1862 and 1863 elections by attacking the president and his party on issues such as the suspension of civil liberties, emancipation, the draft and riots it provoked, and finally, deeply felt war weariness.[103] Grant kept his concerns, and his plans, under wraps: "I did not communicate my plans to the President, nor did I to the Secretary of War or to General Halleck." He even refused to tell Julia, "Don't know exactly the day when I will start or whether Lee will come here before I am ready to move. Would not tell you if I knew."[104]

## Grant Takes Command in the Eastern Theater

Grant established his field office in Culpeper, Virginia, approximately seventy miles outside of Washington and about six miles from Meade's own headquarters. From March 26 through April 4 Grant worked out the details of the upcoming campaigns, sending directives to Stanton, Halleck, Sherman, and other commanders. He secured his senior command appointments, and began to put in action the organizational changes that would streamline the northern armies to bring their combat strength up as much as possible. This was particularly important in light of the huge number of enlistment terms that were going to expire in the spring and summer of 1864. Grant went to work reducing the huge number of Union soldiers (estimated at half of all those in Federal service) who were posted to garrison jobs or guarding supply lines in and around Washington, D.C., and in the Western Theater. Grant ordered every commander to cut his noncombat ranks "to the lowest number of men necessary for the duty to be performed."[105]

Grant's grand idea was to make many Federal armies into one army. To Meade he wrote, "So far as practicable all the Armies are to move together and towards one common center."[106] The defeat of Johnston's and Lee's armies was the centerpiece of his campaign strategy. As expected, the numbers were favorable. At this point Sherman's western army comprised 120,000 men, twice the number of Johnston's. The Army of the Potomac numbered roughly 120,000, opposing Lee's 64,000 effectives. Grant sought to further improve the numbers by coordinating attacks with smaller Union armies. In the West, Grant ordered Maj. Gen. Nathaniel P. Banks to help Sherman by taking Mobile, Alabama, with his force of 30,000 men, while the Army of the James led by Maj. Gen. Benjamin F. Butler threatened Richmond from the South. Grant directed Maj. Gen. Franz Sigel to move up the Shenandoah Valley, severing Lee's communication lines and attacking Richmond from the east, if possible. Armies acting in concert, Grant's strategy brought all possible northern manpower and resource superiority to bear on defeating the Confederates. He explained the rationale:

> There were . . . seventeen distinct [Union] commanders. Before this time these various armies had acted separately and independently of each other, giving the enemy an opportunity often of depleting one command, not pressed, to reinforce another more actively engaged. I determined to stop this. To this end I regarded the Army of the Potomac as the centre, and all west to Memphis . . . the right wing; the Army of the James . . . as the left wing, and all the troops south, as a force in the rear of the enemy. . . . My general plan now was to concentrate all the force possible against the Confederate armies in the field. . . . According, I arranged for a simultaneous movement all along the line.[107]

Grant's approach threatened Rebel armies east of the Mississippi. If all southern forces were endangered, none would be able to send reinforcements to another. Thus, even if Grant's movement on Lee was not successful immediately (as was the case) the simultaneous movements against the rest of the Confederacy, which supplied and supported Virginia in terms of manpower and matériel, would fatally cripple the ability of Lee's army to sustain itself. Grant's knowledge of, and experience with, logistics served him well. Meanwhile, the considerable wealth of the United States poured into Alexandria, Virginia. Its warehouses were filled with provisions of every kind to feed and support 100,000 men and over 60,000 horses and mules. The 4,300 wagons forming the Army of the Potomac's supply trains carried ten days of food, forage, and ammunition. Grant planned to draw his supplies along Virginia's tidal rivers. By advancing by his left flank and using the rivers from the Potomac to the James, he virtually guaranteed that his supply lines would be well protected from Rebel depredations.

### "He looks as if he meant it"

Grant took advantage of his proximity to the men of the Army of the Potomac by getting to know them. He frequently reviewed the various units in their camps. Impressed by their evident discipline and combat readiness, Grant was sized up suspiciously by the officers and enlisted men of the Army of the Potomac. His elevation represented Lincoln's dissatisfaction with the army's previous leadership and its record. At first, many officers offered unflattering comments about their new commander, reflecting their low opinion of the western armies. New York's Col. Charles S. Wainwright, commander of the Fifth Corps artillery, lamented, "It is hard for those who knew him when formerly in the Army to believe that he is a great man, then he was only distinguished for the mediocrity of his mind, his great good nature, and his insatiable love of whiskey." New Englander Lt. Col. Stephen Minot Weld of the 56th Massachusetts sniffed, "He is not fine looking at all; on the contrary he is a very common-looking person." Maj. Abner Small of the 16th Maine observed that "after the debonair McClellan, the cocky Burnside, rosy Joe Hooker, and the dyspeptic Meade, the calm and unpretentious Grant was not exciting in either appearance or conduct." Capt. Charles H. Salter of Michigan expressed the opinion that "the Western rebels are nothing but an armed mob, and not anything near so hard to whip as Lee's well disciplined soldiers."[108]

Others reserved judgment. New Jersey colonel Robert McAllister observed that "Genl. Grant has the secret of keeping his own secrets, which by the way, is a good thing for the success of our cause." Theodore Lyman of Meade's staff recorded that "His face has three expressions: deep thought; extreme determination; and a great simplicity and calmness." Grant, Lyman wrote in a much-quoted passage, "habitually wears an expression as if he had determined to drive his head through a brick wall, and was about to do it. I have much confidence in him." Lyman's friend Capt. Charles Francis Adams Jr. said, "The feeling about Grant is peculiar—a little jealously, a little dislike, a little envy, a little want of confidence." Later, Adams praised him as "a very extraordinary man," who was "cool and quiet."[109]

Many lower-ranking officers and enlisted men were somewhat less critical. They liked Grant's casual style and his way of getting things done quickly and quietly. "He looks as if he meant it," declared a veteran. Another commented on the changes Grant wrought: "Every soldier is in high spirits, and I never saw such confidence in success manifested. General Grant's operations produce no partisan feeling, and that fills all hearts with hope. All are in good spirits, and *confident of success.*" Experienced soldiers were especially gratified to see that Grant turned "easy living artillerists" guarding fortifications into infantry soldiers who would actually be expected to march and fight. Henry Matrau of the 6th Wisconsin approved: "No more passes or furlough's will be granted, & things begin to look some like a move. What will be the next act in this grand drama of war no one can tell, but may God grant success to our Grant." Lt. Charles Wellington Reed of the 9th Massachusetts Artillery declared that "placeing Grant in command is the grandest coup yet. it has inspired all with that confidence that insures success. I have not the slightest doubt but that we shall be gloriously successful this comeing campaign. There will be hard fighting without a doubt."[110]

Soldiers outside the Army of the Potomac chimed in as well. The Union's eastern army and its leadership were often reviled by men in other theaters. A soldier from Illinois believed that the Army of the Potomac "ruined every Gen. Before Grant," but believed that its new commander's "grasp on the Rebel Capitol is like the hand of Fate."[111] Now, with Grant in charge, wrote a California soldier on March 25, the spring campaign

> is likely to open lively. Grant—"Old U.S.—has now the command of the army, and for once we have the 'right man in the right place,' he is going to work in the reorganization of this army in a manner that will insure success. The Army of the Potomac will in a few weeks be numerically one hundred and seventy-five thousand strong, and will be commanded by Grant in person on the field. He will not allow himself to be dictated to by corrupt politicians in Washington. He has the love and confidence of his soldiers, and of the masses of the people, and these will stand by him in whatever he may do.[112]

Whether in the West or the East, Grant's troops seldom cheered his every appearance, as did Sherman's or McClellan's. But that does not mean the men failed to appreciate his steely leadership or notice the quickening of the army's pace. A Massachusetts officer in camp around Brandy Station spoke for many: "We all felt at last that *the boss* had arrived." Another recorded that on May 31, 1864, "General Grant passed by us; many did not know he was near until the cheering commenced, then all joined in the tremendous harrahs for the 'Old man.'" A slightly different perspective was provided by a sergeant observing his new commander in the Shenandoah Valley: "That's Grant. I hate to see that old cuss around. When that old cuss is around, there's sure to be a big fight on hand."[113] Whatever the common soldiers thought of Grant, the time was drawing near for the campaign to commence. The lyrics of a song, "Ulysses Leads the Van," embodied the hopes of the northern nation:

The West has seen his flashing steel,
On many a field of glory;
His soldier tell, around their fires,
The never-wearying story,
Of victories won, and every boast,
With ardor undiminished,
That when Ulysses does a job,
He leaves no work unfinished.

The east extends a welcome hand,
And loads him with caresses;
She's made his name a household word,
That age and childhood blesses;
And now she stands, with beating heart,
Along his war-path gazing,
While at her altars, morn and night,
Her prayers for him she's raising.

CHORUS
Ulysses leads the van.
Ulysses leads the van.
We'll ever dare to follow where,
Ulysses leads the van.[114]

### Grant versus Lee in the Overland Campaign

In a directive to Meade, Grant said: "Lee's Army will be your objective point. Wherever Lee goes, there you will go also"[115] On his forty-second birthday, April 27, 1864, he settled on May 4 as the date when the army would be crossing the Rapidan River. He informed his superiors, his leading generals, and his president. Grant outlined the general scope of his campaign to Lincoln, stressing his desire to defeat the Army of Northern Virginia while activating Union armies on many other fronts. This of course is what Lincoln had been waiting to hear. Employing one of his justly famous metaphors to summarize Grant's plan, he replied: "Oh, yes! I see that. As we say out West, if a man can't skin he must hold a leg while somebody else does."[116] On April 30, Lincoln sent Grant the following letter, which throws light on the bond that had formed between them:

> Not expecting to see you again before the Spring campaign opens, I wish to express, in this way, my entire satisfaction with what you have done up to this time, so far as I understand it. The particulars of your plans I neither know, or seek to know. You are vigilant and self-reliant; and, pleased with this, I wish not to obtrude any constraints or restraints upon you. . . . If there is anything wanting which is within my power to give, do not fail to let me know it. And now with a brave Army, and a just cause, may God sustain you.

Grant thanked him, saying, "Should my success be less than I desire, and expect, the least I can say is, the fault is not with you."[117]

Early on the morning of May 4, the Army of the Potomac moved across the Rapidan River. Grant hoped to get through the Wilderness in open country before giving battle. He took a risk in doing so. The late arrival of wagon trains delayed movements, and on May 5 and 6, in dense thickets of brush and scrubby pines that neutralized Grant's numerical advantage and artillery superiority and disrupted orderly battle plans, Lee attacked. The two armies clashed in some of the most terrible infantry combat of the war, not far from where the battle of Chancellorsville had been fought only a year earlier. Union losses approximated 18,000, including many who were burned to death by brush fires as they lay wounded. Confederate losses exceeded 12,000. Undeterred by the casualties, Grant did not pull back as other Union commanders had, but instead on the night of May 7 ordered Meade to continue pushing his army southeastward toward a strategic crossroads at the small Virginia village of Spotsylvania Court House.[118]

Grant's move south must be judged as a major turning point of the war. This was one time when his men did cheer. They cheered wildly when they saw Grant riding on his big bay horse, Cincinnati, leading them not back to their camps outside Washington in defeat, but South toward a chance at victory. The men hoped they would live to see it, but many did not. Grant's decision had momentous consequences for the course of the war. The ensuing battles tested his mettle as commander as never before. His relentless determination (backed by Lincoln) to save the Union meant that he was

"Hail to the Chief! Grant in the Wilderness" (*Harper's New Monthly Magazine*)

willing to sacrifice the lives of thousands of Union soldiers. Twenty-first-century poet Stephen Cushman contemplated this moment of history:

> Whenever I smoke a cigar I think
> of Grant in the Wilderness writing
> orders out in fatless prose without revision,
> then chewing on a burnt-out stub and weeping
> as numbers flooded in and names piled up
> on lists the Northern papers printed
> along with the outcry Butcher, Butcher.[119]

At the time, many Rebels were disconcerted by Grant's evident determination, but Confederate general James Longstreet suffered from no confusion. He told a friend, "that man will fight us every day and every hour til the end of the war."[120] On May 8, the Army of the Potomac clashed with Lee's soldiers at Spotsylvania, and for the next eleven days the armies fought in a series of battles near that small county seat. The worst clashes occurred on May 12 at a place later dubbed the "bloody angle," where the troops fought for almost twenty hours to stalemate. By May 20, Grant determined that further attacks were useless. The final tally was brutal. The Federal casualties ran to more than 18,000, and the Confederates suffered 12,000 killed, wounded, or captured. "I cannot say how things are going," wrote the 11th New Jersey's Maj. Thomas J. Halsey after the battle. "I only know that we have not been whiped [sic]."[121] Tenacious and determined in the face of frightful losses, Grant resumed his southward movement, retaining the strategic initiative. He and Lee faced each other again at the North Anna River (May 23–26) with costly but inconclusive results. Once more, Grant slipped along the Rebels' right flank.

Back home, citizens were stunned at the sacrifices made, yet most were willing to give Grant's campaign more time. On May 11 Grant sent a message to Stanton, "I propose to fight it out on this line if it takes all summer."[122] Journalist Noah Brooks reported the message's electrifying effect in the capital, "Washington had broken loose with a tremendous demonstration of joy. . . . There was something like delirium in the air. Everybody seemed to think that the war was coming to an end right away." An editorial in *Harper's Weekly* acknowledged the despondency that no clear victory over Lee was achieved, but "the face of General Grant of whom we publish a portrait to-day, is itself a victory. Its fixed resolution is terrible. . . . And what blows he has dealt! How grand the spectacle of the Potomac army, officers and men, inspired by one sublime purpose, and all worthy of each other!" President Lincoln must have had Grant's "fixed resolution" in mind when remarking to his secretary, "It is the dogged pertinacity of Grant that wins." A more sober tone infused one soldier's comment: "That Grant will defeat him [Lee] in the end is the confident hope of the country."[123]

After the battle of the North Anna, an undaunted Grant moved south again, and by month's end the Federals reached a crossroads northeast of Richmond called Cold Harbor. Grant hoped to bring his army through Cold Harbor, turn on Lee's right, and pin the Confederates in a vulnerable spot against the Chickahominy River. Grant believed that Lee's men were weak while his were strong. "Lee's Army is really whipped," he wrote, "The prisoners we now take show it, and the actions of his army shows it unmistakably. A battle with them outside of intrenchments, cannot be had. Our men feel that they have gained the morale over the enemy and attack with confidence. I may be mistaken but I feel that our success over Lees [sic] Army is already insured."[124] By June 3, 59,000 well-entrenched Rebels faced 108,000 Federals across a seven-mile front at Cold Harbor. Grant's massive frontal assault on Confederate lines that day failed miserably. The campaign's previous battles were inconclusive; Cold Harbor was a clear victory for Lee. That terrible day saw some 7,000 Federal causalities (compared to fewer than 1,500 for the Rebels). Grant stopped the fighting. That evening he told his assembled staff officers, "I regret this assault more than any one I have ever ordered. I regarded it as a stern necessity, and believed that it would bring compensating results; but, as it has proved, no advantages have been gained sufficient to justify the heavy losses suffered."[125]

Cold Harbor culminated a month of nonstop campaigning for both armies. The North suffered 50,000 losses and the South 32,000 — 41 percent of Grant's forces and 50 percent of Lee's. These losses were terrible for a South unable to replenish its armies, but also a devastating blow for the northern morale needed to finish the war. Besides the carnage, Cold Harbor was notable as a turning point when defensive fortifications, siege warfare, and daily fighting characterized the war in the Eastern Theater. For soldiers, the war was now a relentless, exhausting, horrific experience, bringing on numerous cases of severe combat fatigue.[126] A growing number of vocal critics deemed the war's costs simply too much to bear. "There is death at the heart of this glory & greatness," declared a New York Democrat. "This war is murder, and nothing else." Another politician declared his disgust with Grant: "I don't think he shows skill in hurrying so many into death & agony. . . . Is it butchery, or—war?"[127] Stronger than before, defeatism and disaffection were rising in the North, especially among so-called "Copperheads" (antiwar Democrats), who enjoyed particular strength in areas of Ohio, Illinois, and Indiana—yet a slight majority of citizens and many soldiers urged fortitude. First Lieutenant James Thomas attacked disloyal behavior back home: "Our Copperheads can't see it that Grant will capture Richmond or that rebels can be subdued yet they scowl and gnash their teeth at each advance which our armies make as a result."[128]

The major Republican newspapers supported Grant, and did so until the end of the war. They urged patience on the part of the people and predicted inevitable Union victory. An editorial in the Philadelphia Daily Evening Bulletin is indicative of the tone: "There must be an end to such a contest, however, and it cannot long be deferred. Lee's army has fought with amazing bravery and endurance; but it must fall to pieces, or waste away under the blows it receives, or else it must surrender."[129] Bruce Catton explained, "Each battle looked very much like a Federal defeat—except that afterward the Army of the Potomac always moved on toward the south, quite as if it had won; and at last there had been set in motion a tide that would sweep the Confederacy out of existence no matter what skill or valor tried to stay it."[130] Grant never intended, as many charged, to engage in a war of "attrition," just throwing more and more men at Lee, not matter what the cost. His goal had always been to meet Lee's army on an open battlefield, where the North's greater strength would prevail. "It was Lee who turned it into a war of attrition," James McPherson argued, "by skillfully matching Grant's moves and confronting him with an entrenched defense at every turn."[131] Lee inflicted great losses, but Grant's overall strategy was working because, despite the losses, in six weeks he moved the army eighty miles to the outskirts of Richmond, where Lee expected the next attack.

One of the most famous photographs of the Civil War shows U. S. Grant leaning against a pine tree in front of his headquarters tent at Cold Harbor. The date of the picture is probably June 11 or 12, just before his departure from the area. The pose is casual, unaffected, and unusual in the Victorian Age, when more formal, dignified photographs were preferred. Grant's leadership style was also casual and unaffected. "Incredible as it may seem," noted Jean Edward Smith, "Grant commanded the Army of the United States from the field with a staff of twelve."[132] With battle raging, Grant often stayed in camp, whittling and smoking one of his two dozen daily cigars (although he tried to cut down). His diet was simple, or more accurately, simply horrible. For breakfast, he ate a sliced cucumber soaked in vinegar, along with cups of strong coffee. At dinner, he ate sparingly, and if the meal included meat, it had to be burnt to a crisp, for the most sanguinary of generals could not stand the sight of blood. With a small staff, he read reports, held conversations with generals, and pored over maps. Not one for holding conferences, he preferred to write out his instructions to subordinates in his concise, clear prose. The most flexible and practical of strategists, he realized well before Cold Harbor that he was never going to remake the ponderous, conflict-ridden Army of the Potomac along the lines of his western forces, and, although he never admitted it, Robert E. Lee proved to be far superior to any Confederate commander he had faced in Tennessee and Mississippi.

But Lee was not unbeatable. "What's wrong with this army?" asked Grant in frustration. Grant detested the fear among many officers in the Army of the Potomac of the general who had bested them in so many battles in 1862 and 1863. "Lee was the one soldier in whom most of the higher officers of the Army of the Potomac had complete, undiluted confidence," mused Catton.[133] Grant believed that fear encapsulated everything that was amiss with the army. One of the few times Grant's temper flared occurred during the battle of the Wilderness when an officer, seized with hysteria regarding grim reports of impending Union defeat, rode into headquarters, and said, "I know Lee's methods well by past experience; he will throw his whole army between us and the Rapidan, and cut us off completely from our com-

In the eye of the storm—
Grant at Cold Harbor,
1864. His unmilitary
pose in this photograph
little suggests the heroic
Grant portrayed in many
paintings, prints, and
illustrations. (Library of
Congress)

munications." Grant responded: "Oh, I am heartily tired of hearing about what Lee is going to do. Some of you always seem to think he is suddenly going to turn a double somersault and land in our rear and on both flanks at the same time. Go back to your command, and try to think what we are going to do ourselves, instead of what Lee is going to do."[134]

That is exactly what Grant did shortly after Cold Harbor, when he stopped flanking Lee and decided to cross the James River and seize the vital communications and rail center of Petersburg. If the Union Army prevailed at Petersburg, twenty miles south of Richmond, the Confederate capital would fall shortly afterward. On June 12, the army marched to the river and crossed a 2,100-foot-long pontoon bridge in a movement that completely fooled Lee. On June 16 the entire Union army was on the south bank. Moving swiftly, the Federals were closing in on Petersburg, defended by a ten-mile line of strongly built fortifications around the city. From June 15 to 18, United States forces, numbering around 63,000, threatened to overwhelm the much smaller Confederate defenders. But Grant watched as his plans floundered, largely as a result of the extreme battle fatigue of the men after weeks of heavy fighting. Repeated Union assaults failed to capture the Petersburg works. The Confederates quickly brought in reinforcements that made their defensive position even more formidable. Four days of fighting left the Federals with a loss of 10,586 compared to 4,000 for the Rebels. On June 18 Lee arrived to direct operations. Convinced that continued frontal attacks would be useless, Grant ordered his men to "use the spade." The ten-month siege of Petersburg had begun. It proved to be the longest military operation of the Civil War.

Grant realized the disadvantages of a long siege. Under heavy pressure to win the war quickly, he knew his prosecution of the war determined the political fortunes of his commander-in-chief. At this point, only victories in the field could sustain the Lincoln presidency and Republican rule, which in turn guaranteed unconditional victory. Ignoring the potential political fall-out, Grant pressed Lincoln and Stanton to replace soldiers lost in the Overland Campaign with 500,000 new men to be raised in the draft. "Prompt action in filling our Armies will have more effect upon the enemy than a victory over them," he explained to Stanton. "They profess to believe, there is such a party North in favor of recognizing southern independence that the draft can not be enforced. . . . The enforcement of the draft and prompt filling up in our Armies will save the shedding of blood to an immense degree."[135] Lincoln agreed—issuing the call on July 18, with some enrollments scheduled just before the election. The president praised his top general to the public: "My previous high estimate of Gen. Grant has been maintained and heightened by what has occurred in the remarkable campaign he is now conducting; while the magnitude and difficulty of the task before him does not prove less than I expected." Privately, the president urged Grant to "hold on with a bull-dog gripe, and chew and choke, as much as possible." His support was echoed among many men in the field. "Everybody here has great confidence in Grant," reported a soldier on June 8. In a letter to his wife dated July 5, 1864, Robert McAllister explained: "It is true we have lost very many men and officers; and with our victories we have had our reverses. But in a campaign like this it can not be expected that all will go in our favor. This is a big work, a glorious undertaking, and you must not expect us to accomplish it in a week or a month."[136]

Grant adjusted to a type of warfare he did not desire. He planned to encircle Petersburg and cut off all of Lee's supply lines. He ordered his soldiers to build a trench system around Lee's line of defensive fortifications stretching from Petersburg to Richmond. By late June the Confederates had approximately 50,000 (the numbers would rise to 66,000) men to 112,000 for the Union. Grant established his military headquarters at City Point, Virginia, on the southern bank of the James River, about eight miles behind the Union army lines at Petersburg. From City Point, Grant directed not only the operations of the siege of Petersburg, but also those of the whole war. As long as Grant fixed Lee's army in Petersburg, Sherman, Sheridan, Banks, and Thomas could move forward with their campaigns in Georgia, Virginia's Shenandoah Valley, Louisiana, and Tennessee. "Grant did not insist that victory come in Virginia," noted Brooks Simpson. "He did insist that wherever it came, it would be in time to keep Lincoln in office for another term and thus ensure that the war would be fought to a successful conclusion." To his sister, a soldier in Petersburg wrote, "I suppose the people of the North are wondering what Grant is doing and why don't the army move. Well the army will move as soon as Grant is ready to move it." Another claimed that "the universal conviction of the army is that the rebellion cannot survive the present Summer and Autumn. Grant . . . is a favorite with all."[137] From City Point, Grant presided over a vast logistical operation that kept the supplies flowing to the troops in the field. Whereas Union soldiers were relatively well fed, clothed, and armed, the southern soldiers suffered from hunger, disease, and other privations. As the siege wore on, as the Union shelling pounded the southern lines and the city behind them day after day, desertions among the Confederates rose and thousands of residents fled the city as refugees, flooding the roads to Richmond.[138]

In July and August, Grant's army extended its lines around the city; Union forays sought to cut the major railroad connections. Lee dispatched mobile forces to stop the Union's expeditions, and many battles took place away from the siege area. Grant periodically authorized attacks, such as the ill-starred "Battle of the Crater," occurring on July 30, 1864. On this occasion, Union soldiers tunneled underneath a Confederate fort and packed the end of the tunnel with 8,000 pounds of black power. When the powder was detonated, the blast created a huge crater, temporarily stunning the Rebels, but gross Federal incompetence failed to secure a success that could have ended the siege. Black soldiers formed an important part of the attack. Afterward, many were shot in cold blood by the Confederates. "It was the saddest affair I have witnessed in this war," Grant wrote of the disaster that claimed 450 lives and wounded 2,000. An investigation followed, with one officer cashiered and one forced to retire.[139]

July 30 was the date of another infamy—the burning of Chambersburg, Pennsylvania, by Confederate cavalry. By such actions, and by defending the vital Shenandoah Valley with Gen. Jubal A. Early's army, Lee hoped to draw Union troops away from Petersburg and Richmond. When Early threatened Washington, D.C., in July, Grant gave Philip Sheridan the command of a newly created Army of the Shenandoah Valley. Grant informed Halleck: "I want Sheridan put in command of all the troops in the field with instructions to put himself south of the enemy and follow him to the death. Wherever the enemy goes let ou[r] troops go also." Grant ordered Sheridan, in addition to clearing the Valley of Confederate soldiers, to "take all provisions, forage and Stock wanted for use of your Command. Such as cannot, be consumed destroy." He cautioned Sheridan: "Bear in mind, the object, is to drive the enemy South, and to do this you want to keep him always in sight. Be guided in your course by the course he takes." Grant wrote, "If the War is to last another year we want the Shenandoah Valley to remain a barren waste."[140]

The raiding strategy that targeted civilians and soldiers alike was implemented by Sheridan (and Sherman) with vigor, but their efforts did not immediately bring good news. Reports from Georgia were depressing. Sherman's campaign toward Atlanta was contested across northern Georgia and featured several notable battles, including Kennesaw Mountain on June 27, 1864, where the Union frontal assaults failed at great cost to the men. Johnston proved adept at eluding Sherman's grasp, but the Rebel army was ever retreating as Sherman maneuvered it inexorably southward. "Uncle Billy," pursued the Confederate army until just outside of Atlanta, where like Grant in front of Petersburg, he laid siege. In July and August, it seemed to some as if Grant's grand strategy lay in ruins. The Democratic *New York World* sarcastically asked, "Who shall revive the withered hopes that bloomed at the opening of Grant's campaign?" while a New Yorker demanded, "Why don't Grant and Sherman do something?"[141]

The absence of good news from the battlefronts brought gloomy prospects for Lincoln. Radical Republicans rejected the president's Reconstruction policy in Louisiana and other southern states, claiming it too generous to the conquered Rebels. While "saving the Union" united Democrats and Republicans, adding emancipation to the Union Cause divided the parties, and the nation, as no other issue. Copperhead partisans jokingly referred to the Emancipation Proclamation as the "Miscegenation Proclamation."

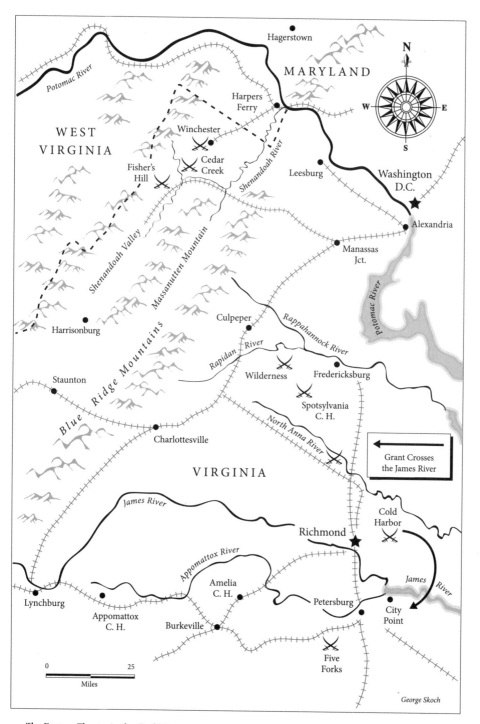

The Eastern Theater in the Civil War

Democrats ran on explicitly racist platforms in 1864, appealing to voters to reject "Abraham Africanus the First," thereby stopping "the accursed slaughter of our citizens."[142] Many Republicans pressed Lincoln to find a way to make peace, some even advocating revocation of emancipation, which he refused to consider. *Harper's Weekly*, ever a staunch supporter of the Union, bemoaned the lack of character in the people: "The apparent unanimity has disappeared; and the party divisions which in every country, at every period, and in every war, have been developed, are evident among ourselves."[143]

High casualty numbers meant low civilian morale, which in turn threatened Republican Party rule and, thus, the drive for unconditional surrender. The tie between the battlefront and the home front was never more powerful, as one Copperhead editor's attack suggests: claiming Grant was "the death's head of a whole people," he asked, "What is the difference between a *butcher* and a *general*? His answer: "A Butcher kills animals for food. A general kills men to gratify the ambition or malice of politicians and scoundrels."[144] The soldiers' favorite, George McClellan, accepted the Democratic presidential nomination in Chicago in late August. A war Democrat running on a strident peace platform, McClellan pledged to carry the war to an honorable conclusion, meaning reuniting the states. Lincoln, however, did not believe his former commander could withstand the majority sentiment in his party for a brokered peace. In that event, Lincoln made plans to cooperate in the transition. He composed a memo for his cabinet members to sign: "It seems exceeding probable that this Administration will not be reelected. Then it will be my duty to so co-operate with the President elect as to save the Union between the election and the inauguration; as he will have secured his election on such ground that he cannot possibly save it afterwards."[145] Grant was worried as well. The South's "only hope now," he stated, "is in a divided North." These sentiments were expressed in a letter widely reprinted in Republican campaign material. He elaborated, "I have no doubt but the enemy are exceedingly anxious to hold out until the Presidential election. They have many hopes from its effects. They hope a counter revolution. They hope the election of the peace candidate."[146]

Just as the Democrats were gearing up for certain electoral victory, Grant's strategy paid dividends. On September 2, 1864, the mayor of Atlanta surrendered the city to Sherman. "Atlanta is ours, and fairly won," exulted Grant's principal lieutenant. Grant sent a telegram to his friend: "I have just received your dispatch announcing the capture of Atlanta. In honor of your great victory I have ordered a salute to be fired with shotted guns from every battery bearing upon the enemy. The salute will be fired within an hour amidst great rejoicing."[147] The good news lifted northern spirits, boosting prospects for Lincoln's reelection, which would ensure the outcome of the war. More good news rolled in from the Shenandoah Valley as Sheridan defeated the Confederates at Third Winchester on September 19, Fisher's Hill on September 22, and Cedar Creek on October 19. Sheridan ended the Confederate presence in the Valley, and in a short time Grant could concentrate his entire force on the Richmond-Petersburg front. "What glorious victories we are having," wrote a soldier with the Army of the Potomac. "The last won by Sheridan, in the valley, is a glorious triumph in the cause. Grant's turn comes next, and I hope it will result grandly to our armies before November. Then we will elect Abraham Lincoln, repudiate McClellan and ignore the Chicago platform, and peace and quite will soon come apace." In late September, a Union officer recounted reading a letter left behind by a Confederate: "The Reb said that Genl. Grant was a smart old fellow, that he had out-generaled Lee . . . that the Rebellion was gon[e] up, and that there was no use fighting longer."[148]

On November 8, 1864, northern voters gave Lincoln a tremendous Electoral College majority of 212 to 21 and 55 percent of the popular vote. Few campaigns in U.S. history have been as dramatic, and few offered choices as stark: yes or no, continue the war; yes or no, support emancipation. More than a few administration officials worried that the heated atmosphere would also lead to domestic disturbances, but in the end, the string of Union victories delivered by Grant, Sheridan, and Sherman ensured both quiet streets and Republican victory. The soldier vote was critical in reelecting Lincoln. Many states during the war had arranged for their "boys" to vote on the battlefield. For other states, the Federal government granted furloughs so that soldiers, by the thousands, could return home to cast votes. Where ever they voted, most chose Lincoln over McClellan. Grant celebrated with Stanton: "Enough now seems to be known to say who is to hold the reins of Government for the next four years. . . . The election having passed quietly, no bloodshed or riot throughout the land, is a victory worth more to the country than a battle won. Rebeldom and Europe will so construe it."[149]

## Appomattox

As fall passed into winter, Union victory seemed imminent despite the Confederate leadership's refusal to give up. Jefferson Davis claimed that the results of the election were irrelevant to the war and vowed to fight on. Leaving Gen. John Bell Hood's army behind to be dealt with by George

*Grant and His Generals* by Ole Peter Hansen Balling (1865) is a group portrait of notable Union army generals led by Grant. William T. Sherman is to Grant's left. (National Portrait Gallery)

Thomas (who destroyed Hood's army in the battle of Nashville on December 15–16, 1864), Sherman vacated Atlanta on November 16, and with Lincoln and Grant's approval began his "march through Georgia." On December 20 he captured Savannah, and he thrilled the United States when two days later he sent a message to Lincoln offering him the city as a Christmas present. Basking in his subordinate's success, Grant sent his appreciation: "I congratulate you, and the brave officers and men under your command, on the successful termination of your most brilliant campaign. I never had a doubt of the result."[150] From Savannah, Sherman planned to march through South Carolina and North Carolina to meet up with Grant in Virginia.

The Confederacy was in its last throes. In January, Grant received three Confederate commissioners at his City Point headquarters on their way to meet with Lincoln to discuss a possible peace agreement. The meeting foundered over Davis's refusal to renounce Confederate independence. In March, Lincoln visited City Point and met with Grant, David Porter, and William Sherman on the steamer *River Queen*. Lincoln discussed what the terms of the impending military surrenders would be for the Confederate armies, emphasizing a generous peace agreement. Lincoln argued for an

"Facsimile of the Celebrated Antrobus Painting of General Ulysses S. Grant Painted on the Battlefield of Chattanooga, 1863–64" (Library of Congress)

"easy" Reconstruction but made two demands of former Confederates: they must accept emancipation and swear a loyalty oath to the United States. As the leaders were concluding their meeting, the Thirteenth Amendment, abolishing slavery in the United States, approved by both the Senate and the House, was going to be voted on by the states. What role the freedpeople might play in the reunited nation does not seem to have been on the agenda; Lincoln was more concerned with restoring stability and civil government in the South. Momentous decisions had to be made, and soon. Anticipating a glorious victory, Lincoln commissioned a Norwegian artist, Ole Peter Hansen Balling to paint a huge canvas of Union military heroes, with Grant featured prominently in the center. Balling also painted a splendid portrait of Grant; both now can be viewed in the National Portrait Gallery in Washington D.C. Another painting of Grant was hung in March in the Capitol rotunda, portraying Grant in formal military attire on the Chattanooga battlefield standing beside cannon, his gloved right hand lightly resting upon the tube, his left grasping a pair of binoculars.[151]

Grant never stopped pressing Lee in the grimmest winter yet for the Army of Northern Virginia. Caught up in the excitement of impending victory, the *New York Times* proclaimed, "WASHINGTON is completing his second cycle. He was with JACKSON in 1832, when he suppressed treason. . . . He has been with ABRAHAM LINCOLN, and has gone with us through the war, teaching us to bear reverses patiently. He was with GRANT at the taking of Vickburgh [*sic*], and will go with him to Richmond."[152] Things fell apart rapidly for the Confederacy in the early months of 1865, as first Petersburg and then Richmond fell to Union forces. The line from Herman Melville's poem on the fall of Richmond, "God is in Heaven, and Grant in the Town," is inaccurate. Declining to appear the conqueror, Grant slipped quietly back to City Point to finish his job. The battle of Five Forks on April 1, 1865, destroyed the last supply line for the Army of Northern Virginia. Lee's subsequent evacuation from Richmond and Petersburg left his fast-dwindling army hungry and weak. Lee's goal was to escape the clutches of the Federals by going southwest to meet up with General Joseph E. Johnston's force in North Carolina, but Grant's cavalry and infantry moved quickly to cut off all routes. A note from General Grant addressed, "General R. E. Lee, Commanding General of the Confederate States of America," was issued on April 7: "The result of the last week must convince you of the hopelessness of further resistance on the part of the Army of Northern Va. in this struggle. I feel that it is so and regard it as my duty to shift from myself, the responsibility of any further effusion of blood, by asking of you the surrender of that portion of the C.S. Army known as the Army of Northern Va."[153]

Although Lee refused Grant's request, by April 9, Palm Sunday, massed Federal power blocked the Confederate army. Lee said, "There is nothing left for me to do but to go and see General Grant, and I would rather die a thousand deaths."[154] Nursing a migraine when Lee's request to discuss surrender was delivered, Grant wrote: "I was still suffering with the sick headache; but the instant I saw the contents of the note I was cured."[155] The two generals would meet in Appomattox Court House, a small community deep in the countryside of Virginia near Lynchburg. A few minutes after 1:30 P.M., Grant and the members of his staff rode into the village and stopped their horses at the two-story brick farmhouse of Wilmer McLean. In the parlor of McLean's residence waited Robert E. Lee and a lone aide. General Lee was dressed in his best uniform and carried a beautiful sword, looking every inch the southern gentleman. The commanding general of northern armies was much less formal. His dress uniform not available, Grant was in his preferred casual field outfit complete with mud splatters from his journey. The two men exchanged some pleasantries. Grant observed his counterpart's emotionless face closely during the conversation: "What General Lee's feelings were I do not know. As he was a man of much dignity, with an impassible face, it was impossible to say whether he felt inwardly glad that the end had finally come, or felt sad over the result, and was too manly to show it."[156]

Ely S. Parker, Grant's military secretary, brought a table for him to begin writing out the terms of surrender. "I only knew what was in my mind, and I wished to express it clearly, so that there could be no mistaking it," Grant wrote in his memoirs.[157] Characteristically direct and simple, Grant's terms reflected President Lincoln's great desire that the beaten Confederates neither be humiliated nor punished. Total defeat was enough. The Rebels were to lay down arms, return home as paroled prisoners, and promise to obey the laws of the United States. Grant did not require Lee to hand over his sword, and southern officers would be able to keep their sidearms. Both officers and enlisted men could keep their horses. "This will have the best possible effect upon the men," Lee said. "It will be very gratifying, and will do much toward conciliating our people."[158] Copies of the surrender terms were then made, and Lee wrote out a letter accepting the terms. Lee's request for rations for his men was approved by Grant, and at 4:00 P.M., the two men shook hands. Lee then mounted his horse and slowly rode back to the Confederate camp. Grant sent a telegram to Stanton tersely informing him that "General Lee surrendered the Army of Northern Virginia this afternoon on terms proposed by myself."[159]

News of the surrender spread quickly through the Union camps. Soon thousands of soldiers were cheering and throwing their hats into the air. Union officer Franklin Dick rejoiced in the news that "our nation is preserved—Slaughter and wounds will cease—tranquility will be restored," adding, "Gen'l. Grant now stands the Greatest General of the World, & one of its greatest men. I honor & love him."[160] A 100-gun salute was begun, but Grant immediately stopped it, saying, "The war is over. The rebels are our countrymen again, and the best sign of rejoicing after the victory will be to abstain from all demonstrations in the field."[161] Although several more Confederate armies surrendered in the months to come, the meeting between Grant and Lee at Appomattox Court House is considered the end of the American Civil War. The news was telegraphed to every northern city, and Washington, D.C., went wild with happiness. "The glorious consummation so long devoutly wished for has at length been attained," wrote a *New York Herald* correspondent, culminating "in the surrender of General Robert E. Lee and his entire army to the victorious legions led on by

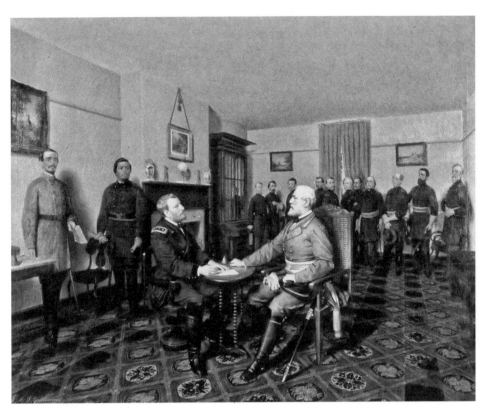

Louis Guillaume, *The Surrender of General Lee to General Grant* (1867): the beginning of a peaceful reunion portrayed. (Library of Congress)

General Grant."[162] Grant met with Lee briefly the next morning and then traveled to Washington, D.C., deliberately missing the formal ceremony of the laying down of arms, which occurred on April 12 in an atmosphere of respectful conciliation. The comments of two Confederate soldiers reveal an appreciative response to the terms and the tone of the surrender conducted by Grant. "When we learned that we should be paroled," a cannoneer recorded, "and go to our homes unmolested, the relief was unbounded. . . . The favorable and entirely unexpected terms of surrender wonderfully restored our souls." The restrained atmosphere drew this begrudging compliment from a South Carolina man: "I am forced to admit that the Federal officers and troops conducted themselves with singular propriety throughout this time."[163]

Appomattox is a sacred symbol of a peaceful reunion after a long and bitter war. Grant and Lee's flawless etiquette during the surrender ceremony and its aftermath has captivated generations of Americans. A more perfect coda to the war cannot be imagined, and immediately it was captured—in paintings, illustrations, prints, poems, and tributes, many of them inaccurately depicting the occasion.[164] Louis Guillaume's beautiful painting, "The Surrender of General Lee to General Grant, April 9, 1865" (1867), replicated widely in cheap prints, is a case in point. Instead of two separate tables, Guillaume placed Grant and Lee sitting together at one, making their union a metaphor for a broken country's healing, the centerpiece of the work. Artists relied on descriptions of the ceremony because right away the McLean house was stripped clean by relic hunters; later the increasingly dilapidated house was demolished. Today, visitors to the Appomattox Court House National Historical Park in a still remote and lovely area of Virginia contemplate the meaning of the surrender in a perfectly reconstructed house.[165] It takes nothing away from the mythic magnanimity of Grant the victorious warrior, or the dignified manner in which Lee accepted that magnanimity, to acknowledge that the transition from waging war to waging peace would not be smooth or easy or bloodless. The fighting had stopped, but the war's death and devastation ensured a difficult aftermath. Back in Washington, Grant ignored the hoopla, waited for imminent news of Johnston's surrender to Sherman in North Carolina, collected materials to write his report to Congress, and eagerly planned for the quick demobilization of the volunteer armies.

There was no time for rest, but perhaps Grant reflected on his journey from obscurity to fame in the past four years. The military hero of the Civil War, Grant was not only a victorious general but also a magnanimous warrior attaining mythic status at Appomattox. Next to Lincoln he was now the most important man in the country, and Grant anticipated working in partnership with the president, securing the fruits of victory over which so much blood had been shed.

chapter three

# A Great Soldier Might Be a Baby Politician

The misleading though popular stereotype of *President* Ulysses S. Grant as a political dimwit, watching helplessly as his administration became awash in corruption and chicanery, has deep roots in the past. Descendant of two presidents, historian, and public intellectual Henry Adams declared, "A great soldier might be a baby politician." Adams spoke for a generation of bitterly disillusioned Gilded Age reformers when he described Grant as "pre-intellectual, archaic, and would have seemed so even to the cave-dwellers." His mocking barb, "the progress of evolution from President Washington to President Grant, was alone evidence enough to upset Darwin," has been widely quoted, as has Adams's statement that the initials "U. S." stood for "uniquely stupid."[1]

Henry Adams was hardly alone in his distain for the eighteenth president. Examples abound to show that many of Grant's contemporaries—and not just his political opponents—thought he was in way over his head. Gideon Welles, Lincoln's and President Andrew Johnson's secretary of the navy, called Grant "a political ignoramus," who was "less sound on great and fundamental principles, vastly less informed, than I had supposed possible for a man of his opportunities," later describing him as "a dangerous man . . . devoid of patriotism." A racist 1868 campaign ditty, sung to the tune of "Captain Jinks of the Horse Marines," went, "I am Captain Grant of the Black Marines / The stupidest man that was ever seen."[2] The Democratic press, including the *New York World* and the *Chicago Sun*, and weekly magazines, such as *Frank Leslie's Illustrated Weekly* and *Puck*, depicted him as venal and stupid in countless columns and editorials. Cartoonists Matt Morgan and Joseph Keppler in *Leslie's* and *Puck*, respectively, added pictures to go with the words, vividly immortalizing Grant's venality. The British-born Morgan and Austrian-born Keppler specialized in savage caricature of Grant and the Republican Party. (Their pictorial critiques were more than matched by the brilliant pro-Grant illustrations of another immigrant, German-born Thomas Nast, political cartoonist for *Harper's Weekly*).[3] The patrician editors of the *Nation* pronounced the epitaph of the Grant administration in 1876: "The crisis came when an ignorant soldier, coarse in his taste and blunt in his perceptions, fond of money and material enjoyment and of low company, was put in the Presidential chair."[4] Three years later, the same influential opinion journal denounced Grant as a puppet of the "Stalwart" faction in the Republican Party, and thought it "difficult to find words of condemnation sufficiently strong . . . for using this simple soldier as the head of The Machine." After Grant died, the *New York Tribune* opined that "the greatest mistake of his life was the acceptance of the presidency."[5]

**THE BABY THAT WON'T TALK AT PRESENT.**

NURSE W——E. "Bless your souls, ladies, the child won't talk for several months yet."
DAME A. J. "Say 'My Policy!' that's a little dear."
MOTHER W. H. S——D. "Yes, Baby: say 'My—my—My Policy!' that's a nice 'ittle darling."
LADY BEN W——E. "Now, my Precious, put down that 'ittle horse one minute, and say 'Con-gress.'"
GRANNY HENRY W——N. "Yes, my Pet, say 'Re-con-struc-tion.'"
MADAME A. T. S——T. "Here's a penny for Baby: say 'Greenbacks,' darling—'Green-backs!'"

The infant Grant tutored by Republican elders dressed as nursemaids (*Harper's Weekly*, February 15, 1868, cartoonist unknown; reproduced by permission of The Huntington Library, San Marino, California)

Adams's phrase "baby politician" was useful for historians trying to explain why the military leader who was strong, fearless, and decisive in war *failed* to show those same qualities as a peacetime leader. This idea carried forward from one century to another. Woodrow Wilson in 1912 damned with faint praise: "The honest, simple-hearted soldier had not added prestige to the presidential office. . . . He ought never to have been made President." In an influential book published in 1928 debunking Grant's reputation, author W. E. Woodard provided this assessment of his lack of political acumen: "I am convinced that he was simply bewildered. He never understood intricate political moves; he was a lost child in the wilderness of politics." Decades later, scholar Vernon L. Parrington provided another harsh assessment, claiming Grant possessed only a "dull plebeian character" and was "unintellectual and unimaginative, devoid of ideas and with no tongue to express the incoherent emotions that surged daily in his heart."[6]

Three widely used textbooks published in the late 1930s and early 1940s demonstrate an entrenched low opinion of President Grant. J. G. Randall, in *The Civil War and Reconstruction*, wrote, "Of Grant's conduct as President it may be said that, by consensus of opinion, he was unfitted for the duties of his lofty office and was so thoroughly involved in partisan politics that his administration became a national scandal." The authors of *America: The Story of a Free People* proclaimed that "Grant was a great soldier, but a sorry Chief Executive," while those of *The Growth of the American Republic* explained that, "Utterly untutored in politics, his political sense was as primitive as that of a Sioux Indian. He was curiously ignorant of the law and even of the Constitution, and he never came to understand properly the relations of the Executive to his Cabinet or to the other departments of the government. . . . Nor did he ever come to understand the character of the Presidential Office."[7] In 1971, the poet Robert Penn Warren commented that in the "memory" wars, "Lee had won a final and inexpugnable victory over Grant by setting his dignity in defeat as a contrast to the corruption and vulgarity in which the victor Grant was basking in the White House."[8]

It did not help that President Grant ushered in the inglorious "Gilded Age," more than three decades (1865–1900) of unparalleled economic boom (and bust) that have become synonymous with the rise of big business led by corpulent robber barons whose lavish lifestyles offered visible proof of a growing gap between rich and poor. Politics and politicians of the era appear in many history books as mere handmaidens or enablers of corporate power in an "Age of Excess." Unbridled materialism, corruption, and money in politics, according to many scholars, degraded the ideals of the Republic, resulting in the "incorporation of America," at the expense of immigrants, the working class, and the poor.[9] One historian proclaimed, "The most significant thing about the politics of the post-war years was their insignificance. Other administrations—those of Pierce and Buchanan, for example—had been dull and incompetent; it was reserved for the Grant administration to be incompetent and corrupt."[10] The above offers only a small sample of history's unflinchingly negative judgment of Grant and his administration. Remarkably for a two-term president, very few studies have been devoted exclusively to Grant's administration.

Two volumes in the highly regarded American Political Leaders series are the exceptions: William B. Hesseltine's *Ulysses S. Grant, Politician* (1935) and Allan Nevins's *Hamilton Fish: The Inner History of the Grant Administration* (1936). Both authors concluded that Grant was an inept, ignorant, and largely ineffective chief executive whose main legacy was to leave the coun-

"The Appomattox of Third Termers—Unconditional Surrender," by Joseph Keppler. The magnanimous general is humiliated in Keppler's devastating pictorial reversal of the role Grant played at Appomattox. Here, the cartoonist portrays anti–third term sentiment as a shame-faced Grant, surrounded by symbols of his administration's scandals, "surrenders" his tarnished sword, with the work "imperial" on it, to the Republican Party's nominee, James Garfield. (*Puck*, June 16, 1880)

try with the promise of Reconstruction tragically unfulfilled and the country in the hands of "the more reactionary economic interests of the day."[11] Calling Grant "a hero no longer," Hesseltine argued that "the cold winds of controversy dissipated his cloud of glory and revealed a man unprepared by the experience and unendowed with the native gifts necessary for a successful political career." Hesseltine admitted that while he strove for a balanced perspective, "the task has been rendered difficult by the almost complete lack of Grant manuscripts. . . . The years of his presidency are singularly barren in documentary remains. Grant himself was a poor writer and had but a limited correspondence with his political associates." Hesseltine's statement about the dearth of Grant materials was simply wrong, as later publications proved. Further complicating matters for him, however, was the fact that "the collected papers of Grant's opponents are voluminous," adding more fuel to the bonfire of Grant's inadequacies.[12]

A consensus emerged, pronouncing Grant's transition from military icon to political leader a failure. A few commentators grudgingly admitted Grant became an expert in navigating the byzantine politics of the wartime years, but they quickly pointed out that his efforts to command and contain the internecine battles of party-driven politics proved far less successful. U. S. Grant switched from "waging war" to "waging peace," and found the latter more difficult and demanding than the former. Reconstruction, many argued, might have proceeded more smoothly if, as president, Grant had applied the same kind of shrewd calculation in the political arena that he had applied on the battlefield. Instead, he openly detested and distrusted the chaotic world of American politics and acted a political innocent at a time when the nation needed a tough and experienced public servant. At best, he became an unwilling tool in the hands of unscrupulous professional politicians and businessmen. At worst, he knowingly allowed corruption to run rampant in both the North and South, and in doing so he frittered away the fruits of Union victory. The chief goal of the Grant administration, one historian argued, seemed to be a Reconstruction policy that would "keep the South subordinate to the North and Democrats subordinate to Republicans. In this it was largely successful. It had behind it the immense prestige of victory and of Grant himself, and its tenure of power was prolonged by the persistent distrust of any party that was connected with slavery and secession, and strengthened by the cheerful support of the business interests which it had served."[13]

Much of the antipathy toward Grant arose from scholars, led by William A. Dunning of Columbia University, propelled by the "Lost Cause" ideology that figuratively whitewashed history to portray Reconstruction as the "tragic era." Pro-Confederate scholar Claude G. Bowers summed up the argument: "The Nation had tired of the bludgeoning of the South; and Northern sentiment was turning against the manipulation of Southern elections through the methods used in Florida and Louisiana. It was disgusted, too, with this constant marching and countermarching of Federal soldiers about the polls. . . . The hour for a change had come."[14] According to Bowers and others, Reconstruction was nothing more than a harsh and corrupt rule imposed on helpless white southerners by a combination of vindictive Radical Republicans, ignorant African Americans, evil carpetbaggers, and turncoat scalawags. Reconstruction directed by Grant's Republicans was an utter, dismal failure. Later, after the turmoil of the second civil rights protest movement, scholars trained in social history rejected the so-called "Dunning School" interpretation and recast the story of Reconstruction. One part of the story remained the same. Still deemed a failure, Reconstruction, as shaped by Grant's shortcomings, was now seen as reflecting the deep racism of northern society. William Gillette claimed that northern prejudice was largely responsible for Reconstruction's "retreat." Gillette drew attention to Grant's own racism as well, and that attention was amplified in William McFeely's *Grant: A Biography* (1981), which damned the president for his inability to secure black civil rights. Grant's historical reputation remained tarnished, McFeely declaring confidently that "no amount of revision is going to change the way men died at Cold Harbor, the fact that men in the Whiskey ring stole money, and the broken hopes of black Americans . . . in 1875."[15] Eminent historian Richard N. Current pointed out an anomaly in the literature: "Grant's low repute among historians has been largely a product of the Dunning school," he noted, adding, "His fame continues to suffer even though the Dunning interpretation as a whole has long been discredited. It is time that revisionist scholars, having already revised practically every other phase of Reconstruction, should reconsider the role of President Grant."[16]

Grant's presidential reputation *is* changing in a more positive direction. A complex depiction of Grant the politician has been rendered by a growing number of scholars, such as Brooks D. Simpson, Jean Edward Smith, and Josiah Bunting.[17] And the fresh direction of Grant scholarship has been influenced by the wealth of information found in the published volumes of the superbly edited and annotated *Papers of Ulysses S. Grant* (of which John Y. Simon was the lead editor). The massive project's origins lie in the Civil War Centennial (1961–65), and the thirty published volumes offer a fascinating documentary history of the United States in war and in peace.[18] Covering Grant's entire career, the *Papers* provide a huge evidentiary basis for the emerging reconsideration of his presidency. The revisionists' Grant is not a politically naïve fumbler who allowed his cronies to lead him around by the nose, but rather someone sensitive to political concerns and passionately committed to pursuing the goals of the war: reunion and emancipation. The new Grant remained a powerful *symbol* of the justice of the Union Cause in his eight years of office. Throughout his administration, Grant labored diligently for *both* sectional harmony *and* the guarantee of the freedpeople's newly gained political and economic freedoms.

Revisionist scholars stress that Grant's acceptance of the Republican presidential nomination in 1868 and his subsequent victory brought to the office the right man at the right time. No one else in the country possessed his unquestioned status as a symbol of unity and reconciliation. An excellent opportunity for enlightened leadership seemed to await Grant, who enjoyed

STATUE OF GEN. U. S. GRANT,
GRANT PARK, GALENA, ILL.—7

Whether cut from granite, carved from marble, or composed of bronze, images of Grant the military hero overwhelmingly outnumbered those of Grant the politician. This Galena, Illinois, monument is one of the few to depict Grant as president, in civilian garb. John Gelert designed the eight-foot bronze statue, resting on a granite pedestal, which was donated to Galena by a wealthy businessman, H. H. Kohlsaart. The figure represents Grant as he appeared in Galena at the end of the war. It is not entirely lacking in appreciation for the military leader—three sides of the monument's bottom feature bas-reliefs of his war career. (postcard, author's collection)

immense popularity with a majority of voters. As is clear, many have contended that he went on to squander his gifts and richly deserves his reputation as one of the worst presidents in history. Others now depict a thoughtful, intelligent, engaged president, fully aware of the responsibilities, duties, and difficulties inherent in the role of chief executive. "Of no president," argued Josiah Bunting, "are biases in judgment less well disguised than in those that inform opinions about Ulysses Grant."[19] Whether struggling to implement Reconstruction policy, advancing the United States' goals in foreign policy, advocating fiscal soundness, or implementing reform for Native Americans, Grant's programs enjoyed some notable successes.

Moreover, Grant possessed a political philosophy, if not Lincoln's expressive eloquence to enunciate it, for subsequent generations. It mirrored that of the triumphant Republican Party that won the war, freed 4 million slaves, and ensured the continuation of the Republic. As Charles W. Calhoun recently pointed out, in a very real sense the old United States was destroyed, replaced with a nonslaveholding republic. "Viewing their party as responsible for the Union victory," Calhoun wrote, "Republicans easily cast themselves as successors to the Founders, and set about to forge a new Republic."[20] The freedoms promised by that new republic—embodied in the Thirteenth, Fourteenth, and Fifteenth Amendments—would be protected by an unparalleled expansion of federal power. This was bound to be controversial, and difficult to implement. President Grant pledged to use that power; and when he did, resistance was fierce, leading to retrenchment and withdrawal after 1876.

The new scholarship does not pretend that the blunders of the Grant administration did not occur and were not serious. But it does contend that some of the failures speak not so much to Grant's incompetence, or to the scandals and corruption that erupted partly due to his lack of judgment, as they do to the incredibly difficult challenges of governing the country at this particular time. Brooks Simpson and Richard Current argued that the issues of war were not resolved at Appomattox. Parts of the South remained in turmoil, and a sizeable number of whites rejected both reunion and emancipation, and they employed violent means to do so. Because of this, one could easily portray Grant, like Lincoln, as a war president: "He was commander in chief during the Reconstruction phase of the continuing Civil War." Few other presidents, Current contended, "carried on such a determined struggle, against such hopeless odds, to give reality to the Fourteenth and Fifteenth Amendments and to protect all citizens of this country in the exercise of their constitutional rights." Simpson's assessment noted that "historians would assail his approach to southern policy, first for being too harsh on southern whites, then for neglecting black interests, and finally for being inconsistent and vacillating. But none were able to suggest how he could have forged a policy that would have achieved both sectional reconciliation and justice for black Americans. Perhaps it was not his failure after all."[21]

Throughout his presidency, Grant remained steadfast in the belief that the goals of the war should be preserved even as the country's enthusiasm for Reconstruction of the South in the North's image faded away. Grant's final task as president harkened back to his first, and perhaps most important achievement: to ensure a stable transition, this time in the disputed election of 1876. He succeeded, and the country reconciled for good. "When the nation almost came unglued following the Hayes-Tilden election in 1876," commented Jean Edward Smith, "Grant's evenhanded mediation of the crisis preserved the peace and paved the way for a successful presidential transition."[22] It is time to replace the caricature of Grant with a more balanced interpretation. Through trial and error, he grew in the office, like his predecessor and political hero, Abraham Lincoln. Henry Adams's "a great soldier might be a baby politician" no longer squares with the emerging scholarship. A brief and necessarily highly selective overview of his experience as a general-in-chief, politician, and president between the years 1865 and 1877 follows, as we continue Ulysses S. Grant's incredible story in which he went from being "first in war" to "first in peace." A short interlude following this chapter provides a transition to the book's second half, examining Grant's legacy.

## "I have a Herculean task to perform"

On April 14, 1865, President Lincoln invited Grant to a morning cabinet meeting where the general recounted the details of the surrender at Appomattox, much to the delight of all in attendance. Afterward, the president asked if Grant and his wife would be his guests that night for a play at Ford's Theater. Grant declined with regrets. He and Julia had plans to leave Washington immediately to visit their children in Burlington, New Jersey. Had Grant accepted, America's (and his own) destiny might have unfolded very differently. News of Abraham Lincoln's assassination on "Black Friday" reached Grant during a stop in Philadelphia. He was also informed that Secretary of State William Seward had been attacked, but survived. Edwin M. Stanton, the secretary of war, had taken charge of the situation, and was assessing the possibility of a widespread southern conspiracy. Grant returned immediately to Washington, later writing his reaction to the terrible news: "It would be impossible for me to describe the feeling that overcame me." Grant also remembered, "The joy that I had witnessed among the people in the street and in public places in Washington when I left there, had been turned to grief; the city was in reality a city of mourning."[23]

A tearful Grant stood alone for several hours at the head of Lincoln's catafalque, stating "He was incontestably the greatest man I have ever known."[24] On April 21 the somber funeral train left Washington to carry the president's body across a grieving country on its way to Springfield. Lincoln's absence cast a large shadow on the Grand Review of the Union Armies held in Washington, D.C., on May 23 and 24. The two-day occasion honoring first the eastern forces and then the western forces had Grant placed next to President Andrew Johnson in the flag-bedecked reviewing stand, receiving the mighty tributes from the seemingly endless parade of soldiers. Swinging by, the men called out, "Grant! Grant! Good bye Old Man!"[25]

After the review, Grant took a vacation, receiving effusive welcomes in his hometowns of Georgetown and Galena, and establishing his official residence in the latter place. Warm welcomes were also extended in cities and towns in New York and Massachusetts, where parades, receptions, and banquets abounded, and everywhere, many thousands of grateful citizens mobbed the general. More and more, Grant appeared to the people as an electable hero who should be the one to carry the Republican banner in 1868. Presidential politics were far from his mind in April and May of 1865. The silencing of the guns saw Grant as commander of the army of the United States, but his role in the Johnson administration lacked precise definition. He remained a powerful presence in the immediate postwar period, officially serving as general-in-chief overseeing the military part of Reconstruction policy yet inexorably drawn into the political maelstrom that engulfed the new administration.

Grant did not start out as an adversary of his boss. Like most, he held a large reservoir of goodwill toward Johnson and hoped for his success. Grant expected to serve him as he had served Lincoln; it was his duty to abide by his civilian superiors. In addition, he had an enormous investment in helping to establish a permanent and solid peace between North and South. Grant assumed that he and Johnson both favored the moderate, conciliatory policy embodied in Lincoln's wartime Reconstruction plan, in his Second Inaugural Address ("with malice toward none, with charity for all"), and in the surrender agreement at Appomattox. Johnson recognized Grant's crucial importance to a successful reunion of the country when he recommended that Grant be made the first four-star general in American history, a recommendation approved by Congress on July 25, 1866.

In the tumultuous months after the war ended, Grant concentrated on the difficulty of administering the military part of Reconstruction policy. He related to Julia: "I find my duties, anxieties, and the necessity for having all my wits about me, increasing instead of diminishing. I have a Herculean task to perform and shall endeavor to do it, not to please any one, but for the interests of our great country that is now beginning to loom far above all other countries, modern or ancient."[26] Grant's comments were on target. War was over, and Reconstruction, the process of bringing the eleven seceded southern states back into the Union, had begun. The goals of Reconstruction—to restore harmonious relations between the sections and to define and secure freedom for the ex-slaves—were daunting. It would be a huge task that involved not only readmitting the seceded states, with their bitter, defeated, impoverished white population, but also reinventing a South without slavery and rebuilding the southern infrastructure that had been destroyed by the war. It would encompass constitutional, legal, economic, and emotional issues. Additionally, as the post-Appomattox victory celebrations abated, divisions in the North between those who favored a lenient policy toward the region and those who advocated punitive measures would surely reemerge. Would the country and its leaders be up to the task?

With Congress out of session, Johnson controlled Reconstruction policy from the executive branch for nearly eight months, creating a firestorm of protest with his actions. He granted liberal pardons to those former Confederates not covered by his original amnesty proclamation issued in May 1865. He went on to appoint provisional governors for any Confederate states that had not already been "reconstructed" by Lincoln. He charged those governors with convening state constitutional conventions that would adopt the Thirteenth Amendment ending slavery, nullify secession, and repudiate all Confederate war debts. Johnson did not demand that the former Confederate states accept black suffrage or protect freedpeople's civil rights, and, in the end, critics charged, the restored South looked very much like the antebellum South without the legal institution of slavery.

## *"A National disgrace"*

At first, Republicans were divided on how to respond, a fact Johnson was counting on to lure moderates to his side. Senators Carl Schurz of Missouri, Charles Sumner of Massachusetts, Benjamin Wade of Ohio, and Congressman Thaddeus Stevens of Pennsylvania—leaders of the abolitionist wing of the Republican Party, dubbed "Radicals"—urged a stern position toward ex-Confederates, who were, they claimed, inciting violence against blacks with little or no expectation of punishment. On November 27, 1865, Grant departed on a trip through the South at the request of President Johnson, who hoped to use Grant's findings to discredit the Radicals' claims and rally the northern people behind his plan. As Grant traversed the region—including stops in Richmond, Charleston, and Atlanta—he viewed for himself the very high price the Confederacy had paid for secession, war, and now utter defeat. Upon his return on December 11, Grant issued a fairly optimistic report (read to the Senate) that pleased his commander-in-chief and disappointed the Radicals. Yes, there were attacks against blacks, he admitted, and "in some form the Freedmen's Bureau is an absolute necessity until civil law is established and enforced, securing to the freedmen their rights and full protection." But, on the whole, Grant concluded, "the mass of thinking men of the south accept the present state of affairs in good faith." He expressed confidence that the ex-Confederates were "disposed to acquiesce and become good citizens." At this point, Grant was more worried about certain Republican politicians whom he felt were being unreasonable in their demands "that the opinions held by men at the South for years can be changed in a day."[27]

Grant soon realized his confidence was premature. During the summer of 1866 riots ravaged Memphis and New Orleans, and scores of freedmen and -women, northerners, and federal soldiers were killed by white mobs. No justice came to those who committed the murders from the newly established civilian court systems. Grant declared the violence made him "feel the same obligation to stand at my post that I did whilst there were rebel armies in the field to contend with."[28] Grant was uncomfortable with the trend of Johnson's Reconstruction policy, which outraged the Radical faction of the Republican Party. Congress pushed Johnson for guarantees of rights for blacks and for the imposition of harsh penalties for former Confederate civil officials and military officers who transgressed laws. Combining idealism with practical politics, Republicans expressed eagerness to establish a viable Republican Party in the South by enrolling black men as voters. The stakes were high and the stage was set for a mandate on presidential Reconstruction in the Congressional elections of 1866.

A reluctant Grant accompanied Johnson on his northern election tour to mobilize voters in the summer of 1866. The hero of Appomattox attracted cheering crowds, but his popularity failed to rub off on Johnson, who often harangued his listeners in what appeared to be a drunken state. Grant increasingly resented being used in such a partisan manner. A reporter quoted the general as saying that he did not "consider the Army a place for a politician."[29] Depressed, Grant wrote, "I am getting very tired of this expedition and of hearing political speeches," calling the tour "a National disgrace."[30] The results of the fall elections supplied the Radicals with an overwhelming mandate to pursue their program. Presidential Reconstruction was dead thanks to a solid, veto-proof Republican congressional majority. Johnson's only recourse was to compromise with congressional Republicans.

Although in late 1865 and through much of 1866 Radical leaders were convinced that Congress needed to seize control of Reconstruction, a sizeable number of Republicans still hoped for a workable compromise with Johnson. The moderates, Grant included, were willing to recognize the new southern state governments as long as they agreed to the acceptance of the Fourteenth Amendment, which granted citizenship to African Americans, and a civil rights bill. Despite Grant's efforts to persuade him of the necessity of the legislation, Johnson refused to bend, arguing that the amendment and the bill represented an unconstitutional expansion of national power over state sovereignty. Johnson vetoed the civil rights bill, and his veto was promptly overridden. Johnson's veto demonstrated that he was not interested in compromise. The fight was now over differing interpretations of how the war's goals—reunion and emancipation—would be implemented during its aftermath. Johnson's political incompetence pushed an even greater number of moderates into the Radical camp. Grant's loyalty to Johnson was dissolving rapidly. Johnson, he believed, acted irresponsibly and placed the Union's victory at risk. The Republicans' program recasting the South in the free-labor style, and establishing a southern Republican Party with the support and the votes of the freedmen made sense to Grant as the method to secure the fruits of Appomattox.

The great political drama that captivated the nation from the fall elections of 1866 through Johnson's impeachment trial in early 1868 intensified when Congress passed the Reconstruction Acts of 1867, casting out Johnson's governments. The acts divided the ten unreconstructed southern states into five military districts, with commanders appointed to oversee the establishment of new civil administrations and the integration of the states back into the Union. These district commanders would report directly to Grant, deliberately bypassing (and embarrassing) Johnson. As one historian summarized the situation, "Early in 1867, the army, the commanding general of the army, and the secretary of war were given an extraordinary role in the governing of the country."[31] Thus, Grant held the overall authority for overseeing the return to the fold of the ex-Confederate states. Under his leadership, conventions drafted new laws and wrote new state constitutions. In his hands rested the ultimate responsibility for enforcing the Thirteenth and Fourteenth Amendments. Johnson tried to block congressional Reconstruction, but his vetoes were overridden. Grant complained that Johnson "seemed to regard the South not only as an oppressed people, but as the people best entitled to consideration of any of our citizens. . . . Thus Mr. Johnson, fighting Congress on the one hand, and receiving the support of the South on the other, drove Congress, which was overwhelmingly republican, to the passing of first one measure and then another to restrict his power."[32]

Grant stood with Republicans in making sure that Union victory was secured on northern terms, restoring the rights and privileges of citizenship of white southerners, but also protecting the rights and establishing the citizenship of southern blacks. "The best way, I think, to secure a speedy termination of Military rule," he wrote, "is to execute all the laws of Congress in the spirit in which they were conceived, firmly but without passion.[33] Something would have to give and soon. Amidst the comic opera unfolding in Washington, Grant performed his job under intense public scrutiny. His duties ranged wider than Reconstruction. He oversaw the demobilization of the Civil War volunteer army, a huge task that was performed with amazing efficiency. In May of 1865 just more than a million men were in the Union army; by November of that same year 800,000 volunteers had been discharged. This was accomplished while reorganizing a much smaller (around 26,000 men) regular army for service in the South and the West. On Johnson's orders, Grant was also planning for a possible military intervention in Mexico to overthrow Napoleon III's puppet, Archduke Maximilian, and force the French to abandon the country.[34] Meanwhile, Grant formed one part of an uneasy ruling executive triangle with President Johnson and Secretary of War Edwin M. Stanton. He could not escape the mounting tensions among Johnson, members of his cabinet, and a growing number of Republicans in Congress.

When Johnson fired Stanton, he violated the Tenure of Office Act passed in March 1867 by a Congress determined to thwart the president's power to remove civilian appointees supportive of the Republican vision of Reconstruction. Grant, who admired Stanton, cautioned Johnson not to fire him, stating that "the loyal people of the country, North & South" might not "quietly submit . . . to see the very man of all others . . . who they have expressed confidence in, removed." The act was probably unconstitutional, and as Grant observed "may be explained away by an astute lawyer," but Johnson's removal of Stanton was illegal until the Supreme Court actually ruled on the law.[35] A period of uneasy ambiguity followed. Grant agreed to Johnson's request to serve as secretary of war ad interim because he thought it crucial that "someone should be there who cannot be used."[36] It was an odd situation. For five months, beginning in August of 1867, Grant served as his own boss, remaining in control of the army.

The tension of holding two such critical positions began to wear on Grant, who spilled out his thoughts to Sherman: "All the romance of feeling that men in high places are above personal conciderations and act only from motives of pure patriotism, and for the general good of the public has been destroyed. An inside view proves too truly very much the reverse."[37] When the Senate refused to accept the president's dismissal of Stanton, Grant sided with the anti-Johnson faction, willingly vacating his office to the former secretary, who never resigned. Grant's action infuriated Johnson. The president claimed that when they met on January 11, 1868, Grant promised to stay in the office to force a judicial decision on the constitutionality of the Tenure of Office Act. Grant categorically denied making such a promise.

The already troubled relationship between Grant and Johnson worsened dramatically after the president accused Grant of treachery in front of the cabinet on January 14. After a series of heated exchanges, Grant wrote Johnson a letter defending his actions, closing with these lines: "And now, Mr. President, where my honor as a soldier and integrity as a man have been so violently assailed, pardon me for saying that I can regard this whole matter, from the beginning to the end, as an attempt to involve me in the resistance of law, for which you have hesitated to assume the responsibility in orders, and thus to destroy my character before the country."[38] The letter was made public, and from that time, the two men were permanently estranged, Grant later calling Johnson "an infernal liar."[39] On February 25, 1868, after Johnson appointed another secretary of war ad interim, the House of Representatives voted to impeach him. As the government ground to a halt, the Senate trial of Andrew Johnson proceeded, and on May 16 he was acquitted by one vote.

## "Let us have peace"

Right after lame-duck Johnson escaped removal from office, Republicans gathered in Chicago's Crosby Opera House to select a candidate for the 1868 presidential election. On May 21 they chose Grant by a wide margin, as expected. His stature and reputation towered above all others', with his name forever linked to the martyred Lincoln and the sacred Union Cause; he had the unqualified support of the vast majority of northern veterans. In the decades after the Civil War, the leaders of the Republican Party crafted a powerful moral, as well as political, message. They sought to unify a divided, diverse country around the symbols of nationhood—the founding fathers, the flag, religion, economic opportunity, and the sacrifice of the Civil War. Grant symbolized that sacrifice, and he enjoyed the trust of millions of Americans. His candidacy did not lack a practical foundation. He handled the delicate political negotiations with Johnson and the Radicals with enough skill to convince the Republican leadership that he would do nicely as president. "Grant's chance for the White House is worth tenfold than of any other man," declared George Templeton Strong. "This is partly due to the general faith in his honesty and capacity, and partly to his genius for silence. . . . I believe seven-eights of the people [of the North] would vote for him tomorrow."[40]

As Strong's assessment suggests, a large number of the electorate embraced Grant as an intelligent man possessed of high character and good moral judgment. Grant's modest origins and struggles with failure and defeat endeared him to northern Americans. Flattering campaign biographies flooded the country, acquainting many with unfamiliar details of his upbringing and stressing his heroic exploits.[41] Citizens read in the newspapers that Grant's little "cabin" at City Point, where he received President Lincoln and other luminaries, and where he plotted the last campaigns of the war, was going to be put on display in Philadelphia. For many years, his City Point headquarters remained a popular tourist attraction.[42] Most of all, voters were confident that Grant shared with Lincoln a belief in the transcendent importance of a vital American democracy. For his part, the general dreaded a life in politics. Why then, did he accept the party's nomination? If we believe his own explanation, he felt an overwhelming *duty* to say yes. Grant's reluctance to run for office was far outweighed by his worry about a resurgent ex-Confederate leadership thwarting and degrading reconciliation. In short, Grant believed that the country was on the precipice of disaster. He privately vowed to do everything he could to arrest the damage, confiding to Sherman that while he felt "forced" to run, nevertheless, "I could not back down without, as it seems to me, leaving the contest for power for the next four years between mere trading politicians, the elevation of whom, no matter which party won, would lose to us, largely, the results of the costly war which we have gone through."[43]

He was no ordinary candidate, nor was he expected to be. No ordinary candidate exuded the strength, the authority, and the power or enjoyed the reputation and the success of General Grant. In his view, he and Lincoln had saved the country from destruction, and now he alone had to secure the shaky peace. Grant's legacy was at stake, but it was still a risky decision. In June 1865 a journalist's prose had captured well the general's unique status:

> Though the war in which he has won his renown is now . . . ended, the future has still much to do in establishing the position which Grant holds in history. To-day he enjoys the confidence of his countrymen to a degree unknown to military leaders during the war. If ultimately successful in the end—if he directs his course through the mazes of the political campaign which is to follow the close of the war as well as he has his military career, posterity will delight, and will find little difficulty, in tracing out a comparison between his character and that of the country's first great leader.[44]

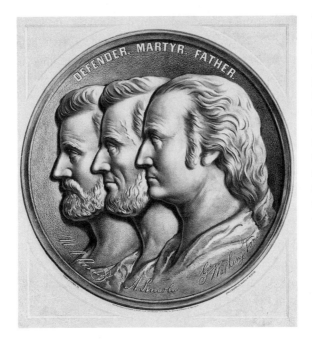

This medallion (struck in 1870 by Charles H. Crosby and Co.) is one of many depictions—in paintings, prints, and popular illustrations—of the three men deemed to be America's greatest leaders that flourished during the war years and in the decade and a half after Grant's death. (Library of Congress)

It is understandable why so many at the time drew comparisons between Washington and Grant. Both emerged as the "indispensable" men of their age, the victorious generals who established or preserved the Republic, and the presidents who led the nation to peace and stability. Many have questioned Grant's stated motivation, implying that he secretly desired continued power and fame that could come only with the highest office. If he did, the overt evidence is scanty. John Y. Simon confirmed that "the documentary record sustains the view that Grant did not seek the nomination, did nothing to enhance his candidacy, and accepted the nomination as an obligation."[45]

And so, Grant accepted, ending his letter to the nominating committee with the famous phrase, "Let us have peace." The phrase delighted Americans by reminding them of the quiet fortitude behind other statements, such as "I propose to fight it out on this line if it takes all summer." The 1868 Republican ticket was set. Grant's vice president was to be Indiana's Schuyler Colfax, who served as Speaker of the House of Representatives. The Democratic ticket was led by the governor of New York, Horatio Seymour, who had opposed many of Lincoln's policies during the war. The campaign was expected to be close, as eager Democrats rallied around a number of explicitly racist campaign slogans, such as could be found in a popular campaign song (one of many such compositions) entitled "The White Man's Banner," and sung to the tune of "Bonnie Blue Flag."

Join with a brave intent
To vindicate our Fathers' choice
A White Man's Government!
No Carpet-bag or Negro rule
For men who truly prize
The heritage of glory from
Our Sires, the true, the wise.
Let Grant and Colfax fight beneath
Their flag of sable hue,
The White Man's Banner we will raise
And conquer with it, too![46]

Democrats, finding Johnson's Reconstruction policy appealing, expected to do well among the newly reestablished southern base, although a significant number of white voters were still barred from participation. William McFeely observed that "the Democrats sought to damn Grant as a black Republican, a latter-day abolitionist . . . and they were not entirely off target."[47]

Grant did not campaign actively, a wise decision given the fact that he was uncomfortable with public speaking. Instead, he reminded voters of his important duties as general-in-chief. Accompanied by Generals Sherman and Sheridan, Grant took an inspection trip of fortifications in the Great Plains, ending up in Colorado. For the remainder of the campaign season, he and Julia stayed in their new residence in Galena, surrounded by family and friends. Wealthy supporters bestowed three houses on the Grants—one in Philadelphia, one in Washington, D.C., and one in Galena. These gifts, accepted gratefully by Ulysses and Julia, would come back to haunt them. Nevertheless, both enjoyed living again in Illinois, and Grant happily left it to Republican orators to make rousing speeches on his behalf around the country. They inspired an already enthusiastic party faithful organizing gigantic marching parades and well-attended patriotic events featuring the usual election hoopla. Friendly newspapers promoted the Republican cause across the country. The *New York Tribune* prominently featured this verse daily before the election:

So boys a final bumper; While we all in chorus chant—
"for next President we nominate; Our own Ulysses Grant!"
And if asked what state he hails from; This our sole reply shall be,

"From Appomattox Court House; with its family apple tree"
For 'twas there to our Ulysses; That Lee gave up the fight.
Now boys, "to Grant for President; And God defend the right!"[48]

On November 4, 1868, the *New York Sun* carried the banner headlines of a Grant-Colfax victory. Editor Charles Dana (soon to become a disappointed office-seeker and Grant's sworn enemy) explained the new president's attraction: "Starting in obscurity, and advancing by slow and sure steps, he has reached an eminence where he challenges the respect and confidence of his countrymen and has made his name a household word throughout the nation. . . . No candid person will for a moment doubt that the interests, the honor, and the glory of the Republic are secure in his hands."[49]

### *"I am afraid I am elected"*

The presidential election of 1868 was a historic contest, the first to be held after Lincoln's assassination and Johnson's impeachment proceedings. It was also the first that included the votes of freedmen, due to a provision of the Fourteenth Amendment enabling black suffrage in the ex-Confederate states. In short, 400,000 African American voters provided Grant with an even more comfortable margin of victory than expected (53 percent of the popular vote) despite facing intimidation and violence from white Democrats. "We have learned of Grant's election," wrote a northern African American missionary, "and all the col'd people's hearts about here have been made glad thereby," to which she added cheerfully, "while on the other hand the Rebs. are quite down in the mouth."[50] Grant virtually swept the Electoral College, 214–80, winning twenty-six states to only six for Seymour. He greeted his election with a typically droll comment. After receiving the news at a supporter's home in Galena, he strolled back to his own house, where he announced "I am afraid I am elected," to his excited wife.[51]

Inauguration Day, March 4, 1869, dawned cold and cloudy; thousands shivered in front of the Capitol as they waited anxiously for the newly elected president's speech. No man other than George Washington had come to the office with expectations as high as those that accompanied the forty-six-year-old Ulysses S. Grant (then, the youngest man to have been elected president) to his swearing-in ceremonies. Some openly worried that Grant's election meant "militarism" would dominate government policy, but most were reassured by Grant's obvious commitment to democracy and to a harmonious Reconstruction. Even the former vice president of the Confederacy, Alexander H. Stephens, praised the Union's hero and pre-

"Victory!" by Thomas Nast. Few pictures better adumbrated the Republican Party ideology of the postwar era. Savior of the Union U. S. Grant rides a magnificent white horse, holding high the precious national flag, with "Union" and "Equal Rights" emblazoned on the stripes, and drives a sword into the throat of Horatio Seymour, representing the Democrats, party of the "rebellion." Note the KKK branded on Seymour's black horse. (*Harpers Weekly*, November 14, 1868; reproduced by permission of The Huntington Library, San Marino, California)

dicted a portentous role. "He is one of the most remarkable men I have ever met," Stephens said. "He does not seem to be aware of his powers, but in the future he will undoubtedly exert a controlling influence in shaping the destinies of the country."[52] Arriving just after noon, Grant took the oath of office from Chief Justice Salmon Chase on the east portico of the Capitol building. With customary reserve of manner, he read his brief handwritten speech to expectant citizens, who pressed in closer to hear his quietly spoken words. Grant began by elaborating on his campaign slogan, "Let Us Have Peace," stressing the urgent need for reconciliation between North and South:

> The country having just emerged from a great rebellion many questions will come before it for settlement, in the next four years, which preceding Administrations have never had to deal with. In meeting these it is desirable that they should be approached calmly, without prejudice, hate or sectional pride; remembering that the greatest good to the greatest number is the object to be attained. This requires security of person, property, and for religious and political opinions in every part of our common country, without regard to local prejudice. All laws to secure these ends will receive my best efforts for their enforcement.[53]

After briefly mentioning his other major goals—a growing, prosperous, stable economy; a reformed policy toward Indians; respect for America abroad; and passage of the Fifteenth Amendment, which would afford suffrage for black men—Grant concluded: "I ask patient forbearance one towards another throughout the land, and a determined effort on the part of every citizen to do his share towards cementing a happy union, and I ask the prayers of the nation to Almighty God in behalf of this consummation."[54] More prosaic than poetic, his speech offered a reassuring, strong pledge to make the nation stable and prosperous, inspired by the principles of Abraham Lincoln's Republican Party—Union, emancipation, economic progress, and American security abroad. Neither the press nor the people expected the silent general to suddenly emerge as a great orator, and he did not. Praise for the address was nearly universal, the New York Times declaring that Grant "said it strongly and well."[55] Grant assumed that he had a mandate from voters to rise above politics to heal the country. "His record of service was transcendently honorable and victorious; like Emerson's Lincoln, he was a native, aboriginal American," noted Grant biographer Josiah Bunting of this moment.[56]

Ulysses S. Grant took the office of the president with an impressive ex-

Grant's inauguration as president on March 4, 1869 (*Frank Leslie's Illustrated Newspaper*, March 20, 1869; reproduced by permission of The Huntington Library, San Marino, California)

ecutive resume. As a commanding general, he strategized, organized, and delegated. Taking the same attitude toward the government as toward army headquarters, Grant appointed men in whom he had trust and in whose loyalty he had confidence. His cabinet officers would be given wide latitude to run their own departments. This management style worked with good appointees but did not work well with those of lesser talents. Departing from custom, Grant made his cabinet choices and announced them without consulting the party elders. If critics portrayed him as a political neophyte, it was a virtue, not a vice, in his estimation. Predictably, his selections prompted a round of outrage. Hypocritical charges of "cronyism" rang through the halls of Congress, especially if expectant appointees were ignored or brushed aside. His longtime congressional supporter from Illinois, Elihu B. Washburne, received the nod for the State Department, and his seriously ailing (from tuberculosis) friend and chief aide John A. Rawlins was appointed secretary of war, with Scottish-born department store magnate (and one of the contributors to Grant's home in Washington) Alexander T. Stewart chosen for the treasury post. For different reasons, several of Grant's appointees were deemed unacceptable and did not survive the fury directed against them.

In the end, Grant's cabinet turned out to be a fairly capable group. The president replaced Stewart with George Boutwell, a Republican politician from Massachusetts, while in Washburne's place the distinguished former U.S. senator and governor from New York, Hamilton Fish, became Secretary of State. Judge Ebenezer Rockwell Hoar from Massachusetts accepted the post of attorney general, and war hero Jacob Cox of Ohio received the appointment as secretary of the interior. As a reward for his support of the Reconstruction Acts, Grant's friend from the "old" army, ex-Confederate general turned Republican James Longstreet, was appointed as surveyor of customs of the port of New Orleans. The fact that these men were all solid Republicans did not assuage the concern of party power brokers like Senators Roscoe Conkling of New York and James G. Blaine of Maine and Congressman Benjamin F. Butler of Massachusetts. They were worried that Grant's independent predilections threatened the future of the Republican Party. Grant soon found that he had to ally himself with these "machine" spoils men in order to get anything done. In doing so, he alienated civil service reform–minded Republicans, who demonstrated increasing concern with the issue of corruption in politics and business and waning support for Republican Reconstruction.

Grant's penchant for appointing friendly businessmen who had given him gifts also came under attack, raising legitimate questions of propriety. Grant, while personally honest, seemed too trusting as supporters, friends, and relations took advantage of him. Charles Dana of the New York Sun charged that Grant's appointments were "chiefly distinguished for having conferred on him costly and valuable benefactions."[57] Grant believed that the gifts bestowed on him for his military achievements came with no strings attached. Appointing family members to civil service positions brought even more scorn. He was neither the first nor the last president to engage in nepotism. Numerous Dent relations received minor positions, and a controversial post went to father Jesse Grant as well. The actions provoked a scathing attack from the New York World: "Civil service examinations would soon have two questions: 'Were you a contributor to either of Grant's three houses?' . . . and 'Are you a member of the Dent family, or otherwise connected by marriage with General Grant?'"[58] Despite attacks, Grant continued to appoint family and friends, raising controversy at various times throughout his administration, although the number of such appointments was never as great as his enemies portrayed. Ignorant at first of Washington folkways, Grant grew more cautious, showing he could discriminate when family was involved. Later, he remarked that "patronage is the bane of the Presidential Office" but added that the majority of his appointments were made "without a personal acquaintance with the appointee, but upon recommendations of the representatives chosen directly by the people."[59]

Historian Mark Summers has written about the postwar sensationalization of the issue of political corruption by an increasingly antagonistic press driven to increase profits. And corruption sold copy. "Time and again," Summers stated, "scandals took front page during the era, and when an investigation resulted, it sometimes uncovered no more than a flowing sink of rumor, disguised as news."[60] More often than not, the press attacks linked Grant's political failings with his alleged addiction to liquor. Julia remembered, "One morning while at Galena, I read the following in a paper: 'General Grant is now lying confined in his residence at Galena in a state of frenzy and is tearing up his mattress, swearing it is made of snakes.' And there sat my dear husband, dressed in his white linen suit . . . smiling at my wrathful indignation, saying, 'I do not mind that, Mrs. Grant. If it were true, I would feel very badly.'" Julia turned to Sherman for advice, delivered bluntly. "It is not what he has done, but what *they will say* he has done," he counseled, "and they will prove too that Grant is a very bad man indeed." She listened, and in time, claimed that she "grew not to mind it."[61] Others were not as sanguine. Distressed at how many caricatures portrayed a drunken president, loyal cabinet member Hamilton Fish defended Grant:

I have known General Grant very intimately since the close of the war. I have been with him at all hours of the day and night—have traveled with him days and nights together—have been with him on social and festive occasions as well as in hourly intercourse of close official relations. I have never seen him in the most remote degree under any excitement from wine or drink of any kind. I have never known exhaustion or fatigue of travel, or of continual anxious labor, to lead him to any undue indulgence in any stimulant of drink. The very close personal association which I have had with him for many years justifies me in saying that the imputation of drunkenness is utterly and wantonly false, and that his use of wine is as moderate and proper as that of a gentlemen needs be.[62]

The Democratic Party and press also accused Grant of anti-Semitism. This charge sprang from his notorious General Orders No. 11 issued on December 17, 1862, which barred "the Jews, as a class" from the Department of Tennessee (consisting of Kentucky, Mississippi, and Tennessee). Although some Jews were among the cotton traders participating in rampant, and illegal, speculation in southern cotton, singling them out was a grievous and flagrant violation. The order was revoked by Lincoln, and Grant, embarrassed by his blunder, apologized. The issue came up in the 1868 election, when Jewish leaders asked Grant to explain his action. Both privately and publicly, Grant expressed his remorse and assured his critics "that I have no prejudice against sect or race but want each individual to be judged by his own merit."[63] The imputations of anti-Semitism did not seriously harm Grant's reputation, either during or after the war, but together with so many other charges, they stung nonetheless.

Summers faults Grant for not responding effectively to both political and personal attacks; instead "The Silent Smoker" refused to acknowledge the hostile press, making more enemies instead of cultivating friendly reporters. "Grant's failure to use the press properly marred his official reputation," Summers wrote, although "it could never quite finish off his personal standing. . . . The president remained widely popular."[64] Previous vicious attacks mounted on his generalship paled before the ignominy heaped on his person and his presidency by the press and by his political adversaries, twisting and tainting, but not destroying, his reputation in the nineteenth century. Grant resolutely ignored the press attacks and began to address the agenda outlined in his inaugural address—strengthening the economy, Indian reform, securing respect for America in the world, and Reconstruction policy.

## West from Appomattox

On May 10, 1876, the grand Centennial Exhibition opened in Philadelphia's 285-acre Fairmont Park, celebrating America's one-hundredth birthday. Officially named the International Exhibition of Arts, Manufactures, and Products of the Soil and Mine, the fair's exhibits featured exciting examples of the industrial power, engineering wizardry, and cultural achievements that pointed toward a united America's destiny as a great international force. At the end of the opening day's ceremonies, a huge crowd watched as President Ulysses S. Grant and Brazil's emperor, Dom Pedro, switched on the gigantic Corliss machine, in turn powering up the other machines at the exposition. By the time the fairgrounds closed exactly six months later, 10 million people had attended and voters had elected a new president, although the results were uncertain. The exposition in a very real sense

"Our Centennial—
President Grant and
Dom Pedro Starting
the Corliss Engine,—
From a Sketch by
Theo. R. Davis."
The machine dwarfs
the president in
this illustration
celebrating America's
industrial might.
(*Harper's Weekly*, May
27, 1876; reproduced
by permission of
The Huntington
Library, San Marino,
California)

represented a consequence and a culmination of the laws and policies set
in motion just before and during Grant's administration, leading to what
one historian has called "The Incorporation of America."[65] In his centennial year Annual Message, President Grant reflected proudly on the country's progress: "It affords me great pleasure to recur to the advancement
that has been made from the time of the colonies, one hundred years ago.
We were then a people numbering only three millions. Now we number
more than forty millions. Then industries were confined almost exclusively
to the tillage of the soil. Now manufactories absorb much of the labor of
the country." In this message, as in many others, Grant reminded citizens
that prosperity and progress were dependent on sustaining a democratic-
republican form of government; through the blessings of such governance,

"our liberties remained unimpaired; the bondmen have been freed from slavery; we have become possessed of the respect if not the friendship, of all civilized nations."[66]

In 1868, Grant believed that a true Reconstruction encompassed far more than a strictly southern policy. The wounds of war would also be healed by a rising tide of prosperity benefiting all citizens and, above all, demonstrating the efficacy of a "free labor vision of economic harmony."[67] This prosperity, and the harmony it would engender, supplied the foundation for the Republican Party's future, once grateful voters realized the benefits of an active government role securing these benefits. Indeed, three of the most important pieces of economic legislation ever passed by a U.S. Congress— the Pacific Railroad Act, the Morrill Education Act, and the Homestead Act—were signed into law by President Lincoln in 1862, fulfilling Republican campaign promises to nationalize economic opportunity. One example of a campaign promise fulfilled occurred on May 10, 1869, at Promontory Point, Utah. There, the Central Pacific and Union Pacific lines met, completing the nation's first transcontinental railroad. The epic event was seen by many as literally knitting together again with iron rails the war-torn nation. In that same year, John Wesley Powell, a one-armed Union veteran, began his survey of the uncharted West, producing detailed information helpful to settlement and development.[68] Grant's 1869 Thanksgiving Day Proclamation encapsulated the party's vision of continued American progress based on development of the country's natural resources.

The year which is drawing to a close has been free from pestilence— health has prevailed throughout the land—abundant crops reward the labors of the Husbandman—commerce and manufactures have successfully prosecuted their peaceful paths—the mines and forests have yielded liberally—the Nation has increased in wealth and in strength . . . civil and religious liberty are secured to every inhabitant of the land, whose soil is trod by none but freemen.[69]

As Grant mentioned, Republicans also stood for protecting and nurturing American manufacturing. They did so by endorsing a system of high tariffs and by advocating adherence to the gold standard, following Europe's example, as a means of securing financial stability. Grant made righting the financial health of the country a top priority. "To protect the national honor, every dollar of Government indebtedness should be paid in gold," he proclaimed.[70] Grant and his treasury secretary, George Boutwell, quickly made progress in paying down the huge national debt incurred during the Civil

War by retiring of some of the paper money, called "greenbacks," that had been issued. This process caused the currency to deflate, harming those groups, like farmers and certain businessmen, who benefited from inflation. Into the late nineteenth century, most Republicans stood for "sound money" (backed by gold), while most Democrats urged debtor relief through the printing of more paper money and injecting higher levels of silver into the monetary system. Positioning himself with the sound-money men, Grant supported the redemption of paper money with coin and on March 18, 1869, signed the Public Credit Act, which called for all federal debts to be paid in gold. His administration also sought to fund Civil War securities with gold, leading to a notable scandal, and a crisis just barely avoided.

Anticipating a huge financial windfall, Wall Street speculators Jim Fisk and Jay Gould planned to corner the gold market by buying up the precious metal, forcing prices up dramatically, and then selling for huge profits. Among the participants in this scheme was Abel Corbin, who was married to Grant's sister, Virginia. In addition, Grant had accepted the hospitality of Fisk and Gould on several occasions. The two speculators assumed incorrectly the president's tacit support in their dastardly endeavor. When Grant discovered their plan, he was outraged and immediately stopped it. On "Black Friday," September 24, 1869, Grant ordered the U.S. Treasury to flood the market with the precious metal, bringing ruin to Fisk and Gould but preserving the country's financial health. Of this action, Jean Edward Smith asserted: "The United States, for the first time, had intervened massively to bring order to the marketplace. It was a watershed in the history of the American economy."[71] A congressional investigation exonerated Grant of all charges of collusion, although it also cast doubt, once again, on his gullible nature and questionable associations. The battle over sound currency continued to rage, as depressions, strikes, and labor unrest roiled the country throughout the decade of the 1870s. Grant resisted cries to inflate the currency to ease the pain of farmers and other debtors, and it took political courage to veto the inflation bill in the spring of 1874. Later he signed the Specie Resumption Act, placing the country firmly on the gold standard by January 1879.[72]

Fiscal responsibility—paying down the national debt, lowering taxes, and cutting budgets—represented only one aspect of Grant's economic vision. As president, he encouraged the development of the vast land held by the federal government in the western territories with the intent of bringing prosperity to all sections of the country.[73] Born and raised in a state not far removed from its frontier origins, and stationed in the Far West as a young soldier, Grant enjoyed an affinity with the region. Favoring irrigation works such as canals, he approved of projects that took great swaths of land and opened them to timber, cattle, land speculators, and millions of settlers from older regions in the United States, and from Europe, who were flooding into the so-called empty spaces. Still, Grant appreciated the West for its majestic beauty, and he signed into law the act that established the country's first national park at Yellowstone on March 1, 1872.

Nonetheless, the idea of preserving the region's environment and concerns about industrial pollution were of much less importance to Grant than cultivating the West's bounty and bringing "civilization" to previously wild and empty spaces. "Grant became President of the United States at a critical juncture in the nation's westward expansion," explained one historian of the region. "His policies, and those of Congress in the 1870s, had a lasting impact on how public lands were divided, sold, and settled. . . . He accepted and allowed expansion, private acquisition, and development to move ahead without doubting its value."[74] Grant presided over the disposition of millions of acres of federal public lands to pioneers and speculators, which encouraged the growth of railroad companies and extractive industries. "Providence had bestowed upon us a strong box in the precious metals locked up in the sterile mountains of the far West," said Grant, "which we are now forging the key to unlock, to meet the very contingency that is now upon us."[75] Signing off on a mining act in the same year that Yellowstone was established, in the following year Grant approved the Timber Culture Act, Coal Lands Act, and Desert Lands Act. All were meant to "unlock" the treasures that would employ thousands and enrich businesses. An examination of his eight Annual Messages to Congress demonstrates the importance Grant attributed to the growth and development of the American economy, especially in the West. His first pointed with pride to the fact that "the quantity of public lands disposed of during the year ending June 30th, 1869, was 7.666.11.97 [sic] acres, exceeding that of the preceding year by 1.010.409. acres. Of this amount 2.899.544. acres were sold for cash, and 2.737.365 acres entered under the homestead laws."[76]

### Civilization and Ultimate Citizenship

Even as he celebrated the progress flowing from economic development, Grant realized that expansionist goals in the postwar period required the removal of Native Americans from desirable land. Indian removal was accomplished largely through treaties, which established a system of reservations where, ideally, tribes would live peacefully while their former lands were settled by the whites. Tribes that did not go quietly faced military actions approved by President Grant. From George Washington's administration to Lincoln's, the federal government had provided for Indians' welfare, but the system, administered by the Indian Bureau, was mired in corruption and humanitarian abuses. In his 1868 Inaugural Address Grant indicated his desire to reform the notorious bureau by formulating a new policy, unique and progressive for his era. "Grant believed deeply in human equality," asserted Jean Smith, "and in his view, the Indian, no less than the former slave, deserved the government's protection."[77] Many might find Smith's assessment too generous—after all, the president did too little to prevent the various tragedies that befell the Native American population during his administration. A scholar of Indian-white relations noted that "Grant as an American and especially as President embodied his culture's values and contradictions" when it came to Indian Policy.[78] Alarmed at the violence erupting over Native American resistance to white settlement in the Plains, Grant's primary concern was that the tribes be treated with dignity and respect. "The proper treatment of the original occupants of this land," he observed, "is one deserving of careful study. I will favor any course towards them which tends to their civilization and ultimate citizenship." Here is how he articulated the challenge in 1869:

The building of rail-roads and the access thereby given to all the agricultural and mineral regions of the country is rapidly bringing civilized settlements into contact with all the tribes of indians. No matter what ought to be the relations between such settlements and the aborigines, the fact is they do not get on together, and one or the other has to give way in the end. A system which looks to the extinction of a race is too abhorant for a Nation to indulge in without without entailing upon the wrath of all Christendom, and without engendering in the Citizen a disregard for human life, and the rights of others, dangerous to society. I see no remedy for this except in placing all the indians on large reservations . . . and giving them absolute protection there.[79]

Dubbed Grant's "Indian Peace Policy," the goals included rigorous agricultural training on reservations, providing ample goods and materials at reasonable costs; replacing the current crop of crooked agents with a cadre of honest and efficient ones; establishing schools and churches that would transform Indians into good Christian farmers and citizens of the United States; and ending the reservation system, allowing Native Americans to blend seamlessly into the general population. "The moral view of the ques-

"Let Us Have Peace," by C. S. Reinhart. President Grant welcomes Sioux leaders Red Cloud, Spotted Tail, and Swift Bear to Washington for their meeting with Ely S. Parker, commissioner of Indian affairs. Many such delegations were warmly received by the president throughout his administration. (*Harper's Weekly*, June 18, 1870; reproduced by permission of The Huntington Library, San Marino, California)

tion," Grant said of Indian citizenship, "should be considered, and the question asked, cannot the Indian be made a useful and productive member of society by proper teaching and treatment?"[80] Implementing the new policy, however, proved vexing, and successes were few. Grant appointed his former aide, Brig. Gen. Ely S. Parker of the Seneca tribe, to be the commissioner of Indian Affairs. Parker was the first nonwhite appointee to a major government position. The Indian Bureau's work was aided by a newly established board of Christian philanthropists who would send missionaries out to the reservations. Under this program, with federal funding, food, clothing, and other necessities were donated under the auspices of church-based charities, houses were built on reservations, farming was encouraged, and schools were established. Some improvements were instituted, but in practice many of the tawdry exploitations of the past continued unabated at the expense of tribal members. In one of the largest scandals of Grant's administration, his secretary of war, William Belknap, was implicated in selling an Indian post tradership, representing the tip of a corrupt iceberg in which contractors, agents, and politicians eluded the reformist agenda set by Grant. In the eight years of his administration, Grant's good intentions with regard to the welfare of Native Americans produced largely poor results.[81]

It is appropriate to contextualize Grant's overall policy toward Native Americans. At no time did he (sharing the sentiment of the vast majority of Americans) contemplate allowing small populations of nomadic tribes to control huge areas of valuable land. Grant's Peace Policy was thus based in a harsh reality where the "past . . . can not be undone, and the question must be met as we now find it."[82] The issue enjoined was not tribal equity, but rather the orderly, nonviolent settlement of the West, fulfilling America's "manifest destiny," combined with humane treatment for the Indians that nonetheless required their forced assimilation. Historian Heather Cox Richardson described his dilemma: "For Grant, the destruction of Indian culture was the only possible chance tribes had to survive."[83] While the majority of tribes went peacefully onto the designated reservations, a few offered active resistance to settlers on the Great Plains and prospectors in the mountains. The War Department, under the authority of Grant's leading Union generals, William Sherman (who succeeded Grant as general-in-chief [1868–83]) and Philip Sheridan (commander of the Department of the Missouri and later Sherman's successor as general-in-chief [1883–88]) fashioned a military response that tried to accommodate the often opposing interests of eastern and western politicians, businessmen, settlers, and advocates of Grant's Indian Peace Policy. Building a string of defensive forts across a wide area, the U.S. military engaged in over 200 pitched battles with defiant warriors in the late nineteenth century. The results of the Apache War of 1871–72, the Red River War of 1874–75, and the Sioux War of 1875–76 proved that, in the end, despite Indian victories such as "Custer's Last Stand," in 1876, resistance to the U.S. Army and government was futile. Summing up the results of over a decade of fighting the Plains Indians, Sheridan said: "This was the country of the buffalo and the hostile Sioux only last year. There are no signs of either now, but in their places we found prospectors, emigrants, and farmers."[84] Domestic policy priorities secured continental sovereignty but at a high cost. Whenever possible, President Grant strongly advocated peaceful methods of influencing both people and land in both at home and abroad.

## Foreign Policy

Grant's foreign policy rested in the capable hands of Secretary of State Hamilton Fish. The patrician Fish served through two terms and became one of Grant's closest friends and staunchest supporters.[85] One great accomplishment and one bitter defeat stake out the parameters of a *relatively* peaceful, successful, and productive era in international relations for the

President Ulysses S. Grant (*A Memorial of Ulysses S. Grant from The City of Boston* [Boston: Printed by Order of the City Council, 1885])

United States, despite tensions with England, Canada, Spain, and Cuba. In a period when the Franco-Prussian War (1870–71) created turmoil in Europe, the United States' growing economic power added to its potential for exerting influence on a world stage. Grant's preference for international arbitration earned the respect of many foreign leaders, undoubtedly accounting for his rapturous reception during his trip around the world almost a decade later. First on the list in 1869 was the solving of the *Alabama* claims controversy. The claims had festered as an issue since the Civil War, when Union shipping suffered damages inflicted by Confederate raiders (of which the *Alabama* was the most famous) equipped and built in Great Britain. When England ignored American requests for a monetary settlement during the Johnson administration, war fever broke out. Among the hawks was the chairman of the Senate Committee on Foreign Relations, Charles Sumner, who emerged as a chief opponent of Grant's foreign policy initiatives. Grant and Fish deftly minimized what they considered Sumner's baneful influence and later engineered his removal from the chairmanship. Restarting the negotiations with Great Britain, Fish skillfully dealt with a number of thorny issues, including disputes over fishing rights in Canadian waters, leading to the Treaty of Washington in 1871. A provision in the treaty submitted the *Alabama* claims to an international tribunal in Geneva, which awarded the United States $15.5 million in damages. Great Britain agreed to pay and apologized for its role in the outfitting of Rebel warships. The Treaty of Washington was hailed as a triumph for America in the short run; in the long run the settlement brought peaceful relations between the United States and England and established a model for international arbitration.[86]

Fish's expertise could not, however, prevent a thundering defeat on the annexation of Santo Domingo (now the Dominican Republic). Wishing to secure a Caribbean base, Grant sent his personal secretary, Gen. Orville E. Babcock, to forge an agreement with the islanders. Babcock returned with a signed treaty of annexation, which Grant promptly sent to the Senate, with a message: "I feel an unusual anxiety for the ratification of this treaty, because I believe it will redound greatly to the glory of the two countries interested, to civilization, and to the extirpation of the institution of slavery."[87] The benefits included trade and commercial prosperity for both countries, securing a foothold for the United States in the Caribbean, and, more controversially, providing a friendly home for freedmen and -women who wanted to leave a place that shunned them. The idea of resettling, or "colonizing" African Americans was one that long captivated some abolitionists and many antislavery politicians, including Abraham Lincoln, as a solution to the country's seemingly intractable racial problems.[88]

Receiving a lukewarm response from African American leaders, Grant nonetheless hoped that blacks might consider taking advantage of brighter opportunities in a Santo Domingo protected by the United States. "I do not suppose the whole race would have gone, nor is it desirable that they should go," wrote Grant in 1876. "But possession of this territory would have left the negro 'master of the situation,' by enabling him to demand his rights at home on pain of finding them elsewhere."[89] Backed by Democrats, Sumner made sure the treaty was voted down by the Senate. Grant dropped the idea of annexation reluctantly, making periodic but futile stabs at resuscitating the proposal. Grant did not advocate using military might to seize Santo Domingo, or another Caribbean island of interest, Cuba. The Cuban revolution that erupted from 1868 to 1878 threatened several times to bring Spain and the United States to war. Fish adeptly maneuvered between the interventionist clique in America and Spanish warmongers to preserve a position of United States neutrality, even during the *Virginius* affair in 1871. With Fish advising neutrality throughout the crisis, in which the Spaniards captured the American ship *Virginius*, Grant resisted pressure from members of his administration to intervene militarily. "I would not fire a gun to annex territory," he explained. "I consider it too great a privilege to belong to the United States for us to go around gunning for new territories."[90] Lacking the extreme bellicosity that characterized Theodore Roosevelt's foreign policy, Grant's policy nonetheless set in motion the age of "democratic-imperialism" that was to come in the twentieth century.[91]

*"Withhold no legal privilege of advancement to the new citizen"*
During Grant's tenure, America's global power was still in its infancy, and foreign relations were overshadowed by domestic concerns. Dramatic changes in the economy reshaping both factories and farms held far more interesting implications for most Americans. Immigration, urbanization, and industrialization brought new challenges and new headaches, requiring new responses. But no issue commanded Grant's attention as much as Reconstruction, and no issue affected his presidency, his reputation, and his legacy more profoundly. It was the reason he sought the office, and he was deeply involved in the implementation of policy—more so than in other areas of his administration. Grant strove for harmony with the white southern population while struggling to establish freedom's meaning for former slaves. Much later, he explained, "I think Republicans should go as far as possible in conciliation, but not far enough to lose self-respect."[92] In 1869, Grant waxed optimistic that blacks could gain a solid footing in the South, with time, and with good faith on the part of whites. "The freedmen, under the protection which they have received," he observed, "are making rapid progress in learning, and no complaints are heard of lack of industry on their part where they receive fair remuneration for their labor."[93] Grant did not advocate social equality between black and white. Rather, he asked that African Americans be given the same "fair chance" to advance that other Americans enjoyed as their right.[94] In the end, the Union held; but full achievement of the war's second goal proved impossible, and white reconciliation trumped black gains. Grant's accomplishments were considerable, but the northern people ultimately withdrew their support for Republican Reconstruction.

With Grant's election, congressional Republicans believed they had a solid friend in the White House working to ensure that their vision of Reconstruction prevailed—reconciliation with whites, a free-labor society in the South, protection and civil rights guaranteed for its freedpeople, and a competitive two-party system. When Grant assumed office in 1869, the majority of the ex-Confederate states had Reconstruction governments in place, thanks to black votes and restrictions on white suffrage, ensuring a fragile Republican presence. The establishment of these so-called "Black Republican" governments met with immediate opposition from violent white supremacists working to overthrow them and reinstitute Democratic Party rule.[95] At the same time, Radicals prodded Congress to take up the suffrage amendment in 1868, and by 1870 it was ratified by the states.

The history of black suffrage suggests the extreme difficulty of fleshing out the meaning of emancipation in the years after Appomattox. White northerners went to war to save the Union, and most were indifferent, resistant, or hostile to emancipation as a wartime measure until circumstances forced the issue. Lincoln's stalwart leadership and U.S. Army victories convinced a majority to endorse emancipation by the election of 1864. Surrender brought an overwhelming desire for a harmonious reunion, and while whites in the North endorsed freedom for southern slaves, few favored equal rights, including suffrage. Advanced by abolitionists, Radical Republicans, and African American citizens, black suffrage was decisively defeated or ignored in northern states (as part of the Fourteenth Amendment), while southern states were forced to accept it as a condition for readmission specified in the Reconstruction Acts. The final version of the Fifteenth Amendment guaranteed the right to vote to all males regardless of "race, color or previous condition of servitude" and included an enforcement clause. Suffrage discrimination based on gender, education, immigrant status, and residence was not specifically prohibited. Still, passage represented another huge advancement for black Americans, which, like emancipation, had been unimaginable a short while before.[96]

When the Fifteenth Amendment became law, President Grant issued a special message stating, "A measure which makes at once Four Millions of people, heretofore declared by the highest tribunal in the land not citizens of the United States, nor eligible to become so, voters in every part of the land . . . is indeed a measure of grander importance than any other one act of the kind from the foundation of our free government to the present day." To those who vociferously opposed the measure Grant cautioned, "To the race more favored heretofore by our laws I would say withhold no legal privilege of advancement to the new citizen. . . . I repeat that the adoption of the 15th Amendment to the Constitution completes the greatest civil change, and constitutes the most important event that has occurred, since the nation came into life."[97]

Under congressional Reconstruction the expansion of the political nation to include black men became a reality. In the decade plus two years

1871 lithograph celebrating "The Fifteenth Amendment, Signed by President Grant." Grant is surrounded by a group of prominent Republicans (including Abraham Lincoln, on his right), abolitionists (note the portrait of John Brown on the wall), and Civil War figures who helped make the moment possible. Illustrations surrounding the central image enumerate the benefits of suffrage for black men. (Library of Congress)

that followed surrender, freedmen joined political organizations, voted in great numbers, and were elected to all levels of government throughout the South. South Carolina and Louisiana had a majority of African American legislators, and sixteen African Americans were elected to the U.S. Congress. As Eric Foner argued, a sizeable number of black officeholders were competent and intelligent men, and the biracial Republican state governments instituted positive changes. These changes included introducing public school education for both black and white children, establishing welfare institutions, and encouraging business investment in the South.[98] In prosperous and depressed times, southerners—white and black alike—suffered from poverty and limited opportunity throughout the Reconstruction period and well beyond. Freedpeople aspired to own their own plot of land. Instead, they settled for sharecropping, a labor arrangement that favored cotton planters. Republican-controlled legislatures offered inducements to northern investors, with scant success. Southern Republicans faced momentous challenges in office. For many reasons, internal divisions instead of unity prevailed, seriously weakening the state governments. Corruption flourished, tainting many of the Republican administrations, and providing the resurgent southern Democrats with popular issues as they campaigned against high taxes and corruption.

But by far the most potent issue was black suffrage and the presumed racial equality it bestowed. Republican power in the South, sustained by African American votes, had to be smashed and blacks returned to a subordinate position. To ensure this outcome, white terrorist groups—most famously the Ku Klux Klan—caused constant turmoil in every election cycle in every ex-Confederate state. Few in the North, including Grant, predicted the rampant lawlessness that threatened to undermine and then destroy Reconstruction policy. KKK-inspired voter intimation, numerous political murders, and widespread terror paralyzed Republican governments in Mississippi, Louisiana, Arkansas, and the Carolinas in the late 1860s and early 1870s. Beleaguered state and local officials pleaded with the federal government for assistance in maintaining order. In response, Grant signed into law three measures known as the Force Acts of 1870–71. These enabled the president to use the power of the federal government to restore order by sending troops, imposing martial law, and suspending the writ of habeas corpus. In addition, Grant appointed a proactive attorney general, Amos T. Akerman, and established the Department of Justice as a part of the cabinet. Akerman wielded his power by using federal marshals and military forces to arrest thousands of Klansmen in several states. Although only sixty-five Klansmen went to federal prison, the specter of a vigorous federal presence in elections made the subsequent 1872 presidential elections the "fairest and freest" in the South until late in the twentieth century.[99]

No student of history should underestimate the Force Acts' negative impact on the fate of Reconstruction. The actions taken under the laws, however justified, violated deeply cherished beliefs in the separation of powers. Most Americans assumed that once the Civil War ended, states' rights and a national government whose powers were limited would once again prevail. Grant was attacked by the Democratic Party and press for "Caesarism" (imposing a military dictatorship) and crushing the right of states to run their own affairs. He defended the actions as undertaken only when "acts of violence . . . render the power of the State and its officers unequal to the task of protecting life and property and securing public order therein."[100] His proclamation fell on deaf ears across the white South. Grant pleaded with ex-Confederates to "treat the Negro as a citizen and as a voter—as he is and must remain—and soon parties will be divided, *not on the color line*, but on principle. Then we will have a Union not calling for interference in one section that would not be exercised under like circumstances in any other."[101] Democratic voters overwhelmingly rejected the rationale of intervention, but it was also offensive to a small but influential number of Republicans and other northerners. President Grant, still backed up by a majority of Republicans, disagreed. While stating "it will be a happy day for me when I am out of political life," he insisted that "I do feel a deep interest in the republican party keeping controll of affairs until the results of the war are acquiesced in by all political parties." Grant agreed to seek a second term in 1872. John Simon explained, "Recognizing the unfinished work of his presidency, Grant pressed on with a dogged sense of responsibility."[102]

### *"He is a better President every day than he was the day before"*

Grant pressed on even as he had come to despise life in the White House: "Who ever has the place will have a slaves life," he remarked.[103] Backing Grant's candidacy were party officials from coast to coast, reassured by his continued high personal popularity among voters. Meeting in Philadelphia, the Republican convention delivered a unanimous renomination for his candidacy in June of 1872. Friendly dailies declared enthusiastically for another Grant run. The *New York Times* asked, "Was anyone ready to trust the Democrats with power?" *Harper's Weekly* premier cartoonist Thomas Nast placed his considerable talents at the disposal of Grant and the Republican Party. America's most influential minister, Brooklyn's Henry Ward Beecher, declared that there "had never been a President more sensitive to the wants of the people."[104] Grant's supporters in Congress included two of the most powerful and controversial politicians in the country—Massachusetts's Benjamin Butler and New York's Roscoe Conkling. Both were the kind of politicians despised by reformers because of their blatant use of the "spoils system" to cement loyalty to the party. Senator Conkling built an impressive Republican machine in New York. Asked to assess Grant's candidacy, Conkling reported that he "made a better President than . . . we had any right to expect, and he is a better President every day than he was the day before."[105] Conkling's aspiration for higher office was in part thwarted by his break with senatorial rival James G. Blaine of Maine. Their rivalry split the party into Conkling's supporters, called "Stalwarts," and Blaine's followers, known as "Half-breeds."

More serious than the divide between the Stalwarts and Half-breeds was the emergence of a disaffected wing within the Republican Party contesting Grant's nomination in 1872. Sumner and Schurz led the Liberal Republicans, who demanded tariff and civil service reform (ending the spoils system and installing a merit-based system for most government positions based on competitive examinations), and a "New Departure" in Reconstruction policy. Grant stole some of their thunder when he approved civil service reforms, sought tariff reductions, and supported the sound-money platform.[106] Liberal Republicans scoffed at his gestures and broke decisively with the president. In a letter to Senator Henry Wilson of Massachusetts, nominated to replace Colfax as vice president, Grant expressed his utter contempt for Liberal Republicans, particularly Sumner: "They have all attacked me without mercy. . . . Mr. Sumner has been unreasonable, cowardly, slanderous, unblushing false. . . . I feel a greater contempt for him than for any other man in the Senate."[107]

Unable to win regular Republicans over to their side, the Liberals formed an independent movement attracting the disaffected from both major parties. Appealing to Democrats, reformers declared themselves in favor of white southern "home rule" with a restoration of all citizenship rights to ex-Confederates, in essence calling for an end to "bayonet rule." Fiery orator Anna E. Dickinson broke with the Republicans when she called for the defeat of a president who had a "greater fondness for the smoke of a cigar and the aroma of a wine glass" than for running the country. Articulating the platform of the Liberals, Dickinson demanded the end of "special legislation" for blacks and asked for "the democratic process to work its magic in the South."[108] In return for this "New Departure," southern Democrats, regaining local power, would pledge to uphold freedpeople's rights. The Liberal Republicans nominated *New York Tribune* owner and editor Horace Greeley as their candidate. Selection of the eccentric Greeley, ill and grieving from the sudden death of his wife, spelled certain defeat, even with the endorsement of the Democratic convention. "Sheer insanity," snorted a prominent editor. Grant had an equally trenchant comment about Greeley: "He is a genious without common sense."[109]

Genius or not, Horace Greeley, along with his managing editor, Whitelaw Reid, denounced the Grant administration in the pages of the *Tribune* as one of "plunder, waste and corruption." Another headline predicted, "Despotism Ahead; The Plot to Overthrow the Republic; Honest Election Stifled by Fraud."[110] Worse, a bombshell unleashed by the press held the potential

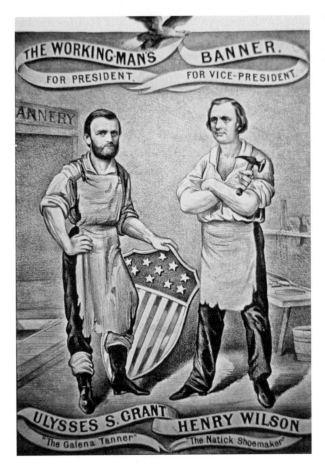

The 1872 Republican ticket stressed the working-class background of both Grant and Senator Henry Wilson of Massachusetts, a Radical Republican, who had replaced Colfax as the vice presidential nominee. (Library of Congress)

to do serious damage to the campaign, even though most of the wrongdoing happened before Grant was president. The Crédit Mobilier scandal involved corruption by businessmen and Republican politicians in the building of the Union Pacific Railroad. Republican speakers defended their party by carrying the Union banner high into the election, persuading voters that the country was still too unstable to be left in the hands of "treasonous" Democrats and their allies in the Liberal Republican Party. The abandonment of Reconstruction by some former antislavery leaders such as Sumner and Theodore Tilton was not accepted by the majority of ex-abolitionists, who supported Grant in 1872. Declaring his preference for the Grant ticket with eloquence, Frederick Douglass stated, "Whatsoever may be the fault of the Republican Party, it has within it the only element of friendship for the colored man's rights."[111]

Ulysses and Julia with their children (left to right: Jesse, Fred, Ulysses Jr., Nellie). Another side, the family man, softened the stern hero of the war. Countless images such as this one bridged Grant's transition from military leader to president. (author's collection)

Election results validated Grant, who easily defeated Greeley by a popular landslide of 56 percent to 44 percent (600,000 more votes than he had received in 1868) and an even larger Electoral College majority of 286 to 66. His coattails were long, with Republicans winning a two-thirds majority in both houses of Congress. The anti-Grant press refused to back down. Indicating rough times ahead, the *Sun's* headline blared: "Greeley Defeated: Four More Years of Fraud and Corruption."[112] Grant, though gratified by the scale of his victory, ended his second Inaugural Address with a plaintive tone, "Throughout the war, and from my candidacy for my present office in 1868 to the close of the last Presidential campaign, I have been the subject of abuse and slander scarcely ever equaled in political history, which today I feel that I can afford to disregard in view of your verdict, which I gratefully accept."[113] Grant hoped that his second term could bring progress on the thorny problems still threatening the country. "I do now," he claimed, "as I did four years ago, sincerely believe that the interests of the whole country demand the success of the Republican Party."[114]

### "A bright and beautiful dream"

By 1872 Grant had established a comfortable routine in the White House. He woke up early and read the newspapers before eating breakfast with his wife. His meals were decidedly more abundant than they had been during the war, accounting for the thirty-five pounds gained in eight years. Unless a special occasion or crisis beckoned, he worked in his office from 10:00 A.M. to 3:00 P.M., except on Tuesday, when he held cabinet meetings. Julia's brother, Col. Frederick Dent, was Grant's appointment secretary, and his other two secretaries, Orville Babcock and Horace Porter, conveniently lived in White House quarters. Often, Grant would go for buggy rides in the late afternoon, or just walk, unguarded, along the capital's pleasant streets, occasionally stopping along the way to light up a cigar. For entertainment, Grant enjoyed dinners and evenings with Julia and the children, attempting to maintain a viable family life in the White House. The activities of their attractive young family were faithfully, and usually favorably, recorded by the press. Numerous illustrations and photographs of Ulysses, Julia, and their four offspring were published, humanizing Grant as a doting husband and father. Some images showed Grant in military garb and others in civilian clothes, but all served to change his image from that of a stern, mythic military hero to that of a president, who was expected to appeal to ordinary people.

Grant lived up to his reputation as a good family man. He cherished his wife and children, as well as the twelve grandchildren that would come, and was happiest when they were around him. Author Ishbel Ross described Ulysses and Julia's devotion to each other: "Her faith in him was like a charm throughout his life. His love for her was a shield against destruction."[115] A beautifully refurbished White House became the center of a lively, youthful hospitality, a stylish Julia happily presiding over numerous social events. Indeed, Ulysses and Julia set a new trend of friendly, casual, and constant entertaining. Julia positively relished the duties of first lady. "My life at the White House was like a bright and beautiful dream and we were immeasurably happy," she recalled in a newspaper interview.[116] Guests were frequent, including many friends and relatives. Less enamored than Julia of the Washington social scene, Ulysses plotted his escape from the capital's hot and humid summers to their spacious cottage at the New Jersey seaside resort of Long Branch.

Like most married couples with children, Julia and Ulysses alternated between pride and anxiety as their children enjoyed successes or suffered failures or setbacks. Their eldest son, Frederick Dent (1850–1912), graduated from West Point in 1871 and established his military career in the next two decades, retiring from active service as a lieutenant colonel in 1881. In 1874 he married Ida M. Honore, the daughter of a prominent Chicago business-man. Fred, Ida, and their two children frequently visited Ulysses and Julia. Like Fred, Ulysses S. Jr. (1852–1929), known in the family as "Buck," did not reside at the White House. He was educated at exclusive schools, including Harvard and Columbia. A businessman and investment banker, he married Fannie Chaffee, with whom he had five children. The Grants' daughter, Ellen (1855–1922), called "Nellie" was not only the apple of her father's eye, but of the nation's as well. In a manner that anticipated the coverage of Theodore Roosevelt's daughter, Alice, reporters doted on every move of the pretty teenager, such as when she traveled to Europe in 1871. Nineteen-year-old Nellie's White House wedding to wealthy Briton Algernon Sartoris on May 21, 1874, produced much sensational coverage. Reluctant to give his approval to the marriage, a saddened father accepted her departure to England, where the couple would make their home. During the ceremony, Jesse remembered his father as "silent, tense, with tears upon his cheeks that he made no movement to brush away."[117] It turned out to be an unhappy union, and Nellie and her three children returned to America in the 1880s. The baby of the family, Jesse Root (1858–1934), was a lively and endear-ing young man, who attended Cornell and Columbia law school. In 1880, Jesse married Elizabeth Chapman, with whom he would have two children. Along with Buck, he moved to San Diego, California, after their father's death. The two youngest sons prospered in real estate and other business activities in southern California. In 1910, Buck opened the beautiful U. S. Grant Hotel in San Diego. Still standing, the hotel recently underwent a $52 million renovation, restoring its former luxury and prominence. Its new owners? An Indian tribe, the Sycuan Band of the Kumeyaay Nation, whose casino profits generated the cash to help bring the U. S. Grant Hotel (and San Diego's downtown) back to life.[118]

## Sacrificed on the Altar of Radicalism

Grant's goals for his second administration were similar to those for the first—promote a prosperous economy as well as peace at home and abroad. "My desire is to see harmony, concord and prosperity exist everywhere in our common land," he proclaimed.[119] Regardless of his desire, unstable fi-nancial markets and overproduction led to the Panic of 1873, followed by a severe depression. The exposure of leading administration officials in scandals obliterated much of the good feeling that had been engendered by his 1872 victory. The infamous "Whiskey Ring" is one example. The scandal involved a conspiratorial network of distillers and federal revenue agents that stole millions of dollars from the government treasury. Grant's stout defense of his personal secretary, Orville E. Babcock, accused of participating in the ring, made him seem naïve to the point of stupidity. Depression, corruption, and continued white resistance to Reconstruction measures in the South, prompting disaffection and apathy in the North, spelled trouble in the upcoming elections. By the mid-1870s, the northern people tired of the continual fight to reconstruct their former foes. Other issues, like the Indian Wars in the West and the Crédit Mobilier scandal, drew attention and energy away from southern problems. Republicans were soundly defeated in the election of 1874, returning the Democratic Party to control in the House of Representatives for the first time since before the war and dooming Grant's Reconstruction policies. Afterward, an exultant *New York Sun* urged Grant's impeachment, editorializing that "the overthrow is complete and terrific. . . . It is impossible to enumerate the names of the great mass of hypocrites, adventurers and rogues which the work of Monday and Tuesday has put under the sod to never rise again."[120] Soon, Grant's reputation was being pummeled by former friends as well as expected enemies. Even Thomas Nast's cartoons began to reflect disillusionment. On July 18, 1874, a devastating pictorial in *Harper's Weekly* portrayed "Columbia" hanging her head in shame over yet another scandal. The caption, "Don't let us have any more of this nonsense. It is a good trait to stand by one's friends; but . . . ," expressed the frustration many were feeling toward Grant. His friends in Congress—Roscoe Conkling, Michigan senator Zachariah Chandler, and others of the Stalwart wing were attacked as corrupt, vicious, and antiprogressive. His critics slammed him on his choice of appointments and his crony-driven administration. Most telling and urgent, however, was the nation's demand that Reconstruction come to an end.

The southern Republican coalition was coming apart under relentless pressure from white Democrats who railed against "Black Republicanism" and fought against "Negro rule." Replacing the Ku Klux Klan, other terrorist organizations sprang up to commit acts of violence against African American officeholders, Republican politicians, and voters. Louisiana's crisis reached epic proportions, providing a case study as to why Reconstruction failed. Both Democratic and Republican governments claimed victory in the 1872 state elections. The disputed results were decided in favor of the Republicans, but the appearance of the White League paramilitary group

"Murder of Louisiana: Sacrificed on the Altar of Radicalism" shows the disaffection with how Grant and Congress handled the disputed elections in the state. (Library of Congress)

made governing impossible. The league was implicated in two shocking massacres of blacks at Colfax in 1873 and Coushatta in 1874. Elections held in 1874 were again disputed; federal troops were sent to arrest several Democratic members of the legislature and restore order. With chaos spreading, Grant authorized the sending of 5,000 soldiers to crush the rebellion. In addition, he sent General Philip Sheridan to the Pelican State to defeat the White League. Calm temporarily prevailed, but popular revulsion over the extent of northern interference with Louisiana — and other ex-Confederate states — had reached a boiling point. This revulsion boded ill for the political fortunes of the Republican Party.[121]

The perception that southern Republicans could not win elections except at the point of a gun guaranteed the reemergence of the Democrats. White southerners "redeemed" their state governments one by one, and when they did, African Americans were removed from office and denied their newfound voice in politics. Despite the northern electorate's lack of interest in helping the freedpeople, Grant signed the Civil Rights Act of 1875 guaranteeing blacks equal rights in public places. By 1876, only three Republican governments remained in the South—in Florida, Louisiana, and South Carolina—all sustained by military power, but not for much longer. Historian George Rable, author of a book about Reconstruction violence, pointed out that "in the middle decades of the nineteenth century, the American people and their political leaders were neither united nor patient enough to carry a radical policy to completion."[122] As Grant's second term neared its end, a boomlet for a third term emerged, but he refused to consider another four years. In a letter published in the *New York Tribune* on May 29, 1875, he declared, "I am not, nor have I been, a candidate for a renomination."[123] To an astonished Julia, who loved being first lady, he revealed his torment, "I wish this was over. I wish I had this Congress off my hands. I wish I was out of it altogether. After I leave this place, I never want to see it again."[124]

Was Grant's Reconstruction a success or a failure? His dream of peaceful reconciliation based on Republican principles floundered as his presidency polarized an already deeply divided country, pitting Republicans against Democrats, northerners against southerners, and whites against blacks. Yet if one of the goals of Reconstruction was to reconcile the North and the South, to restore political, economic, and social relations between them, then on that score it was a success. By 1876, the nation was relatively stable and strong. If another goal was to bring justice to the freedpeople, then in that regard Grant's Reconstruction was a failure. Four million Americans were newly free from the bonds of slavery, but poverty and racism severely limited their freedom. The foundation was laid for black advancement, but it would take place in another century. Historian of the Republican Party Lewis L. Gould assessed the effort: "But when all justifiable historical reasons for the Republican abandonment of black Americans have been recalled, there remains the hard truth that a party committed in its origins to human freedom came up short on that issue at a crucial time in its history."[125]

Historians have long debated the merits of Reconstruction, but President Grant went on the record in 1879. Expressing disappointment and bitterness at the outcome, he suggested that military Reconstruction should have been continued for at least a decade. Denying ex-Confederates suffrage, he claimed, "was a mild penalty for the stupendous crime of treason. Military rule would have been just to all, to the negro who wanted freedom, the white man who wanted protection, the Northern man who wanted Union." Grant regretted black suffrage because it gave "the old slave-holders forty votes in the electoral college. They keep those votes, but disfranchise the negroes."

He added sadly, "The trouble about military rule in the South was that our people did not like it. It was not in accordance with our institutions. . . . But we made our scheme, and must do what we can with it. Suffrage once given can never be taken away, and all that remains for us now is to make good that gift by protecting those who have received it."[126] Josiah Bunting argued that despite the errors, in the end President Grant "had surely fulfilled his commitment to those his service as a soldier had helped make free men and women."[127]

Voting was close and results quickly disputed in the 1876 presidential election. The Democrats campaigned on a platform of change and reform from "Grantism," an epithet that stood for his alleged corrupt government. The Republicans reminded voters of their unquestioned role in preserving the Union, and also promised more civil service reform. Violence and intimation kept many black voters from the polls in several southern states. The nation held its breath as to whether the nineteenth president of the United States would be Republican governor of Ohio (and former Union general) Rutherford B. Hayes or Democratic governor of New York Samuel B. Tilden. The electoral votes from Florida, Louisiana, South Carolina, and Oregon were claimed by both parties. From November 1876 to March 1877 the outcome of the election remained in doubt, with no end in sight. The country once again experienced perilous times. Some even suggested that another civil war might break out over the controversy. Grant performed his role as a mediator with dignity and tried to assume an air of careful neutrality, although the specially appointed "Electoral Commission" (eight Republicans and seven Democrats) cast its votes along strict party lines. In the midst of chaos, Grant assuaged worries that he would use the army to ensure the election victory for Republicans. "I think the entire people are tired of the military being employed to sustain a state Government," Grant declared to reporters.[128] The victor was Rutherford B. Hayes, who officially ended Reconstruction when he pulled the army out of the South. By April of 1877 "Redemption" was complete and all of the states of the former Confederacy were again under Democratic rule.[129]

In his final address, Grant uttered an extraordinary, but also refreshingly candid, apology: "It was my fortune, or misfortune, to be called to the office of Chief Executive without any previous political training." His message shows that even after two terms he rejected political verbiage for honest assessment. "Under such circumstances," he recalled, "it is but reasonable to suppose that errors of judgment must have occurred. . . . Mistakes have been made, as all can see and I admit." Grant insisted, "I have acted in every instance from a conscientious desire to do what was right. . . . Failures have been errors of judgment, not of intent." He reminded his audience, "My civil career commenced too at a most critical and difficult time." Commenting on the speech, the *New York Tribune* described it as "that of a man who is weary of public life and tired of political strife."[130] Ohio Republican congressman and former Union general James Garfield, often a bitter critic of Grant, recorded in his diary: "I was again impressed with the belief that when his presidential term is ended, General Grant will regain his place as one of the foremost of Americans. His power of staying, his imperturbability, has been of incalculable value to the nation, and will be prized more and more as his career recedes."[131]

Appreciation of Grant's presidency—sometimes lavish, sometimes grudging—appeared in a small number of works published between 1885 and 1920. James Penny Boyd praised him as the "chief representative of a nation preserved intact by his valor, unified by his wisdom, presided over by his firm, conciliatory and enlightened sway."[132] These appreciative authors usually pointed out the partisan nature of the attacks on Grant and the Republican Party and predicted that history would judge him more fairly. Journalist Frank A. Burr believed that "when the future historian studies calmly and impartially the story of General Grant's presidential terms, he will place him among the great civil rulers of the nation," while the writer of a beautiful volume in the Lives of the Presidents series, William O. Stoddard, judged him "the right man in the right place," and General Charles King declared that "in spite of all the alleged mismanagement the nation throve, the country prospered, the debt was greatly lessened, the people reasoned for themselves, and though many fell away from their allegiance, more stood firmly by the soldier-leader of their original choice."[133] The distinguished author Hamlin Garland attributed Grant's continued popularity to the fact that "a campaign of abuse, which loaded all responsibility upon the Executive and denied him all credit, was too bitterly partisan to make any permanent impression upon the minds of the people." Garland concluded, "But in the main all the great features of his public policy, and all the measures really vital in the progress of the nation, will be remembered and approved by the statesmanship of the future." A study of Grant's presidency yielded this assessment from Massachusetts politician and scholar Louis A. Coolidge: "It has not been the literary fashion to commend him much for his achievements after the Rebellion; yet his success as President in setting our feet firmly in the paths of peace . . . is hardly less significant than his success in war." Coolidge argued future generations would come to see that "Grant's Administration ranks second only to that of Washington."[134]

In 1888, the eminent Scottish-born scholar James Bryce published *The American Commonwealth*. In many respects comparable in scope, quality, and brilliance to Alexis de Tocqueville's *Democracy in America* (1835), the three-volume work explored in great detail the political institutions and practices of the United States. Lord Bryce believed that America was on the cusp of achieving a power unknown in all of recorded history. He explained in his introduction, "Thoughtful Europeans have begun to realize, whether with satisfaction or regret, the enormous and daily increasing influence of the United States, and the splendor of the part reserved for them in the development of civilization."[135] In Chapter 8, "Why Great Men are Not Chosen President," Bryce discussed how democracy's process often dismissed the "best men" in favor of lesser candidates. He then ranked America's presidents. The first generation to 1828 had all been, he wrote, "statesmen in the European sense of the word, men of education, of administrative experience, of a certain largeness of view and dignity of character," while presidents of the second period, 1829–1860, "were mere politicians . . . or successful soldiers" who stood as "intellectual pigmies beside the real leaders of that generation—Clay, Calhoun, and Webster." Finally, Bryce proclaimed, "A new series begins with Lincoln in 1861. He and General Grant his successor, who cover sixteen years between them, belong to the history of the world." In Bryce's estimation Grant deserved accolades because his presidency, with all of its flaws, completed Lincoln's vision of a reunited country. Of the American presidents elected from 1788 to 1900 Bryce wrote, only Washington, Jefferson, Lincoln, and Grant "belong to a front rank."[136] It is worth noting that in placing Grant with the three men who are generally agreed to hold the "front rank," Lord Bryce departs dramatically from most of the historical assessments of his generation, of the next three generations, and indeed even of those who are presently revising Grant's presidential reputation.

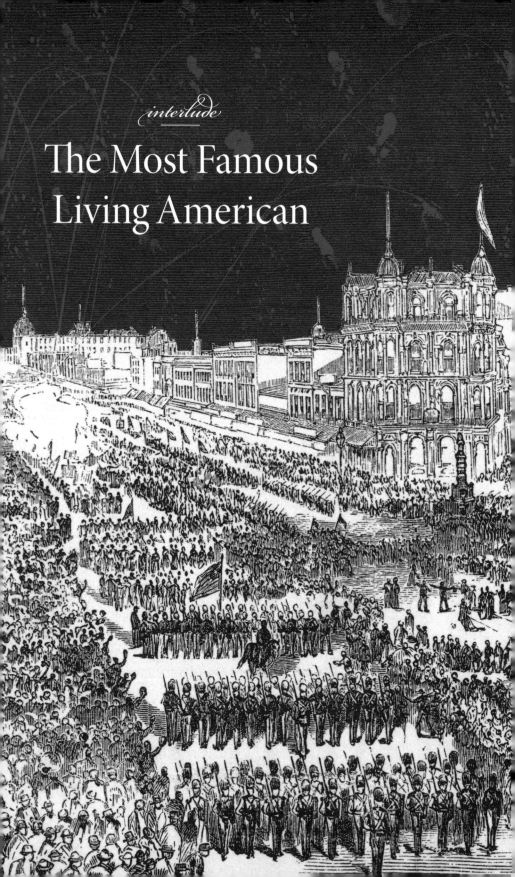

*interlude*

# The Most Famous
# Living American

In stark contrast to what the literature might suggest, Grant retained much of his iconic status during his presidency and regained what had been lost in his postpresidential years, becoming a global celebrity and international statesman. On his world trip of 1877–79, the first time any ex-president traveled so extensively, Grant was hailed everywhere by rapturous crowds and saluted with splendid reviews, parades, and speeches; he was wined and dined by kings and queens, generals and prime ministers, chancellors and potentates. Historians usually either ignore Grant's trip altogether or dismiss it by describing it as meaningless, or bizarre, or a callous lark undertaken by a typically smug Victorian leaving behind "a legendary trail of gaucheries."[1] At the time, it was not dismissed. American newspapers eagerly chronicled the triumphant receptions for Grant, beginning in England, then continuing in France, Switzerland, Denmark, Italy, Germany, Austria, Russia, Holland, Spain, and Portugal, and finally ending in China and Japan. To his hosts, Grant symbolized a new American identity born of war, freedom, economic prosperity, and a nationalism and internationalism leavened with democratic ideals. Grant represented the wave of the future to many admiring nations. His triumphant two-year trip abroad, his return in 1879 to masses of adoring crowds, and his near nomination for the presidential ticket in 1880 chronicle another rise to the top that would be sustained for more than a generation after his death.

### Around the World with General Grant

On March 4, 1877, fifty-five-year-old Ulysses S. Grant was finally free of the grave responsibilities of the White House. "I was never as happy in my life as the day I left the White House," he told a reporter. "I felt like a boy getting out of school."[2] Grant was now truly a private citizen, a general only by courtesy since he had relinquished his position (and his pension) in the army to serve as president. Ulysses and Julia left Washington and traveled to Georgetown, Ohio; to their Missouri farm; to Galena; and to several other cities as well. Everywhere wildly enthusiastic crowds greeted their arrival. Ulysses and Julia would leave for their world tour from Philadelphia, where they booked seats on the warship *Indiana* sailing for Europe on May 17, 1877. The happy couple's immediate destination was England. They planned to see every country in the Old World, and perhaps extend their trip to the Far East, if their funds allowed. Jesse Grant would accompany them, as would Fred for a year; Buck was charged with taking care of family business while they were out of the country. John Russell Young, a thirty-seven-year-old journalist for the popular *New York Herald*, also accompanied the Grants.

GENERAL GRANT'S TOUR AROUND THE WORLD.

Route of Grant's world tour (L. T. Remlap, ed., *General U. S. Grant's Tour Around the World*
[Chicago: J. Fairbanks and Company, 1880])

Young's accounts of the general's exotic trip captivated the paper's readers,
driving up circulation rates. Later, Young published a lavishly illustrated
two-volume account of the trip, *Around the World with General Grant*, one
of several available to late nineteenth-century readers.[3]

The arrangements were surprisingly casual. No official functions or receptions were anticipated; the State Department alerted the various embas-
sies of Grant's imminent departure. Before Grant sailed, several hundred
thousand lined the Philadelphia wharfs to bid him farewell. Fellow *Indiana*
passengers delighted in seeing the general walking on the deck, smoking
his cigars, and willingly engaging in light conversation. A week and a half
later the ship docked in Liverpool, where an immense gathering cheered the
former president's arrival. Grant's first taste of elaborate ceremonies came as

the mayor bestowed on him the "Freedom of the City" (a ceremonial honor dating back to medieval times), while tens of thousands of working-class people stood in line to shake the hand of a man they considered to be one of their own. Grant gave a small speech of appreciation. One British newspaper described the general approvingly as "open-browed, firm-faced, blunt, bluff and honest, and unassuming, everybody at once settled in his own mind that the General would do."[4] Slowly making his way to London, Grant received an enthusiastic welcome—in city after city—featuring parades, banquets, speeches, and receptions worthy of an honored head of state.

The adulation continued in London, though the royal family was puzzled as to exactly how to respond to the ex-president. Etiquette had to be devised to accommodate the visit. U.S. minister Edwards Pierrepont and consul Adam Badeau (Grant's former aide) worked with British officials and came up with the designation of "ex-sovereign" for Grant, sparking off a round of invitations from royalty, intellectuals, and political leaders. Fancy receptions and elaborate dinners with the Prince of Wales, the Duke of Wellington (son of the victor at Waterloo), and Queen Victoria ensued. The queen and her prime minister, Benjamin Disraeli, viewed Grant's "ordinariness" with as much distain as their constituents in Glasgow, Edinburgh, and Newcastle embraced it. Grant, dressed in a stiff black suit, endured rather than enjoyed the festivities.[5]

American reporters following Grant were amazed to note that the silent general was not only delivering on average three speeches a day but, joyfully liberated from the straitjacket of his former position, freely gave interviews to foreign reporters. A rarely glimpsed Grant emerged—relaxed, genial, and expansive. Breakfast with Matthew Arnold, Robert Browning, and Anthony Trollope impressed, but his favorite audience continued to be working-class Britons. A few days after his meeting with the queen at Windsor Palace, he welcomed a deputation of workers warmly, telling them, "I have received attentions and have had ovations and presentations from different classes, from the governing classes, and from the controlling authorities of your cities as well as from the general public; but there is no reception that I have met with which I am prouder of than this one to-day."[6]

The clamor for Grant among common people was explained by their view of him as a humble man who scaled the heights of society without any help from family or royal relations. As such, Grant represented the triumph of free labor and free men in a true democracy. Writing to a friend, Grant humbly noted: "The attentions which I am receiving are intended more for our country than for me personally. I love to see our country honored &

Ulysses (seated), with Julia on his right, at the pyramids, Egypt (Library of Congress)

respected abroad, and I am proud to believe that it is by most all nations, and by some even loved.[7] Gratifying to the ex-president was the fact that formerly hostile American newspapers "filled long editorial columns with spread-eagle gratulations over these old-world demonstrations." Biographer Hamlin Garland explained that the press now realized that "General Grant represented the power of the American nation . . . and the honors he was receiving were gratifying to all Americans." Garland analyzed the foreign newspaper coverage and found that the English regarded Grant not only as a great general, but also as a statesman and a man of peace, who favored arbitration over war and had sought to bring justice to the former slaves during his two terms.[8] Wherever he traveled, Grant represented the emergent power and democratic possibilities of the United States.

In early July, Grant and his party left England for a tour of every country of the continent. In Belgium he met with King Leopold, in Germany with composer Richard Wagner and Chancellor Otto von Bismarck, in France with President Maurice de MacMahon and Premier Georges Clemenceau, and in Rome with Pope Leo XIII. Grant never seemed to tire of bustling ports, exotic landscapes, and bountiful banquets, or of receiving an ever-increasing load of lavish gifts and expensive souvenirs.[9] Whether consulting with world leaders, conscientiously visiting museums in Paris and Rome, engaging in a vigorous excursion to Mount Vesuvius, sailing leisurely down the Nile, viewing the Holy Land, or watching the dancing girls provided by the Maharajah of Jeypore in India, Grant displayed a boundless appetite and energy for discovery, though he enjoyed some things more than others. "He liked men and women better than scenery, great engineering works better than cathedrals," wrote Garland, adding: "He was undoubtedly the greatest traveler that ever lived; that is to say, no other man was ever received by both peoples and sovereigns, by scholars and merchants, by tycoons and sultans and school-children and work-people and statesmen as was General Grant."[10]

Visiting Berlin, Grant found himself both fascinated and repelled by Germany and its "Iron Chancellor," Otto von Bismarck. What struck him as chilling was the militarization of the country—uniforms everywhere. Telling Bismarck that he only reluctantly agreed to witness a military review, he said, "The truth is, I am more of a farmer than a soldier. I take little or no interest in military affairs. . . . I never went into the army without regret, and never retired without pleasure."[11] During his trip Grant's counsel had been sought by many world leaders, prompting reams of admiring, even gushing newspaper prose back home. His political star ascended once again. In the parlance of twenty-first-century pollsters, his positives were astronomically high and his negatives low. Stalwarts led by Roscoe Conkling eagerly plotted a third Grant term. To Adam Badeau, Grant wrote, "Most every letter I get from the States asks me to remain abroad," urging him to delay returning until just before the 1880 convention was to take place.[12] This crafty scenario would capitalize on his surging popularity at home before the inevitable opposition mobilized. John Y. Simon, however, claimed that "such considerations played no role in Grant's thinking" regarding his travel plans.[13]

Given Grant's relief to be out of the White House, it seems incredible that he would consider running again. Near the end of his trip, Grant told Young: "I never wanted to get out of a place as much as I did to get out of the Presidency. For sixteen years, from the opening of the war, it had been a constant strain upon me."[14] What were his true intentions? Grant's letters and published conversations (with Young) clearly indicate that he did not wish to be considered. "I am not a candidate for any office," he wrote to Adam Badeau.[15] The constant travel delayed troubling decisions about his uncertain future. But they loomed larger the longer his trip went on. What would he do? How could he provide the kind of comfortable life that he and Julia had become accustomed to? He told Elihu Washburne, "I am both homesick and dread going home. I have no home, but must establish one after I get back, I do not know where."[16] Meanwhile, Ulysses and Julia had decided to extend their trip another year, planning to visit India, China, and Japan, by way of the Suez Canal. On January 24, 1878, Ulysses and Julia, joined by Fred Grant (Jesse returned to America), Adolf E. Borie (former secretary of the navy) and Dr. John M. Keating of Philadelphia, proceeded to India. "We visited the Taj and admired it as everyone does," remembered Julia. "We went again to visit it by moonlight. Everyone says it is the most beautiful building in the world, and I suppose it is."[17] The next stop was Hong Kong, and from there, the Grant party sailed to Canton, China, where the general was "carried by porters through a crowd of 200,000 and feted with sumptuous state banquets."[18]

Last stop on the itinerary was Japan. On June 21, 1879, the Grant party sailed into Nagasaki on the 225-foot USS *Richmond*. Author Dallas Finn wrote: "The Grants could not escape the contagion of excitement caused by their visit to a nation so long isolated. Crowds waved from the cliffs, junks circled the *Richmond*, and bonfires lit their route at night."[19] Grant was as-tonished by the welcome they received everywhere in Japan, prompting them to extend their visit to two months. "Can I ever forget the many civili-ties and kind attentions we received from these charming people?" Julia asked in wonderment. "My visit to Japan has been the most pleasant of all my travels," Grant wrote to Badeau. "The country is beautifully cultivated, the scenery is grand, and the people, from the highest to the lowest, the most kindly . . . in the world." Grant also admired the proud display of new railroads demonstrating the country's mastery of Western technology.[20] While Grant was in China, Viceroy Li Hung-chang asked him to deploy his diplomatic skills in negotiating a peaceful treaty between China and Japan regarding a dispute over the Ryukyu Islands, which he accomplished suc-cessfully. Modest in (civilian) dress and demeanor, the quiet-spoken Grant impressed the Japanese people and their rulers. Emperor Meiji asked for a private meeting with Grant before he left the country. The two men con-versed pleasantly, and at the conclusion shook hands. Both the meeting and the handshake represented a great honor conferred on a foreigner.

*The Most Famous Living American*

Grant steamed home from Japan, arriving to cheering crowds in San Fran-cisco on September 20, 1879. Traveling across the country, he was greeted by

Grant meets with the emperor and empress of Japan. This illustration portrays the emperor wearing a western military outfit. (John Russell Young, *Around the World with General Grant*, 2 vols. [New York: American News Company, 1879])

throngs of people everywhere, giving evidence that, while he had become a world figure by 1879—seen by untold millions outside the country—he remained a huge figure in the United States as well, and indeed was the most famous living American. The ecstatic receptions back in the United States only underscored the scale of his fame, as countrymen and -women welcomed him back after various nations of the world had affirmed his international reputation. The mayor of Philadelphia declared a holiday for Grant's arrival in that city, where an estimated 350,000 citizens hailed the returning Grants in a parade that lasted for much of the day. As the couple toured the country, similar huge demonstrations greeted the returning ex-president. If another term was his goal, Grant returned far too early, giving the opposition to his renomination time to gather steam. His old enemies in the press once again loaded up their cannons and fired away. The *New York Sun* exclaimed: "Ulysses S. Grant is a man driven mad by ambition. He now seeks to grab the government of the United States—a thing unprecedented—for a third term."[21]

Grant avoided the critics by embarking on yet another tour, accepting invitations to visit Florida, Cuba, and Mexico.[22] The usual elaborate ceremonies greeted Ulysses and Julia—and guests Fred and Ida, and Philip Sheridan—throughout their trip. Grant enjoyed visiting Mexico. It brought back

San Franciscans welcome the returning hero. (L. T. Remlap, ed., *General Grant's Tour Around the World* [Chicago: J. Fairbanks and Company, 1880])

many memories of when he was a young soldier, as his party traveled from Veracruz to Mexico City. After Mexico, the group traveled to Texas, Louisiana, and Tennessee, where Grant's appearances were greeted by surprisingly large, cheering audiences, lending truth to the idea that sectional reconciliation was finally on the upswing. He ended his trip in Galena, waiting for news of his fate at the June 1880 convention. Would he accept the nomination if offered? Could he win a third term? Despite the attacks, his popularity with voters remained undimmed. Brimming with enthusiasm at the thought of another four years in Washington, Julia urged him to run again. At fifty-eight, her husband was rested and in good health. Adam Badeau, who believed Grant *did* desire another term, advanced a motive: he had become a profound thinker and an international statesman during his travels. "He had seen other countries, both the peoples and the rulers. . . . His views were widened, and his whole character changed. . . . In the East, [he] had obtained his knowledge of China and Japan, and conceived an Oriental policy for this country which he believed so important that a desire to achieve it was certainly one reason why he was so eager to return to power."[23] Grant refused to openly encourage his supporters, following his pattern in 1868 and 1872. But he did not categorically ask them to stop. Roscoe Conkling, Senator John Logan of Illinois, and Senator James D. Cameron of Pennsylvania went to work on his behalf; the trio proved inept campaign managers. The Chicago meeting opened strongly for Grant, with 306 votes in his supporters' pockets, but a deadlocked convention coalesced around a dark horse candidate, Ohio congressman and former Union general James A. Garfield, giving him the Republican nomination, with Chester A. Arthur, former collector of the port of New York, as his running mate.[24] This was the end to Grant's official political career, prompting Badeau's witty observation that "he was never so fit to be President as when his party rejected him."[25]

Grant campaigned enthusiastically for the Garfield-Arthur ticket. Indeed, this was the first time he had actively participated in any political campaign. His fall calendar was filled with meetings, speaking engagements, and frequent appearances at banquets and parades on behalf of the Republican Party. In Massachusetts, Connecticut, Illinois, New York, and New Jersey, Grant urged voters to return the Republicans to the White House, often calling for fair elections in the South, where "our fellow-citizens of African descent, and of every other class who may choose to be Republicans, shall have the privilege to go to the polls, even though they are in the minority, and put in their ballot without being burned out of their homes, and without being threatened or intimidated."[26] Biographer Geoffrey Perret wrote of his efforts: "In the North . . . Grant remained the most popular man there was. There wasn't even a close second. Huge crowds turned out to hear him speak. . . . He never spoke for more than ten minutes, and he invariably stressed unity—of nation, of party." New Yorkers were invited to "honor" the general in a political parade on October 12, 1880. Over 60,000 citizens marched in the parade before an estimated 300,000 spectators. An editorial published in the Republican-friendly *New York Times*, anticipating the crowds, declared: "A demonstration will be witnessed in this City tonight great in numbers, more important in character, and more brilliant as a show than any political turn-out in this country." Grant reviewed the parade from a grandstand to the constant roar of cheers and huzzahs. With Garfield's victory secured a few weeks later, Grant turned to building a new life for himself and Julia.[27]

Ulysses and Julia did not want to live in Galena, but their finances could not support residing in New York City, their favored spot for retirement. Presidents did not have pensions in those days, and Grant needed a secure income. Fortunately, two separate trusts were established for him by two sets of wealthy supporters, enabling Grant to buy a house in Manhattan. The couple moved to their new residence in August 1881, with an income of approximately $6,000 per year from the trusts, still not enough to pay their bills. Grant accepted an honorary executive position with the Mexican Central Railroad, a business with bright promise that soon faltered in bankruptcy. More promising was an invitation from Ferdinand Ward, an up-and-coming Wall Street financier, to come aboard as a "silent partner" in a profitable enterprise. The fact that Buck was in business with Ward made his proud father predisposed to accept, investing every last penny of his funds in the enterprise. Dividends paid handsomely between 1881 and 1884. Grant settled in to life in New York, blind to the gathering storm.[28]

## chapter four

# Historian of the
# Union Cause

The *Personal Memoirs of U. S. Grant* is a powerful testament to the Union Cause and may be Grant's most influential memorial, self-made. The two-volume work is accorded high rank as both literature and history. The *Personal Memoirs* surpasses any other military memoir of the Civil War and stands alone as the best presidential autobiography ever published.[1] In his memoirs, Grant painstakingly recorded his role in the history of the great conflict despite suffering through months, then weeks, then days, then hours of indescribable agony from throat cancer. The story is a riveting, gut-wrenching tragedy ending with his death on July 23, 1885. His family's financial future depended upon the successful completion of the book, and he could not let them down. But the *writing* also took on a special urgency; he felt an obligation to tell what he knew to be true about himself, about the war, about America. Even as he faced death, Grant openly relished his role as a writer of history. U. S. Grant became a "man of letters," declared Bruce Catton.[2]

The *Memoirs* fall short of modern professional standards for writing history, but Grant is a historian if defined as someone who is "a writer or student of history."[3] Grant's account of the war conveyed what he himself called "truthful history." It can be simply put. According to Grant, the northern cause—union and emancipation—was the morally superior one. The interpretative significance of the *Personal Memoirs of U. S. Grant* is best judged within a careful elucidation of the *process* that led to the massive work, including its reception, reputation, and evaluation. Grant's interpretation and exposition of the war were interwoven with and reactive to issues, controversies, and events in his military and political career that explain Grant's "writing of the civil war."[4]

## The Ailing General

Grant's troubles began on a festive holiday. Christmas Eve in 1883 was cold and rainy, and by late evening the sidewalk was frozen in front of Grant's four-story house at No. 3 East 66th Street in New York City, near Central Park. Stepping out of a rented carriage, Grant slipped on the ice and sustained a painful injury. As the formerly robust general struggled to regain his health, another blow struck. In May 1884 he learned that Grant and Ward, an investment firm that held his and many others' fortunes, had failed. Friend and New York banker Henry Clews commented wryly on the debacle, "The great captain of the Union's salvation was as helpless as a babe when Ferdinand Ward and James D. Fish moved upon his works."[5] Ward and Fish were eventually jailed and Grant's reputation dragged through the mud. The Democratic *New York Sun*, an old adversary, demanded that criminal charges be leveled against the ex-president.[6] Grant was proved innocent of all wrongdoing other than being duped by financial tricksters. Aged sixty-two, Grant was penniless, humiliated once again as he had been in his thirties. Friends and supporters rallied around Ulysses and Julia. William H. Vanderbilt lent him $150,000. He offered to forgive the loan, but Grant refused, instead signing over to Vanderbilt all of his property, including his military trappings and the gifts bestowed on him during his European trip. He was able to keep his residence, but little else.[7]

The family's poverty stirred efforts in the U.S. Congress to establish a "Presidential Retiring Fund," while some of Grant's supporters called for the restoration of his military status so he could receive a pension.[8] Unfortunately, the immediate cash Grant desperately needed was not forthcoming. In the midst of depression and despair, he was persuaded to write an article for *Century Magazine*. It was the right time for such an effort. Civil War literature was pouring forth from the popular presses: books, newspaper and magazine articles, and serials. Most of the material was military in nature—descriptive accounts of battles, fictional portraits of soldiers coming to grips with the war, biographies and memoirs of soldiers, unit histories—and it fed a hungry public's insatiable appetite. Scribner's profited greatly with its well-received *Campaigns of the Civil War*. Then, in 1884, the first issue of *Century Magazine*'s serial *Battles and Leaders of the Civil War* appeared. The series, conceived by editors Robert Underwood Johnson and Clarence C. Buel, sought contributions from leading Union and Confederate soldiers, emphasizing reconciliation between former enemies. "On the whole 'Battles and Leaders of the Civil War,'" Johnson declared, "is a monument to American bravery, persistence and resourcefulness, and has the additional distinction of having struck the keynote of national unity through tolerance and the promotion of good will. We rightly judged that articles celebrating the skill and valor of both sides would hasten the elimination of sectional prejudices and contribute toward reuniting the country by the cultivation of mutual respect."[9]

The authors of the *Century* series benefited from a momentous decision made by the U.S. government in 1864 when it chose to pursue the goal of making the history of the war permanently accessible by publishing the complete records (battle reports, telegraph messages, and so on) of both armies. The history of the funding, the debates over records' location, and the editorial politics surrounding the publication of the 128-volume *War of the Rebellion: A Compilation of the Official Records of the Union and Con-*

*federate Armies* is fascinating. The editors of the *Official Records* selected for publication materials that they deemed "significant, official, and produced during the war."[10] Officials in the Civil War were required to keep copious records, which then had to be copied, recopied, and stored, with the result that a huge amount of paperwork was generated. Maj. Gen. Henry Halleck, who served as President Lincoln's chief of staff, realized the significance to history of Confederate records and ordered them retrieved from the burning ruins of Richmond. Grant lent his strong support to the effort, calling it "desirable to have all rebel documents Captured in Richmond and elsewhere in the South examined and notes made of their contents for convenient reference."[11] By 1877, work on forty-seven volumes of the *Official Records* was completed, and the first volume published in 1881. Subsequent generations of historians have used the *Official Records* as an indispensable reference for the war.

The War Records Office decided to make the project as nonpartisan and as nonpolitical as possible. Throughout the 1870s and 1880s, over fifty tons of materials were stored in various buildings in the Washington area. From the beginning, then, the *Official Records* set a high standard for evenhandedness in the war's portrayal. Every effort was made to locate and include Confederate military records and publish them alongside the more voluminous Union records. The War Records Office hired former Union *and* Confederate officers as editors. Government officials formed a liaison with former Confederate brigadier general Marcus J. Wright, who scoured the South for hidden records. This liaison led to an agreement between the *Southern Historical Society Papers* and the War Records Office for "reciprocal free access" to each other's Confederate documents. Generally, the *Official Records* volumes were praised in the journal's pages.[12]

The influential publishing project's emphasis on fairness to both sides was echoed in the larger society's desire for reconciliation, as exemplified in Johnson's description of the *Century* project. As the extreme bitterness of the war years receded, another interpretation, or "truth," about the Civil War emerged. It took the least controversial elements from both perspectives in an effort to bolster an official national ideology upon which a majority of citizens could agree. This interpretation, rising in popularity by the 1880s, can be described as promoting "sectional harmony." Increasingly, the idea that slavery caused the war, and that the Union army became a revolutionary instrument in bringing freedom to millions of slaves, became an impediment to reconciliation. Thus, the African American presence before, during, and after, the war was deemphasized.[13] This denatured revisionism encouraged a professional and nonpartisan approach to writing the war's history. The emphasis on reconciliation was supported by important elements of the northern and southern press and public, and to a limited extent by veterans. Sectional harmony was highlighted in the blue and gray reunions that were regularly held on anniversaries of important battles. A less divisive reconciliationist explanation proposed that both sides fought for noble causes; the controversial issues of slavery and emancipation were rarely mentioned.

The *Century*'s *Battles and Leaders* prompted an extraordinary rise in subscriptions for the magazine, coinciding with Grant's need to earn money for his family. The editors specifically targeted him, knowing that Grant would endow the whole project with prestige, ensuring even larger profits for the magazine. "With all his faults and shortcomings," *Century*'s senior editor Richard Watson Gilder sniffed, "he continues to be the most eminent and interesting of living Americans."[14] Early in the summer of 1884 Grant contracted to provide four accounts of major battles and campaigns (Shiloh, Vicksburg, the Wilderness, and Appomattox) for $500 (later raised to $1,000). Associate editor Johnson dealt directly with Grant, whom he admired. In his own memoirs, Johnson described his relationship with Grant as "one of the most fortunate experiences of my life, since it revealed to me the heroism and the integrity of a much misrepresented man." Grant's first submission, "The Battle of Shiloh," was disappointing. Johnson judged the Shiloh piece too stilted and formal. He suggested Grant adopt a more casual, entertaining style. Grant quickly rewrote the article to everyone's satisfaction. It was a smashing success, prompting an immediate offer from the Century Publishing Company for a whole book.[15] Soon, several firms were bidding for the honor of being Grant's publisher, much to the consternation of the *Century* editors. To his surprise, Grant enjoyed the writing, almost as much as the paychecks that arrived with reassuring regularity. Elsie Porter, daughter of Horace Porter, recorded that her father and Adam Badeau, both former aides, met with Grant daily in the summer of 1884. She described Grant writing with his pencil "racing over his pad."[16] He usually worked at a table, in the kitchen or on the pleasant piazza overlooking the sea at his summer home in Long Branch, New Jersey.

A brief period of happiness ensued, but fate once again intervened. The story is well known. A delightful summer dinner ended with the serving of a plate of fresh peaches. Julia recalled the particulars. "Helping himself, [Grant] proceeded to eat the dainty morsel; then he started up as if in great pain and exclaimed: 'Oh my. I think something has stung me from that peach.'" A drink of water felt like "liquid fire."[17] The pain in his throat did not abate. He was having trouble swallowing. A doctor recommended an immediate appointment with his family physician, Fordyce Barker, and a throat specialist. Grant procrastinated, downplayed the symptoms, not wanting to interrupt his work. It could wait until the family's return to the City in the autumn. Waiting was a mistake. October 22, 1884, was the day that Grant arrived for his first appointment with a preeminent throat doctor, John H. Douglas. A quick but thorough examination revealed the worst. Recorded Douglas, "I found the velum inflamed, of a dark, deep congestive hue, a scaly squamous inflammation, strongly suggestive of serious epithelial trouble. . . . I requested permission to examine the parts with my finger, and found the tongue swollen and hard at the base, and to the right side." The word "epithelial" meant cancer. Terrified, Grant managed only one question "Is it cancer?" Dr. Douglas did not utter the dreaded word to his eminent patient, but he did say it was "serious." He assured Grant that *sometimes* people with his condition could be cured. Douglas knew better. A later biopsy confirmed that Grant had contracted a fatal inoperable tongue and throat cancer. His death would not be easy, and would probably come within a year. He would suffer, enduring illness and depression along with brief periods of hope, even improvement.[18] His outward appearance would be transformed. He would lose weight, cough incessantly, and submit to undignified invasive procedures. His hair and beard would go from brown to heavily flecked with white. Every pleasure of life would be diminished, or banished, including eating, conversing, walking, and smoking cigars.

It was a grim prognosis. Douglas, who would serve as Grant's main physician, met with the family and told them how to make him as comfortable as possible. Julia, shocked and disbelieving, recalled asking "again and again if it were not curable and was answered that there had been instances when it had been cured." She clung to hope because "down in my heart, I could not believe that God in his wisdom and mercy would take this great, wise, good man from us."[19] At first, it was not so bad. Grant continued to see friends, to go on carriage rides and occasional outings, and to enjoy dinner with his family even if his aching throat could tolerate only milk and cold soup. He visited Dr. Douglas twice a day in the physician's New York office, receiving blessed relief with applications of cocaine. Soon, however, he could not leave his house. Another distinguished physician, Dr. George Shrady, joined Dr. Douglas in treating Grant.[20] Together, these two headed Grant's basic medical team, which also included a number of other specialists and Dr. Barker, and together they dealt with an increasingly suspicious press and a public growing ever more alarmed about Grant's condition. Rumors that he was ill abounded throughout the winter of 1884–85, but when the family refused to confirm them, the interest temporarily abated. That changed in February when the *New York World*'s front-page headline blared, "General Grant Very Ill." Not long afterward, the *New York Tribune* stated, "General Grant is a very sick man, and his death apparently not far distant." On March 1, the *New York Times* announced unequivocally that Grant would die of throat cancer.[21] From that time, Ulysses S. Grant's illness became the obsession of the nation, via the aggressive New York press.

Two authors who published books on Grant's death, Thomas Pitkin and Richard Goldhurst, provided details of the growing circus around Grant's 66th Street brownstone, just off Fifth Avenue. The street was clogged with the curious, groups of school children, veterans, representatives of patriotic organizations, cranks who promoted cancer cures, and visitors who were admitted to the house, if Grant felt well enough to receive them. Julia recalled, "The sympathy we met with from every source cannot be written: kind messages and great bouquets of flowers sent from the hothouses of friends, little boxes of trailing arbutus gathered from beneath the snow and sent from far and wide by schoolchildren with loving messages to the General. Beautiful letters came from many schools offering prayers for his recovery, and this same prayerful petition was offered by every denomination throughout the country."[22] Fred, his wife Ida, and their children moved into the third floor of the house, lending their support to Julia and Ulysses. The family was literally under siege from the press for much of the time from February to late June, when Grant left for Mount McGregor, a summer resort. New York City was the home base for the national press services as well as for a cluster of powerful newspapers—the *Times*, the *Tribune*, the *Sun*, the *Herald*, and the *World*. Streams of information regarding General Grant went directly to the homes of people living far from Gotham. "All the metropolitan newspapers had special telegraph wires to their downtown offices, and reporters patrolled the street in front of Grant's house," noted Pitkin.[23]

During periods of high activity, meaning when it was thought Grant might die, three "bulletin boys" were allowed in the main hall of the house—one for Western Union, one for Associated Press, and one for the United Press. No family member, physician, friend, or visitor eluded the press gang. Vying for the best stories, reporters often combined the ludicrous and fanciful with very accurate depictions of Grant's condition. Selected headlines from a survey of 102 *New York Tribune* articles published about Grant's illness from February to July 1885 provide insight into the frenzy. There were good days to report—"General Grant's Condition Unchanged: sleeping well and eating heartily," "General Grant Improved: he sleeps well and feels brighter," "General Grant More Cheerful," "General Grant Goes Out Twice," "General Grant sure that He will Recover" and "General Grant More Hopeful." These articles were filled with cheery details of diet, exercise, visitors, and time spent with family members. "Judging from the face of the patient, no one would pronounce him the sick man that he is," concludes one piece.[24] The bad days came more often, and of course produced lurid, dramatic stories and, with them, the hope of higher circulation rates—"General Grant Depressed," "General Grant Gets Little Sleep," "General Grant Still Alive," "General Grant's Throat Irritable," "General Grant Not So Well," and "General Grant Unable to Speak." These articles were filled with depressing details of the desperately ill man's condition. "From 1 to 6 a.m. the General slept most of the time, but not soundly. He muttered at times, and at others lay with his eyes wide open staring at the ceiling. When asleep he twitched and moved as if disturbed by unpleasant dreams." Many accounts described his medical treatment in detail: "The doctor then thoroughly washed the throat and mouth and painted the mucous surface with a soothing solution. The soreness did not abate at once, but was much relieved when some phlegm that had become hardened and adhesive was removed."[25]

A few reporters, unsatisfied with secondhand accounts, even posed as patients, pretending to share the same symptoms as the ailing general. When one or the other of Grant's doctors failed to produce enough information for good copy, they were accused of incompetence and cries went out for replacements. Doctor Shrady recalled Grant's asking how *he* was holding up under the fierce criticism. Shrady responded by asking advice from the general. Grant replied that when it mattered he never read the newspapers and told Shrady to remember that "one does the work, and the other does the guessing."[26] After some consideration, Grant gave out a statement supporting his medical team and then suggested the physicians hold regular meetings with reporters to control the flow of information. As a result, the doctors became celebrities, keeping extensive notes on their service that resulted in publications after Grant's death. By virtue of their frequent reports to the press on Grant's health, Drs. Douglas and Shrady also educated the American public on a disease that had remained hidden from public discourse. In many parts of the country, stores posted huge pictures of Grant with detailed and explicit information regarding his health below. Historian James Patterson's study of cancer in the United States showed that for most of the nineteenth century, the disease was rarely spoken of by name when doctors were dealing with patients, let alone discussed in newspapers. "The great exception to this virtual conspiracy of silence was the illness of Grant. Once the story broke that he had a malignant tumor, there was no sating the appetite of the reporters," Patterson claimed. "Until President Ronald Reagan developed a malignancy in his colon a century later, no case of cancer received more thorough coverage in the press."[27]

## Man of Letters

The same day that Grant learned of his cancer, he verbally accepted a *Century* book contract that provided him with 10 percent royalties on an expected subscription sale of 25,000 sets. It was a bad deal, deliberately underestimating potential profitability. The editors at *Century* had been salivating over the prospect of a book for months. In July, Gilder speculated on the interest Grant's memoirs would generate: "I do not see how it could fail to attract attention throughout the world. It should be translated at once, into French and German. It ought to sell in England—& in America it would of course be a standard work. . . . His . . . book would command unusual respect and attention." In a damning admission, Gilder warned, "[Grant] ought not to be permitted to get too high an idea of immediate sales and profits." Johnson exulted, "We have never had such a card before as Grant . . . we mustn't let that slip!" In a meeting held in early September, Grant questioned the Century Company's president, Roswell Smith, "Do you really think anyone would be interested in a book by me?" Smith issued an immediate and flattering response: "General, do you not think the public would read with avidity Napoleon's personal account of his battles?" He left Grant confident that *Century* would publish the book.[28] Grant was still entertaining other offers, however, and working hard on the manuscript, expanding the *Century* articles, and planning to divide the memoirs into two volumes. It is worth pointing out that Grant was emphatically not, as is sometimes portrayed, starting his career as a writer from scratch, nor was the autobiography written by ghostwriters. Importantly, the volumes were the last stage of a process that began during the war and continued, gathering steam, in the decades of Grant's postwar career. He explained his literary credentials in the following way:

I have to say that for the last twenty-four years I have been very much employed in writing. As a soldier I wrote my own orders, plans of battle, instructions and reports. They were not edited, nor was assistance rendered. As president, I wrote every official document, I believe, usual for presidents to write, bearing my name. All these have been published and widely circulated. The public has become accustomed to my style of writing. They know that it is not even an attempt to imitate either a literary or classical style; that it is just what it is and nothing else. If I succeed in telling my story so that others can see as I do what I attempt to show, I will be satisfied. The reader must also be satisfied, for he knows from the beginning just what to expect.[29]

Grant's late-blooming literary masterpiece therefore represented a culmination, by one of the major figures in the conflict, of twenty-four years of thinking, writing, and talking about the meaning of the Civil War for the preservation of the United States.

Grant's experience laid the foundation for the memoirs; his pen first captured that experience in formal battlefield reports. The documents of the Civil War and its individual battles began as soon as the muskets and cannons fell quiet on the conflict's battlefields. The old saying "The pen is mightier than the sword" applies to the official reports that had to be written by the leading battle participants to justify their successes and failures to their military and political superiors. Grant's major (and minor) battles and campaigns from Fort Donelson through Shiloh and Vicksburg and Chattanooga to the major battles of the Overland Campaign had to be analyzed, explained, and defended, with blame cast and praise awarded to the major officers. Casting blame upon others and awarding praise for oneself was a motif for many postwar reminiscences, as Robert U. Johnson knew only too well. He observed that every battle has at least four points of view: that of the man who gets credit for the victory, that of the man who thought *he* should get the credit, that of the man who is blamed for the defeat, and that of the man who is blamed by the man who is blamed for the defeat. Out of such confusing elements, Johnson mused humorously, history is written.[30] During the war, many reputations were advanced or damaged by the official reports, and if a high ranking general was perceived as committing a serious blunder on the battlefield, he knew that his actions would be written up immediately and he could expect to be rebuked, at best or, at worst, to be fired or court-martialed.

General Grant was no different from any other officer in the Civil War in this regard. Like other generals, he suffered from negative reports and evaluations, as well as from vicious attacks in the press. Like other generals, he cultivated certain politicians and reporters who unfailingly supported him and to whom he would explain and justify controversial actions. Unlike many other generals, however, Grant became a master of writing clear and forceful battle reports, presenting his views so successfully that his superiors—President Lincoln, Secretary of War Edwin Stanton, and Lincoln's chief military adviser, Henry Halleck—rarely disputed them. An aide observed Grant at his desk during the war: "His work was performed swiftly and uninterruptedly. . . . His thoughts flowed as freely from his mind as the ink from his pen."[31] The same clarity of thought that marked his official reports was also present in his instructions to his subordinates in written orders, telegrams, and letters. A member of Gen. George Meade's staff remarked: "There is one striking feature of Grant's orders; no matter how hurriedly he may write them on the field, no one ever has the slightest doubt as to their meaning, or even has to read them over a second time to understand them." Examples of his superior prose—clear, incisive, and terse— abound.[32] During the Chattanooga campaign, a clearly unhappy Grant sent a brigadier general the following message:

Your dispatch of yesterday to General Halleck has just been repeated to me. If you had shown half the willingness to sacrifice yourself and command at the start, [as] you do in your dispatch, you might have rendered Burnside material aid. Now I judge you have got so far to the rear, you can do nothing for him. Act upon the instructions you have, and your own discretion, and if you can do any thing to relieve Burnside, do it. It is not expected you will try to sacrifice your command, but that you will take proper risks.[33]

In the midst of the bloody battle of Spotsylvania, Grant dashed off a communiqué to Stanton that demonstrated his resolve to fight to the end:

We have now entered the sixth day of very hard fighting. The result to this time is much in our favor. Our losses have been heavy as well as those of the enemy. I think the loss of the enemy must be greater. We have taken over five thousand prisoners, in battle, while he has taken from us but few except stragglers. I propose to fight it out on this line if it takes all summer.[34]

Grant sent an urgent telegram to General Sheridan after the battle of Cedar Creek:

If it is possible to follow up your great victory until you reach the Central road and Canal do it even if you have to live on half rations. I say nothing about reaching Lynchburg with a portion of your force because I doubt the praticiability of it. If the Army at Richmond could be cut off from Southwest Va it would be of great importance to us but I know the difficulty of supplying so far from your base."[35]

Grant's farewell message to Union soldiers, issued on June 2, 1865, was written with heartfelt precision, anticipating the themes of his later history of the war:

Soldiers of the Armies of the United States! By your patriotic devotion to your country in the hour of danger and alarm—your magnificent fighting, bravery and endurance—you have maintained the supremacy of the Union and the Constitution, overthrown all armed opposition to the enforcement of the Law, and of the Proclamations forever Abolishing *Slavery*, the cause and pretext of the Rebellion, and opened the way to the Rightful Authorities to restore Order and inaugerate Peace on a permanent and enduring basis on every foot of American soil.

Your Marches, Seiges, & Battles, in distance, duration, resolution and brilliancy of result, dim the lustre of the world's past military achievements, and will be the Patriot's precedent in defense of Liberty and Right in all time to come.

In obedience to your country's call, you left your Homes and Families and volunteered in its defense. Victory has crowned your valor, and secured the purpose of your patriot-hearts; and with the gratitude of your countrymen, and the highest honors a great and free nation can accord, you will soon be permitted to return to your homes and families, conscious of having discharged the highest duty of American citizens.

To achieve these glorious triumphs and secure to yourselves, your fellow-countrymen and posterity the blessings of free institutions, tens of thousand of your gallant comrades have fallen, and sealed the priceless legacy with their lives. The graves of these a grateful nation bedews with tears—honors their memories, and will ever cherish and support their stricken families.[36]

The constant stream of reports, orders, and letters issuing from Grant's headquarters sharpened his perceptions of the larger issues of the conflict— loyalty, preservation of the Union, freedom, political democracy—as well as demonstrating his mastery of military strategy, thus uniting what Horace Porter called Grant's "singular mental powers and his rare military qualities."[37] By the end of the war, Grant had accumulated a treasure trove of materials from his headquarters records to draw upon when he wrote his report on the campaigns of 1864–65. In that document Grant laid out for the nation's review and for posterity the winning strategy of the war and how it was implemented in 1864–65. First, he stated, "I . . . determined . . . to use the greatest number of troops practicable against the armed force of the enemy; preventing him from using the same force at different seasons against first one and then another of our armies, and the possibility of repose for refitting and producing necessary supplies for carrying on resistance." Second, he decided "to hammer continuously against the armed force of the enemy and his resources, until by *mere attrition*, if in no other way, there should be nothing left to him but an equal submission with the loyal section of our common country to the constitution and laws of the land."[38] The phrase "mere attrition" was, and still is, a gift to pro-Confederate writers and is repeated endlessly in their case against Grant's generalship. But did "mere attrition" represent Grant's admission that the North won by sheer numbers, and brute force? Did Grant diminish his own prowess as a military leader? Hardly. He immediately pointed out the fact that no northern military leader (except him) had been able to use the numerical superiority in the most effective way to achieve total victory. Grant alone of all the northern generals had been fearless in pursuit of Lee's army.

Moreover, Grant argued that the South, in fact, enjoyed significant *advantages*: a vast territory, a largely united and supportive population, and long lines of river and railroad commerce. The North, Grant remembered, had huge *disadvantages*, beginning with a fractured, disaffected population politically represented by the Democratic Party. The Democrats, he observed, had had an excellent chance to win the 1864 presidential election, and perhaps end the war on terms unfavorable to the Union. In addition, the 1862 enlistments were ending, and too many experienced soldiers had been honorably discharged and thus lost to the army when they were needed the most. In contrast, new voluntary enrollments were down. The people, he wrote, were sick and tired of the war. "It was a question," Grant reminded readers of his report, "whether our numerical strength and resources were not more than balanced by these disadvantages and the enemy's superior position."[39]

Presaging his later criticisms of the "marble man," Grant disparaged the generalship of his southern counterpart, Robert E. Lee. While praising Lee's dignity at Appomattox Court House, Grant criticized Lee's defensive strategy during the Overland Campaign, arguing that it had unnecessarily and tragically prolonged the war. Instead of meeting Union forces face-to-face in battle, Grant claimed, "he acted purely on the defensive, behind breastworks, or feebly on the offensive immediately in front of them, and where, in case of repulse, he could easily retire behind them."[40] The northern general also made clear his low opinion of the Confederate nation: "In the South, a reign of military despotism prevailed, which made every man and boy capable of bearing arms a soldier; and those who could not bear arms in the field acted as provosts for collecting deserters and returning them. This enabled the enemy to bring almost his entire strength into the field."[41] Grant concluded his lengthy report with a tribute to the armies he commanded and a call for reconciliation by stating, "Let them [Union soldiers] hope for perpetual peace and harmony with that enemy, whose manhood, however mistaken the cause, drew forth such herculean deeds of valor."[42] Grant's 1866 report provided the "larger truth" of the war that for him no new information or factual evidence would ever change: the Union had justice on its side; the cause of the war was slavery; Confederates had advantages that offset Union superiority in both numbers and resources; northern soldiers fought just as well as southern soldiers, and under more difficult conditions; and Robert E. Lee's generalship was deeply flawed.

Eighteen years later, the report was just one of thousands of documents Grant drew on for reference, many of them written by his own hand. It was a daunting task. Most men under a death sentence would have abandoned an ambitious writing project at such a time. Not Grant. Famed for his quiet determination on the battlefield, he had to finish the manuscript before he died, but even he faltered. In late November and December 1884 he had trouble sleeping, and felt low. He stopped working for a while. Some family members approved, worried that the writing was making him weaker, while others were convinced that it helped keep him stronger. When his dear Philadelphia friend George Childs urged him to visit, Grant declined, vividly capturing his symptoms in shocking prose, "If you could imagine what molten lead would be going down your throat, that is what I feel when swallowing."[43]

Christmas brought an improvement in spirits and the courage to take up the task again in January. The two doctors who attended to Grant daily— Douglas and Shrady—were enjoined to do everything in their power to keep him alive and functioning until he completed the manuscript. Their job was to free him from pain as much as possible and to make sure that he would not choke to death while swallowing food. They did that and much more. They displayed devotion and duty well beyond professional requirements, at the cost of personal strain and exhaustion. Douglas gave an interview acknowledging the momentous charge: "I felt that I was representing to Gen. Grant the love and sympathy of 50,000,000 of the American people, and my sense of responsibility to him and to them has nerved me to a degree of physical endurance that might otherwise have been impossible."[44] Thomas Pitkin commented, "Grant had come to look upon them [Douglas and Shrady] almost as brothers."[45] He needed and received support from his physicians, from a loving family, from loyal aides, and from devoted friends and acquaintances who visited him, such as Hamilton Fish, Matías Romero, Rufus Ingalls, Jerome B. Chaffee, Roscoe Conkling, James Grant Wilson, Cyrus Fields, Daniel Sickles, Mrs. Leland Stanford, William Sherman, and Mark Twain.

A deeply affectionate friendship had sprung up between the silent general and the forty-nine-year-old humorist, satirist, lecturer, and novelist Samuel Langhorne Clemens, who, under the pseudonym Mark Twain, published a series of novels that became American classics, including *Innocents Abroad* (1869) and *The Adventures of Tom Sawyer* (1876). The two had met a couple of times during Grant's presidency but did not connect until Twain accepted an invitation to speak at a formal dinner of the annual reunion of the Army of the Tennessee in Chicago held on November 13, 1879. The reunion celebrated Grant's return from Europe, and, the event, as described later by one scholar, generated an enthusiasm "reserved in these more jaded times for rock musicians," attracting thousands of Chicagoans to watch a gigantic procession led by Grant before the dinner to honor him.[46]

Scheduled at the end of a long evening, Twain's hilarious speech previewed the infant Ulysses's future: "And in still one more cradle, somewhere under the flag, the future illustrious Commander in Chief of the American Armies is so little burdened with his approaching grandeurs and his responsibilities as to be giving his whole strategic mind, at this moment, to try and find out some way to get his big toe in his mouth—an achievement which, meaning no disrespect, the illustrious guest of this evening turned his whole attention to some fifty-six years ago." Master of comic timing, Twain paused and let the gales of laughter subside before delivering the final line, "And if the child is but the prophecy of the man, there are mighty few that will doubt that he succeeded." The next day Twain wrote his wife that "the house came down with a crash." Twain was openly delighted when the impassive Grant revealed that "he laughed until tears came and every bone in his body ached."[47]

From that time, the two were bound together in a friendship marked by mutual respect and admiration. Twain often visited Grant, sharing cigars and congenial conversation. Noted for his cynical treatment of Gilded Age politicians, reformers, and corruption, Twain stood in awe of Grant, stating, "He was a very great man and superlatively good."[48] Mark Twain heard about the *Century* contract and while chatting with Grant in November 1884, ventured his opinion that the offer was ridiculously low. Twain and his brother-in-law, Charles L. Webster, had recently established their own New York–based publishing house, Webster and Company. Its first publication, *Adventures of Huckleberry Finn* (1884), was selling briskly. Twain proceeded to offer Grant a $10,000 advance, with the promise of 70 percent of the net profits. The overly generous terms sprang from Twain's desire to help his friend escape poverty. He wrote later, "It had never been my intention to publish anybody's books but my own. An accident diverted me from this wise purpose. That was General Grant's memorable book."[49] After consulting with friends and family, Grant happily signed with Webster and Company in February 1885 (the official announcement was made on March 2, 1885) dashing the hopes of the Century Company. Robert U. Johnson described the decision as one that "cast a gloom over the younger members of the Century Co., who never ceased to think that in our hands this phenomenal book would have reached as phenomenal a sale as it did in Mr. Clemens's."[50] Grant would still produce the remaining articles owed to Century, adding another burden. Twain knew he was risking Webster's future on the hope that Grant would remain alive to finish his book. His motives were not entirely philanthropic. He expected that the memoirs would be a huge best seller with copies on the bookshelf of every northern veteran, generating enough profits for both Grant and Webster and Company.[51] It certainly did not hurt that Grant was the object of constant attention and scrutiny by the press. Twain planned a vigorous subscription campaign to sell the volume. In the end, he was right. "The announcement [of Grant's memoirs by Webster] produced a vast sensation throughout the country," remembered Twain.[52]

## The Union Cause versus the Lost Cause

Webster and Company hired many salesmen to sell subscriptions to an eager audience, with northern veterans especially targeted. Understandably, Grant enjoyed a special relationship with Union veterans, who had voted for him in great numbers in 1868 and 1872. During the Civil War, northern soldiers not only formed powerful bonds with each other, but also with some of their officers, which would have been unthinkable during peace-

Profits as well as pathos as the general lay dying (author's collection)

able times. For them, saving the Union had been a noble cause sanctified by the blood and sacrifice of their dead comrades. The meaning behind the words on the huge banner that greeted the men who marched in Washington's Grand Review, "The Only National Debt We can Never Repay is the Debt We Owe to the Victorious Union Soldiers," was embraced by veterans.[53] The survivors, from the humblest to the highest-ranked soldiers, had a stake in preserving the memory of the war for future generations in history books, such as school textbooks; on preserved battlefields, such as those at Gettysburg and Vicksburg; and in national cemeteries, such as the one in Arlington, Virginia. In the spring of 1866 the most prominent of the northern veterans' groups was founded in Illinois. Inclusive (every soldier was welcomed, including black veterans) and democratic (officers were granted no special status, and working-class veterans were welcomed), the Grand Army of the Republic (GAR) emerged as an interest group whose political power extended widely around the country. Although tipping heavily toward the Republican Party, the GAR embraced Democratic members, and its endorsement was courted enthusiastically by both parties. While often divided at the ballot box, veterans united on other issues, such as pensions and the building of old soldiers' homes.[54]

A review of President Grant's calendar and correspondence for just one year, 1873, provides compelling evidence of the amount of time, energy, and passion he invested in maintaining ties to veterans. Of course he strove to keep veterans within the Republican Party fold, but also wished to keep the Union Cause honored in history's judgment.[55] Although he accepted many fewer invitations than he received, Grant made frequent appearances at veterans' reunions and other commemorative occasions, striking a balance between the Union army's eastern and western wings. On February 6 "The Great Commander" attended a meeting in Wilmington, Delaware; May 15 found him at an Army of the Potomac reunion in New Haven, Connecticut; on September 17 the veterans of the Army of the Cumberland enjoyed their former top general's presence at an event in Pittsburgh; and on October 15–16 Grant joined the two-day reunion of the Army of the Tennessee in Toledo, Ohio. He relished being with "his old comrades in arms," declaring the meetings as being "attended . . . with a revival of old associations and sympathies, formed in such trying times."[56] Historian of the GAR Mary Dearing claimed Grant ranked first in veterans' esteem. He became an official, dues-paying member of the organization in 1877.[57]

President Grant sanctioned a new holiday commemorating the deaths of Union soldiers. Unofficially celebrated in the North as early as spring 1866,

Decoration Day (later Memorial Day) honored fallen soldiers by reminding the living of their sacrifices. The occasions were solemn, featuring processions, speeches, and sermons and drawing large crowds. The president and Mrs. Grant were among the 5,000 people who attended a commemoration in Arlington National Cemetery on May 30, 1868.[58] On May 21, 1873, the president issued an order closing government offices "in order to enable the employees of the Government to participate, in connection with the Grand Army of the Republic, in the decoration of the graves of the soldiers who fell during the rebellion."[59] But Grant did more than attend celebrations, commemorative occasions, and banquets, and support holiday status for Decoration Day. He appointed thousands of veterans, and their widows, to government jobs, especially in postal and customs offices. He answered letters from veterans asking for government pensions for injuries or losses, both during and well after he left the White House. The outpouring of affection Grant received from veterans' associations when he traveled around the country in the decade and a half before his death is well documented, as when he attended a reunion of 40,000 ex-soldiers in Milwaukee in 1880.[60] What is less well known are the numerous demonstrations of concern and loyalty—letters, petitions of support, flowers, groups marching in front of his house in New York City and his cottage in Mount McGregor—shown to Grant by veterans when his illness was made public. On May 30, 1885, General Grant was resting in his room when he heard the familiar strains of "Marching through Georgia." Four hundred GAR members were passing in front of his house. The general pushed back the curtain and saluted the veterans.[61] As these gestures suggest, northern veterans were adamant about keeping the memory of the Union Cause burning brightly. When veterans honored U. S. Grant, they were also honoring their war service and honoring the goals that they fought for. In doing so, Union veterans were demonstrating a loyalty to values and principles in stark contrast to the rise of a pro-Confederate memory of the Civil War that disparaged Grant's generalship, the fighting qualities of Union soldiers, and the northern version of the war's history.

The North's, and Grant's, interpretation of the war's righteousness was challenged by an ideology about the Confederate nation called the "Lost Cause." The elements that define the Lost Cause are familiar: the war was caused not by slavery but by states' rights; southern armies were never defeated, but instead were overwhelmed by numbers; the southern soldier was brave and true, echoing the perfection of the patron saint of the Lost Cause, that courtly Virginia gentleman of impeccable lineage, Gen. Robert E. Lee.

Jubal A. Early, Lee's former general, and his supporters actively and successfully promoted their version of "truthful" history in the pages of the influential *Southern Historical Society Papers* and in numerous speeches to southern veterans' groups. For the "unreconstructed," it was not enough to idolize Robert E. Lee; Ulysses S. Grant's reputation had to be destroyed.[62] Lee's and Grant's historical reputations assumed distinctly different trajectories at this time, Lee's ever upward, Grant's downward. Lee's General Orders no. 9 issued on April 10, 1865, provided Lost Cause partisans with an explanation and a platform for Confederate defeat and Union victory. In that farewell message, Lee honored his soldiers for having displayed "unsurpassed courage and fortitude," arguing that they had been "compelled to yield to overwhelming numbers and resources."[63] Taking his cue from General Orders no. 9, as well as conversations and correspondence with Lee himself, Early claimed, in speeches and in print, that Grant was a bloody butcher who was not even remotely equal to Lee as a military strategist or tactician. Moreover, he presented an impressive array of facts and figures to support the Confederate side of the story.[64]

The negative portrayal of Grant that emerged not only tarnished (in the long run) Grant's national and international military stature, but also increased Lee's, which was the true goal of this effort. Referring in part to the pro-Confederate histories that were critical of him, an irritated Grant said: "The cry was in the air that the North only won by brute force; that the generalship and valor were with the South. This has gone into history, with so many other illusions that are historical."[65] This seemingly unstoppable and, to Grant, grotesque adulation of the aristocratic Lee was neatly summed up by the English writer Matthew Arnold, who explained that in his view Grant "is not to the English imagination the hero of the American Civil War; the hero is Lee."[66] Just as Lee was presented as a flawless icon, so the Confederate cause was whitewashed. The preservation of states' rights was elevated as *the* southern cause, not the defense of the Confederate slave republic. Reflecting the sectional divide during the war, two sharply differing interpretations of the conflict emerged in full force only a decade after Appomattox.

Grant was aware that Lee's reputation was overshadowing his own. The growing influence of the Lost Cause owed much to the power of the criticisms hurled against Grant's hated Reconstruction policy in the South. Jubal Early wrote in 1870, "We have just witnessed the elections throughout several States of this 'Free Republic,' some of which are called 'loyal States' superintended by armed agents of the United States Government, backed by U.S. troops, for the purpose of perpetuating the power of the ruling faction, through the instrumentality of the ballot in the hands of an ignorant and inferior race." From the pen of ex-Confederate general Dabney H. Maury in the *Southern Historical Society Papers* came a typically hostile evaluation of Grant's presidency: "In reviewing the history of this century it will be impossible to find a rule so barren of statesmanship . . . as Grant's has been. . . . It is uncharitable and of little profit to speculate upon the remnant of his life left to him. But we may well believe 'his [remaining] days will be few and evil!'"[67] White southerners connected Grant's brutal generalship with his so-called imposition of Republican rule on the defeated region. Grant, however, connected the war's goals—reunion and emancipation—with an attempt, very imperfect, to make the South a place where black and white, Republican and Democrat could live together. He failed. "There has never been a moment since Lee surrendered," Grant remarked ruefully, "that I would not have gone more than halfway to meet the Southern people in a spirit of conciliation. But they have never responded to it. They have not forgotten the war."[68]

Over the next century, understanding or appreciation of the Union Cause steadily declined against the appeal of southern nobility and romanticism. Although the Lost Cause ideology has been thoroughly discredited by scholars, it retains a powerful grip on the popular imagination, albeit in a less racist form than it took during the last decades of the nineteenth century. The myth of Robert E. Lee is still immensely appealing to large numbers of Americans, and not just southern Americans. Lee's brilliant generalship, his stainless character, his supposed old-fashioned and gentlemanly style of warfare, and his noble acceptance of defeat commend him to us. In contrast, the warfare conducted by Ulysses S. Grant, "the butcher," is repellent because it has been deemed modern. In his lifetime and afterward, Grant has been portrayed as having only luck on his side in the Western Theater and having only the advantage of vast numbers and unlimited resources in the Eastern Theater. The southern journalist and Lost Cause historian Edward A. Pollard's cruel but widely quoted assessment of Grant as "one of the most remarkable accidents of the war . . . a man without any marked ability, certainly without genius, without fortune, without influence" has retained its force over decades of Civil War historiography.[69] Winston Churchill, heavily influenced by Lost Cause writers, wrote of Grant's "unflinching butchery," arguing that "more is expected of the high command than determination in thrusting men to their doom," and concluding that Grant's generalship, when compared to that of the incomparable Lee, "must be regarded as the negation of generalship."[70]

Clearly, Grant's reputation was tied to the Union's numerical superiority. According to this view, a less talented general who has more soldiers can beat a more talented general who has fewer soldiers. Yet many historians have demonstrated the military advantage of holding the interior lines during the Civil War.[71] This advantage, used adeptly by Lee against a series of bumbling Union generals, made his small army more than equal to a larger one. William T. Sherman weighed in on the controversy, refuting the British depiction of Lee's superiority to Grant. Acknowledging Lee's standing as a "gallant general," Sherman said, "He never rose to the grand problem which involved a continent and future generations. His Virginia was to him the world." Sherman claimed that Lee lacked aggressiveness in the last year of the conflict, "and in war that is the true and proper test. . . . Grant's strategy embraced a continent; Lee's a small State. Grant's 'logistics' were to supply and transport armies thousands of miles, where Lee was limited to hundreds."[72] Grant would say of Lee: "I never could see in his achievements what justifies his reputation. The illusion that nothing but heavy odds beat him will not stand the ultimate light of history. I know it is not true."[73] How wrong he was in this assessment. One could argue that Grant's genius was the opposite of Lee's. As Sherman suggested, his great test came in successfully directing several armies comprised of almost a million soldiers over great swaths of the country. Grant struggled to make that point in many venues. It disturbed and distressed him to think that future citizens would forget about the hardships of the Union army (and of course his role) in winning the conflict. To some extent, his worst fears have been realized. Today, many are hard pressed to articulate what exactly the northern side was fighting for beyond emancipation. Preserving the Union to keep democracy alive in the world does not resonate in a time when American exceptionalism is in poor repute. Today, the revolutionary, progressive impact of the Union army's role in bringing a victory that kept the country whole and brought freedom to millions of slaves is often brushed aside or ignored, especially in light of Reconstruction's failures. Today, scholars emphasize what divides, not what unites, Americans. The stance is appropriate for skeptical times. Grant and Americans who lived through the Civil War did not, as a rule, embrace either skepticism or moral relativism. That is what, for them, made the stakes so high and so meaningful in the effort to control the historical memory of the war for future generations.

## Truth in History

Grant did not often respond personally to criticisms of his military leadership; a president engaging in such defenses would be undignified. But he did review manuscripts and weighed in on some of the numerous controversies about the war.[74] He defended his reputation indirectly, and by doing so, influenced the writing of Civil War history. John Simon wrote, "Grant's apparent indifference to what was said about him masked reality."[75] He lent his prestige, his oral recollections, and his collection of wartime materials to reporters and partisans who wrote important defenses of his generalship.[76] The first significant volume to appear was that of Adam Badeau in 1868. Badeau, Grant's military secretary during the last year of the war, challenged Edward A. Pollard's *The Lost Cause* and William Swinton's *Campaigns of the Army of the Potomac*, both published in 1866. Swinton, a northern journalist banned by Grant during the war, agreed with Pollard that in the 1864 Overland Campaign, Lee, although vastly outnumbered, outgeneralled the blundering Grant. Then, instead of certain and relatively painless victory, Lee forced the Union commander to settle for a costly siege at Petersburg. Not surprisingly, Swinton's work was highly praised by the southern press, and also in many northern circles unfriendly to Grant.

Badeau's work (eventually the three-volume *Military History of Ulysses S. Grant*, 1868–82) was bitterly denounced by that same southern press, outraged by his claim (which was Grant's) that pro-Confederate historians inflated Union troop numbers while minimizing their own. Jubal Early's fiery refutation of Badeau's numbers was published in the *London Standard*, providing insight into the passion driving Lost Cause historians: "To a people overpowered and crushed in a struggle for their rights, there is still left one resource on earth for the vindication of their conduct and character: that adopted by England's great Philosopher—an appeal to 'foreign nations and to the next age.'" Early continued, "A persistent and systematic effort to falsify the truth of history has been made, since the close of the late war in this country, by the adherents of the United States Government in that conflict."[77] Badeau's volume was also the object of attacks in northern newspapers allied with the Democratic Party, hostile to Grant. One such attack claimed, "It is in everything but name the carefully prepared memoir of Grant, by himself." Calling the history a "panegyric and special pleading," the reviewer commented: "For his own good name and fame it is to be lamented that he did not put the task in more competent hands."[78] This unfriendly review provided evidence that Grant was almost as controversial within some parts of northern society as he appeared to be in the South.[79] Documentation of Grant's active involvement in Badeau's work can be found in many letters he wrote to the author. One begins, "Dear Badeau, I have read with great pleasure your chapter on the Cold Harbor Campaign. . . . I have no criticisms to make, and think it not only very accurate but that it will explain many existing misapprehensions in regard to that Campaign."[80] Badeau himself confirmed Grant's interest, stating that "Indeed every line in my history was read by him before it finally went to the printer, and had his sanction as completely as any portion of his more 'Personal Memoirs'"[81] The evidence shows that Grant *was* most definitely the guiding force behind the volumes, expressing satisfaction that Badeau had rebutted Swinton effectively and had put down the circle led by Early.

Strictly military accounts such as Swinton's and Badeau's were complemented by general histories of the war that held the Union Cause, and U. S. Grant, in high esteem. Both popular and academically trained writers united in agreeing that the Confederate experiment in rebellion was a disaster. Gearing their argument toward a northern audience, authors such as Benson J. Lossing and John W. Draper blamed southerners for starting the war and identified the cause of the conflict as slavery. Other histories came from the pens of prominent politicians and public figures. Most notable among them was the three-volume work written by Grant's vice president and former Massachusetts's Senator Henry Wilson. Wilson, an opponent of the "slaveocracy," and a proponent of black equality, devoted an unusually sizeable space in his volumes to African American soldiers and their fight for freedom.[82] Military accounts, however, tended to sell better then general ones, and other Grant partisans cashed in on the opportunity. Two of them who published admiring accounts of Grant's wartime achievements were Horace Porter and John Russell Young, the latter the reporter for the *New York Herald* who accompanied Ulysses and Julia on their world journey. Grant gave Young a series of remarkable interviews in which he offered candid reflections on the art of war, Union and Confederate generals, other Civil War leaders, and important battles. Aware of their wide readership, Grant reviewed Young's articles of his "conversations," soon published in the *Herald* (and later in a book, *Around the World with General Grant*).

Many of Grant's pronouncements caused controversy and discussion back home, including his thoughts about Lee's generalship. Grant's analysis printed in Young's interviews formed the basis for his evaluation of Lee found in the *Personal Memoirs*. His assessment of Lee was harsh:

Lee was a good man, a fair commander, who had everything in his favor. He was a man who needed sunshine. He was supported by the unanimous voice of the South; he was supported by a large party in the North; he had the support and sympathy of the outside world. All of this is of an immense advantage to a general. Lee had this in a remarkable degree. Everything he did was right. He was treated like a demi-god.[83]

Grant rejected categorically the Lost Cause claim that the two sides fought for equally honorable causes. Although Grant lauded the courage of southern soldiers, he attacked the idea that *only* they were admirable: "When I look for brave, noble characters in the war, men whom death has surrounded with romance, I see them in characters like McPherson, and not alone in Southern armies." He was also distressed by attacks on his character and military abilities, and by extension, on the typical northern citizen soldier. "While I would do nothing to revive unhappy memories in the South," Grant declared, "I do not like to see our soldiers apologize for the war."[84]

In a conversation with Otto von Bismarck in Germany, Grant made the case for his deeply held conviction that the Union's cause was the just one because it came to stand for freedom as well as for preserving the Republic. It began when the Iron Chancellor offered his regrets that such a terrible war between peoples of the same country had to be fought. Grant agreed, stating, "But it had to be done." Bismarck interjected, "Yes, you had to save the Union." Immediately Grant replied, "Not only save the Union, but destroy slavery." Bismarck, not persuaded, insisted, "I suppose, however, the Union was the real sentiment, the dominant sentiment." Grant responded, "In the beginning, yes, but as soon as slavery fired upon the flag it was felt, we all felt, even those who did not object to slaves, that slavery must be destroyed. We felt that it was a stain on the Union that men should be bought and sold like cattle. . . . We were fighting an enemy with whom we could not make a peace. We had to destroy him. No convention, no treaty was possible—only destruction." Grant also expressed his opinion that the length of the war was in some way "providential" because a brief conflict might have left slavery intact.[85]

Quite obviously, there was sharp contention over which version of history was "truthful." For Grant, as for others who wrote about the war in the two and a half decades immediately following 1865, there were "facts," which were verifiable, quantifiable, recoverable, objective, and rational. When writing his memoirs, Grant sought the most accurate and up-to-date factual information with which to make his case. These facts, this "evidence" could be retrieved from memory, conversations, written and published reports, letters, maps, telegrams and diaries. Facts were supposedly objective and formed the narrative of history. There was also a "truth." Truth was derived from facts, but not dependent upon them. Truth was subjective, and morally based. Truth had a higher meaning. Truth was based in the facts but ultimately not answerable to them. Today, professional historians call truth "interpretation."[86] That Grant read, digested, and was displeased with published accounts of the war showed in an 1879 interview. In it, he described how these accounts "only show how often history is warped and mischief made." The writers, he claimed, "study out dispatches, and reach conclusions which appear sound, and are honestly expressed, but which are unsound in this, that they only know the dispatches, and nothing of the conversations and other incidents that might have a material effect upon the truth." In his memoirs, Grant pronounced, "Wars produce many stories of fiction, some of which are told until they are believed to be true."[87]

## "I shall reach a period in a moment"

Sick as he was, Grant surely took strength and inspiration from an opportunity to refute all the criticisms, and in turn, his work methods inspired admiration. "General Grant was a sick man," Twain recorded in his autobiography, "but he wrought upon his memoirs like a well one and made steady and sure progress." Julia stated, "The General's memoirs occupied every leisure moment. He even wrote at night sometimes when sleep would not come to him. It was a happy thought that suggested that book. He worked on and on in his labor of love, his health gradually failing."[88] Just as the press reported on his health, so too did they issue constant reports on the progress of his book, as these headlines record: "General Grant at Work on His Book," "General Grant Working on His Book: his throat more irritable by talking," "General Grant's Condition—Revising His Manuscript," "General Grant Well Enough to Resume Work," and "Grant Writes a Chapter. He Works for Four Hours over His book. Wonderful Will Power." On May 5, as one journalist described, "His easy chair was wheeled up to the table in the library, where a large pile of manuscript lay, and after giving a glance at the morning papers and commenting upon the war cloud that hung over Europe, he turned his attention to his manuscript and laid out the plan to be followed in dictating to the stenographer."[89] Dr. Shrady commented that Grant "would sit and write when most men would have been abed and under the influence of an anodyne."[90]

Both with pen and through dictation, Grant provided the narrative structure of the book. In Manhattan, his writing table was set in a small room at the head of the stairs. In the cottage at Mount McGregor, when he was too weak to sit at a proper desk, a specially constructed lap table was made available to him. In both places, Grant's surrounding "office" space was crammed with his maps, his primary materials, and his books. A naturally restless man, Grant found the increasing confinement almost unbearable. He needed vistas, and the memoirs provided a way to see them, reeling in the years. A friend, visitor, and former Union general, James Grant Wilson, noted the obsessive nature of Grant's writing: "His mind was absorbed with the one subject of his military autobiography and a desire to be accurate in the most minute particulars. . . . In all matters aside from his book Grant took but a slight and passing interest."[91]

The evolution of the *Personal Memoirs* from September of 1884 to March 1885 went fairly steadily. The first completed part—up to the battle of Vicksburg—was almost entirely done, and Grant was proofreading parts of it for the printer by late April 1885. The process was established early. Grant's written or transcribed draft would be passed along to his staff. Grant had a small group of researchers and assistants to help him revise, edit, check facts and dates, and procure needed papers. "What part are you reading up and verifying?" he asked Fred, who emerged as his principal assistant.[92] Other staff at various times included Adam Badeau and Horace Porter; Fred's wife Ida; Grant's other sons, Buck (Ulysses Jr.) and Jesse; Harrison Tyrell, his personal valet; and Nathan E. Dawson, his stenographer. When possible, Badeau recalled, "He liked to have his pages read aloud to the family in the evening, so that he might hear how they sounded and receive their comments. He worked . . . from ten or eleven in the morning until two or three in the afternoon, and sometimes again later in the day."[93] Mark Twain also played an important role in facilitating the publication of both volumes, although he was not, as is sometimes asserted, their "ghost writer." In mid-March, Twain checked the manuscript's progress almost daily, and by mid-April, he was correcting the galley proofs for grammatical and other errors.[94]

The second volume did not proceed steadily. Grant wrote, or dictated, it while suffering from intense pain, diluting the clarity of the prose and the smoothness of the narrative. The period from late March to his death in July was punctuated by constant medical crises big and small, with periods of relief. After Ulysses's death, Fred continued to edit Volume 2 before giving the final version to Webster and Company. The dosages of cocaine and morphine given by Grant's doctors prevented him from working with a clear head, yet without drugs neither sleep nor rest was possible. As the cancer worsened, his throat was swabbed with cocaine to relieve the immediate pain; a nighttime's rest increasingly required injections of morphine. Grant considered the effects of the cocaine on his concentration. In a note to Douglas, he judged cocaine as providing "a wonderful amount of relief from pain." Admitting that he had to fight against the desire to take greater and greater amounts, he summarized its effects: "On the whole, my conclusion is to take it when it seems to be so much needed as it was at times yesterday. I will try to limit its use. This latter you know how hard it is to do."[95] The description of his physical discomfort continued to be published in the press in graphic and discomfiting detail. Anxious citizens read that Grant was subject to paroxysms of choking and coughing and bouts of vomiting. Terrified of choking to death, he preferred to sleep sitting up. Enfeebled and incapacitated, Grant struggled through, sometimes staying up all night writing. One of Dr. Douglas's journal entries recorded that the evening of March 23 was a "restless night." Grant, however, was able to write "some manuscript in the morning. At 2 p.m. [sic] longing for sleep but not able to get it."[96]

Grant's condition declined swiftly between March 26 and 29; a choking fit caused a sudden huge hemorrhage, bringing him to the brink of death. Douglas recorded the advent of another hemorrhage, a few days later: "General Grant slept well until 4:00 A.M., when he awoke and took his nourishment. Immediately after, in a paroxysm of coughing, he had a slight hemorrhage. . . . The hemorrhage was at first quite abundant, and alarming. It [blood] came in great mouthfuls." Grant did not desire to live after such experiences. He described for Dr. Shrady the feeling of almost dying, "I was passing away peacefully and soon all would have been over. It was like falling asleep. I am ready now to go at any time. I know there is nothing but suffering for me while I do live."[97] Incredibly, he experienced a rapid recovery—doctors speculated that the hemorrhage might have relieved the pressure—resuming his writing with excellent results. Grant also managed a few short trips, carriage rides, and enjoyed dining with his family, which now included his daughter Nellie Grant Sartoris, arriving in March from her home in England. He spent his sixty-third birthday, on April 27, reading a flood of goodwill messages from all over the country. The *New York Tribune* reported, "Hardly had daylight come when messenger boys began to run up the front stoop, carrying dispatches to the ex-President. The neighborhood presented a busy appearance, crowds of people passed up and down the

Grant leaving his brownstone for a last ride in Central Park in April 1885. The streets surrounding Grant's home were often crowded with well-wishers. (*Frank Leslie's Illustrated Newspaper*, May 2, 1885)

street, watching the house and the floral emblems that were almost constantly passing in."[98]

On twenty-four-hour call, Drs. Douglas and Shrady redoubled their efforts, enabling their famous patient to work. They both expressed amazement at his dedication. Dr. Douglas remembered the care they took to keep Grant writing: "We had always taken this [his ability to write] into consideration in determining the treatment. . . . All we could do was to aid him as far as lay in our power." Douglas recalled a typical consultation during which they "found the General engaged in writing. As we entered he raised his hand and said, 'I shall reach a period in a moment' . . . after the consultation, he resumed his literary work, and I learned, at my evening visit, that he had worked in all four or five hours."[99] The two doctors, along with members of Grant's close circle (especially Fred and Harrison Tyrell), provided the controlled and supportive environment that allowed the desperately ill general to complete his memoirs. Drs. Douglas and Shrady felt keenly their historical role. Along with clinical information, their depictions provide an intimate window into the day-to-day life of the invalid. Knowing that his charge would soon be unable to speak, Shrady described Grant's voice as "soft, deep, and distinct."[100] One of his most poignant memories is of what occurred Easter Sunday, April 5, 1885:

> The morning came, beautifully bright and clear. The General's room was a fine, large one with a bay window overlooking West Sixty-Sixth Street and Fifth Avenue. The warm sunshine flooded the room, but the patient's vitality was so low that it was deemed necessary to have a fire in the grate. He sat before it in his favorite armchair, apparently oblivious to his surroundings. . . . He looked intently in the fire and gradually his lids drooped and he fell asleep. . . . I walked over to the window and saw there were thousands of people, looking up in hushed awe. There was a reverence and hush upon the assemblage that was very impressive. They had come to pay homage to the great soldier who lay dying. The General slept on quietly while the crowd grew to such proportions that it extended almost from Madison Avenue to Fifth Avenue.
>
> When he awoke he came to the window and stood beside me, looking down on the people below. The curtain screened him and those outside could not see him. "What a beautiful day it is," he said.
>
> "Yes," I answered, "and it has brought a great throng of people. They are all very fond of you. They come here day after day to quietly gaze up at your window, as a mark of their sympathy."
>
> "I am very grateful to them, very," he said sadly, and then walked back to the seat near the fire. He was silent for a moment and then said: "I am sure I should like them to know that I am appreciative." It was then that the General dictated to me his famous "Easter Message," where he said he desired the goodwill of all people.[101]

The eventful month of April brought more trouble. Grant headed off a potentially disastrous threat to the integrity of his authorship. Badeau became unhappy at his increasingly marginalized status within the Grant household. He considered himself the expert on Grant's military career since publishing his three-volume military history. Contemptuous of the idea of Grant writing his memoirs, he fought bitterly with Fred, who replaced Badeau as main assistant. Additionally, Badeau was worried that the publication of Grant's books would cut into his own books' profitability. Finally, he informed Grant that the general's memoirs would damage "my reputation as your historian."[102] Badeau demanded a renegotiation of his contract, which Grant refused. His unhappiness found its way into a newspaper article printed in the *New York World* that implied strongly that Badeau, not Grant, was the author of the forthcoming memoirs. Hurt and angry, Grant immediately wrote a rejoinder in which he unequivocally stated, "The Composition is entirely my own."[103] Badeau was fired from the project, and the bitter feelings between him and the Grant heirs lingered for years.[104] For Grant, however, the painful issue was resolved with satisfaction, and with continued support and perseverance, he strove with every hour left to him to complete his memoirs. As William McFeely observed, "The book was now his life."[105]

In early May, Grant finished fifty pages for the second volume, covering the Wilderness and Appomattox, having dispensed with Sherman's 1864–65 campaign before his grave crisis in March. On May 23, The *New York Tribune* wrote, "The story of the General's campaigns is about finished." However, Grant was not quite ready to relinquish the manuscript. On June 8, unable to speak, he signaled to Twain that Volume 2 was in rough draft form. Webster and Company went into high gear. Twain announced the dates— Volume 1 to be published on December 1, 1885, with Volume 2 available by March of the following year. In anticipation, the subscription campaign was ginned up, advertisements paid for and placed, and press and binderies secured for the massive printing. By mid-June, an unheard of 60,000 sets of the *Personal Memoirs* had been preordered by subscription. "General Grant," wrote an Ohio veteran, now an agent selling subscriptions for the books, "the people are moving *en masse* upon your memoirs."[106]

*"I am a verb instead of a personal pronoun"*

By mid-June, Grant left his home in New York City for the last time for the cooler, drier, and more healthful clime of Mount McGregor, a beautiful resort just opening in New York's Adirondack Mountains, near Saratoga Springs. Arrangements had been made for the family to stay for the summer rent free in a spacious cottage owned by the resort's promoter, W. J. Arkell. He later bluntly admitted his intentions: "I thought if we could get him to come here to Mount McGregor, and if he should die there it might make the place a national shrine, and incidentally a success."[107] Mount McGregor had plenty of competition for the "honor," but Julia and Fred were reassured by the fact that Arkell's wealthy business partner was an old family acquain-

Cottage at Mount McGregor, New York, where Grant completed his memoirs
(Library of Congress)

tance, Joseph W. Drexel of Philadelphia, and by the fact that Dr. Douglas knew the area well and recommended it enthusiastically. On June 16, Grant boarded a private train provided by W. H. Vanderbilt at Grand Central Station. Accompanying him in the luxury car were Julia, daughter Nellie, Fred and Ida, his nurse Henry McQueeny, and his valet Harrison Tyrell. A suite of rooms had been reserved for the remaining Grant children and grandchildren at a local hotel. Dr. Douglas and his family would stay there as well, and Dr. Shrady would be on-call from his nearby summer residence. Crowds gathered to wave at every stop, and when the train pulled into Saratoga, the party switched to a narrow-gage train, arriving at their destination by late afternoon. The two-story Queen Anne–style cottage had been freshly repainted and refurbished for Grant's stay. Nestled in a grove of beautiful maple, pine, and oak trees, the cottage's most attractive feature was the spacious piazza around three sides of the house.[108]

Grant settled into a large corner room on the first floor, enjoyed a good night's sleep, and the next evening announced his intention to stroll on the path from the cottage to the "Eastern Lookout," which offered a splendid view of the mountains. Using his cane, and leaning heavily on Tyrell, Grant managed the distance (described by the newspapers as the equivalent of five city blocks) to the lookout, where he rested on a bench, but he could barely make it back to the cottage.[109] The effort left him exhausted and dejected. Perhaps the last illusion left him was that fresh air and a change of scenery might revive his health if only for a while. If that was the case, it was thoroughly dispelled. While he recuperated that evening, he wrote two notes, one to Dr. Douglas and one entitled, "Memoranda for my Family." To his doctor he said, "I feel plainly that my system is preparing for dissolution." He predicted three ways that death might come—hemorrhage, choking, or exhaustion. He told Douglas, "I do not want any physician but yourself," and made clear his distaste for active medical intervention that would result in yet "another desperate effort to save me, and more suffering."[110] Fred opened up his father's note to read explicit instructions for burial, mentioning as possible sites St. Louis, Galena, and "New York, where I have made my home for several years past, and through the generosity of whose citizens I have been enabled to pass my last days without experiencing the pains of pinching want." Distressed, Fred indicated to his father that it was most likely he would be buried in Washington. After a minute's thought, Grant scribbled, "It is possible my funeral may become one of public demonstration, in which event I have no particular choice of burial place; but there is one thing I would wish you and the family to insist upon and that is wherever my tomb may be, a place shall be reserved for your mother."[111]

Both notes caused uproar. Already devastated by her impending loss, Julia redoubled efforts to make her husband as comfortable as possible, as she had always done, but with a sorrow evident to all. She refused to leave the cottage for the duration.[112] For his part, Douglas assured Grant he was in no immediate danger of dying and urged him to reserve his energy for the memoirs. His reassurances comforted the general. Communication at Mount McGregor between Grant and others (primarily Dr. Douglas and Fred) was conducted entirely by the writing of notes, now in the Grant Family Collection in the Library of Congress, Washington, D.C. The notes between doctor and patient, family and visitors testify to Grant's renewed obsession with the memoirs. "I pray God," Grant wrote to Julia on July 8, "that [my life] may be spared to complete the necessary work upon my book."[113]

His unfinished work kept him alive. The days assumed a familiar routine. Despite a frustrated Twain's best efforts to wrestle the memoirs away, Grant revised the page proofs for the first volume, adding new material and pointing out errors that should be corrected. Fred and Dawson entered his revisions on the galleys. "I said I had been adding to my book and to my coffin," Grant remarked.[114] Explaining the delays, Grant wrote, "My work [on Volume 2] had been done so hastily that much was left out and I did all of it over from the crossing of the James river in June/64 to Appomattox. Since then I have added as much as fifty pages to the book I should think."[115] He continued working on the second volume, still in manuscript, adding pages, a new chapter, providing detailed commentaries. On June 28, he finished a 500-word preface. Pleased, he wrote to Douglas on July 5, "I feel much relieved this morning. I had begun to feel that the work of getting my book to-gether was making but slow progress. I find it about completed, and the work now to be done is mostly after it gets back in gallies. It can be sent to the printer faster than he is ready for it. There [are] from one hundred and fifty to two hundred pages more of it than I intended."[116]

While Grant was concentrating on his memoirs, the nation was preparing for his death. Mount McGregor had now become a shrine.[117] As with his New York home, the area around the cottage swarmed with reporters wiring daily reports to their newspapers. Some protection was provided Grant by the local GAR, but people—from nearby and far away—flocked to Mount McGregor, and long lines paraded in front of the cottage daily. Generally quiet, citizens were thrilled when Grant occasionally acknowledged their presence. The family sent out telegrams asking their friends not to visit, but many came anyway. Mark Twain and Robert U. Johnson combined business with their farewells, and Johnson arrived to pick up the final revision for the Vicksburg piece. He recalled, "I could hardly keep back the tears as I made my farewell to the great soldier who saved the Union for all its people, and to the man of warm and courageous heart who had fought his last long battle for those he so tenderly loved."[118] Other visitors who came to Mount McGregor to say goodbye included Sherman and ex-Confederate general Simon B. Buckner.

When Grant felt well enough, he liked to sit on the large and comfortable piazza to read newspapers and enjoy the cool air. One last poignant photograph showed the frail, shrunken Ulysses, writing intently, while seated in a wicker chair on the porch. Swathed in scarves and shawls, with a woolen cap perched on his head, and propped up by a pillow, he was simply unrecognizable as the strong general who led the Union armies to victory. But a sharp observer of the image will note the resolution in his ravaged countenance. On July 20, Grant announced that he was finished. That same day he asked to be taken to the lookout. This time Grant was transported in a specially ordered "Bath chair" to enjoy one last time nature's beauty. When

"I said I had been adding to my book and to my coffin": Grant at Mount McGregor (Library of Congress)

he returned, he was ready to die. The suffering was destined to end. "I am a verb instead of a personal pronoun," a pain-wracked Grant scribbled in one of his last notes to Douglas. "A verb is anything that signifies to be; to do; or to suffer. I signify all three." Mercifully, Ulysses S. Grant died on July 23, 1885.[119]

## Personal Memoirs of U. S. Grant: *An Evaluation*

The *Personal Memoirs* can be said to offer many things to many people. Grant's volumes are a history of the Civil War, an unmatched military narrative of the conflict, a carefully constructed autobiography of a man, a commentary on American character and institutions, and an exegesis of the Union Cause. They provide a comprehensive and rich story of the war between the United States and the Confederate States of America. The volumes—with Volume 1 covering birth to Vicksburg and Volume 2 going from the Chattanooga Campaign to Appomattox—follow the war chrono-

The bedroom in which Grant died, which has been preserved at Mount McGregor (U.S. Instantaneous Photographic Co. [Boston, 1886]; reproduced by permission of The Huntington Library, San Marino, California)

logically, providing commentary, information, documents, maps, analysis, and background on specific battles and on overall military strategy, as well as incisive portraits of people and description of political events.[120]

Grant portrays himself as a representative character of the victorious North. His writing style is simple and clear, even conversational at times and utterly disarming. In adopting this style, he consciously invites the reader to appreciate the good, solid, unthreatening virtues of a typical northerner, who, like himself, lived in a free-labor society. Volume 1 opens with a brief but compelling account of his family history. Grant takes pains to point out his simple and rustic background, his trusting nature, and his unmilitary bearing. His legendary personal simplicity endeared him to his soldiers and retained their loyalty to his death. The same simplicity is present in his writing and is similarly endearing. Grant continues the tale of his early youth by remarking that he did not at all want to go to West Point, but did so only because his father, Jesse, "thought I would go." He did middling well there but was uncertain if he would continue in the professional army at all. His simple statement, "A military life had no charms for me" establishes his unabashed ordinariness and is designed to downplay any connotations of an elite education and expectations of high position.[121]

Although Grant distinguished himself in the Mexican War of 1846–48, he did not support that effort. Yet he devoted many pages to the conflict, and his account is told in riveting prose. Grant's hero, the reader is informed, was not the tall, aristocratic Winfield Scott. Grant admired Scott's abilities, but his model was the plain, simple soldier, later president, Zachary Taylor, who rejected the pomp and circumstance of military life.[122] Most important, Grant revealed that the lessons he learned in Mexico had a much greater impact on him than did his four years at the U.S. Military Academy, underscoring the importance of real life over book learning, and building anticipation toward the account of the Civil War. "My experience in the Mexican war," he wrote, "was of great advantage to me afterwards. Besides the many practical lessons it taught, the war brought nearly all the officers of the regular army together so as to make them personally acquainted. It also brought them into contact with volunteers, many of whom served in the war of the rebellion afterwards."[123]

Slavery, interwoven with Grant's discussions of the causes and consequences of the Civil War, is addressed—directly and indirectly—throughout the memoirs. In one such discussion Grant links the southern states' desire to expand their slaveholding territory to the war against Mexico, ending with this observation: "The Southern rebellion was largely the outgrowth of the Mexican war. Nations, like individuals, are punished for their transgressions. We got our punishment in the most sanguinary and expensive war of modern times."[124] Grant presents an articulate overview of the events that led to the outbreak of war in 1861. From his perspective in 1885 (and not in 1856, when he voted Democratic) the overview reflected exactly the antislavery position of the 1850s Republican Party. In two substantial segments covering the causes of the Mexican War and "The Coming Crisis," Grant addressed the root of secession, leaving no doubt as to his position. To protect slavery, the foundation of its prosperity, the South needed to control the national government. To protect free labor, the North was compelled to prevent the extension of slavery. Secession and the rebellion that followed were treasonous, and had to be stopped. The subsequent detailed unfolding of Grant's wartime career provides his firsthand view of the inexorable march toward slavery's end, first as a military and political necessity, and then as a moral imperative. Brushing aside the rationale for the Lost Cause, Grant summed up in his conclusion a message that was conveyed earlier, that "the cause of the great War of the Rebellion against the United States will have to be attributed to slavery."[125]

There were other issues to contend with in the *Personal Memoirs*. As the leading Union general, Grant was influential and so was his portrayal (both facts and truth) of the war, but by no means was it universally accepted by northerners, and it was certainly not accepted by most ex-Confederates. His actions sparked controversy, and criticisms of Grant's generalship—particularly surrounding the battle of Shiloh in April 1862 and the Overland Campaign in the spring of 1864—appeared in newspapers, magazine articles, and books.[126] Indeed, Shiloh is a good example of facts/truth as played out in the *Personal Memoirs*. The battle was critically important for Union fortunes, and Grant's. His critics leveled two charges. First, Grant was unprepared for the Confederate attack on the morning of April 6, 1862. Second, his failure to prepare the ground defensively resulted in an initial defeat redeemed by the timely arrival of Gen. Don Carlos Buell's Army of the Ohio, and thus the credit for the victory should have gone to Buell, not Grant. In response, he offered a strong rebuttal: he was not surprised by the attack; he himself was all over the field deploying "green" troops and preventing disaster; Buell's troops, while welcome, did not "save" the battle because the Confederates clearly were going to be defeated the following day. His factual account did not sway those who were already convinced otherwise. Facts were disputed bitterly in histories of the battle, and oppositional points of view remained entrenched.[127] By the time he wrote on Shiloh, however, Grant recanted his earlier criticism of another general, Lew Wallace, since new information on Wallace's role at Shiloh had come to light.[128]

He never, however, wavered in his larger truth about Shiloh. After that battle, he wrote, "I gave up all idea of saving the Union except by complete conquest."[129] Was this an accurate statement? Perhaps; only Grant knew for sure. But the accuracy is irrelevant because he meant to convey a deep truth. Indeed, "I gave up all idea of saving the Union except by complete conquest" proved an adept literary strategy because the reader is alerted to the author's perspective on the American Civil War, a perspective that shaped and leavened the military narrative of the volumes. Union motives and strategy, Grant claims, responded to southern intransigence: "The Northern troops were never more cruel than the necessities of war required."[130] The early Federal war effort was not guided by the desire to destroy the Confederate nation by "complete conquest." This idea (aptly summed up in an oft-used phrase among white southerners, "the War of Northern Aggression"),

Grant implied, came later, put forth by apologists. He stood strong in his belief that the South was to blame for starting the war, and for prolonging the war. The blood is on southern hands, Grant made clear, not on northern hands. The *Personal Memoirs* plainly demonstrate that as military commander Grant was guided by this belief, and that Shiloh was the moment of its crystallization. Although the volumes barely cover the period after 1865, the reader knows that Grant's vision of reconciliation and Reconstruction was similarly informed. The South was wrong, and the North was right. Mistakes were made on both sides, but, in the end, the United States won the war, unconditionally. Victorious, the Federals welcomed the rebellious states back to the Union, but the nation must never forget that justice and morality were on the side of the United States.

Whether writing about Shiloh, the Vicksburg Campaign, or the Overland Campaign, Grant explains his actions and defends them against newspaper charges that he considered shoddy, inaccurate, and defeatist. Indeed, Grant's sensitivity to press coverage showed a keen appreciation for the political nature of the Civil War. His depictions of military clashes draw attention to the "big picture," never allowing readers to forget that battlefield fortunes were linked to the home front. Vicksburg's treatment is typical: "The campaign of Vicksburg was suggested and developed by circumstances. The elections of 1862 had gone against the prosecution of the war. Voluntary enlistments had nearly ceased and the draft had been resorted to; this was resisted, and a defeat or backward movement would have made its execution impossible. A forward movement to a decisive victory was necessary." Commenting on Lincoln's chances of reelection in 1864, he reminds readers that Sherman's and Sheridan's "two campaigns probably had more effect in settling the election of the following November then all the speeches, all the bonfires, and all the parading with banners and bands of music in the North."[131]

There is an obvious connection in the *Personal Memoirs* between Grant's personal memories, the era's social or historical memory (the memory of millions in a generation who shared war experiences), his ability to turn those experiences into meaningful narratives, and history (written accounts purporting to be objective). In so many ways, the nineteenth-century audience for the *Memoirs* was remarkably attuned to the text. Scott E. Casper's examination of nineteenth-century biography (of which autobiography was considered a "subset") revealed the extent to which the popular genre was expected to uplift and instruct readers. For example, few readers would have been disappointed that the autobiographical volumes did not offer personal revelations, or apologies for Grant's mistakes. Grant expresses regret only for two failed and costly assaults. One was the May 22 attack on Vicksburg. "If Vicksburg could have been carried in May," he writes, "it would have not only saved the army the risk it ran of a greater danger [illness] than from the bullets of the enemy, but it would have given us a splendid army, well equipped and officered, to operate elsewhere with." Grant then hedges his regret for the terrible casualties suffered, claiming that morale might have been severely compromised: "Had the assault not been made, I have no doubt that the majority of those engaged in the siege of Vicksburg would have believed that had we assaulted it would have proven successful, and would have saved life, health and comfort." The other was Cold Harbor, and his apology for that battle is chillingly brief, offering no mitigating explanation: "I have always regretted that the last assault at Cold Harbor was ever made. . . . At Cold Harbor no advantage whatever was gained to compensate for the heavy loss we sustained."[132]

Other embarrassments were left out, including his infamous General Order no. 11 of December 1862 barring Jews from his command, and his struggle with alcohol. Mark Twain wished that Grant had written openly about his fondness for drink, and about how he conquered the desire. It would have added, not detracted, from Grant's laurels. "I wish I had thought of it!" Twain lamented, "I would have said to General Grant: 'Put the drunkenness in the Memoirs—and the repentance and reform. Trust the people.'"[133]

Grant declined the opportunity to bare his soul, but he nonetheless managed to infuse his memoirs with a uniquely personal tone. Particularly poignant are the asides that remind readers of the grisly sacrifices endured by the men who fought. One example came after the battle of Champion Hill on the night of May 16, 1863. Grant installed his headquarters on a homely porch of a house that served as a Confederate hospital. Surrounded by wounded and dying men, Grant observed, "While a battle is raging one can see his enemy mowed down by the thousand, or the ten thousand, with great composure; but after the battle these scenes are distressing, and one is naturally disposed to do as much to alleviate the suffering of an enemy as a friend."[134] Imbedded in the narrative, adding to the intimate touch, are many deft and revealing portraits of his fellow top-ranking Union officers—such as favorites William T. Sherman, Philip H. Sheridan, and James B. McPherson—that by themselves make the memoirs worth reading. Few fictional or film depictions of male bonding can rival that of Sherman's and Grant's in the Civil War. Grant describes the warm and generous friendship deeply cherished by both. Comrade, compatriot, and confidant, Sherman served an indispensable role for Grant, and vice versa. In many chapters, Grant recounts their growing mutual respect and loyalty—from just before Shiloh to war's end. He expresses gratitude for Sherman's unstinting support though the ups and downs of campaigns, giving full credit to "Uncle Billy's" successful exploits, and puts to rest a rumor that Sherman was not the architect of the "March to the Sea." Grant said, "It was clearly Sherman, and to him also belongs the credit of its brilliant execution."[135]

For the most part, Grant refrained from settling old scores, and his memoirs are noticeably free of the rancor that infected so many of the genre. Even so, few readers finish the volumes unaware of who stood where in his sharply drawn portraits of the leading officers on both the Union and Confederate sides. For example, Grant's exasperation with Maj. Gen. George H. Thomas's characteristic slowness in protecting Tennessee during the winter of 1864 is barely contained. "Thomas's dispositions were deliberately made, and always good," wrote Grant, adding, "He could not be driven from a point he was given to hold." Having made clear that Thomas was too conservative when the times called for speed, Grant asserts, "He was not as good, however, in pursuit as he was in action. I do not believe that he could ever have conducted Sherman's army from Chattanooga to Atlanta against the defences and the commander guarding that line in 1864."[136]

Grant vigorously defended controversial actions, offering insight into his management of men and his leadership style under the stress of war. His treatment of Maj. Gen. Gouverneur K. Warren, commander of the Fifth Corps, is illustrative. Phil Sheridan relieved Warren of his command just before the battle of Five Forks in March of 1865, with Grant's approval. Warren was personally humiliated, and spent twenty of his postwar years trying to correct what he felt was a gross injustice to his career record. Grant defended his and Sheridan's decision in the pages of his memoirs. He provided a close analysis of Warren's leadership flaws that led to his dismissal. "He was a man of fine intelligence, great earnestness, quick perception, and could make his dispositions as quickly as any officer, under difficulties where he was forced to act," Grant wrote, concluding, "but I had before discovered, a defect which was beyond his control, that was very prejudicial to his usefulness in emergencies like the one just before us. He could see every danger at a glance before he had encountered it. He would not only make preparations to meet the danger which might occur, but he would inform his commanding officer what others should do while he was executing his move." Grant penned a devastating critique. Warren simply could not be trusted to finish the job; he was incapable of corps command. Despite his

First edition of the *Personal Memoirs of U. S. Grant*, known as the "shoulder strap" edition because it reproduced the insignia of rank on the binding. (author's collection)

honorable record and service, "his removal was necessary to success." Grant ended his harsh judgment thus: "I was very sorry that it had been done, and regretted still more that I had not long before taken occasion to assign him to another field of duty."[137] In portraying Warren's weaknesses so candidly and convincingly, Grant justified a decision that still troubled him twenty years later.

The last pages of the *Personal Memoirs* provide interesting reflections on some of the notable political leaders of the Civil War—Lincoln, Stanton, and Andrew Johnson among others. Lincoln's assassination clearly left Grant desolate. Writing of his commander-in-chief, Grant declared, "I knew his goodness of heart, his generosity, his yielding disposition, his desire to have everybody happy, and above all his desire to see all the people of the United States enter again upon the full privileges of citizenship with equality among all." In a brief look at early Reconstruction, Grant described how the best hope for reunion was dashed by the bungling of the Johnson administration.[138] He scarcely touches on his two terms as president. The *Personal Memoirs* was about the war, not about the peace. A little conclusion offered a summary of America's progress since 1865, finding much to commend. Grant declared: "The war has made us a nation of great power and intelligence. We have but little to do to preserve peace, happiness and prosperity at home, and the respect of other nations. Our experience ought to teach us the necessity of the first; our power secures the latter."[139]

### Reviews and Legacies

The posthumous publication on December 10, 1885, of the *Personal Memoirs of U. S. Grant* (1,231 pages in total) proved a spectacular popular and critical success. Costing $9.00 in cloth and $25.00 in leather binding, the volumes eventually sold more than 300,000 sets. Within the first two years, royalties totaled over $450,000, bringing financial security to Grant's widow and four children. With the publication of his memoirs, "historian" could be added to the list of Grant's professions. The *Personal Memoirs* elicited praise from prominent journals and intellectuals. With exceptions, reviews were effusive, and many compared the *Personal Memoirs* favorably with Caesar's *Commentaries*. Mark Twain pronounced, "General Grant's book is a great unique and unapproachable literary masterpiece." Gilded Age novelist William Dean Howells wrote Twain, "I am reading Grant's book with the delight I fail to find in novels," adding, "The book merits its enormous success, simply as literature." The *New York Tribune* and the *New York Times* ran favorable reviews that occupied whole pages, while the *Atlantic Monthly* announced that "fifty years hence . . . the mind of the nation will distinctly recognize only two figures as connected with all that great upheaval, Lincoln and Grant."[140] *Harper's New Monthly Magazine*'s reviewer captured the book's essence:

> But these Personal Memoirs of U. S. Grant, written as simply and straightforwardly as his battles were fought, couched in the most unpretentious phrase, with never a touch of grandiosity or attitudinizing, familiar, homely, even common in style, is a great piece of literature, because great literature is nothing more nor less than the clear expression of minds that have something great in them, whether religions, or beauty, or deep experience.[141]

U. S. Grant, historian, was almost universally praised for his simple and direct portrayal of the Civil War, and for his modesty in downplaying his own considerable role in bringing about northern victory. Many readers observed that Grant's memoirs, above all other accounts of the war, told the "truth" about the nation's greatest conflict.[142] People were impressed by his ability to write a compelling, readable narrative of the war's battles. His account seemed calm, measured, objective, and buttressed by solid documentation.

There were dissenters only too happy to point at weaknesses, perceived flaws, and mistakes, or outright lies. Perhaps a few southerners bought the *Personal Memoirs* as a gesture to the magnanimous victor at Appomattox. More white southerners probably agreed with the dismissive review given by an ex-Confederate officer in the *Southern Historical Society Papers*. That review described the *Personal Memoirs* as "a book full of blunders and flat contradictions of the official reports (both Federal and Confederate), and the future historian who attempts to follow it will be led very far astray from the real truth."[143] As discussed earlier, the war's official reports were often the starting, not the ending, point of debate and argument for many participants in the conflict. Thus it should not surprise that General Grant's account did not go unchallenged. The lengthy two-part review penned by the English poet, essayist, and Confederate sympathizer Matthew Arnold prompted some controversy as well. He was not impressed with the volumes, finding them written in "an English without charm and without high breeding." Finding little to recommend in the American civilization that triumphed with the northern victory, Arnold concluded, "Modest for himself, Grant is boastful, as Americans are apt to be, for his nation."[144]

The *Personal Memoirs* sold briskly into the first decade of the twentieth century before falling into obscurity by the late 1920s and 1930s. It was no coincidence that Grant's reputation reached a nadir in those particular decades, as the popular culture celebrated the romantic image of the Confederacy epitomized in Margaret Mitchell's novel *Gone with the Wind* and immortalized in its movie adaptation.[145] When interest revived in Grant's life and career, it sparked a reappraisal of his military and political record and a renewed appreciation for the virtues of his memoirs. Although the *Personal Memoirs* never again achieved its late nineteenth-century "best seller" status, modern writers, scholars, and critics have turned to it to help explain the man and the war and the country. Improbably, Grant's *Memoirs* was beloved by Gertrude Stein, the American modernist writer who lived and worked in Europe. She believed the volumes to be the ultimate expression of the country's purity of language. Known for her stylistically idiosyncratic prose, Stein wrote, "Grant was first an army officer, then not an army officer. Then he was a general and then a lieutenant general. This was rank which was made for him especially. It meant that he was alone in this way."[146] Edmund Wilson's classic volume *Patriotic Gore* more famously described Grant's memoirs as "a unique expression of national character." Wilson expanded on why they remained so compelling after nearly eighty years. "Perhaps never has a book so objective in form seemed so personal in every line, and though the tempo is never increased, the narrative, once we get into the war, seems to move with the increasing momentum that the soldier must have felt in the field." Wilson perceptively asserted, "What distinguished Grant's story from the records of campaigns that are usually produced by generals is that somehow, despite its sobriety, it communicates the spirit of the battles themselves and makes it possible to understand how Grant won them."[147]

Never out of print, the volumes continue as a valuable source to scholars, writers, and students. The editor of *The Papers of U. S. Grant*, John Y. Simon, asserted that the *Personal Memoirs* offer "candor, scrupulous fairness, and grace of expression."[148] Bruce Catton called the memoirs "a first-rate book—well written with a literary quality that keeps it fresh." The prestigious Library of America published a one-volume, selectively annotated edition of the *Personal Memoirs* in 1990, edited by William S. McFeely and Mary Drake McFeely. Grant's Library of America volume regularly appears in the "top ten best sellers list" almost two decades after its publication date. James McPherson and Brooks D. Simpson have singled out Grant's memoirs as a historical and literary tour de force, and both wrote introductions to new editions. Finally, the editors at the *Papers of U. S. Grant* are preparing a fully annotated edition of the *Personal Memoirs* as the final volume of the project. This edition will replace all others as the authoritative text.[149] In short, the strong consensus is that the *Personal Memoirs* offers a literate and indispensable resource for understanding the military and political history of the war that neither the professional historian nor the amateur can afford to ignore. But it offers much more than that. For the modern reader, the *Personal Memoirs* can also explain two interrelated questions: "Why they fought" and "Why the North won."

The *Personal Memoirs of U. S. Grant* presented the moral, political, economic, and social argument for waging war against the rebellious states, and touted the benefits of slavery's destruction for the southern people. Yet, more often than not, Grant's memoirs are also celebrated for the theme of reconciliation. In an oft-quoted passage, Grant commented: "I feel that we are on the eve of a new era, when there is to be great harmony between the Federal and the Confederate. I cannot stay to be a living witness to the correctness of this prophecy; but I feel it within me that it is to be so."[150] Embedded within the style and substance of Grant's *Memoirs* is a contradiction that was also played out in his public actions. On the one hand, Grant was the magnanimous victor of Appomattox who said, "The war is over. The rebels are our countrymen again." The chief goal of the war was reunion. On the other hand, Grant was the head of the Union army responsible for smashing the institution of slavery and bringing a revolution in race relations. There is no doubt that Grant deeply hoped for a permanent and genuine restoration of "great harmony" between North and South. But what, exactly did he mean by expressing that desire? Did he mean that sectional peace (which all agreed was a good thing) should deliberately elide a still widely accepted belief among northerners in 1885 that it was the Union, and not the Confederate cause, that was noble? Do the *Personal Memoirs* reflect this sentiment?

In the pages of his volumes, Grant promoted reconciliation—but on northern terms. "I would not have the anniversaries of our victories celebrated, nor those of our defeats made fast days and spent in humiliation and prayer; but I would like to see truthful history written," he declared; "such history will do full credit to the courage, endurance, and ability of the American citizen, no matter what section of the country, he hailed from, or in what ranks he fought." What follows is crucial: "The justice of the cause which in the end prevailed, will, I doubt not, come to be acknowledged by every citizen in the land, in time."[151] True enough, the *Personal Memoirs*, which was "dedicated to the American soldier and sailor," contained much about Civil War battles and saluted the courage and valor of the soldiers on both sides. But by describing what happened on those battlefields, Grant tellingly emphasized that citizens can learn about the history of a nation, a nation that was forged anew at Appomattox with Union victory.

Thus, readers of the *Personal Memoirs of U. S. Grant* will note Grant's contempt for the southern cause of slavery, and for the general so associated with that cause, Robert E. Lee. He explained why the "complete conquest" was necessary to destroy slavery, save the Union, and restore harmony. The victor, not the vanquished, Grant claimed, should dictate the terms to end the war and should define the conditions for the reestablishment of peace and harmony within the Union. Grant's memoirs offer readers a stark and ugly depiction of a southern society mired in backwardness and deeply tainted by slavery. The thrust of his history emphasized the best qualities of northern free democratic society, deflecting serious criticism. He concluded that the modern war waged by the United States benefited, and would continue to benefit, the former Confederate nation: "The war begot a spirit of independence and enterprise."[152] Indeed, through his frequent tributes to northern character and civilization Grant not only highlighted the superiority of wartime Union strength and resources, but also asserted the ideological superiority of northern free labor over southern slave labor.

The essence of the *Memoirs* went beyond a definition of autobiography, "the writing of one's own history."[153] The eminent military scholar John Keegan commented that Grant had provided, "an enthralling history of one man's generalship, perhaps the most revelatory autobiography of high command to exist in any language." Grant's volumes were a deliberately triumphal narrative of the Civil War written from the viewpoint of the man, after Abraham Lincoln, most closely identified with bringing about northern victory. But the individual is merged with the event and the era, leading Keegan to conclude rightly: "If there is a single contemporary document which explains 'why the North won the Civil War' it is the *Personal Memoirs of Ulysses S. Grant*."[154] If the memoirs tell the history of the Union Cause, Grant's funeral pageant illuminates the rise of reconciliation in the 1880s.

*chapter five*

# Pageantry of Woe
## The Funeral of U. S. Grant

*Is it so small a thing*
*To have enjoy'd the sun,*
*To have lived light in the spring,*
*To have loved, to have thought,*
*to have done;*
*To have advanced true friends,*
*and beat down baffling foes.*

Matthew Arnold, "Hymn of Empedocles"

---

On August 8, 1885, Americans awoke to the solemn sound of tolling bells. Most needed no reminder that this was the day of the funeral of Union general and two-term president Ulysses S. Grant. Befitting Grant's already larger-than-life legacy, a million and a half people gathered in New York City to view the funeral procession and burial ceremonies. The spectacle, replete with religious, patriotic, and nationalistic imagery and rhetoric, was but the biggest of the thousands of memorial ceremonies held in the United States on that sad day. In large and small cities, in bustling towns and dusty hamlets, citizens prepared and planned their own commemorations that complemented New York's. In charge of the ceremonies in Providence, Rhode Island, the GAR proudly recorded, "In this city the formal observance of the obsequies was civil and military; as spontaneous as it was general." These commemorations—lavish or simple—were much the same and usually included a procession lasting several hours that ended at a church or other public building. There, against a backdrop that included a large picture of Grant, a floral decoration, and a black-draped pulpit, a minister, a veteran, and an elected official would each offer eulogies. Prayers, music, and poems completed the memorial services. "No death in our day and generation has called forth more full, just, and admirable tributes, by type and tongue, in the newspapers, in the pulpits, and in public assemblies, in all parts of our own country, and in not a few parts of other countries," declared one speaker. "There is perhaps no parallel in the history of state funerals," another observer stated, "where so many orations were delivered as at yesterday's obsequies." The thousands of eulogies and obituaries for Grant stressed his good Christian moral character, his role in saving and preserving the Union, and his magnanimity at Appomattox.[1]

The praise for the last was especially loud, as eulogists likened the sentiment for sectional reconciliation engendered by Grant's death to a final, and happy, ending to the tragic national drama begun by the Civil War. One

All the nation's newspapers and journals had special editions, such as this one, devoted to Grant's death and funeral. (*Frank Leslie's Illustrated Newspaper*, August 8, 1885)

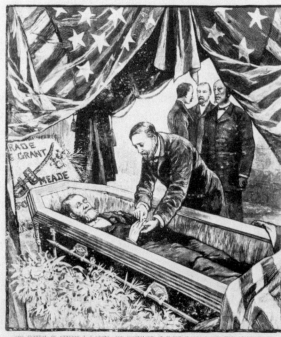

minister captured a powerful and popular theme of Grant's life: "By a single act Gen'l Grant put himself above the wisest of American statesmen. That act was the terms he offered to Lee for the surrender of his Army. . . . In a few, clear, simple lines [he] solved at once the problem of peace, and the possible unity and fraternity of the American people." A speaker at a memorial service declared, "That grand funeral pageant . . . owed its main impressiveness to the evidence it afforded . . . [of] a restored National Union, a renewed brotherhood among the people, and a renewed sisterhood among the States." From San Francisco came this tribute: "Federal and Confederate officers, Northern and Southern cities, republican and monarchical governments, men of all faiths and of all trades, princes and peasants, war torn veterans and little children unite in common sorrow." A newspaper editorial reflected the prevailing sentiment across the country when it proclaimed that Grant's life did not need to be remembered in sculpture, pictures, prose, or poetry, because "The Union [is] His Monument."[2]

The death and funeral of Ulysses S. Grant became a vehicle for a religiously tinged emotional and political reconciliation of North and South. A northern minister said, "But, great soldier as he was, nothing will be longer remembered of him that he was a magnanimous conqueror. . . . When the rebellion was broken, his enmity ceased." Proclaimed ex-Confederate general and pallbearer Simon Bolivar Buckner, "I am sorry General Grant is dead, but his death has yet been the greatest blessing the country has ever received, now, reunion is perfect." Gen. William Henry Fitzhugh ("Rooney") sent a telegram: "As the son of Robert E. Lee, I send my most profound sympathy. The whole South mourns the nation's loss."[3] Such statements were issued by former Civil War generals and prominent politicians, spoken by ministers of every denomination and region, and splashed across the headlines of major newspapers. They claimed Grant, in life and in death, forged reconciliation between the sections ensuring the emergence of a powerful and united American nation. "From Appomattox dates the end of sectionalism and no one man did more to bring about this result as Ulysses S. Grant," a proclamation issued from The Tammany Society, New York's Democratic Club, explained, continuing, "To-day the Unionist and Confederate are united in the universal sorrow which all citizens feel at his death, and join hands over his bier in one sacred pledge of devotion . . . to the Union to which his life was so earnestly devoted." Grant became a symbol of unionism, unity, reconciliation, and nationalism in the political culture of the era, as this speaker suggested: "The political storms and partizan clouds are swept out of the horizon now, and in the calm, clear light, we are able to see the full and noble qualities of the man . . . he was the Savior of the Republic. He must sit in the chair of the Father of his Country."[4] Indeed, the reaction to his death can be seen as a critical component in bringing about what Nina Silber has so aptly described as "The Romance of Reunion."[5]

As a rite of passage and memory, the funeral of U. S. Grant was a momentous event. Grant's funeral did not, all by itself, end the bitter feelings created by the Civil War. But situating the funeral in its political context, as well as its religious, emotional, and cultural context establishes its importance as a benchmark event for sectional reconciliation. The mourning for U. S. Grant unified the North and South. How could this be? His name was firmly linked with total Union victory and Republican rule in the South. Even as the nation underwent the swift changes and dislocations brought by massive industrialization, urbanization, and immigration in the decades after Appomattox, the old hostilities between the regions still cast a dark shadow over the political landscape. The Civil War was refought in many local, state, and national contests, alongside other important issues, such as civil service reform, the tariff, labor conflicts, and the currency question.[6] In the North, people swelled with pride over the memory of the Union victory. Republican politicians in particular, many of who were ex-soldiers, seized upon this feeling to "wave the bloody shirt" in election after election. They argued that when and if a "solid South" should rise again, based on the votes of ex-Confederates, it would spell great trouble for a typically divided North. If the Democrats won control of the national government, voters were warned, the Confederate debt would likely be repudiated, black people's civil rights would be utterly destroyed, and perhaps former slaveowners would vote themselves compensation for their ex-slaves. In short, all of the hard-won goals of wartime America would be lost, this time forever. Certainly these and similar arguments were familiar to northerners through Grant's two presidential campaigns in 1868 and 1872.

The political capital to be made through waving the bloody shirt had a solid basis in northern emotions and memories. Two million men had fought in the war for the Union Cause, and most northern families were touched by the conflict. The country's largest and most powerful civic and philanthropic organizations were those of the Union veterans—particularly the Grand Army of the Republic, which by 1885 had over five thousand posts and a membership of nearly half a million.[7] The GAR was only the biggest of many such veterans' groups. Northern veterans were in their vigorous middle age in 1885 and considered themselves transmitters of living history. They spoke, wrote, and commemorated their own roles in the war, and in turn, celebrated the Union Cause. By participation in public events, such as Grant's funeral procession, veterans preserved a personal relationship to historical events and personages.[8]

Northern images and emotions were matched in the South through the "Lost Cause" ideology. This sentimental view of the war arose out of bitterness over the terrible losses suffered by southern white people during and after the conflict.[9] According to Lost Cause adherents, brave southern soldiers lost the war only because they were outnumbered and outgunned by the overwhelming forces arrayed against them. The ex-Confederate soldiers joined the United Confederate Veterans and other soldiers' organizations whose influence was similar to that of the GAR, if less centralized. Southern politicians waved their version of the bloody shirt when they demanded recognition of their now reestablished rights as citizens and members of a reunited government. In short, Democrats and Republicans were still winning elections urging men to "vote as they shot." The funeral of U. S. Grant, therefore, is especially noteworthy because it came in the wake of repeated failures to solidify reconciliation.

Surprisingly, scholars who have studied Civil War memory have either ignored Grant's funeral altogether or mentioned it only in passing. The same is true of the funerals of other notable Union heroes—George G. Meade, George B. McClellan, Winfield Scott Hancock, and William Tecumseh Sherman.[10] Yet recent studies have highlighted the importance of festivals, holidays, celebrations, and funerals in Victorian American culture.[11] Christian rituals of bereavement and mourning customs occupy a large place in the literature. Indeed, throughout the nineteenth century, funerals for well-known people infused religious traditions with nationalistic symbolism, thereby elevating the public and political importance of funerals. The funeral's emotional combination of the public with the private, of the religious with the secular, was expanded dramatically during and after the Civil War. The huge number of deaths alone guaranteed that this would be so. Historian Gary Laderman observed, "Funeral processions for fallen soldiers were elaborate affairs replete with patriotic symbols and rites. American flags, national guards, funeral dirges, reverential crowds, and speeches and sermons all contributed to the solemn proceedings and ensured that the bodies evoked ideas of national unity and the righteousness of the Union [or Confederate] cause."[12]

Such rituals, called by one contemporary writer the "Pageantry of Woe," played a critical role in the creation of a collective historical memory for the generation of Americans who lived through the war, and carried political repercussions.[13] Grant's funeral plainly demonstrates the connection between private and public memory and private and public commemorations. Understanding this connection is important especially for analyzing the reaction to Grant's death and the following ceremonies. The formal state funeral for General Grant was unique, even in a time when funerals for famous figures were spectacular events.[14] Grant's funeral was unique because of his status as "savior" of the Union, president of the United States, and, by the time of his death, beloved symbol of the American nation. This status differentiated his funeral from other popular Union generals' as well as from Lincoln's and Garfield's, the two other state funerals in the nineteenth century that are comparable to Grant's. President (and former Union general) James Garfield was felled by an assassin's bullet in 1881, and his two-month deathwatch gripped the nation. Republican Garfield was neither

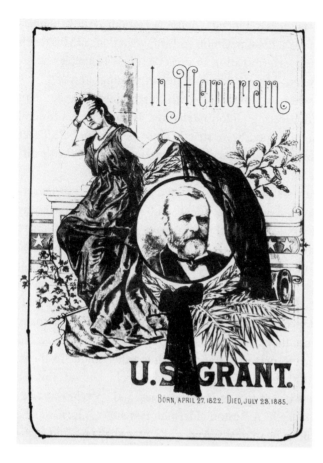

Typical
commemorative
broadside (Grant
Monument
Association Archives,
New York City)

In Memoriam

U.S. GRANT.

BORN, APRIL 27, 1822. DIED, JULY 23, 1885.

a great general nor (yet) a great president; his assassin was motivated not by the high drama of Civil War but by the disturbed anger of a disappointed office-seeker. Garfield became a martyr to the cause of civil service reform, an important issue in the Gilded Age; but his reputation faded over time. It is more illuminating to compare Grant's death with Lincoln's.[15]

The assassination of President Abraham Lincoln on April 14, 1865, Good Friday, was a stunning tragedy that called forth a vast public demonstration of grief—from the North. The cataclysmic nature of the assassination as well as its occurrence just before Easter Sunday was deemed providential by a majority of northern ministers and politicians. In the tidal wave of eulogies that followed Lincoln's death, he was portrayed not only as a tragic symbol of the bloodshed that had gone on for four years, but also as a more hopeful symbol of the national redemption that lay ahead.[16] Lincoln's quick apotheosis ensured that he would be remembered as a godlike figure in

American history. Immediately, Lincoln's memory embodied the principles for which the North fought the war, Union and emancipation, and his death provoked a widespread determination to preserve those principles in reconstructing the country. His sudden and violent passing, however, was not mourned in the white ex-Confederacy, which remained sullenly silent if outwardly respectful, fearing Union retaliation. Thus, Lincoln's funeral ceremonies, while monumental, were strictly a northern affair.[17] This fact alone made Grant's funeral and immediate commemoration markedly different from Lincoln's.

In 1885, when many southerners participated in Grant's memorial services, they commemorated one transcendent symbol of Unionism in a way they could not, and would not, for Lincoln twenty years before. Grant's memorialization included further acknowledgment of his elevation to the first rank of American heroes, alongside Washington and Lincoln. Today, it would be shocking to suggest that Grant (often the lowest-rated president, save for Buchanan or Harding) and Lincoln (the highest-rated president) were of equal importance in American history.[18] It did not seem so to many citizens in 1885 because they were not just judging Grant's presidency, but his overall importance to preserving and sustaining the Union. To them, Grant was every bit the equal of Washington and Lincoln, and this linkage was made in countless newspaper articles, eulogies, and speeches just before and after Grant's death. A Boston alderman lamented: "Great was he in life, but greater will he be in death. And while time shall last, and mankind shall hear of the deeds of Washington, Lincoln, and Grant, they will stand out as the three great characters of American history." Along the same lines, a speaker declaimed that there were three true "heroes" in U.S. history: "Washington, who was the father of his country; Lincoln, who guided the Ship of State through the late storm of civil strife; and Grant, the Great General, who saved the nation from over-throw in the sanguinary struggle for national life." The *Weekly Graphic's* two-foot cover page for a lavish commemorative issue was adorned with the headline, "Washington–Grant–Lincoln: A Nation's Heroes."[19]

Americans honored Washington the Father, Lincoln the Martyr, and Grant the Savior. Eulogists did not claim that Grant was one of the greatest presidents in United States history. "He had his faults, who has not?" the *New York Herald* reminded its readers, yet "we cannot see them because the brilliancy of his deeds shines in our eyes." Democratic newspapers tended to be more critical. The *New York Sun* editorialized: "Unfortunately for the country . . . the luster of his great fame as the conqueror of the rebellion has since been dimmed by his conspicuous failure as a statesman and business man." Even the most stalwart of Republicans waxed restrained about his two terms in office. "He must sit in the chair of the Father of his Country," began a memorial speaker, who stated, "For eight years he was elected President by overwhelming majority. Not trained in political science and statecraft it was inevitable that he would make some mistakes."[20] Yet the eulogies suggested a shrewd appreciation of the difficulties Grant faced as he struggled to carry out reconstruction policies. The one delivered by Brig. Gen. John Sanborn, who led a division at Vicksburg, was typical. "On the field at Appomattox, in the confusion and excitement of battles and surrendering of armies, he adopted a policy in relation to the conditions of surrender that made the reconstruction of the government possible," he said, adding, "to build up and restore the broken fragments of a government is the most difficult task that men or statesmen are ever called on to perform."[21]

Moreover, prominent speakers—leading political figures, ministers, military officers, and veterans—universally praised Grant as one of the greatest generals in the history of the world, and the general who, along with Lincoln, preserved the Union for all time. The fact that Grant was both a general and a president prompted southerners to emphasize the connection with Virginian George Washington. The *Montgomery Advertiser* proclaimed "His death a National Affliction" and stated: "Looking at the life and character of General Grant from the broadest national standpoint, it is true to say that no man since Washington has better illustrated the genius of American institutions or the temper of Americans as a people."[22] The majority of Southern eulogies made no mention of Lincoln at all—one of the notable differences between white northern and southern commemorations of Grant. While the passage of time ensured that reconciliation between the sections was under way by 1885, it was by no means fully secured.

### A State Funeral

Surrounded by his family, his doctors, and his minister, the Reverend John Newman, Ulysses S. Grant died on July 23, 1885, in his summer cottage at Mount McGregor, New York. Colonel Fred Grant reached over and stopped the clock to mark the exact time—8:08 A.M. Shortly afterward, news of Grant's death sped across the continent via telegraph. By 8:14 A.M. the *New York Times* prominently displayed the death announcement in its office window, with a special edition of the newspaper already printing. Everywhere, newspapers sold out as fast as they ran off the presses. Within an hour New York City's flags were at half-mast and ordinary business came to a standstill. In every state capital, legislatures adjourned for the day after send-ing messages of condolence to the Grant family, flags were lowered, and arrangements were made for public and private buildings—stores, hotels, and newspaper and government offices—to be swathed in black material. Department stores quickly emptied supplies of the traditional emblems of mourning—black crepe, armbands, and ribbons. "Never in the history of the trade has there been so sudden and rapid an increase in the demand for black and white cambrics, which are the principal materials used in drap-ing buildings."[23] New York City's wealthiest residences were unadorned, as their owners were out of town, but modest displays of commemoration were noted approvingly in many working-class neighborhoods.[24] Acting swiftly, President Grover Cleveland released a proclamation of condolence previewing the themes of numerous eulogies yet to be delivered:

The President of the United States has just received the sad tidings of the death of that illustrious citizen and ex-President of the United States, General Ulysses S. Grant, at Mount McGregor, in the State of New York, to which place he had lately been removed in the endeavor to prolong his life.

In making this announcement to the people of the United States the President is impressed with the magnitude of the public loss of a great military leader, who was, in the hour of victory, magnanimous; amid dis-aster, serene and self-sustained; who, in every station, whether as a soldier or a Chief Magistrate, twice called to power by his fellow-countrymen, trod unswervingly the pathway of duty, undeterred by doubts, single-minded and straightforward. The entire country has witnessed with deep emotion his prolonged and patient struggle with painful disease, and has watched by his couch of suffering with tearful sympathy. The destined end has come at last, and his spirit has returned to the Creator who sent it forth. The great heart of the nation that followed him when living with love and pride bows now in sorrow above him dead, tenderly mindful of his virtues, his great patriotic services and of the loss occasioned by his death.

In testimony of respect to the memory of General Grant it is ordered that the Executive Mansion and the several departments at Washington be draped in mourning for a period of thirty days, and that all public business shall, on the day of the funeral, be suspended, and the Secre-taries of War and of the Navy will cause orders to be issued for appropri-ate military and naval honors to be rendered on that day.[25]

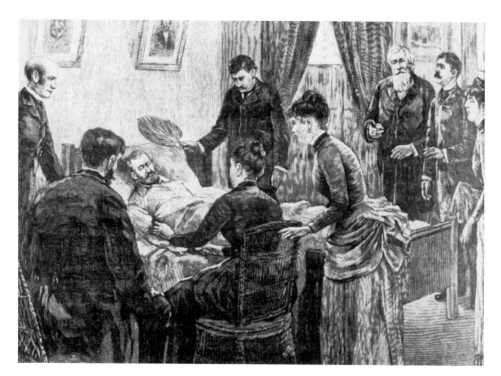

"The Death of General Grant." Surrounded by his family, doctors, and minister, Grant died at 8:08 A.M. on the morning of July 23, 1885. (*Harper's Weekly*, August 1, 1885)

---

The president's message was the first of many thousands of condolence letters and resolutions the family received. The *Tribune* related, "Letters and messages of condolence are still being flashed over the wires and come by mail from everywhere each moment of the day and night."[26] Reporters complained that telegrams flooding into the nearby Hotel Balmoral's telegraph office prevented their stories from being filed as quickly as editors demanded. Condolences came from friends and strangers, from black and white, from mighty and humble, from Democrats and Republicans, from North and South, and from national and international sources. Every city's mayor and every state's governor sent a message. After ordering the firing of guns, and state flags at half-mast, Louisiana's governor, Samuel D. McEnery issued, a proclamation: "A great American captain has fallen. The brave and magnanimous leader will be remembered with honor by soldiers of all countries." New York's Governor James Hill announced: "Ulysses S. Grant, twice President of the United States, the defender of the Union, the victorious leader of our soldiers and General . . . is dead. To the last he was the true soldier, strong in spirit, patient in suffering, brave in death."[27] The Mayor of Bradford, Pennsylvania, hand wrote a letter to Julia and placed in the envelope a newspaper clipping that described the large public meeting called by himself in which was made a proclamation that began, "Whereas, the foremost citizen of the Republic, the hero of its latest story, the choice exemplar of its institutions, the marvel of its military annals, the idol of its civic life, fearless soldier, patriotic sage, most honored son, Ulysses S. Grant, has passed from the scene of his shining career . . ."[28] A package from Nevada officials enclosed the "Senate Memorial and Joint Resolution, No. 32," proclaiming: "The services of General Grant cannot be estimated by any standard of value. . . . He was the foremost General in the greatest war that ever moved the destinies of the world." The Kingston, New York, Board of Education sent a copy of its condolence in which the board "adds its unanimous expression of sorrow to that so universally felt at the death of the great Soldier, Statesman, the exemplary Citizen . . . whose bravery on the field of battle, magnanimity in hour of victory, and devotion to every duty of American citizenship, will forever make his life a model example for the youth of this Republic."[29]

From Indian Territory, Dennis W. Bushyhead, the principal chief of the Cherokee Nation ordered the distribution of the following: "The Cherokees and other Indians have especial cause for sorrow in the fact that Gen. Grant was at all times, and especially when their rights were in peril, their firm and consistent protector and friend."[30] Working-class organizations were well represented in expressing sympathy to the Grant family. Some recalled Grant's humble status with affection: "Citizens of St. Louis still remember the rough backwoodsman who sold old wood from door to door, and who afterwards became a leather seller in the obscure town of Galena."[31] Groups such as the United American Mechanics of Wheeling, West Virginia, the Union of Locomotive Engineers of several states, and the Essex County Trades Assembly of Newark sent effusive proclamations. The Newark message stated:

At a meeting . . . the following resolutions were adopted in the presence of 10,000 in memory of U. S. Grant. From the ranks of wage-workers he rose to command the armies of this republic in war, and to preside over its affairs in peace. His life will be through all history an incentive to every citizen of the United States. It is an illustrious example that under our government there is no royal road to honor, and that the highest dignities man can attain on earth [are] possible to all, irrespective of birth or fortune. We testify our gratitude for the part he bore in a strife which made three millions of slaves free men."[32]

Grant's global prominence brought condolences from across the border and overseas. Great Britain's Queen Victoria, Mexico's President Porfirio Díaz, and Japan's Prince Towhit offered sympathy, as did dignitaries on behalf of Brazil, China, Egypt, Italy, France, Germany, and many other nations. Not all the messages came from the highest officials. The mayor of Tynemouth, Northumberland, England reminded Julia, "It was our proud privilege to welcome General Grant when he visited the Banks of the Tyne in our Borough a few years ago."[33] The European press recognized Grant's contributions in many admiring obituaries. England's *Daily Telegraph* printed a long review of Grant's career, and summarized his life in an editorial: "Yesterday the greatest and most successful soldier that the United States has produced breathed his last. . . . Beyond all others he was best fitted to cope with the tremendous crisis which made him, and when the grave closes over all that is mortal of Ulysses Simpson Grant, it will be felt that he leaves behind him no man cast in a simpler, sincerer or more heroic mould." Another British paper, the *Daily News*, commented, "It is as a soldier that he will be remembered. It is on his military services that his fame will rest. After Lincoln's death Grant was decidedly the most popular man in the United States." Every seat was taken at a memorial service held at Westminster Abbey, bringing together "the largest assemblage of Americans that has ever met in London." All the messages were sent to the cottage at Mount McGregor, where Fred read them to his mother. He released a statement to the press: "Such a flood of world-wide sympathy has probably never before been told by the electric spark to suffering hearts, and the family is profoundly grateful." A day later, he added, "In due time, it will be a part of Colonel Grant's pleasure to acknowledge the tokens and tributes to his father."[34]

Official funeral preparations began when President Cleveland sent his adjutant general to Mount McGregor offering the services of the government in providing a state funeral honoring the man who served both as commanding general of U.S. forces and as president of the United States. Family members conferred and decided the funeral and interment would be in New York City. A temporary tomb would be erected in Riverside Park and, later, a permanent tomb constructed in the same area. Thus informed, the president placed Maj. Gen. Winfield Scott Hancock, a hero of Gettysburg and currently commander of the Division of the Atlantic headquarters on New York City's Governor's Island, in charge of supervising the funeral arrangements. Cleveland could hardly have made a better choice. Hancock, a Democrat (and the party's candidate for president in 1880), enjoyed widespread popularity and respect for his lengthy military career. Relations between Grant and Hancock had been tense dating from Hancock's prosouthern Reconstruction policies in Louisiana. In an 1880 newspaper interview Grant described Hancock as "ambitious, vain, and weak," just the type of northern Democrat, Grant declared, "who would do the South's bidding in every area."[35] Previous bad feelings between the men were erased during Grant's illness, and Hancock worked smoothly with Fred Grant to hammer out a schedule for the funeral ceremonies announced on July 25. Private services were to be held at Mount McGregor on August 4. (The delay allowed time for the building of the temporary tomb.) The next day, Grant's body would be transported by train to Albany, where it would lie in state for twenty-four hours. On August 6 the remains would travel to New York and lie in state at City Hall. On Saturday, August 8, a gigantic funeral procession would accompany the body to the temporary vault in Riverside Park.[36]

Plans for the complicated funeral arrangements needed to be organized and executed with dispatch. The scale of the commemoration is suggested by Lt. Gen. Philip A. Sheridan's orders for the national military funeral:

In compliance with the instructions of the President, on the day of the funeral, at each military post, the troops and cadets will be paraded and the order read to them, after which all labors for the day will cease. The national flag will be displayed at half-staff. At dawn of the day thirteen guns will be fired, and afterward, at intervals of thirty minutes between the rising and setting of the sun, a single gun, and at the close of the day a national salute of thirty-eight guns. The officers of the army will wear crape on the left arm and on their swords, and the colors of the Battalion of Engineers, of the several regiments and of the United States Corps of Cadets will be put in mourning for the period of six months."[37]

Hancock gathered a staff of forty, working out of Governor's Island and offices in the downtown Federal Building. Many long days and nights of work lay ahead. The public ceremonies attending a state funeral required a mastery of both logistics and diplomacy—and Hancock triumphed in both areas. One newspaper headline summed up Hancock's duties perfectly: "Bring Order out of Chaos."[38] A great number of requests were received from organizations—civic and military—for positions in the funeral procession in New York City. Hancock had to make many hard decisions as the New York procession was limited to 60,000 participants. A few of the organizations winning approval included the Knights of Sherwood Forest, the Volunteer Firemen of New York, the Boy's Temperance Organization, and the United German Singing Societies of New York. Northern veterans' groups clamored for special attention. Eighteen thousand marched, with the biggest number from the GAR, but with numerous representatives of the Societies of the Army of the Potomac, of the Army of the Cumberland, and of the Army of the Tennessee as well.[39] And there was another procession to plan—in Albany, to accompany the casket to and from the railway station—although the procession in New York City, from Grand Central Station to City Hall and from City Hall to the temporary tomb, would be much larger. Both required pomp and circumstance, and the delicate handling of dignitaries representing the federal, state, and local governments.[40] A military funeral for a person of Grant's rank required an escort for the casket carrying reversed arms and a riderless horse, with boots turned backward in the stirrups. The order of Grant's funeral procession commenced with the regular or official military units representing the U.S. Army, Navy, and Artillery—followed by the casket, resting on an elaborate catafalque pulled by twenty-four horses. Next in order came the family members, the president and his cabinet, the veterans division, and the civic division.[41]

### "My Faith Looks Up to Thee"

At Mount McGregor, two GAR posts vied for the honor of guarding Grant's remains—the Wheeler Post 92 from Saratoga and the U. S. Grant Post of Brooklyn. An unseemly competition was avoided by dividing the duties between the two posts. Tents were set up in the area behind the cottage to accommodate the veterans' sleeping arrangements. Hancock also ordered a unit of U.S. Regulars from Governor's Island adding to the security of the area and the solemnity of the occasion.[42] The most pressing duty was the embalming of the body and its placement in the specially constructed polished oak casket. The casket was made by the Stein Manufacturing Company in Rochester. Public demand led to its being put on display, and 15,000 people rushed to the factory to view the casket before it was shipped to New York City. In the city, undertaker Stephen Merritt made provisions for the casket to be seen by 70,000 citizens before its arrival at Mount McGregor. Merritt also traveled to the cottage on Wednesday, July 29, to preside over the embalming process, which took two days.[43] A death mask was fitted by Karl Gerhardt, a young sculptor recommended highly by Mark Twain. The general's cancer-ravaged body, weighing less than one hundred pounds, was dressed in a suit of black broadcloth, with his feet encased in white stockings and black patent leather slippers; "a white linen standing collar, and a black silk scarf ... tied in a plain bow at the throat" completed the burial attire. No military accoutrements — such as Grant's sword — graced the casket. They were now the property of the Smithsonian Institution, and thus the federal government, under an agreement Grant had signed with William H. Vanderbilt to secure a loan. Fred lifted his father's right hand and placed it across his breast and arranged the left arm by his side. He slipped in mementoes, including a varnished wreath of oak leaves collected and fashioned by a granddaughter, just before the casket's heavy plate glass top was screwed into place. Covered with an American flag, the casket stood in the parlor room when the Tuesday, August 4, funeral obsequies commenced with a thirteen-gun salute at dawn.[44]

Services were attended by family members and friends, including Julia's sister, Nellie Dent Wrenshall; Grant's sister, Virginia Corbin; Admiral Stephen C. Rowan; and Generals William T. Sherman and Horace Porter. General Hancock was there to supervise the removal of Grant's body from the cottage. The ceremony began with the recitation of the Ninetieth Psalm by the Reverend Dr. Benjamin L. Agnew of Philadelphia, followed by a prayer and the song "My Faith Looks Up to Thee" performed by a group of singers from Boston, Brooklyn, and New York. Reverend Newman delivered an hour-and-a-half eulogy, taking as his text Matthew, 25:21: "Well done, thou good and faithful servant, enter thou into the joy of the Lord." Newman paid lavish tribute to Grant's service to the country but singled out his spiritual journey for special attention. Admitting that the late general was not baptized until recently, the minister nonetheless insisted, "The principles of Christ were deeply engrafted upon his spirit. ... His faith in God as the Sovereign Ruler and the Father Almighty was as simple as a child's and mighty as a prophet's."[45]

Despite Newman's portrayal, it was no secret that the military hero was at best a nominal Christian. Yet his disease-ridden body became a Christlike symbol for both human suffering and absolution. Congregations across the country prayed in Sunday services that Grant's physical suffering would be mitigated, even cured, by God's power as medical science failed. Reverend Newman told the ailing general: "You are a man of Providence; God made you His instrument to save a great nation; and now He will use you for a great spiritual mission, in the skeptical age."[46] Exuding both charisma and pomposity, Newman inserted himself into the newspaper frenzy that surrounded Grant's household. He issued daily bulletins to reporters on

Grant's spiritual state that quite clearly were meant to match the physicians' reports. Mark Twain, horrified by the way the minister (in his view) shamelessly portrayed Grant as a dutiful Christian, retorted, "It is fair to presume that most of Newman's daily reports originated in his own imagination."[47]

Reverend Newman created a newspaper sensation when he claimed that it was prayer, and not a timely injection of whiskey administered by Drs. Shrady and Douglas, that saved Grant from near certain death on the evening of April 1, 1885. That same night, Newman, at the request of the women of the family, baptized a barely conscious Grant. Dr. Douglas remembered: "The scene was solemn and impressive but as quiet and free from excitement as it possibly could be. From the silver bowl, which the clergyman held, he took the water and gently applying it to the General's brow, reverentially said: 'I baptize thee Ulysses Simpson Grant, in the name of the Father, in the name of the Son, and of the Holy Ghost,' following these solemn words with a brief and appropriate prayer." Later a close relation remarked of Grant: "He did not care how much praying was done around him if it made his wife feel better."[48] That Grant lacked devotion was of small consequence to the country; his character was formed in a Christian crucible, and he clearly honored and respected, and tried to live by, the Bible. "I believe the Scriptures," Grant said, "and whoever lives by them will be benefited." The New York Times ran a story on "The General's Sturdy Piety," and the Pittsburg Christian Advocate promised "Recollections of General Grant's Church Life." From his Brooklyn Plymouth Church pulpit, the Reverend Henry Ward Beecher assured his Sunday parishioners that Grant was going to heaven, and then commented, "I trust that Gen. Grant in the essential element of his character is Christian."[49]

Inevitably, Grant's relationship to God and religion became an object of interest, widely discussed by the press and public. Protestant newspapers played up his spirituality: "And where in all the annals of the Church shall we find a dying hour so full of divine repose?" asked the Christian Advocate, while the New York Evangelist complimented Grant on his "natural" religious faith. Chicago's The Standard praised the general's evident embrace of God and noted "the growing impression becomes a conviction, and he evinces the temper of a lovely, earnest Christian."[50] Both as general and as president, Grant encouraged vigorous expression of religion. His parents Methodists, the adult Ulysses attended church to please Julia. During the war, Grant supported warmly the work of the U.S. Christian Commission among the soldiers of the Union Army.[51] He could hardly do less in a country where Protestant Christian ideals and practice lay at the center of community life.

Characterized by religious diversity, even divisiveness, and challenged by a growing number of Catholic immigrants, Protestant churches—which included Baptists, Methodists, Presbyterians, Congregationalists, Episcopalians, and Lutherans—played a major role in the cultural, social, and political life of the nation. Though newspapers, journals, missions, revivals, and educational and welfare organizations, church leadership both articulated and reflected middle-class ideals and values against a backdrop of dramatic transformations brought on first by war and then by industrialization.[52]

The politician Grant knew well that churchgoers voted in great numbers, and many in the North voted solidly for the Republican Party, the party that stood for low tariffs, a sound currency, a strong national government, and Protestant-based moral values and reforms. As president he cultivated the support of powerful ministers, including American Methodist Bishop John Heyl Vincent, one of the founders of the Chautauqua Christian summer camps in New York. Vincent and Grant first met in Galena in 1859, when the former served as pastor in the town's Methodist church. At Vincent's request, Grant helped to inaugurate the Chautauqua movement when on August 14, 1875, he spoke before 30,000 Protestant campers. "Grant had never warmed to the evangelical style," commented a scholar of the movement, "but Chautauqua appealed to him as a way to exhibit kinship with Protestants without requiring too much in the way of public devotion." During that same period, he attended a huge revival meeting presided over by the evangelist Dwight Moody, whose compelling message stressed religious reconciliation between North and South.[53] In his adult lifetime Grant witnessed, and symbolized, the growth of a "civic religion" that blended patriotism, loyalty, and sacrifice to forge a distinctive and powerful American nationalism. Horace Bushnell, the Massachusetts clergyman and reformer, asserted that the Civil War made the United States into "a nation—God's own nation."[54]

Ulysses S. Grant occupied a special place in the hearts and minds of American citizens living in 1885. The *Richmond Dispatch* proclaimed, "He was so pervaded by greatness that he seemed not to be conscious that he was great." A southern editor admitted: "General Grant was the foremost and most prominent figure among those who employed arms to crush the Southern effort for separate and independent existence. No other military chief engaged in the task of coercion, no leader battling for the maintenance of the Union and the supremacy of the Federal Government, accomplished any thing like so much. No man was so thoroughly identified as he, in the estimation of both sections, with the triumph of the one and the defeat of the other."[55] Citizens felt as if they knew him, whether or not they admired him or scorned his reputation. The *New York Tribune* published one such citizen's sentiments. "This generation will never appreciate fully General Grant's greatness," said Levi M. Bates. "That will remain for . . . the future. He did more for his country than any man since Washington, not even excepting Lincoln, who could have done little without Grant. His only mistake of civil career was in trying to do too much for his friends."[56] There was no other American public figure that was as famous, and as well loved by so many as Grant, both at home and abroad.

## *"The Great Captain is dead"*

After the service ended, Julia remained behind in seclusion; her sons, daughters-in-law, and daughter accompanied the body to New York, along with a small delegation of friends and invited dignitaries. First out of the cottage were soldiers carrying reversed arms, followed by buglers playing a dirge. The next to emerge were the clergymen, and then Dr. Douglas, Fred, Ulysses Jr., and Jesse Grant, followed by the guard of honor carrying the casket, which they loaded carefully onto the funeral car. The three-car train carried Grant's remains down the mountain to Saratoga, where they were transferred to a nine-car funeral train, all covered in black, that made the forty-mile journey from Saratoga to Albany at half-speed. At every crossroads and town, people gathered to pay their respects, often numbering in the thousands. Arriving in Albany in the late afternoon, the casket was removed from the train to the sounds of a thirty-eight-gun salute. The *Albany Argus* reported that 50,000 visitors flocked to the city for the "ever-memorable day." A whole issue of the *Albany Evening Journal* was devoted to Grant, his death, his legacy, and the funeral ceremonies at Mount McGregor and pending ones in Albany. The *Journal* editor reminded readers that "we are learning every day how much Gen. Grant did to cement in peace a union he had wrought in war, and the generations shall delight to point to the consistent development of love of country that began when at Appomattox he told Lee's soldiers to keep their horses and return to their farms, and ended at Mount McGregor with his words to Gen. Buckner." Over 130 military and civic organizations formed two divisions in the procession that accompanied Grant's body to the executive chamber in Albany's capitol building, covered in black for the occasion. By the time the room was closed at 3:00 A.M., 80,000 mourners had filed through to view the general.[57]

Early the next morning, the procession, reconstituted, accompanied the

Albany funeral procession (U.S. Instantaneous Photographic Co. [Boston, 1885]; reproduced by permission of The Huntington Library, San Marino, California)

casket back to the railroad station. Cannons boomed as a vast sea of spectators watched the train slowly move out of the station, carrying the general to his final destination in New York City. Inside, passengers viewed crowds packed on the roofs of local buildings and massed along both sides of the railroad's footpaths. There were many such memorable views as the funeral train crossed the bridge spanning the Hudson River and wound its way down the Hudson Valley and through the Catskills, passing towns and villages where large numbers of people stood in silence, men removing their hats in a gesture of respect. Two fleeting scenes included passing by the small station at Hudson, where buildings could be glimpsed draped in black, and in Fishkill, where a huge black-bordered banner emblazoned with "The Great Captain is dead" expressed the sorrow of loss. A touching ceremony unfolded at the general's alma mater, the U.S. Military Academy. As the funeral train neared West Point's railway station, the sounds of booming cannon preceded the sight of the entire cadet corps, led by Cadet Captain

John J. Pershing (later a World War I hero and four-star general), drawn up in line at "present arms," while the band played "Sweet Spirit, Hear My Prayer."[58]

## The General Returns to New York

Leaving West Point amid heavy rain and lightning storms rattling windows, the train managed an on-time arrival at Grand Central Station in New York City, at 5:00 P.M. Passengers were met by representatives of the Citizen's Committee of One Hundred, wearing black suits and crepe armbands. Governor Hill and his staff took their places in the procession that accompanied the remains to City Hall. General Hancock led the pageant, with regiments of the National Guard, arms reversed and wearing mourning colors marching behind. The large black catafalque, drawn by twelve black horses, received the casket, and the procession proceeded from the Forty-third Street side of the station, watched by massed crowds along the way. The distinctive sounds of mourning accompanied the procession—the rolling of muffled drums and the tolling of bells. Arriving at black-swathed City Hall Square, the horses pulled up in front of the building. The Brooklyn GAR guard carried the casket from the catafalque into City Hall as the band played a dirge. Inside the building all the public rooms were draped in black. The room set aside for viewing the remains contained a bust of Grant, a large bronze medallion featuring the general's likeness, and a huge, elaborate floral tribute with a banner reading "'8:08,' 1822–1885" sent by the Women's Relief Corps of New York and Brooklyn. For two days, citizens filing past the casket paid their respects in great numbers—on Thursday, 150,000 and on Friday, 100,000. Double lines extended far up Broadway for more than a mile. Newspapers filled their columns with fulsome descriptions of, and interviews with, the visitors. In the early morning, a reporter noted, "about two-thirds of the visitors were of the masculine gender, and these were mostly of middle age . . . most of them being apparently of the class that labors for its bread." Later in the day, women and children joined the throngs, and "a long row of parasols" appeared. Excepting the very wealthy, they hailed from all walks of life—working men carrying their lunch pails, shopgirls, prosperous-looking parents with their children, hardened veterans, and older folks who all claimed feelings of a great loss in Grant's passing.[59]

New York City's pageant deliberately showcased reconciliation. Both President Cleveland and General Hancock were delighted to accommodate Fred Grant's request to include one or two ex-Confederate generals as

The commanders and their causes on an equal footing (Library of Congress)

pallbearers. Cleveland formally appointed Joseph Johnston and Simon B. Buckner, who were paired with Union generals William T. Sherman and Philip H. Sheridan. There were twelve pallbearers in all, including two admirals and six civilians. Hancock went one step further in inviting the country to view the funeral as an important touchstone for reconciliation between North and South. He sent a telegram to General Fitzhugh Lee, ex-Confederate cavalry officer and nephew of Robert E. Lee, asking, "Would it be agreeable to you to be appointed as aide on the occasion of the ceremonies in connection with the obsequies of General Grant? If it would you will be so announced." Lee replied: "I accept the position, because by so doing I can testify my respect for the memory of a great soldier and thus return, as far as I can, the generous feelings he has expressed toward the soldiers of the South."[60] Despite the solemnity surrounding the event, a humorous exchange briefly captivated the press. It occurred when somebody came up with the bizarre idea that sectional reconciliation could be promoted best by disinterring Robert E. Lee's body and burying it together with Grant's remains in a glorious monument to be built in Washington, D.C. Reporters asked a nonplussed Gen. Fitzhugh Lee what he thought of this idea. His reply was tactful but firm: General Grant should be buried in Washington, D.C., but alone.[61]

General Lee was criticized by some in the South for participating so enthusiastically in the funeral activities. At the time, he was running as the Democratic candidate for governor in Virginia, and the *Raleigh Chronicle* asked in an editorial if he really deserved the votes "of the naked, hungry, footsore Virginia veterans that wept when their flag went down at Appomattox?"[62] Two prominent and unrepentant ex-Confederate generals expressed their disgust with the commotion over Grant's death in private correspondence. Jubal Early cast doubt on whether Grant deserved to be called "magnanimous," declaring, "I have no doubt his [Grant's] anxiety to have the glory of General Lee's surrender to him, and his fear of failure to obtain it, induced him to consent to the terms granted." D. H. Hill asked Early sarcastically: "Cannot you and I get up some quote over the 'late lamented,' 'the second Washington' the 'greatest captain of any age?'"[63] Other dissident voices expressed anger at the "hypocrisy" and "mockery" of gestures of southern respect toward Grant. "Stop with all these false prasis [*sic*]" cried one Georgian.[64] These dissenters, however numerous, only underscore the surprising strength of official, public demonstrations of southern bereavement for Grant.

### "The North and South are reunited forever"

Fitzhugh Lee, not Jubal Early, represented the way in which white southerners—in newspaper coverage, in political speeches, and in memorial services—participated in the mourning for U. S. Grant. General Lee dramatized his own participation in the funeral ceremonies as evidence that "the North and South are reunited forever." When asked by a reporter to account for the surprising demonstration of southern sorrow at Grant's passing, he replied: "It means that the Union is now more firmly and inseparably united than it was twenty years before Buchanan's administration."[65] All stressed the magnanimity of the victor of Appomattox. "General Grant was a brave and successful soldier and a generous adversary, remembered General P. G. T. Beauregard. "We of the South," declared a New Orleans newspaper, "forget the stern General who hurled his terrible masses upon the ranks of our fathers and brothers, whose storms of shot and shell mowed down our friends like wheat before the gleaner, remembering only the manly soldier who, in the hour of triumph, displayed the knightly chivalry that robs defeat of its bitterest pang."[66] Southerners saluted the Christian compassion of the Union commander whose written terms of surrender provided leniency for the Confederate army from the top down. It was as if General Grant "the butcher" and President Grant who enforced "Negro rule" had been erased from southern memory, *at least for the purposes of participating in the national mourning.*

A selected "forgetfulness" was critical in the construction of a shared memory of the Civil War in the late nineteenth century. Historians David Blight, Reid Mitchell, and Nina Silber have made this point persuasively.[67] Blight in particular demonstrates that a national memory based on reconciliation triumphed over at least several other competing and equally important "memories" of the war. Sectional harmony, which emphasized the valor and courage of soldiers, emerged as the dominant motif in many (although by no means all) contemporary histories, commemorations, reunions, monuments, and novels. Other narratives were diminished or erased as the century came to a close. One of those narratives was the story of slavery, emancipation, and freedom. If, by the dawn of the new century, the luster of the Union Cause was increasingly diminished, that of the Lost Cause gained strength, and that of the Emancipationist Cause had almost disappeared. Mitchell shows the importance of the family as a metaphor for bringing the American political nation back together at the familial table. Silber enlarges upon Mitchell's insights: "The family could . . . nurture and regenerate the type of emotional bonds that would truly and completely heal the national rift." She notes that forgiveness and forgetfulness became the watchwords for many northerners. These northerners sought to integrate ideas of harmony and ideals of an "imagined community" for a truly united country. Blight, Mitchell, and Silber demonstrate that this type of reconciliation was precisely what northern and southern whites needed to be able to forge a new nation out of the bitter ashes of the old one.[68]

The funeral's commemorative motif of sectional harmony sprang from Grant's reaction to the overwhelming rush of support and warm wishes he received during his illness. He particularly relished those from the South. In June, a long and thoughtful editorial on Grant's career appeared in the literary journal, *Southern Bivouac,* beginning this way: "The universal expression of interest and sympathy during General Grant's illness, and the testimonials of regret his anticipated death has elicited from the people of the whole country, and all classes of political opinion, are very significant. The feeling has been indubitably cordial and genuine, and unmistakably evinces that we have really entered upon an era of national reconciliation."[69] Grant's former aide and military biographer Adam Badeau noticed how dramatically the messages affected his boss's morale for the better, so much so "that his whole nature, moral and physical, became inspired and renovated." Badeau continued, "Few men, indeed, have known in advance so nearly the verdict of posthumous fame. No deathbed was ever so illumined by the light of universal affection and admiration."[70]

Basking in an unanticipated but welcomed wave of tributes from former enemies, the adulation tipped Grant's inclination toward embracing sectional harmony. Ben Perley Poore, journalist, author, and friend of Grant, commented, "The South seemed to vie with the North in flooding his room with telegraphic messages of condolence and sympathy and prayer." The city fathers of Louisville, Kentucky, urged the nation's cities to follow their example to make Grant's birthday a national holiday, drawing praise from a northern newspaper, which declared that such a holiday "is destined to become popular like the 22nd of February or 'Washington Day' as it has been happily styled." An avid newspaper reader, Grant may have read this report from the *New York Tribune*'s correspondent in Columbia, South Carolina: "Upon all sides and from all classes of people throughout this state are heard expressions of sympathy for General Grant." A newspaper reported Grant reading a letter from a former Rebel soldier thanking him effusively for his actions at Appomattox, assuring him "that I am not the only ex-Confederate who sends his prayers daily to the Throne of Grace for the restoration of [our] grandest . . . statesman." Ex-Confederates Jefferson Davis, Alexander Stephens, and Thomas Rosser are three of many who gave public interviews expressing southern sympathies for Grant.[71]

Badeau recalled, "I had been greatly struck by the universal watching of a nation, almost of a world, at his bedside, and especially by the sympathy from former rivals and political and even personal adversaries; and I recounted to him instances of this magnanimous forgetfulness of old-time enmities. When I told him of the utterances of . . . Jefferson Davis, he replied: 'I am very glad to hear this. I would much rather have their good-will than their ill-will!'" On Easter Sunday, Grant prepared a thank-you letter to all the people who expressed their sympathy: "I am very much touched and grateful for the sympathy and interest manifested in me by my friends, and by those who have not hitherto been regarded as friends."[72] In July, Grant visited with old friend and former antagonist Simon B. Buckner, and spoke of reconciliation. Later he allowed his message to Buckner to be widely publicized: "I have witnessed since my sickness just what I have wished to see ever since the war—harmony and good feelings between the sections."[73] In an oft quoted passage of the *Memoirs*, the ailing general wrote:

I feel that we are on the eve of a new era, when there is to be great harmony between the Federal and Confederate. I cannot stay to be a living witness to the correctness of this prophecy; but I feel it within me that it is to be so. The universally kind feeling expressed for me at a time when it was supposed that each day would prove my last, seemed to me the beginning of the answer to "Let Us Have Peace."

The expressions of these kindly feelings were not restricted to a section of the country, nor to a division of the people. They came from individual citizens of all nationalities; from all denominations—the Protestant, the Catholic, and the Jew; and from the various societies of the land—scientific, educational, religious, or otherwise. Politics did not enter into the matter at all.

I am not egotist enough to suppose all this significance should be given because I was the object of it. But the war between the States was a very bloody and a very costly war. One side or the other had to yield principles they deemed dearer than life before it could be brought to an end. I commanded the whole of the mighty host engaged on the victorious side. I was, no matter whether deservedly so or not, a representative of that side of the controversy. It is a significant and gratifying fact that Confederates should have joined heartily in this spontaneous move. I hope the good feeling inaugurated may continue to the end.[74]

Memories of controversial figures soften with the passage of time, more so if the person has endured tragedy. Annoyances fade, quarrels are forgotten, mistakes forgiven, sanctity conferred. By the time of his funeral Grant had become as much a symbol of national reconciliation as he was earlier a symbol of uncompromising Union victory. Poet, novelist, journalist and Civil War veteran Ambrose Bierce cast aside his bitterness to write a poem commemorating Grant. The last two stanzas pay tribute to the magnanimous general:

His was the heavy hand, and his
The service of the despot blade;
His the soft answer that allayed
War's giant animosities.

Let us have peace: our clouded eyes,
Fill, Father, with another light,
That we may see with clearer sight
Thy servant's soul in Paradise.[75]

Grant's funeral marked an important milestone on the road to white sectional harmony, a harmony increasingly commonplace by the early

Beginning of the funeral procession, with view of City Hall, New York City (U.S. Instantaneous Photographic Co. [Boston, 1885]; reproduced by permission of The Huntington Library, San Marino, California)

twentieth century.[76] General Hancock seized upon the good feeling for Grant displayed by southerners and made sure that Confederate units (two companies of the First Virginia Regiment—the Richmond Grays and the Walker Light Guards) were guaranteed prominent places in the otherwise northern-dominated funeral procession. An observer later commented approvingly: "It was quite a sight to see the Stonewall Brigade [march] up Fifth Avenue with their drums marked Staunton, Va. They wore the grey, with a black and brass helmet. There were several companies of Virginia and Southern troops."[77] Hancock also ordered advertisements to be placed in New York newspapers advising that "all ex-Confederate soldiers residing in New York City and the vicinity who desire to participate in the funeral are requested to send their names and addresses" so that they could march in the procession.[78]

### "Broadway moved like a river"

The day of the funeral dawned sunny and blessedly mild. Before first light, the military units camped at Governor's Island landed at Battery Park, filling New York with the sounds of horses and marching men. The great event brought hundreds of thousands of visitors, many of them arriving early in the morning by ferries coming from Jersey City and Hoboken. Others took the trains, and every coach and taxi in the city had been reserved by the Central, the Pennsylvania, the New Haven and other railroad companies for their customers' use. The elevated trains were packed (a record 600,000 transported), so thousands walked the Brooklyn Bridge's footpath, flooding into the city from that direction. At sunrise, minute guns were fired from Maine to California, announcing the beginning of the funeral activities. Major General Hancock and his retinue, which included General Fitzhugh Lee, arrived at City Hall at 8:30 A.M. A reporter described Hancock and company as wearing "gold helmets with white plumes, gold epaulets, white gauntleted gloves, and shining medals [that] became incandescent in the bright morning." Mayor William R. Grace led a delegation of ministers up the City Hall steps, followed by the pallbearers, including Sherman and Sheridan, Johnston and Buckner, Admirals David D. Porter and John L. Worden, Senator John A. Logan, and former secretary of the treasury George Boutwell. As the casket was removed from City Hall, twenty members of the Liederkranz Society sang Schubert's mournful "Geisterchore" and the "Pilgrims' Chorus" from Tannhäuser. The men of the Grand Army Guard grasped the silver bars on either side of the casket carried it down the steps, and carefully placed it on the catafalque. The funeral hearse, covered by a black canopy, was led by twenty-four black horses, each attended by an African American groom. Albert Hawkins, who had served as Grant's driver while he was president, drove the hearse.

At 9:30 A.M. all was in readiness when General Hancock gave the order "Forward March," and the parade moved to the sound of bands playing funeral dirges. The moment of Hancock's order a signal flashed from Western Union to St. Paul's and Trinity Church, and then to the city's other churches so that the sound of tolling bells filled the air. That sound echoed across the country as sextons in many states waited for the electronic signals to sound their church's bells. The procession left City Hall, beginning its line of march up Broadway, buildings decked out in black crepe and flags flying over rooftops, to Fourteenth Street, west to Fifth Avenue, north to Fifty-seventh Street, again to Broadway, north to Seventy-second Street, and west to Riverside Drive, ending at 122nd Street and the temporary tomb in Riverside Park. From its start at City Hall the procession moved with flawless precision as units filling fifty side streets waited patiently for their cues and then fell into their assigned place in the procession. First came Hancock, then the military units represented, including the "U.S. 22nd Infantry with four battalions of artillery, sailors, marines, national guard regiments, black soldiers stationed in the southwest, and brigades from every state that fought in the Union." Marching with fixed bayonets, this martial body preceded the catafalque, which was flanked by an honor guard, then came the carriages filled with pallbearers. President Cleveland's carriage, "drawn by six bay horses, was followed by others filled with cabinet members, senators, congressmen and governors." Next came 18,000 GAR men led by colorful former major general Daniel E. Sickles, riding on his horse with the remains of his amputated leg (lost at Gettysburg) strapped on the back of the saddle. Toward the end of the parade New York's mayor, William Grace, led a contingent of 8,000 civic and municipal officials. "And so they passed," wrote an observer, "the legions of New-York, Pennsylvania, Massachusetts, Virginia, Connecticut, Georgia, Minnesota, New Jersey, and the District of Columbia—all martial and reliant, for East or West, North or South, the soldier of this flag is the same . . . [with] the same harmonious flowing of sparkle and color." Marching bands and fife and drum corps were interspersed throughout the nine-mile procession.[79]

More than a million and a half spectators jammed the streets, perching on window ledges, climbing on statues and up trees, sitting on the porches of empty houses, straddling the tops of lampposts and telephone poles, crowding dangerously onto rooftops. By early afternoon, people backed up along the bluffs above the Hudson River, where numerous sailboats bobbed on the sparkling water, and five men-of-war waited in line for the signal to fire their salutes. A journalist captured the scene: "Broadway moved like a river, a river into which many tributaries were poured. There was one living mass choking the thoroughfare from where the dead lay in state to the grim gates at Riverside open to receive him. From 14th street to the top of the hill—pavements, windows, curbs, steps, balcony, and housetop teeming. All walls and doorways were a sweep of black."[80]

Enterprising vendors sold three-legged wooden stools for twenty-five cents and souvenirs such as black silk mourning ribbons, busts, and pennants with "Grant" emblazoned across the front. Others sold lemonade, cider, and food, offering relief for the hungry and thirsty. Twenty miles of crowds, respectful and subdued (the New York City police had arrested all

Funeral procession with catafalque, August 8, 1885, at Fortieth Street and Fifth Avenue (National Park Service)

Catafalque passing A. T. Stewart's department store on Fifth Avenue (U.S. Instantaneous
Photographic Co. [Boston, 1885]; reproduced by permission of The Huntington Library,
San Marino, California)

known pickpockets and troublemakers) watched as the seemingly endless
procession of soldiers, distinguished men, veterans, and civic organizations
wound their way to Riverside Park. Thousands consulted the programs sold
for the occasion or the free maps in the newspapers to check on the identi-
fication of the marching units. Many hoped to catch a glimpse of one of the
numerous carriage-borne dignitaries.

General Hancock reached Riverside Park at 2:30 P.M., with the tail end
of the procession finally arriving a little before 5:00, when the burial service
was scheduled to begin. Hancock and the honorary pallbearers strode into
the temporary tomb, a small and unpretentious brick structure facing the
Hudson River. It was covered by a barrel arch with a cross in front and iron
gates, with a big "G" on the front closing, for protection. It was amazingly
modest given the scale of the funeral ceremonies, and someone remarked
irreverently that "the whole thing looked like a bake oven."[81] At the end,
prayers were said, and Reverend Newman offered a benediction. Reporters noted that pallbearers Johnston and Sherman, Sheridan and Buckner,
heads collectively bent, were solemn and tearful. Afterward they all shook

Temporary vault for General Grant (Library of Congress)

hands. Flowers were placed on the casket; it was locked in the tomb, the crowds melted away, and U. S. Grant passed into legend and memory. "The great scene is over," wrote ex-Union general Joshua Chamberlain to his wife, Fanny. "Grant is laid in his tomb. You may imagine—few others can—how strange that seems to me. That emblem of strength & stubborn resolution yielding to human weakness & passing helplessly away to dust."[82]

## *"Engraved upon our hearts"*

The funeral of U. S. Grant was a moving and significant event in the lives of Americans, evoking different responses but a common loss. The commemorations in New York City and around the country combined genuine grief, unabashed patriotism, serious reflection, and crass commercialism in a vast outpouring of religious sentimentality. Grant's achievements and failures, so intertwined with the new nation that had been forged since the northern victory some twenty years earlier, were discussed and debated endlessly in newspapers and other public forums. "Such a funeral never before occurred in America and never will again," wrote General Sherman to Julia.[83] The *New York Times* headline on August 9 proclaimed: "A Nation At A Tomb" and "The Reunited Republic Buries General Grant." Another postfuneral headline put it succinctly: "If the War Did Not End In 1865, It Certainly Ended Yesterday."[84] Along with thousands of lesser poets, Walt Whitman paid tribute to Grant:

As one by one withdraw the lofty actors,
From that great play on history's stage eterne,
That lurid, partial act of war and peace—of old and new contending
Fought out through wrath, fears, dark dismays, and many a long
    suspense;
All past—and since, in countless graves receding, mellowing.

"Victor's and vanquish'd—Lincoln's and Lee's—now thou with them,
Man of the mighty days—and equal to the days!
Thou from the prairies!—tangled and many-vein'd and hard has been
    thy part,
To admiration has it been enacted![85]

To modern sensibilities, the dimensions of Grant's funeral may appear to be extreme. The national memorial was replicated in ceremonies staged in Philadelphia, Denver, Chicago, Cincinnati, Cleveland, Los Angeles, Sacramento, and San Francisco, many of them replete with huge processions and overflowing crowds in churches and town halls. Services often occurred on the days leading up to the national funeral, while others followed the date. Boston's memorial ceremonies are a good example. The City Council met immediately after hearing the news of Grant's death to plan the commemorations, with the mayor and each alderman making remarks that would later be preserved in a specially printed volume. Two large ceremonies were planned, the first on July 27 in Faneuil Hall featuring speeches by prominent politicians, such as the governor, the mayor, and congressmen as well as by ministers. Meanwhile, thousands of Bostonians watched as the First Massachusetts Regiment marched down State Street to the railroad station on its way to participate in New York's procession. The second memorial service took place on October 22 in Tremont Temple, where Henry Ward Beecher held his audience spellbound with a lengthy eulogy and Julia Ward Howe offered an ode:

A conqueror crowned for deeds of might,
But happiest in the Victor's might,
When the strong arm that dealt the blow,
Might lift and help the prostrate foe.[86]

The First Massachusetts Volunteer Regiment marches down Boston's State Street to the train station, their destination the national funeral for Grant in New York City. (U.S. Instantaneous Photographic Co. [Boston, 1885]; reproduced by permission of The Huntington Library, San Marino, California)

The reportage of the numerous local and state events offered the same kind of lavish detail given to New York's.

Whether national or local, the funeral and the attendant memorial ceremonies are representative of the kind of highly sentimentalized, religious, patriotic event that was so typical of ritualized mourning in the Victorian era. However, for Victorians in general, and for the Civil War generation in particular, the relationship between the private person or citizen and public life, as represented by U. S. Grant—and in this case, his dead body on display in New York's City Hall, or within the catafalque in the parade, or in a blown-up illustration in an obscure veterans' hall—was profoundly meaningful. "No pen could touch the depth of that spectacle," wrote one awed witness to Grant's funeral procession. "Men without whose names the history of America cannot be written, watched the great soldiers of the North and South reunited over the corpse of the foremost warrior of the continent."[87] The obituaries for Grant reveal a desire to analyze with some precision not only the meaning of his life and death, but also to bestow nobility on the era in which he lived, and the country at large. They linked Grant's idealized individual characteristics with the traits that every American might possess—simplicity, honesty, and a devotion to democracy. These traits explained both his wartime achievements and the persistence he displayed during his presidential struggles and his postwar travails. "The career of this great man," advised a eulogist, "is not fully measured until it is set amidst the great conflicts through which God is bringing in His Kingdom of truth and love." Another claimed that "his military character . . . contributed to his military genius."[88] The conventions of mourning and loss connected private sentiments and sadness to public commemorations and political concerns. Elements of the "Pageantry of Woe," such as processions, black crepe, memorial cards, pins, flowers, and so on invested individual citizens with a public role to express personal loss, and, just as important, a chance to claim their place in national history.[89]

North and South, veterans and their families were haunted by the tragedy and loss of the war, and their feelings had repercussions in every aspect of public and private life, nowhere more prominently or profoundly than in the events surrounding Grant's death and funeral. The funeral demonstrated the creative tension that exists between the past and the present, in which a familiar history is reworked to accommodate new meanings. This is especially true of the American Civil War, where individual memory was linked with the collective historical memory in powerfully evocative ways. Many scholars have analyzed the impact of the historical memory of the Civil War on art, culture, and politics in the nineteenth and twentieth centuries. Their work delineates the myriad ways in which historical memory has been artificially constructed to suit the needs of different groups. Often history was used to legitimate an elitist, racist, exclusive view of American society. Significantly, there is general agreement that all historical memory is as much about the present as it is about the past. Historians persuasively argue that traditions are "invented," that mainstream and popular history favored white over black and men over women, and that the elevation of one kind of collective memory inevitably built on the suppression of others.

The creation of a collective historical memory of the war to the generation who lived through it was a profound and meaningful exercise. This exercise should not be dismissed as simple oppression, escapism, or nostalgia. Millions of ordinary Americans cared deeply about the war's history and sought to memorialize it. They understood the symbols and achievements of Union victory not only as articulated by their leaders, but by their local organizations as well. Members of the GAR's Custer Post No. 6 of Tacoma, Washington, expressed their sentiments on the war and on Grant:

> That we recognize that the fame of the Union Army and volunteer soldier, which has become the wonder and admiration of the world is largely due to the gallant and brave hero whose military career was without spot or error and who was always triumphant. . . . That while with his brilliant and successful civil service to the nation, which will be gratefully remembered as long as the republic endures, we are content yet for his pre-eminence as winner of hard fought battles. In the interests of human freedom and perpetuation of our glorious union his memory will remain with us, fragrant, bright and dear forever; and his name be engraved upon our hearts as the greatest, grandest hero the world ever saw.[90]

Another GAR post, the Robert Anderson Post of York, Nebraska, sent the Grant family a handwritten copy of their resolutions that demonstrated how cherished was the memory of the sacrifices of the men who had fought and died, and of the man who led them: "We will guard faithfully the record of his fame and the merit which made him the most illustrious Commander of his time, whose leadership gave victory to a cause founded upon the unity of the American nation and the liberty of the people."[91] Just a month before his death, Grant sent a message to the annual GAR encampment in June of 1885: "Tell the boys that they probably will never look into my face again, nor hear my voice, but they are engraven on my heart, and I love them as my children."[92] Members of GAR posts from all over the country paid their own expenses to march in Grant's funeral procession in New York City. It is hardly surprising that the GAR and other veterans' organizations, such as those of the Armies of the Tennessee, Potomac, Cumberland, and Ohio, enthusiastically commemorated the legacy of "their" general on August 8, 1885, and as long as they lived. But within twenty-five years, most of the Union veterans would be dead. Perhaps feeling history's cold shoulder, and clearly reaching the limits of his capacity to withstand sentimental outpourings toward the South, William Sherman huffed to his friend Grenville Dodge, "The line of Union and Rebel, of loyalty and treason, should be kept always distinct." Dodge replied, "As long as our veterans live it will be; but the tendency all the time is, to wipe out history, to forget it, forgive, excuse

George G. Meade GAR Post, Philadelphia, honors "Our Hero." Note that the celebration of the Union Cause includes appreciation of southern involvement in the funeral. (U.S. Instantaneous Photographic Co. [Boston, 1885]; reproduced by permission of The Huntington Library, San Marino, California)

and soften, and when all the soldiers pass from this age it will be easy to skip into the idea, that one side was as good as the other."[93]

## "The grief is as widespread as the Union"

Saturday, August 8, was the day set aside for a national commemoration that would be observed in many places in the South. White southerners echoed Fitzhugh Lee, remembering Grant as the magnanimous victor at Appomattox as they contemplated the meaning of his death. Analyzing southern reaction to Grant's death, the New York Tribune intoned, "The South Remembers only the Manly Soldier."[94] A reporter described commonplace scenes: "Throughout the entire South yesterday universal respect was paid to the memory of General Grant. Funeral services were held in every prominent city and town, all of which were participated in by prominent ex-Confederates. At Chattanooga, Tennessee, members of the Grand Army of the Republic marched arm-in-arm with ex-Confederates to the memorial services."[95] As in the North, citizens draped buildings in black, closed businesses, fired cannon, formed processions, and scheduled church services. In Richmond, Virginia, flags flew at half-mast, and "the Richmond Howitzers at sunrise fired guns on Capitol Square, and this was continued every thirty minutes."[96] Memorial pageants were held in Baltimore, Louisville, Memphis, Galveston, and Dallas. These events featured the pairing of ex-Confederate units with ex-Union ones, ex-Confederate ministers with ex-Union ones, and so on, in a show of unity. Five thousand gathered in Vicksburg, Mississippi, to offer a memorial to the city's former conqueror.[97] As the South Carolina News and Courier expressed it: "Had his life ended but a few years since, the mourning for the great leader would have been more or less sectional in its manifestation. Dying as he now dies, the grief is as widespread as the Union, and the sorrow as national as his fame. In his last days, he was the foremost citizen of the United States."[98]

The national figure remembered by the South was the hero of Appomattox, the magnanimous general who gave Johnny Reb back his horse and, symbolically, his right to begin his life again as a welcomed citizen of a restored Union. John S. Wise, a Confederate veteran and politician from Virginia, explained:

> Between Grant and the Confederate Soldier, even in time of war, there was ever a feeling of mutual respect, and much that was akin to kindness. Towards Grant, for gentleness and magnanimity which surprised and touched them inexpressibly, there went forth from the hearts of the

Typical portrayal of
southern reaction
to Grant's death.
(Grant Monument
Association Archives,
New York City)

"THE SOLID SOUTH."

soldiers of the Army of Northern Virginia, even at the hour of their surrender to him, a feeling which they entertained towards no other Federal
Commander. Thenceforth, there sprung up between them and him, a
kindness which grew and waxed stronger as the years rolled on, until,
when he died, his coffin bore as many flowers of the South as of the
North; every State of the Union stood around his bier; and the old Confederate veteran had a feeling at his heart such as he had not known
since he stacked arms at Appomattox, or wept at the tidings that Lee was
Dead.[99]

The Woman's Christian Association of Utica, New York, editorialized in
a local newspaper: "There must be a sad satisfaction in seeing how now, all
men, of every party, and of every section from one end to the other of our
regenerated Union, unite to do him reverence who saved it from destruction."[100] U. S. Grant's legacy of Christian mercy and kindness was the one
on which both northern and southern white Americans could agree, and
which provided the basis for the emotional reunionism of the funeral and
its role in cementing the nation even more tightly together.

### "Freedom had no stronger champion"

The white northern public accommodated honoring the Union Cause (unity and freedom) within a strongly reconciliationist sentiment. The Reverend C. L. Woodworth's eulogy delivered on August 8 in Watertown, Massachusetts, commended the lessening of sectional differences but reminded his audience of the role Grant played in ending slavery: "In this awful reckoning Abraham Lincoln was God's mouth to proclaim liberty to the captive, and Ulysses Simpson Grant was God's right arm to smite the fetters from the slave." Union general Charles Devens, a former abolitionist, emphasized emancipation over reunion in his tribute: "As he was the chieftain so he was the representative of the Federal Army; that army which, springing from the people itself, vindicated the integrity of the American Union, swept from its States the curse of slavery and lifted a nation to a higher and nobler life."[101]

African American commemorations emphasized emancipation and its benefits. Black veterans, ministers, journalists, and politicians stressed General Grant the liberator of their people, and President Grant the political deliverer of suffrage and of the protection of liberty and freedom in peacetime. A black-run newspaper announced a July 27, 1885, "Meeting of Sorrow, held by the Colored Citizens of Birmingham, Alabama," while a similar gathering met at the Colored Methodist Episcopal church in Brownsville, Tennessee. "He was truly a great man—called by God to do the work of a patriot," intoned the Reverend T. J. Searcy at the Brownsville service. The newspaper account described how black veterans who served under Grant during the war "spoke of him as a father and as the greatest benefactor of our race."[102] Another eulogist claimed "Lincoln signed the emancipation proclamation. Grant made emancipation a fact. What wonder that in the negro's heart the two names lie side by side." The distinguished African American leader John Mercer Langston offered up his assessment: "General Grant is the American statesman to whom especially belongs the honor of inducting the colored citizen of the United States into national official life."[103] Langston, unlike his white counterparts, did not mention Appomattox, but instead remembered Grant's firm support of the Fifteenth Amendment and his successful prosecution of the Ku Klux Klan. A former slave, Kate Drumgoold, described Grant in her autobiography: "Another one who will ever be shining bright in the hearts and minds of the whole negro race, and what shall I say of him who lead us to the greatest victory the world has ever known—Ulysses S. Grant, the loved of all nations and the pride of all lands; he whom the world admires, to call the blessed, who mourned for this land to see the end, and God did help him in ways that man know not, save himself and his God."[104]

Black Union veterans such as the members of the GAR's John A. Andrew Post, No. 186 (Colored) marched in the New York procession, and such units were represented in a majority of northern processions and in many southern ones as well.[105] This participation fit into a larger pattern. John Neff, Barbara Gannon, and Donald Schaffer have explored the progressive stance toward race shown in the GAR, the only major social organization in the nineteenth century that welcomed African Americans consistently on a basis of social and political equality.[106] In the North, and to a lesser extent in the South, integrated posts were common. This contention runs counter to much of the received scholarly wisdom positing an automatic white racism, even among former comrades in the war. It is true that the handshake extended by white to black northern veterans was tragically limited. It emphasized the benefits of emancipation brought by the war, but did not support either social equality (in the North) or continued northern intervention in southern affairs to ensure political equality. There were also many all-black GAR posts, but Gannon's research finds that the majority were formed by proud consent rather than as a result of deliberate segregation. Black and white ex-soldiers shared the same reverence for their sacrifice and contributions in the Civil War, and they united on issues important to veterans' health and welfare, such as pensions. They also joined in many of the parades and reunions that appeared with increasingly regularity on the GAR calendar in the 1880s and 1890s. Most of the northern Memorial Day activities were integrated affairs, and in the ex-Confederate states, "The African-American community honored the Union Army's dead of both races in the South because they were the only part of the local community that observed the day."[107]

At Grant's national funeral, African Americans were very well represented indeed, and in a few southern memorial services, they appeared to be the only participants. In Charleston, South Carolina, the remembrance was entirely run by the African American community. A Charleston newspaper reported that "The First Brigade, National Guards (colored) paraded the principal streets, with full ranks, with colors, draped and arms reversed . . . [then] . . . attended the memorial services at Zion (colored) Presbyterian Church where a memorial service was preached. . . . 2,000 people there." The college town of Charlottesville, Virginia, announced the closure of businesses, banks, and government offices on the day of the funeral, but the only ceremonies described were those held by black churches. In Atlanta,

Georgia, church bells and fire bells rang throughout the city, while the biggest procession was when "the colored military paraded the streets" and huge crowds attended the "Big Bethel Colored Church where Bishop Turner spoke." In Savannah, Georgia, "memorial services were held in the colored churches. . . . Flags were at half mast, and half hour guns were fired from sunrise to sunset by the colored artillery."[108] When southern parades and processions were racially mixed, memorial services were held in separate places. Likely, African American churchgoers heard very different eulogies and tributes from those heard in white venues. The Rev. W. B. Derrick of Bethel Church on Sullivan Street in New York City provided a typical eulogy of Grant's achievements that stressed the fruits of freedom, not reconciliation. "We consider ourselves a part and parcel of this Nation," he observed, "and feel our loss with as much tenderness as any other part." Derrick summarized Grant's real contribution thus: "He was a leader of leaders; he was a great and noble man. Freedom had no stronger champion."[109]

The reaction to Ulysses S. Grant's death reveals much about a generation's connection between the memory of an event (in this case the Civil War), a commemoration (in this case Grant's funeral), and the articulation of a new, or renewed, basis for American nationalism. A close examination of the funeral activities, however, demonstrates a more complex picture than an uncomplicated orgy of approval for reconciliation. Beneath the rising tide of sectional harmony relentlessly pushed by the political elites and the press lurked still-strong sectional animosities. The funeral was largely a northern affair. Among northern participants, praise for the Union Cause predominated, and among white southern participants, alongside praise for the reunited nation, loyalty to the Lost Cause was strongly expressed, while African Americans embraced the emancipation memory. What if any attitudes were changed? Despite differences in responses, the deathwatch and funeral of U. S. Grant exemplified the desire of the white nation to forge an emotional bond of Unionism. We see it in Grant's longing for reconciliation when he lay dying, and in the response of the northern and southern political and religious leaders who shaped the funeral ceremonies. Grant's funeral offered a window for looking at how some southerners viewed a more thorough national unity based upon mutual affection and respect.

## "The Union His Monument"

The 1880s provided a propitious moment for the South to reintegrate itself into the nation as sectional issues seemed to recede in favor of other, more pressing, concerns. Proponents of the "New South," led by the Atlanta-based newspaper editor Henry Grady, accepted the romanticism of the Lost Cause but tempered its conservative, backward message. Grady and the more progressive elements of the South sought to integrate their region with an industrializing national economy. Intent on expanding an economic base beyond cotton cultivation and manufacturing to promote a South vitalized by railroad, timber, coal, and iron industries, they stressed the region's willingness to seek harmonious economic, social, and political equity in the postwar Union.[110] And the election of 1884 paved the way for the kind of orchestrated harmony demonstrated at Grant's funeral. In that presidential contest, the Republicans and their standard bearer, Senator James G. Blaine of Maine, built a campaign around the positive virtues of the tariff and the prosperity it would bring to the whole country, rather than conducting another waving-the-bloody-shirt campaign. Race and sectional issues, however, still made a campaign appearance. There were politically inspired race riots in Louisiana, and many reports of the suppression of Republican black voters in other areas of the South were publicized and investigated. Some southern blacks were said to be fearful that if a Democrat were elected president, they would be reenslaved, an idea evidently encouraged by a few Republicans.[111]

Blaine was plagued by charges of corruption, and he was anathema to liberal Republicans, the so-called "Mugwumps," who once again, as they had in the election of 1872, broke with the Republican Party. This time, they supported Democratic governor Grover Cleveland of New York. Cleveland had established a record as a civil service reformer and swayed "independent" Republicans, who joined forces with northern and southern Democrats to defeat Blaine by a very slim margin.[112] President Cleveland, who had hired a substitute during the war, assumed office in January 1885, pledging to heal any lingering wounds of the war and the Reconstruction period. He also pledged to protect the rights of black citizens in the South. While the latter pledge was ignored, Cleveland did appoint a number of prominent ex-Confederates to his cabinet. Indeed, ex-Confederates were now common in the cabinet, in the House, in the Senate, and, of course, in statehouses across the South. The Democratic presidential victory, the first since 1856, signaled a new and important phase of political conciliation for the nation. "The Southern states," remarked Alabama educator, minister, and politician Jabez Curry, "feel that the Union is really restored." The happy result of the contest, continued Curry, "produced a satisfaction, nay, an exhilaration of feeling in the South which has not been felt for many years," creating "an opportunity for the display of the patriotism which really exists."[113]

Southern Democrats had every reason to feel triumphant. They had assured the North that they would treat their "colored people" kindly, and northerners accepted their word. "The race question is eliminated from national politics, and with it sectionalism is destined to a final disappearance," crowed a *New York Times* editorial.[114] As this representative quotation indicates, northern newspapers and political observers believed it a sign of progress that southern Democrats could now be trusted to take care of their own problems, particularly their racial problems. The bitterly partisan politics of Reconstruction led to the withdrawal of northern support for black suffrage and economic independence. Many in the North, fearful of labor disturbances and popular antibusiness movements, moved quickly to forge cross-sectional ties that emphasized reconciliation and downplayed the controversial issues that gave rise to the Civil War. Now, as in the antebellum era, the political parties could disagree on partisan issues that would not be sectional in basis but national: tariffs, civil service reform, and the monetary question.

President Cleveland and the Democrats clashed with Republicans, but clearly the danger of breaking up the nation over sectional conflict had passed. And so, out of a newly forged political and cultural consensus came the first agreed-upon revisionist view of the Civil War. Northern and southern whites argued that secession was wrongheaded but honorable; the war was fought between brave soldiers who, on both sides, believed in their respective causes; Reconstruction was a failure and a sordid page in the nation's history, best forgotten. There were many dissenters to this interpretation, but their voices would dim as the years passed. Perhaps one of the most pointed scenes of political reconciliation came when the newly installed President Cleveland happily signed the commission to restore General Grant to the retired list, so that he could get his pension. This commission, passed by the previous Congress, was delivered to the White House by the previous administration's secretary of war, Robert Todd Lincoln.[115] As Gaines M. Foster observed, "the election of Cleveland helped convince southerners that they had a political future within the union."[116] In other words, 1884 promoted a sectional harmony between North and South that reflected the South's full postwar position in the nation. The year 1885 was the perfect time for U. S. Grant, that symbol of a hard northern victory and a hard northern peace, to die, and to be commemorated by the whole country.

Less known and less appreciated is how Grant's funeral, *as an event*, was interpreted in a similar manner. Grant himself did not abandon his deepest beliefs about what the Union Cause represented. Indeed, he never backed down either in public or private on his firmly held belief that slavery was the cause of the war and that emancipation was a glorious, if unfulfilled, consequence of the conflict.[117] Yet Grant's actions before his death spoke most powerfully to white reconciliation, with the overwhelming sentiment stressing reunion and sectional peace. An editorial in the *New York Herald* encapsulated this idea: "There is nothing more gratifying to the nonpartisan American than the rapid change which is going on in the Southern States. . . . The great soldier who won this tremendous victory for our institutions lies dead, and over his bier are bending, not the North alone, but the North and South in common sorrow and admiration. As we drape the city in token of our sorrow at the nation's loss, we wonder that the cataclysm and the recovery should be embraced in the last twenty-five years of that worn out life." The editorial concluded: "General Grant's best monument will be the grateful remembrance on the part of the whole people that he drew the sword when his country was in danger and sheathed it the moment the danger was over."[118] While white southern demonstrations of goodwill toward Grant faded after his funeral, the nationalism forged by reconciliation would be on full display in the building and dedication of Grant' Tomb in New York City.

## chapter six

# The Nation's Greatest Hero Should Rest in the Nation's Greatest City

Before it was the General Grant National Memorial it was officially called Grant Monument. Visitors dubbed it "Grant's Tomb," and the nickname stuck. Commanding a hill on the north end of Manhattan's Riverside Park, 270 feet above the Hudson River, the huge 160-foot gleaming granite and marble mausoleum is one of the most impressive Civil War monuments ever built and the largest tomb in North America. Opened with great fanfare on the seventy-fifth anniversary of Grant's birthday on April 27, 1897, and funded entirely by popular subscription, the neoclassical building was designed deliberately to inspire awe. "His grave, his monument, his fame," predicted a contemporary, "will transcend all other attractions." Another predicted that people would forever learn "lessons of patriotism and fidelity from his monument."[1] Grant's Tomb quickly became a sacred pilgrimage spot for Union veterans and their families from all over the country. Many thousands gathered for regularly scheduled ceremonies on Grant's birthday, Memorial Day, and the Fourth of July. Presidents and other prominent politicians selected the spot for speeches and important announcements. Foreign dignitaries visited frequently to pay their respects. Until 1916 it remained New York's most visited monument attracting 500,000–600,000 people annually, outdistancing the Statue of Liberty, and it maintained extremely high levels of visitation to 1929.[2]

That year, aged survivors of the Grand Army of the Republic, the North's most powerful veteran organization, conducted their final ceremony at the tomb. The veterans, their families, and their immediate descendants declined in number afterward, and the monument languished. Attendance dropped dramatically through the decades. Where the monument once stood alone, now the surrounding built landscape, including the towering Gothic Riverside Church, crowded it out, diminishing its presence. The lovely and remote rural park in which it was placed in the 1890s turned into a dangerous crime-ridden neighborhood, called Morningside Heights, in the 1960s and 1970s. Additionally, the structure designed to summon feelings of reverence and contemplation, seemed old-fashioned and ugly to modern sensibilities. One critic called it "clumsy, tasteless," while another described it as "pompous beyond even the requirements of a Mausoleum for a national hero."[3]

The Grant Monument Association, the private organization responsible for its upkeep, could not raise enough money to stop the building's deterioration. Nor did the situation change much for the better when the National Park Service took over the monument's care in 1958. By 1988, one scholar wrote that Grant's Tomb was the "least appreciated national monument in the country." Another observer was more graphic, calling Grant's Tomb

Crowd at the 1897 dedication of Grant's Tomb (National Park Service)

a "graffiti-scarred hangout for drug dealers and muggers."[4] The defaced monument offered little to the casual history buff.

Unlike at other important national park sites, there were, and are, no visitors' center to interpret Grant's career and no restrooms to accommodate tourist comfort. As interest in Civil War sites increased in the 1990s due in part to Ken Burns's PBS documentary, *The Civil War*, the monument's decay became a minor, and then a major, scandal. Frank Scaturro, a Columbia University student volunteer at the tomb, went public with a scathing report charging neglect and abuse by the federal government that in turn generated media attention.[5] A 1994 *New York Times* editorial entitled "Dishonor for a Hero President" enumerated a sad list of woes that befell his tomb and called for the National Park Service to redress what had become a disgrace attracting widespread attention.[6] Family descendants, led by Ulysses S. Grant Dietz, the great-great-grandson of the general, threatened to remove Grant's body from New York City and reinter his remains (along with Julia's) in Illinois, when that state's legislature offered a burial

Postcard of Grant Monument, with Riverside Church (built 1930) in the foreground (author's collection)

place. In a Manhattan courtroom, the family charged that the tomb was "neglected and being abused by graffiti writers, skateboarders who use its stairs as a ramp, drug users and homeless people who urinate on the monument's wall." Responding to a chorus of protests, the Park Service embarked on a $1.8 million restoration project finished in time for the 100th anniversary commemoration of the monument's opening on April 27, 1997.[7]

Despite the improvements, Grant's Tomb remains an undervisited, underfunded, and ignored national monument. Where thousands once visited, now only hundreds do, except for busloads of schoolchildren. Why is this so? The vagaries of New York's urban development combine with another plausible answer.[8] Grant did not evolve into the mythological figure envisioned by the monument's supporters. In 1897, Grant was equal in history and memory to Abraham Lincoln. He has not been so regarded for many decades. One historian observed, "At the dawn of the twentieth century, Grant's Tomb stood as a central site of Civil War Commemoration, for national as well as New York audiences."[9] Lincoln transcended the Civil War, but Grant did not. Many if not most New Yorkers, as well as out-of-town tourists, are largely unaware of Grant's achievements. They do not know

Graffiti-scarred
monument, 1970s
(Frank Scaturro,
Grant Monument
Association)

where Grant's Tomb is and most do not care. In the 1990s, people expressed their opposition to using federal, state, or local funds for the tomb's improvement. "Are we so cowardly," a *New York Times* writer demanded, "that we can't stand up to a man who's been dead for a century? Are we going to let a corpse extort money from us?" Furthermore, the same author declared, "At a time when schools and parks are badly neglected, we shouldn't spend millions renovating a building that attracts so few visitors and has so little to do with the city's character."[10]

The columnist John Tierney articulated the above sentiments in an article published in the *New York Times Magazine* urging the removal of Grant's body from the tomb. When that occurred, he suggested, the monument could be turned into a memorial for the fallen of World War II. To the old question from Groucho Marx's quiz show, "Who is buried in Grant's

Recent photo of Grant Monument — the Hudson River and the Henry Hudson Parkway are to the left. (National Park Service)

Tomb?," Tierney sneered, "The correct answer today is, Who Cares?"[11] That attitude, magnified many times, is why the modern public response to the General Grant National Monument falls amazingly short of the expectations held for it by the Civil War generation. In the late nineteenth century, New York and New Yorkers embraced Grant in life and in death. At his death in 1885, Grant was world famous — his funeral in New York *seemed* an unforgettable spectacle. What a contrast between now and then. Now, New Yorkers turn a cold shoulder to the monument and to General Grant. Then, everyone knew him and knew that without his victories at places like Shiloh and Vicksburg and Chattanooga and staying the course through places like Spotsylvania and Cold Harbor and Petersburg, the Union might never have been preserved.

But this is the story of the building of Grant's Tomb, not its decline. Immediately after Grant's death, there was a concerted effort made by political, military, and cultural leaders ensuring that the "Great Commander" was permanently entombed in an edifice worthy of his legacy. New York City emerged as the permanent burial site. Amid often-bitter debates regarding the so-called New York Takeover, funds were raised, plans were approved, an architect was hired, and a monument was erected. Public art emerges from a complex and contentious process involving businesspeople, politicians, city and state government officials, artists, and the general public, organized into interest groups such as the Grand Army of the Republic. In examining the building of Grant's Tomb, attention is drawn to the relationship between memory and history expressed in monuments—a topic that has attracted much attention among historians—especially in monuments like Grant's that are deliberately designed to foster a sense of national identity and unity.[12]

## "Grant's Memorial: What Shall It Be?"

Grant's Tomb, like most major "national" monuments, took a long time to finish, evoked controversy at every stage of its development, and finally, at its completion, fell short of expectations. Despite such difficulties, there was never any doubt that Grant's monument would be built. Some background is necessary. Monuments are structures that honor an individual or an event. They range from the unaffected gravestone in a lonely cemetery to an elaborate mausoleum, the latter serving both as tomb and memorial. Buildings, sculptures, and battlefields are also designated as monuments. Before 1865 Americans had commemorated important events and persons in history, but the Civil War, understandably, brought a huge increase in memorials and dramatically reshaped America's "landscape of memory." The sheer scale of tragic death and heroic sacrifice drove the honoring of both leaders and ordinary soldiers by erecting statues and other structures in many venues. Where before there were few, now there were thousands of such memorials. A relatively small number of Civil War monuments were dedicated in the 1860s and 1870s. The rapid expansion began twenty to twenty-five years after Appomattox, coinciding with the building of Grant's Tomb and rising to a climax in the 1890s. Humble, inexpensive statues honoring the common soldier predominated, although many grander monuments offered tribute to military and political heroes, while still others were elaborate commemorative arches straddling urban thoroughfares. Typically, monuments grand or humble were placed in battlefields and cemeteries, small-town squares and splendid urban plazas.[13]

Civil War monuments were built sometimes with public expenditures and sometimes with private financing but often with a combination of the two. The federal government backed the construction of Washington, D.C.'s, first two Civil War monuments (to Maj. Gen. John A. Rawlins and Lt. Gen. Winfield Scott), both erected in 1874. Individual states frequently bankrolled the ubiquitous "regimental" monuments dotting preserved battlefields such as those at Gettysburg, Pennsylvania, and Vicksburg, Mississippi. The victorious North had the resources to build many more than the South, although that changed by the 1880s. David Blight claimed that in the former Confederacy, "by the 1890s hardly a city square, town green, or even some one-horse crossroads lacked a Civil War memorial of some kind."[14] In both sections, veterans' groups, church or civic associations, and women's organizations held fund-raising events and donation drives to pay for statues commemorating war-related activities. Unveilings featured patriotic ceremonies and speeches, reverberating with political and social meaning, and revealing much about the war's legacy to the generation who lived through the era.[15]

The Grant Memorial easily fit and even surpassed the requirements for an important national monument. The man who led the northern armies to victory and guided the country through Reconstruction both as general and as a two-term president deserved the most awe-inspiring memorial the country could furnish. "The interest in General Grant's death has been very great," explained former president Rutherford B. Hayes. Hayes, who had ended the war as a brevetted major general, made two speeches on the day of Grant's death at different GAR posts in Ohio. On both occasions, he urged veterans to support construction a memorial that would "be worthy of the Republic, worthy of General Grant, and worthy of the righteous cause of which he was the most illustrious soldier." Hayes wrote a letter published by the New York newspapers and carried nationwide in which he pleaded for a concerted effort by northern veterans in raising funds to erect a national monument at whatever site was chosen for Grant's burial. "If the matter is promptly pushed by the Grand Army of the Republic while the public mind is intensely interested in all that concerns Gen. Grant," Hayes noted, "there is every reason for confidence that a national monument can be built."[16] Hayes's comments were echoed in numerous public forums enjoining the issue of how to honor Grant's legacy.

The results of one forum appeared in several *North American Review* "round table" discussions with selected public figures, cultural critics, painters, sculptors, and architects. The stated purpose was to answer the question, "Grant's Memorial: What Shall It Be?"[17] Although the combined background of the discussants revealed an elitist perspective, they also shared their generation's war experiences. Architect Henry Van Brunt had served as a Union soldier, and Democrat Horatio Seymour had been elected wartime governor of New York. Many, like sculptor Launt Thompson, had completed significant Civil War commemorative projects. They expressed a belief in Grant's importance to history as shown in this commonly expressed sentiment, "We should erect to his memory the grandest mausoleum or temple of modern times."[18] For all, Grant was a towering national icon whose achievement in preserving the Union deserved one of the greatest memorials in history. The published comments of these professional artists and prominent public figures illuminated the widely shared assumption that drove a similar but much broader public discussion on the monument's design.

Reflecting the tone of many funeral orations, the roundtables heavily emphasized Grant's magnanimity at Appomattox. According to the painter and author Clarence Cook, the monument's national focus automatically lessened the impact of Grant's battlefield exploits in favor of the harmonious, peaceful reunion of North and South. Cook summed up his position: "The military career of General Grant being safe in the hands of history, there ought not to appear upon his monument the name of any battle of our Civil War." The well-known artist John La Farge expanded on Cook's viewpoint: "Both the South and North and the whole Union should be represented, inside or out, of the building."[19] Recommending a monument of colossal proportions, several participants urged that Grant's memorial herald a new era in American art. Karl Gerhardt, the young sculptor who molded Grant's death mask boldly proclaimed, "Let the memorial be worthy of the man, the nation, and American art, equally and alike." The painter W. H. Beard declared that Grant's monument should "fix an epoch in American art—a most fitting time to give the nation its first (single statues excepted) great monument." Grant's memorial presented a unique opportunity to meld art and architecture because it encompassed both memorial and tomb. The Garfield Memorial (1885–90) located in Lake View Cemetery in Cleveland, Ohio, was the country's first large-scale mausoleum. Still in the early stages of construction, the plan for Garfield's memorial was mentioned as a possible model for Grant's. Launt Thompson—who produced statues of Winfield Scott in Washington, D.C., and Ambrose Burnside in Providence, Rhode Island—urged a mausoleum over other memorial forms. In the end, his vision for Grant's monument proved remarkably accurate: "As the monument under consideration is to be National, and to serve the double purpose of honoring the hero's memory and protecting his mortal part for future ages, I would suggest a mausoleum, of Roman or Grecian Doric architecture, solid and simple, crowned with a dome, surmounted by an allegorical statue."[20]

In their comments, Gerhardt, Beard, and Thompson suggested that the tomb blend European neo-classicism with American-inspired themes and resources. The so-called Beaux-Arts movement of the late nineteenth century did not reject Old World forms but rather injected New World creativity and exuberance into monumental buildings and structures.[21] The architects' magazine *Building* offered advice: "In the natural order of the career of such a prosperous people, it is certain that they are turning to outward manifestations to commemorate the deeds of our great men, and to satisfy the natural human love of display, and the desire to beautify the public parks, squares and highways. . . . To this end the monumental spirit latent in each true architect should be nourished by a faithful, earnest study of the purest classic work, to catch its spirit." Indeed, roundtable critics suggested that Grant's resting place should be comparable in majesty to the magnificent tombs of European military heroes such as Nelson, Napoleon, and Wellington. Beard revealed the prevailing sentiments and hopes of himself and his colleagues when he said, "A loved and honored son of the nation has gone out from among us. . . . There is no doubt but the nation at large will pour out from its abundance ample means to erect a structure adequate for the purpose. . . . It should be simple, though full; pure, grand, unique." A cynic might dismiss Beard's words as an exercise in empty rhetoric. Monuments dedicated to great heroes evoke passionate declamations and fervent hopes before the reality of restricted budgets appear. Nevertheless, conversation about Grant's memorial continued unabated within and without the lofty halls of academe and sumptuous boardrooms, spilling over to newspapers, veterans' meetings, and private correspondence. On August 12, 1885, a reporter captured the tone of the debates engaging a public eager to shape Grant's memorial, writing, "It is fitting, therefore, that it should be a modern and not a classic edifice, and that its emblems and friezes and tablatures should represent scenes from the life of the nineteenth century and on the physical plane of the American continent." Considerable newspaper space was given to the imminent monument, right alongside the endless newspaper columns devoted to the story of Grant's death and funeral.[22]

### The New York Takeover

Before any memorial could take shape, Julia and her family had to decide on a place of interment. Grant himself did not strongly favor one place over another. His only desire was that Julia be buried next to him. Grant wrote a note on June 23 to Fred mentioning three possible burial sites, among them New York City, "because the people of that city befriended me in my need."[23] Interment in New York would be breaking with tradition, however, as previous presidents had been buried in their state of birth. After Grant's death, immediate competition broke out among various towns in Illinois and Ohio and Washington, D.C. Above all others, New Yorkers were organized and aggressive in pressing their case. Just hours after Grant passed away, a telegram arrived from New York's mayor, William R. Grace, offering land for Grant's burial in any city park the family designated. In a letter later published in the papers, Grace wrote to Julia: "I have already communicated to you . . . the informal desire of the authorities of this city to have National honor done to it by making it the last resting place of General Grant." New York was first, but its offer was quickly followed with one from the Soldiers' Home in D.C., offering a prime interment site overlooking the capital city. Soon the family was inundated with applicants. As Fred remembered, "Upon the death of General Grant . . . many telegrams were immediately received, containing offers for various pieces of ground for his last resting-place."[24]

Fred asked Mayor Grace to send a representative to Mount McGregor to make a full report to the family. In a meeting held on July 24, a city official guaranteed that land in a public park would be set aside upon which a "grand tomb" would be built.[25] Credit for swaying the Grant family in New York's favor must go in part to Democrat William Russell Grace. Born in Ireland, he was a wealthy businessman who became New York's first Roman Catholic mayor in 1880. He served with distinction for two terms, running as an independent in 1884. A deft and charismatic reform politician who opposed the Tammany Hall machine, Grace was supported by many Republicans, and his courteous missives to Julia and her family were warmly received. Grace's considerable skills went to making sure that the sprawling and contentious New York political establishment presented a united front for securing Grant's monument. The Park Board, the Board of Aldermen, and the Board of Commissioners all passed resolutions that enabled the city's offer to be as pleasing as possible for Grant's family.[26] Fred recalled, "It was decided that the offer made by New York was the most desirable one, as it included the guarantee . . . that his wife should be provided with a last resting-place by his side—there, this offer was accepted." Ending the suspense, Fred Grant (serving as the official family spokesman) announced to the public that his father would be buried in New York City. Empire State newspapers expressed jubilance upon hearing the decision. The *New York Times*'s headline blared: "A Most Fitting Burial Place: The Nation's Greatest Hero Should Rest in the Nation's Greatest City."[27]

New York papers also joyously reported a national consensus. Testimony from eight-six New Yorkers—the mayor, other politicians and government officials, businessmen, bankers, ex-generals, and lawyers among them—referred to Gotham as the nation's "real capital," while Washington was dismissed as the nation's "nominal capital."[28] New Yorkers stood on solid ground. In their massive study of New York's architectural and urban development, Robert Stern, Thomas Mellins, and David Fishman stated, "In the twenty-five years following the Civil War, New York had transformed itself into the nation's richest and most important city, surpassing its former rivals, Boston and Philadelphia." More tellingly, the authors claimed, "Given that New York was not a state capital, its sense of itself as the representative American city was critical, giving rise to what might be called its metropolitan destiny: New York saw itself as a quasi-independent political and cultural entity that was both a microcosm of and a model for the nation as a whole."[29] New York's explosive growth was aided by an ever-expanding infrastructure that drove building and development downtown and into the hinterlands. The profits generated by wealthy and philanthropic-minded businessmen built important cultural institutions and beautiful architectural landmarks such as the Metropolitan Museum of Art (1880) and the American Natural History Museum (1877). The Statue of Liberty (1886) and the Brooklyn Bridge (1883) in different ways demonstrated the economic, political, and industrial preeminence of the city. Manhattan's Central Park was the stunning jewel in New York's crown, completed just after the Civil War. These massive projects of civic triumphalism demonstrated that New York, passing the 1 million population mark, was already a cosmopolitan world-class city. It seemed only fitting to New Yorkers that General Grant, a national and international icon, would be buried and memorialized with a monument befitting and alongside the city's other landmarks.[30]

Pleased, Mayor Grace knew that the family's decision would not be final until they formally approved a site and signed a contract. Moving seamlessly into the next phase, he recommended the family consider "the prominent height in Riverside Park, on the banks of the Hudson."[31] The mayor believed that Central Park was unsuitable because it had already become so familiar to New Yorkers that a tomb would seem intrusive, possibly even offensive. Grace gave an interview to a reporter in which he waxed eloquent on the virtues of Riverside for Grant's burial place. He said that "the greatness of the man should call for a structure unique, and magnificent, to which the surroundings should be fitted, and that a place should be selected in which the monument could stand . . . as the only structure, in isolated grandeur."

Grace's view was supported by Parks Commissioner John D. Crimmins, who tersely stated, "Riverside is the proper place."[32] The family at first demurred. They reminded the mayor of General Grant's love for Central Park. They also objected to Riverside's remote location. The family's reservations were echoed by the *Times*. "It is here in the vernal beauty of Central Park," an editorial rhapsodized, "surrounded by the most peaceful and tender woodland scenery, yet lap in the arms of this great population . . . that the great soldier should rest at last."[33] After conferring with Julia, whose grief would keep her at Mount McGregor until after the funeral ceremonies, Fred and Jesse Grant left for the city. On July 27, officials arranged a tour of several possible interment sites. Besides the two Grant sons, the small delegation included trusted family friends Horace Porter, William T. Sherman, and former Colorado senator Jerome B. Chaffee, Grant's political ally, whose daughter Fannie married Ulysses Jr. (Buck).

The group visited several sites, mostly in Central Park and Riverside Park. As Grace anticipated, the former was deemed too noisy, while the latter was greeted with approval by one and all. After returning to Mount McGregor and consulting with his mother and family, Fred decided in favor of Riverside Park. The next day, July 28, the mayor received a telegram from Fred: "Mother Takes Riverside Park."[34] Approval for the scheme by the Board of Aldermen was immediately forthcoming, as was their approval of Julia's resting place next to Ulysses. Beautiful and rural, Riverside Park seemed an ideal location. It was also historical. In 1776 George Washington fought the battle of Harlem Heights within the environs. Officially established in 1873, Riverside Park was designed by Frederick Law Olmsted and Calvert Vaux. A local writer praised its serene beauty: "The view from this Mecca of the American traveler is one of the finest in the world—for thirty miles, on a clear day, up the Hudson toward West Point, and southward toward the Battery, and across the Bay to the Narrows. The East River and Long Island Sound may be seen in the East, and the Palisades, Fort Lee, and the bold, steep leafy shores of New Jersey on the West."[35]

Others were less enamored with the choice. Upon hearing the news, Grant's minister, the Reverend John Newman, blurted out, "Oh, it is such a lonely place there; and he was thoroughly a man of the people."[36] Some criticized the site as benefiting the wealthy, as at that time only carriages could get to Riverside Park, although soon public transportation improved access. A disgruntled doubter noted the barren look of much of the park, describing it as "a neglected strip of unimproved land" and intimating that pressures by city officials to increase real estate values might have played a role in its selection. Undoubtedly profit motives did play a role; the area was designated as early as the 1860s as a prime target of real estate development for the wealthy. Olmsted and Vaux both expressed concerns (soon assuaged) regarding placing Grant's memorial in a park meant for enjoyment and not solemn contemplation.[37]

## The Grant Monument Association

Mayor Grace proposed forming an organization to facilitate the planned monument while public sentiment "was at its highest." He sent letters to a carefully selected list of prominent New Yorkers requesting their support for a Grant memorial. More than eighty gentlemen attended a meeting on July 28, 1885, and on that day the Grant Monument Association was officially established, its members united in their goal to build "a great national monument which shall appropriately testify to future ages" for "the grandest character of the century."[38] Among the founders were former Republican president Chester A. Arthur, Cornelius Vanderbilt II, and powerful banker J. P. Morgan, the latter serving as treasurer. Although Republicans were well represented, the list also included New York City Democratic Party operative Samuel S. M. Barlow. Approximately six months later, the Grant Monument Association was officially incorporated by the state legislature, with twenty-nine trustees and four ex-officio members. The latter included the mayor of New York City and the governor of the state. Among the trustees were President Arthur, Hamilton Fish, and three prominent newspapermen—Charles Dana of the *Tribune*, James Gordon Bennett of the *Herald*, and Joseph Pulitzer of the *World*. Arthur served as president for several years, followed by a succession of dignitaries, including Vanderbilt, William Grace, and Horace Porter.[39]

The Grant Monument Association immediately announced a campaign to raise $1 million. This was an unprecedented sum, easily surpassing that raised for any previous memorial. Further details revealed that the entire cost of the monument would be borne by the private sector. Some marveled at the inappropriateness of the amount. "Why a million dollar monument . . . a memorial to the great soldier's great weakness?" protested an unhappy citizen, referring to Grant's infamous lack of business sense. Protests brushed aside, the Grant Monument Association's function was threefold: get the money, build the monument, and "maintain the structure after it was completed."[40] Past experiences with large memorial structures, such as the Bunker Hill Monument, or Lincoln's Springfield memorial, or the Washington Monument (completed in 1885 after forty years) suggested that the Grant Monument would experience typical delays and failures along the way, but in late July and early August of 1885 all signs seemed auspicious for a speedy outcome. There was even talk that the Grant Monument would be finished in five years. That prediction proved optimistic. The wealthy and prominent men occupying the association's top leadership roles did not have time to run an effective and efficient organization dedicated to fund-raising. Indeed, their failure to muster a quorum in many of the earliest, and most critical, executive committee meetings (between October 1885 and February 1886) seriously hampered the efficacy of fund-raising and drew much unfavorable notice in the press.

Appointed by Mayor Grace to the board of trustees, forty-one-year-old African American Richard Theodore Greener handled the day-to-day administration. Greener, elected to the salaried position of secretary, worked in office space donated by the Mutual Life Insurance Company in midtown Manhattan. Greener was the first black graduate of Harvard College, and his distinguished résumé included service as an educator, lawyer, professor, and diplomat.[41] As a high-profile leader in the African American community, Greener campaigned hard for the Republican Party in the early 1880s and professed admiration for President Grant, with whom he forged a personal acquaintance. Finding his salary inadequate for his large family's needs, he also served for several years as New York City's chief examiner of the Municipal Service Board. Greener's most important task by far was to raise money *nationally* for the "Grant Fund." His highest accomplishment came in mobilizing the black community to support the monument. Members of the African Methodist Episcopal Zion Church in New York sent in their contributions, and small donations poured in from many other states, as well as from the citizens of Monrovia, Liberia. One South Carolinian, Edwin J. Dickerson, explained why so many blacks sent money: "We are grateful to and appreciate General Grant for the valuable service which he rendered the erection of that great and glorious monument of freedom . . . of the American Negro."[42]

Greener and the Grant Fund enjoyed the unqualified support of the influential New York press. Whether Republican or Democrat, newspapermen happily served as the association's willing handmaiden in publicizing the Grant Fund. "An Appeal to the Country: The People asked to Aid in the erection of the Monument," ran an early headline. The reporter noted that the Monument Committee emerged from Mayor Grace's office to invite "the people of the United States to participate in the erection of a suitable memorial in honor of Gen. Grant by the contribution of such sums as they may feel able and willing to devote to this great purpose."[43] The name of every donor was printed in the papers, and the majority of contributions were sent to newspapers such as the *New York Tribune*, the *New York Times*, and the *New York World* and forwarded on to the association's offices. Larger amounts from wealthy businessmen and corporations were lavishly praised in print. Western Union provided the first significant contribution, $5,000, and, in addition, offered its lines free of charge for citizens who wished to wire funds. A popular device proved to be the issuance of an elaborate "certificate" thanking the donor. Most people sent modest sums ranging from pennies to $10. "Two Yankee Women" donated 20 cents, while "A German Who Gives up his Beer" contributed 15 cents. Often notice of a larger contribution was placed near that of smaller ones, evoking a poignant contrast. Rutherford Stuyvesant's $250 was listed next to "Johnny's Mite's" ten cents and five cents from "A poor Soldier's Orphan." Donations came from veterans from all over the country, including the states of Iowa, Louisiana, Pennsylvania, and Alabama.[44]

## Missteps and Controversies

The most cursory analysis of the contributions, however, revealed that, except among the African American populace, a clear majority of the subscriptions emanated from New York City, a troubling sign. The sad truth emerged that several weeks into the campaign only $50,000 had been raised, scandalously less than needed if the target of $1 million was going to be reached in a timely manner. A Connecticut paper stated the dilemma succinctly: "The New York Monument Committee have voted to raise one million dollars for a Grant Monument. They have raised about $50,000 which will probably be spent in sending begging letters to other parts of the country."[45] Knowledgeable supporters worried that a relatively brief window of opportunity existed for gathering funds expeditiously. In mid-August Rutherford Hayes warned in a private letter that "the golden moment has already passed," adding, "further delay imperils all. . . . Experience [with monuments] shows that the funds, if raised by popular subscription, must be obtained at once."[46] The association's campaign faltered badly despite the stupendous outpouring of love and affection for General Grant. To the astonishment of many New Yorkers, the monument's placement in their city posed a serious public relations dilemma, starting from the day the news broke. Simply put, a majority of Americans rejected New York's self-proclaimed status as a national city. They did not open their wallets for a Grant memorial that few, at least for now, expected to visit. An Indiana newspaper declared "we have not a cent for New York and would advise that not a dollar of help be sent to the millionaire city."[47] Jealousy, resentment, or frustration led to accusations that New York "seized" Grant's body for its own aggrandizement.

Sensing looming disaster, New York City–based journalists opened fire early with trenchant criticism. A *New York World* editorial lambasted the Grant Monument Association for being entirely made up of New Yorkers. If it was the national monument it pretended to be, the *World* asked scornfully, then why not recruit men from all over the country? The paper concluded: "If Washington had been selected as the place of interment the Monument Committee would of course have been National in its composition. But it is to be hoped that the selection of New York as the burial place will not in any degree lessen the desire felt in other States to share in the erection of a fitting monument over Gen. Grant's grave. That ought to be a National Work." Another view was expressed by *Harper's Weekly* editor George William Curtis, who observed sorrowfully that "New York City is widely disliked by the rest of country." He urged that its citizens remember that "General Grant was especially and symbolically a national man. His grave and his monument should be national. But New York is not a national city, and Grant was not born there, and his association with it is the most painful of his career."[48]

Echoing Curtis's sentiments, numerous out-of-state newspapers recorded with pride that their citizens were ignoring New York's entreaties and building *their own* Grant monuments. Just a month into the Grant Monument Association's fund-raising drive, Philadelphia had raised roughly the same amount of money toward a Grant monument. Likewise, Chicago's city fathers proudly announced that their Grant fund effort reached the princely sum of $45,000. One contemporary author recalled: "The popular sentiment clearly demanded his burial at some site near Washington. There he had won his imperishable renown; there was the nation's governmental centre."[49]

Gotham editorials expressed the shock of many New Yorkers to the opposing, and competing, forces. Three examples provide the common tone. The *New York Post* responded in kind, describing the claims of other cities as "the most astonishing of all the manifestation of the curious jealousy excited by General Grant's desire that his body should lie among the people of New York."[50] Another editorial, appropriately entitled "The National Monument," argued that "there is something particularly discordant in the querulous tones of petty jealousy and local spite. The choice of New York as the burial place of Gen. Grant, by the free and unbiased decision of his widow

Postcard of Chicago's monument to Grant (author's collection)

Postcard of Philadelphia's Grant monument (in Fairmount Park) by Daniel Chester French and Edward Clark Potter. Many cities and towns erected Grant statues in the aftermath of his death. (author's collection)

and eldest son, has provoked a bitter and wholly unnecessary outburst of spleen on the part of the press of other cities, notably Philadelphia. . . . Every city can have its Grant monument, if it wishes, but the one which will obtain a national importance will be that erected over his grave." Another asserted that "It is fitting that the tomb of the greatest soldier and citizen of our later history should be in the commercial metropolis of the nation, where it will be visited and seen by the greatest number from all parts of our country as well as from foreign lands."[51]

The controversy swirled; the critics refused to be silenced. The *Cincinnati Commercial Gazette* fumed, "If it were not for the fact that he lies in his coffin, the deep feeling aroused by the news that he is to be buried in Central Park would break out in a general expression of undisguised indignation and disgust." An editor from the *Indiana Enterprise* echoed the sentiment: "The feeling is pretty general in the West that as the Empire City secured the remains of General Grant over the protests of 9/10th of the citizens of the United States she is in duty bound to place a monument over the grave of the grand old commander at her own expense."[52]

A most worrisome aspect of the controversy was the solid opposition from northern soldiers' organizations, which overwhelmingly preferred Washington, D.C., to New York City. An Ohio citizen summed up the sentiment" "Our people are of the opinion that Washington is the proper location for a monument to so distinguished a character as the late General Grant and are willing to contribute to any other location believing that New York has no claims that are as prominent as other locations that have been mentioned."[53] The Grand Army of the Republic's commander-in-chief Samuel S. Burdette spoke for his constituency when he demanded Grant's burial in the true "national" city, Washington. He further rejected the Grant Monument Association's request to merge resources and thus denied it a quick and lucrative fund-raising asset. Many had already pointed out the logic of Washington, D.C., for Grant's mausoleum. Arlington National Cemetery had been formally established in 1865 and was the burial place of many Civil War soldiers, as was the slightly older Soldiers' Home Cemetery. The *Seattle Daily Post-Intelligencer*, on July 26, 1885, urged that Grant's body "ought to be placed in state in New York, Philadelphia, and Washington, and then be buried there beside the soldiers who fought with him." Washington, D.C., newspapers expressed disgust immediately after the decision for New York was announced. They attacked New York's proposal as nothing more than a scam imposed by local politicians, conveniently ignoring or playing down the Grant family's stated preference.[54] In addition, prominent generals and politicians, such as John A. Logan and Philip Sheridan, pushed for their former commander to be interred in Washington, D.C. Ex-senator Roscoe A. Conkling wrote to Sheridan that "The Soldiers' Home would be a perpetual resting-place. Like Washington, Grant belongs to the country and should be buried where the pilgrims of all ages can visit his tomb, as they have for nearly a hundred years the tomb of Washington."[55] It seemed reasonable to veterans living outside of New York City and State that they would be just as likely, or more likely, to visit Grant's memorial in the national capital.

Two beloved figures among veterans, Rutherford Hayes and William Sherman rallied to New York's defense. Hayes worked hard to arouse enthusiastic GAR efforts in support of New York, "where General Grant last resided and where more soldiers and citizens will see and enjoy it than would be the case in any other locality."[56] Hayes sent a sharply worded letter to Burdette urging him to give up all opposition. The Grant family was not going to bend on this issue, Hayes insisted, telling Burdette that he was being "misled by a temporary local delusion. General Grant's remains will forever rest on the banks of the Hudson."[57] Staunch New York monument supporter Sherman tried to win veterans over to his point of view in a speech to the Eighteenth Annual Reunion of the Society of the Army of the Tennessee in Chicago. Sherman reassured veterans that "each city, town and even hamlet may have whatever monument they are willing to erect"; then he cautioned, "but it seems to me better that all should unite and build a strong, solid, simple monument, characteristic of the man, over his grave on the banks of the Hudson."[58] He reminded his audience that Riverside Park was "the spot selected by his son, approved by the entire family, and accepted by all who had a right to be consulted." Sherman recounted the pleasant features of the park for the many unacquainted with its virtues. Grant's monument, he said, will be built "on the banks of the Hudson, at the upper end of Riverside Park—not a park in the sense of a pleasure ground, but a hill, as yet in the rough and susceptible of infinite embellishment, which will remain as firm as the granite on which it stands till the earth shall give up its dead and time shall be no more." Finally, Sherman said that Grant himself would be pleased. "If the spirits of the dead have the privilege of contemplating their own tomb, then will Gen. Grant's be content, for from the pedestal, he can look upon the old revolutionary forts, Lee and Washington, at his very feet—the beautiful Palisades just across the river; Tappan Zee and the Highlands above; the mighty city of New-York, with its busy harbor, below, and Long Island Sound Across the peninsula."[59]

Julia Grant served as the ultimate arbiter. Seeking to put an end to the debate, Richard Greener and Mayor Grace asked Julia in late October 1885 to write a letter indicating her strong support of New York. In a widely published reply, she pronounced Riverside Park in New York City the ideal spot for her husband's remains. Julia explained firmly that "Riverside was selected by myself and my family as the burial place of my husband, General Grant. First, because I believed that New York was his preference. Second, it is near the residence that I hope to occupy as long as I live, and where I will be able to visit his resting place often." Julia dampened the criticism. Earlier, the *Kansas City (Mo.) Journal* voiced a call for sanity on the issue. "It matters little where Grant may be buried, after all," it editorialized, "no matter where his tomb may be it will be visited, will become a hallowed spot. . . . Let the people unite in determining to help New-York to keep the trust she has assumed—the care of the tomb of Grant." Mark Twain added his support as well. "I observe that the common and strongest objection to New York is that she is not 'national ground,'" he observed. "Let us give ourselves no uneasiness about that. Wherever General Grant's body lies, that is national ground."[60]

The leadership of the Grant Monument Association used the support of Sherman and Hayes to smooth out relations between the association and the veterans. To some extent they succeeded. John Cameron, the GAR adjutant general in Washington, D.C., issued a general order that suggested a donation of 15 cents be raised from every member toward the national monument. The suggestion was only that, and was resisted by most veterans, even as one Grant insider reminded the organization that "The G.A.R. Comrades bore the General to his grave, he was buried with its ritual, he was an early member of the order and his body bears pinned upon the bosom the Grand Army Badge."[61] The majority of veterans still preferred Washington, D.C., as the place of interment, although time would soften their stance toward visiting the monument in New York. But they would not give enough money. Thus, the underlying problems of funding the monument nationally persisted. By Thanksgiving of 1885, the association announced that it had reached the $100,000 mark. The figure was impressive but for the fact that another $900,000 was needed to reach the target. Worse, the New Year, 1886, saw donations slow to the barest trickle. The association faced a dilemma. It did not have enough money to begin construction, and, worse, it lacked an actual plan. Why should citizens give money to build a monument whose shape was still a mystery? Gloom had settled over the whole project by the time the veterans of U. S. Grant Post no. 327 held a ceremony at Grant's temporary tomb on Decoration Day in 1886. Reporters noted sarcastically that even as huge crowds visited Grant's temporary tomb that day, no concrete progress had been made toward a permanent resting place.[62]

## The Winning Design

Attempting to reinvigorate the process three years after Grant's death, the Grant Monument Association formally invited competitive designs from any and all prominent architects in June 1888. Entries were to be judged by an independent six-member panel of architects and academics. Specifications were drawn up, with cash prizes for the best entries. The prospect of a harmonious search withered when some in the architectural community attacked the contest's vague specifications and wide-open competition. Potential applicants were advised only that Grant's memorial should include a "monument, library, [and] mausoleum," but otherwise left in the dark.[63] Unfortunately, the quality of the sixty-five submissions proved shockingly poor, with the majority of them favoring an obelisk over a mausoleum. The association was compelled to delay the announcement of the winning design due to confusion over the entries. Alarmed architects warned against selecting an obelisk for the Grant memorial. Sometimes called funereal shafts, columns, or towers, obelisks originated in ancient times and were the preferred monument for military heroes but, in more modest form, were also commonly found in antebellum cemeteries. The obelisk was chosen for Washington's monument, the Soldiers' and Sailors' Monument in Boston, and the 117-foot National Lincoln Monument in Springfield, Illinois, completed in 1869. Obelisks were also favored for the countless regimental monuments on national battlefields, as well as the South's burial grounds. Their ubiquitous presence led one architect to denounce obelisks as mere "votive piles."[64]

In 1890, the Grant Monument Association brought the design competition to an end by awarding first prize to a submission featuring an obelisk rising to an astounding 240 feet. Adding insult to injury, the design (which was rejected) was as expensive as it was hideous. The results of the competition frustrated the public. Five years after Grant's death, his body still lay in an unsecured temporary tomb. Some disgruntled congressmen introduced a bill in August 1890 threatening to remove Grant from his temporary tomb and bring his body to Washington, D.C. Outraged New Yorkers blocked the attempt but that it even occurred indicated the persistence of anti–New York feeling, and the impotence of the association.[65]

Plans for a second competition were made within months of the comple-

tion of the first. Learning from experience, the association invited only five prominent architectural firms to submit, four from New York City and one from Philadelphia. The specifications were clearly elucidated this time. The design called for a "large, imposing structure," with room for the display of war relics and an observatory. The cost was scaled down to $500,000. Limiting the quantity ensured a higher quality of plans received by the association.[66] On September 9, 1890, the winning design was announced, unanimously awarding the job to the firm of thirty-six-year-old John Hemenway Duncan. A well-regarded New York City architect, Duncan designed the Washington Monument at Newburgh, New York. By the time he submitted his plan for Grant's Tomb, he had already garnered several other major commissions, including the Soldiers' and Sailors' Memorial Arch (based on the Arc de Triomphe in Paris) at the entrance to Prospect Park in Brooklyn.[67] Duncan's Grant memorial was a neoclassical design inspired in part by one of the Seven Wonders of the World, the ancient tomb of King Mausolus at Halicarnassus in Asia Minor, the very structure that gave rise to the word "mausoleum." Other influences included the tomb of the Roman emperor Hadrian, lending credence to Duncan's later confirmation that his design was "rooted in the most substantial tradition of funerary memorials." Borrowing from Greek, Roman, and French architecture as well as from the design for President Garfield's mausoleum, Duncan's imposing and impressive monument plan consisted of three levels, all to be constructed from light granite.[68]

The exterior featured a massive rectangular first level that soared to 100 feet. Placed on top of it was a seventy-foot dome supported by Ionic columns, and on top of the dome, a "conical roof." Six enormous Doric columns preceded the main entrance (one of three) located on the tomb's southern side. Duncan envisioned equestrian statues of Grant's four division commanders to be placed above the entrance portico. In addition, a bronze equestrian statue of Grant was planned for the mid-plaza area. Like many other recommended embellishments, the statues were later eliminated due to lack of funds, although the basic structure remained the same. Duncan's interior plan was equally elaborate, drawing inspiration from that of Napoleon's tomb in Paris. Once inside, visitors would enter a memorial hall large enough to hold roughly a thousand people. The upstairs gallery was lined with coffered barrel vaults and offered spectacular views of the Hudson River, the New Jersey coastline to the west, and the Long Island Sound to the east. Duncan later stated that his intention was "to produce an edifice which shall be unmistakably a Monumental Tomb, no matter from what point of view it may be seen."[69]

Across from the entrance and down a marble staircase lay an open crypt where Ulysses and Julia would be entombed side by side in identical sarcophagi. The design provided ample space for displays of Civil War relics. Duncan's vision for the Grant Monument suited the association and the Grant family perfectly. They felt it reflected the gravity necessary to truly honor Grant, fusing the spiritual and practical elements. Richard Greener, one of Duncan's biggest supporters, remarked proudly that "I was one of the first to point out the simplicity, dignity, and fitness of [Duncan's design], as presenting the characteristics of the Conqueror of the Rebellion." Architectural historian Robert A. M. Stern presented a different view: "Duncan grasped the fundamental issue: to make a building that embodied not so much the character of Grant . . . but to create an American Valhalla, a shrine to American power." Montgomery Schuyler, an architectural critic, commented that "there is no question among those who saw the designs submitted for the Grant Monument, that the accepted design was by far the best of them, the only one, in fact, that could be seriously considered. The others were either unduly wild or unduly tame."[70] An added attractive feature of Duncan's design was that the construction could unfold in separate stages, so fundraising could continue throughout the process.

### Horace Porter Takes Control

The crowds viewing the groundbreaking ceremonies on April 27, 1891, might be forgiven for breathing a collective sigh of relief that the tomb construction had finally begun. Only a select few, however, knew that the association's coffers were so low that the entire sum collected since 1885 registered only $155,000. If more money was not raised, the construction would halt. As the desperate situation was publicized, criticism mounted once again from the press, the public, politicians, and veterans' groups. "For seven years," fumed one ex-soldier, "the body of our old General-in-Chief had been allowed to remain in an open city park in a rude temporary shelter. This neglect had become a standing reproach and humiliating to every surviving Comrade."[71] The object of their combined wrath was the leadership of an inept and inert Grant Monument Association.

The Grant Monument Association was not up to the task of finishing the memorial. Fund-raising continued to lag, given the stiff national resistance to the monument's site in New York City. "Financially, Grant's tomb had become a local memorial honoring a national hero," declared G. Kurt Piehler, author of *Remembering War the American Way*.[72] Yet the association's wealthy members eschewed aggressive measures, preferring to let the pennies and dollars trickle in slowly. Passivity was not the only problem. Political infighting erupted in the fall and early winter of 1892 and flowed into disputes over employee salaries and high expenses, further diminishing the capacity for effective direction. Two factions emerged to contest for the soul of the organization. One was led by the "old guard" and included Mayor Grace and Richard Greener. The other was led by former brigadier general, Grant aide, wealthy businessman, and prominent Republican trustee Horace Porter, asserting that a significant shakeup was needed. This shakeup occurred between the groundbreaking ceremony and the more elaborate ceremony held the following year to lay the cornerstone of the monument. Former Union general Grenville M. Dodge, an ally of Porter's, remembered exactly when the Grant Monument's fortunes rose. After the annual meeting of the association on February 18, 1892, "General Horace Porter called

Grant Monument under construction, 1891, with temporary tomb at right (National Park Service)

together a small number of Gen'l Grant's friends at the Union League Club, in New York," he wrote, "and an organization [GMA] was [re]made of which Gen'l Porter was president, and I was vice president."[73]

Porter assumed complete command of the association in the spring of 1892 after a bloodless but nonetheless ruthless takeover in which many officers and trustees resigned, including Greener. "In thoroughly reorganizing the Grant Monument Association," Porter wrote, "new trustees were elected. . . . Every one is an intimate friend or personal acquaintance of mine, and went on the board at my request. . . . They are the heart and soul in the work."[74] Porter cut the executive committee to six and streamlined the board of trustees, while simultaneously enlarging the organization's support circle by personally lobbying wealthy businessmen and prominent politicians to join the organization among the business and political leaders he recruited were Dodge, Whitelaw Reid, Elihu Root, and members of New York's GAR, which greatly improved relations with the latter organization. Indeed, Porter eagerly embraced the idea of an "autographic Honor

# w national champion rower at Washington

ow Husky rower
, who hails from

ot really think-
d at rowing.
ter Christ-
d down
. He

as "pure pain." He also said it was
the hardest sport he's ever played.

A typical day in Schroeder's
life goes like this: Wake up at 5
a.m. for early-morning practice;
attend class from 9:30 a.m. to
12:30 p.m.; work on technique at
Conibear Shellhouse, the
university's rowing facility; eat

# business

August 5, 2010

## Send us your business brief

If you have business news to announce regarding your operation, such as an award, a promotion or a new location, please write to us at the *Thousand Oaks Acorn*, Attention: Business Briefs, 30423 Canwood St. Ste. 108, Agoura Hills, CA 91301. Or you can e-mail tonewstip@theacorn.com.

Certain promotional information may not be accepted and items cannot exceed 150 words.

"Probably the most distinctive characteristic of the successful politician is selective cowardice."

**— Richard Harris**

805

Roll" of every GAR veteran placed in a special repository in the monument building.[75]

It is hard to imagine that the tomb could have been finished successfully without the charismatic leadership of Horace Porter. National Park historian Eric A. Reinert correctly dubbed him "the man most responsible for the Grant Monument."[76] Born in Pennsylvania in 1837, Porter graduated from West Point in 1860, serving in both the Eastern and Western Theaters of the war. He attracted Grant's favorable attention for his actions during the battle of Chickamauga (for which he received the Congressional Medal of Honor in 1906) and in the Chattanooga campaign. In April 1864 Grant appointed Porter his aide-de-camp, and Porter served ably in that capacity until the end of the war, ending his service as a brevetted brigadier general. Porter continued working for Grant, filling the position of presidential executive secretary from 1869 to 1873. Turning then to business, Porter became wealthy as a banker and financier whose talents were eagerly sought after by insurance and transportation companies. A conservative Republican, Porter actively supported Ohio congressman and former Union officer William McKinley's successful presidential campaign in the heated election of 1896. In that campaign, Porter used the war's memory to give meaning to present troubles. "During the heroic age of the country, in 1861, the old soldiers went to the front to save the nation's life," he told voters, describing the "redhanded anarchy" of the 1890s as every bit as serious as rebellion. He added diplomat to his résumé when President McKinley appointed him as the United States Ambassador to France, a position he held from 1897 to 1905.[77]

Porter was a trusted friend, adviser, and admirer of Grant until the latter's death, and afterward remained close to the family. Tall and distinguished-looking, with a bristly mustache, Porter was a gifted orator, much in demand at memorial occasions and dedication ceremonies. In 1897 he published a classic of Civil War literature, *Campaigning with Grant*, and also penned numerous articles about aspects of Grant's life, career, and character. In one such publication, Porter listed the five traits that in his opinion defined Grant: "Truth, Courage, Modesty, Generosity, and Loyalty."[78] In short, Porter enjoyed access to, and commanded respect from, the highest levels of the American business, political, and military worlds. His unstinting loyalty to Grant strengthened the family's favorable impression of Porter's ability to make sure the monument was built. Fred Grant, who previously worried that his father's monument would never be finished, provided enthusiastic backing. "I feel assured," Fred wrote to Porter, "that this matter will reach a successful end soon now, with you in charge—all the world knows of your ability and energy, and I know of your devotion to my dear father."[79]

Fred Grant was correct in his assessment. Horace Porter brought to the task passion, keen intelligence, and a willingness to work as long and as hard as necessary. Porter set himself an exhaustive schedule of letter-writing, meetings, and speeches. He acted swiftly to ensure a streamlined organization. Operating costs were cut drastically. "I had an amendment made to the by-laws that no officer or member of the Association should receive any compensation for his services," Porter explained.[80] He arranged for rent-free office space and installed James C. Reed as secretary and prominent banker Frederick D. Tappen as treasurer. Both men were trusted colleagues and played key roles in implementing Porter's directives, including his new campaign for raising money.

In short, Porter was the right man at the right time to lead the Grant Monument Association. He articulated and implemented a winning strategy for finishing the memorial. He abandoned the pretense that "the nation" was going to pay for the edifice. Porter instead turned the country's anti–New York sentiment into a potent fund-raising tool, appealing to the pride, generosity, and duty of all New Yorkers. In speech after speech, he reminded various groups that the city made a sacred pledge to build a magnificent memorial to General Grant. "Let it be remembered," Porter said, "that our city authorities invited the family of General Grant to make the metropolis of the nation his permanent place of burial. . . . We have contracted a debt and like honest men we must pay it." He further warned that "in this crisis it is not the reputation of Gen. Grant which is on trial, it is the reputation of New York."[81] Anything less than meeting the original obligation, Porter concluded, would bring shame to the city and state. Armed with his message—the tomb was still a national monument, but New Yorkers must bear the costs—Porter endeavored to make sure everyone who could contribute something did.

Porter audaciously announced a goal of raising $350,000 in sixty days. Then he laid the foundation to achieve that goal. Running the effort like a military campaign, Porter appointed committees and subcommittees identifying and targeting specific city businesses from plumbers and policemen to bankers and lawyers. Regular executive oversight meetings were instituted to assess progress and make changes if needed. He hired a professional fund-raiser to make sure that every legitimate source could be tapped. Thus, all classes of people were targeted—businessmen who could afford gener-

Horace Porter,
ca. 1899 (National
Park Service)

ous donations of $5,000, humble and wealthy church congregations asked
to give according to their means, veterans who could afford only smaller
contributions, and working men who could offer just pennies. Thousands
of schoolchildren participated in a citywide essay contest on Grant's contribution to American history, an effective publicity stunt that kept the cause
fresh in people's minds. Porter especially liked having children participate
in some way. "The greatest satisfaction I have in seeing the Grant Monument completed," he stated to the president of the National Educational
Association, "is that it will be an object lesson to the rising generation in
loyalty, patriotism, and self-sacrifice."[82] Leaving no stone unturned, Porter
ordered subscription books printed and placed in public places like train
stations, hotels, and banks. Finally, he orchestrated a daily publicity barrage
in the newspapers, constantly pushing the plight of the memorial before
the New York public. "It actually became a fad to raise money for the Grant
Monument Fund," noted one newspaper account. The next big ceremony
marking the progress of the tomb occurred on April 27, 1892, and Porter
used the occasion to announce some good news.[83]

Grant Monument Association certificate issued in return for a contribution to support construction of the tomb (National Park Service)

The May 7 cover of *Harper's Weekly* featured a solemn illustration by Thure de Thulstrup of President Benjamin Harrison laying the cornerstone of the Grant Monument. Standing beside him was Horace Porter, and, in military attire, General Dodge. Julia was seated in a place of honor, along with two of her sons and their families. Other distinguished guests included the vice president, the secretaries of war and the interior, and Gens. O. O. Howard and John M. Schofield. Four thousand guests, flanked by two thousand veterans, were seated in anticipation of the ceremonies. Beyond them an estimated fifty to seventy thousand people waited, enjoying the warmest of spring days at "the site of the monument [which] was the natural goal and culmination of one of the most delightful of suburban drives."[84] The program was short and simple and, although the president's speech was more anticipated by the crowd, Porter's oration was also enthusiastically received. The association coffers had added roughly $200,000 to the $150,000 already collected, Porter proudly announced. He radiated confidence that the target would be met in thirty days, by the next Decoration Day, and exhorted the crowd to keep the money flowing. He reminded them of the progress accomplished—the foundation finished and the superstructure begun—and the progress anticipated. Porter asked the gathering to cherish the significance of the project they were all dedicated to finishing.

In countless speeches such as this one, Porter articulated a reverent vision for the Grant monument. "The Monumental Sepulcher erected here will be the shrine at which American patriots will worship," he stated in typically florid prose. "Generations yet to come will pause to read the inscription on its portals, and the voices of a grateful people will ascend from this con-

Coin receptacle for
contributions to
the fund to build
Grant's Tomb
(Grant Monument
Association Archives,
New York City)

secrated spot as incense rises from holy places, invoking blessings on the memory of him who had filled to the very full the largest measure of human greatness and covered the earth with his renown."[85] Soon after Porter finished, President Harrison awkwardly spread mortar over the bed of the cornerstone with a golden trowel, and to thunderous applause, offered his own tribute to Grant.

In the weeks that followed, Porter intensified his relentless fund-raising campaign, achieving spectacular results. In a letter written to a possible donor in early May, Porter provided this financial assessment: "The trustees of the Grant Monument Association have succeeded in raising the entire half million required to complete the tomb," he began. "A thorough canvas has been made of the different trades in the city, and the money thus far has come largely from the working classes and shop people, and the old soldiers who have contributed their mite. Nothing more can be secured from this source; and we shall have to depend for the remainder largely upon individual subscription from our prominent New York citizens."[86] By Decoration Day 1892 all of the $350,000 — the majority from New Yorkers — was collected and secured. Together with interest, the entire sum available for the construction of Grant's monument would total $600,000. Overall, 90,000 individuals donated to the popular subscription drive. "Our citizens have contributed a fund larger than any ever received from voluntary contributions for any similar object in history," Porter proudly wrote.[87] It was a remarkable achievement, and Horace Porter deserved much of the credit.

## Construction of the Monument

Brimming with confidence and buoyed by a clear vision of what needed to be accomplished, Porter turned his formidable skills toward finishing the construction within a strict budget that had once been envisioned at $1 million. The Grant Monument Association was divided into three sections— the board, the trustees, and the "building committee." Porter, Duncan, and Dodge were among the five members of the latter who shouldered the burden of completing the monument, and the work of the building committee now stepped up to the forefront. The committee oversaw all facets of construction, including contract approval. Porter's "Letter Books" from 1892 to 1896 record numerous communications with Duncan, other architects, artists, contractors, Grant family members, politicians, engineers, and government officials on the federal, state, and local levels. Although the association was entirely responsible for the tomb's construction, the city had agreed to pay for certain necessary improvements. Porter negotiated with the New York City Department of Public Works to remove an unsightly hotel and to grade a hill that impeded the view of the tomb. On the latter topic, he wrote that "Both artistic taste and common sense demand that any monument should stand upon the highest ground in its immediate vicinity and the most conspicuous monument of the nation should not be subordinated to a miserable hump in the ground."[88] Almost all of Porter's business correspondence stressed the gravity of the undertaking. He hoped that construction would be completed by 1896, but he had to settle for a year later, making the building time roughly six years, not at all bad compared to that of other national monuments. Delays occurred as a result of spates of unusually bad weather, a six-month strike by quarry workers, and the normal cessation of work during the winter.

Porter had to be cautious with expenses. Money was saved when the structure was made slightly smaller than originally envisioned. Many other features of Duncan's original design were eliminated outright. The proposed exterior equestrian statues; a bronze figure, "Union," at the very top of the dome; and most of the interior sculpture and art work could not be funded, making the shining white memorial rising on a hill seem starker than nec-

Recent photograph of the sarcophagi holding Ulysses's and Julia's remains
(Grant Monument Association Archives, New York City)

essary. Both Porter and Duncan agreed that the embellishments would be added later, as more money was raised. Indeed the future promised endless fund-raising, as Porter and the association knew well that beyond the dedication lay the challenges of maintenance and preservation.

Outwardly, Porter was ever the enthusiastic leader, constantly assuring the public that the memorial would open on schedule. A master of public relations, he arranged for impressive ceremonies at the building site every April 27 and May 30—the anniversary of Grant's birthday and Memorial Day. In 1893 Porter learned that a Naval Review was going to take place in New York on Grant's birthday. He wrote the secretary of the navy and suggested that they use the occasion to fire a salute opposite the tomb. The Navy was amenable, and the ceremonies had an added touch of pageantry.[89] Porter continued his endless round of speeches at venues in New York City and beyond, delivering elegant exhortations to the memory of his late commander. More privately, Porter bargained for time, sending pleas to contractors to lower their prices, with varying levels of success. In 1896 Porter's letter to the treasurer of the Berlin and Montello Granite Company revealed his plight: "We will have left in the Treasury of the Association after completing the

Photograph of the Grant Monument under construction (National Park Service)

entire work, involving an outlay of nearly $600,000.00, $3,500.00, and this the only amount which can be devoted to procuring the two sarcophagi."[90] Between 1893 and 1897 he raised another $50,000, enabling the association to meet unexpected cost overruns.

At the same time, Porter was determined to bring the great promise of Grant's memorial to fruition. "The monument shall be flawless," he declared in a letter to the *New York World*.[91] Following Duncan's counsel, Porter kept a close watch on the excavation of the granite for the structure. The Maine and New Hampshire Granite Company was awarded the contract for the 8,000 tons needed for construction. The light-colored granite was cut and carved at a quarry in North Jay, Maine. By the spring of 1893, Porter wrote that the "granite is nearly all set and the backing of the concrete will soon be finished." In a long letter to Julia, Porter asked for patience. He explained that although the project was moving ahead, there were obstacles that had to be dealt with in order to ensure that the Grant Monument would meet all expectations. No expense was spared with the granite and marble that would comprise the exterior and adorn the interior.

For example, Porter and Duncan frequently personally inspected the granite samples to make sure no subgrade material found its way into the monument. This careful inspection was absolutely necessary, Porter informed Julia. One illustration is instructive. The portico of the monument would be supported by ten fluted Doric columns twenty-four feet in height. Carving the columns was a delicate business, and any one of them could be damaged by frost, so the work had to stop for months at a time. Porter pushed the contractors as far and fast as he dared, but "I could not afford to take any chances of failure for the purpose of making undue haste in the construction." The interior facade featured the finest marble available from Italy and Massachusetts.[92] Toward the end, two polished Wisconsin red granite sarcophagi weighing nine tons each were placed in the crypt. Fred Grant made the decision that his mother would rest to the right of his father.

The only interior art to survive the 1890s budget cuts was that of the New York sculptor J. Massey Rhind, who completed the doors of Trinity Church on Wall Street, the Soldiers' and Sailors' monuments for Philadelphia and Syracuse, and the John C. Calhoun monument in Charleston, South Carolina.[93] Inside the rotunda in four triangles (or pendentives) between the arches, Rhind designed and sculpted allegorical figures, representing the phases of Grant's life—"Youth," "Military," "Civic Life," and "Death." Rhind's beautifully wrought bas-reliefs represented the felicitous blending of sculpture and architecture. Thus they added a graceful educative, emotional, and human element to the tomb. Rhind also contributed to the exterior artwork. Above the entrance, flanking Grant's famous words, "Let Us Have Peace," are two carved figures—representing "War" and "Peace," symbolically linking the general and the president, the military and the civic parts of Grant's career and emphasizing the reconciliation of the country.

## The Dedication, April 27, 1897

In the month before the opening, finishing touches were applied to the tomb and preparations made for the parade and the program. Under conditions of secrecy, Grant's body was removed from the temporary tomb and placed in his sarcophagus a week and a half before the dedication. Thousands of people flocked into the area trying to catch a glimpse of the interior of the memorial. Anticipating huge crowds, Mayor Josiah Strong appointed 300

"Let Us Have Peace"—a message of peaceful harmony between North and South above the entrance to Grant's Tomb (National Park Service)

prominent citizens to the Municipal Grant Monument Committee. Armed with $50,000 for expenses, the committee was charged with responsibility for the planning and execution of the ceremony. New York City officials declared a holiday, "Grant Day," and ordered schools, stores, and businesses closed. In contrast to the black-clad buildings of Grant's funeral, the City's streets were swathed in the bright national colors. "Stars and Stripes Everywhere," ran the headline in the *New York Herald*.[94] Indeed the newspaper's own headquarters in Herald Square was just one of numerous buildings, stores, and private residences—especially along the parade route—lavishly decorated for Grant Day.

At least from early April, anticipation was running high as reported in the press. Day after day, newspapers across the country devoted major coverage to the finished Tomb, and, again as in the case with his funeral, Grant's historical reputation was the subject of a national discussion. Before an overflow crowd in Carnegie Hall, Professor Felix Adler delivered a talk to the Society for Ethical Culture entitled "The Debt of the American People to Ulysses S. Grant." "Grant's Tomb the Mecca" and "Gathering to Pay Honor to the Dead Hero, Warrior," ran the banner headlines in the *San Francisco Chronicle*.[95] Many newspapers and journals offered special supplements, with numerous pictures of the general and his family, lengthy biographies, discussions of his military campaigns and presidency, and usually, headlines and articles featuring the theme of reconciliation—"The Gray Has Blended With the Blue," proclaimed the *Los Angeles Times*.[96]

A few days before the unveiling, the city's railroad stations and ferries disgorged legions of soldiers and ex-soldiers—regular army, National Guard, and veterans' units—who marched through the festively decorated streets on their way to quarters. Marching along with them were ex-Confederate veterans from Maryland and Virginia, and a unit of 150 "Sons of Confederates," accompanied by the "Stonewall Brigade Band." Virginia's contingent, led by the Richmond Light Infantry Blues, featured a battalion of black (U.S.) troops bringing up the rear.[97] Along the way, all surely observed construction of the parade route bleachers—with seats going for 50 cents and boxes ranging from $1 to $50. Takers were fewer than might be expected—most of the 1 million plus spectators preferred to stand rather than pay. Perhaps they were thinking of saving their money to buy some of the souvenirs—badges, pictures, little biographies of Grant—sold from stands lining the way up to the monument. One of the most popular souvenirs proved to be cheap copies of an official medal struck for the occasion. One side of the medal showed the newly built tomb, while the other side depicted the familiar profiles of three presidents—Washington, Lincoln, and Grant. The motto below the profiles read: "Father, Savior, Defender."[98] As more and more visitors thronged into the city, hotel rooms were impossible to find, at any price. Distinguished guests were greeted by reporters jostling for the best interview. The day before the ceremony a special train arrived in New York via Jersey City carrying President McKinley and his family in the first car and, in the second car, Julia Grant and her daughter and three granddaughters, accompanied by Secretary of State John Sherman.

April 27 opened bitterly cold and windy, with occasional bursts of rain. The weather did not deter the 50,000 who began marching at 9:30 A.M. The solemn parade proceeded slowly from Madison Square, winding its way over to Riverside Drive. The front of the procession arrived at the Tomb around 1:00 P.M. but the end did not arrive until 7:00 P.M., long after the ceremonies were over. At the tomb, huge grandstands seated a crowd of 5,000. Reserved seats in a special section found President William McKinley, Vice President William Hobart, ex-president Grover Cleveland, the Grant family, cabinet members, justices of the Supreme Court, thirteen governors, and twenty-eight representatives of the Diplomatic Corps waiting expectantly for the program to begin. The invited military officials included some familiar names of the aging Civil War generation—William Rosecrans, Horatio Wright, Don Carlos Buell, Franz Sigel, Lew Wallace,

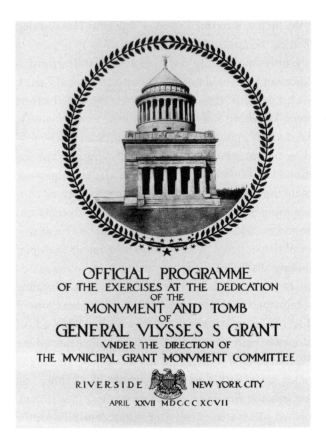

OFFICIAL PROGRAMME
OF THE EXERCISES AT THE DEDICATION
OF THE
MONVMENT AND TOMB
OF
GENERAL VLYSSES S GRANT
VNDER THE DIRECTION OF
THE MVNICIPAL GRANT MONVMENT COMMITTEE

RIVERSIDE     NEW YORK CITY

APRIL XXVII MDCCC XCVII

Grenville Dodge, Oliver O. Howard, Daniel E. Sickles, James Longstreet, and Simon Buckner among them. Behind the crowd, the magnificent ships of the U.S. Atlantic Fleet sailed up the glistening silver thread of the Hudson River. The ceremony at the tomb featured hymns, prayers by Reverend Newman, a few remarks issued by President McKinley, and a longer oration given by General Porter.[99] Afterward, most agreed that President McKinley's short but graceful tribute best captured the occasion.

> Let us not forget the glorious distinction with which the metropolis among the fair sisterhood of American Cities has honored his life and memory. With all that riches and sculpture can do to render an edifice worthy of a man, upon a site unsurpassed for magnificence, has this monument been reared by New York as a perpetual record of his illustrious deeds, in the certainty that as time passes around it, will assemble with gratitude and reverence and veneration men of all times, races, and nationalities. New York holds in its keeping the precious dust of the silent

soldier, but his achievements—that he and his brave comrades wrought for mankind—are in the keeping of seventy millions of American Citizens, who will guard the sacred heritage forever and forever more.

## Afterword

Grant's Tomb was complete. The monument was impressively austere, meant to inspire reverential reflection from endless generations of Americans. At least it started out that way. Union veterans and tourists came to the tomb to pay their respects to the general who won the war and secured the peace—their war, their peace. In the early days, gentlemen were required to remove their hats, and a quiet, reverential atmosphere prevailed. In the first months, 560,000 men and women visited. New Yorkers were vindicated. It seemed, after all, that New York City was the right place for Grant's national memorial. (Now, it seems that the veterans' earlier reservations were right. Arguably, the Great Commander's remains would be better off entombed in Arlington National Cemetery.) Not surprisingly, given the high expectations, reviews were mixed. The *New York Times*, which devoted a whole magazine supplement to the dedication, decreed the monument "too plain," yet, it added, "the tomb of Grant is upon the whole honorable alike to the community which possesses it and to the hero whom it commemorates."[100] In other words, it was more than a work of art, and as such, could not be judged solely on aesthetic qualities. Nearly thirteen years earlier, *Harper's Weekly* had called for Grant's memorial to embody a "massive simplicity," and somehow that phrase seemed just right for the tomb that commemorated "a modest man, a simple man, a man believing in the honesty of his fellows, true to his friends, faithful to traditions, and of great personal honor."[101] The spirit of the hugely successful memorial was captured by the novelist and expatriate Henry James, who, after walking on the broad plaza leading up to Grant's Tomb, described it as "a great democratic demonstration caught in the fact, unguarded, and unenclosed . . . as open as a hotel or a railway station to any coming and going."[102]

Another evaluation came from Lt. Gen. John M. Schofield, who reasoned why the Tomb spoke to the common people: "It has been said that Grant, like Lincoln, was a typical American and for that reason was most believed and respected by the people. . . . Soldiers and the people saw in Grant . . . not one of themselves not a plain man of the people, nor yet a superior being whom they could not understand, but a personification of their highest ideal of a citizen, soldier or statesman, a man whose greatness they could see and understand as plainly as they could anything else under the sun." Most of

Postcard of the Grant Monument, ca. 1906 (author's collection)

all, Grant's Tomb represented a nation reunited — its creed, its ideals, its past and its future. "It is to be our one great memorial of the struggle for union," declared an editor, "a monument not only to the foremost of our generals, but to the cause of 'liberty and union' and, in a sense, to all who fought and died for that sentiment."[103]

Despite the controversies that had surrounded the planning and construction of Grant's Tomb, veterans, their families, and their immediate descendants embraced the monument's celebration of national pride and patriotic values. Horace Porter's words and actions evoke this, as did many other declarations regarding the meaning of Grant's Tomb. Grant's was only the most impressive of the numerous Civil War art monuments constructed in the late nineteenth century. In total, these monuments called forth huge investments of money and of artistic effort, but, more important, they reflected the larger society's desire to immortalize the nobility and high ideals of the war. This desire to memorialize the deep appreciation so many people had toward those who sacrificed their lives drove the honoring of dead presidents, generals, and ordinary soldiers by erecting statues and other structures in so many places. U. S. Grant instinctively knew how tightly his part in the war bound him to veterans, and vice versa. In a speech delivered near Hamburg, Germany, on July 4, 1878, Grant responded to his host's effusive remark that he had "saved the country during the recent war."

If our country could be saved or ruined by the efforts of any one man we should not have a country, and we should not be now celebrating our Fourth of July. There are many men who would have done far better than I did under the circumstances in which I found myself during the war. If I had never held command; if I had fallen; if all our generals had fallen, there were ten thousand behind us who would have done our work just as well, who would have followed the contest to the end and never surrendered the Union. Therefore, it is a mistake and a reflection upon the people to attribute to me, or to any number of us who held high commands, the salvation of the Union. We did our work as well as we could, and so did hundreds of thousands of others. We deserve no credit for it, for we should have been unworthy of our country and of the American name if we had not made every sacrifice to save the Union. What saved the Union was the coming forward of the young men of the nation. They came from their homes and fields, as they did in the time of the Revolution, giving everything to the country. To their devotion we owe the salvation of the Union. The humblest soldier who carried a musket is entitled to as much credit for the results of the war as those who were in command. So long as our young men are animated by this spirit there will be no fear for the Union.[104]

The National Park historian and Grant's Tomb expert David M. Kahn summed up an era's position when he stated that "the tomb is not a mere building. It is a monument, and as such it embodies the spirit and ideals of the American people at a particular point in history. The mammoth and costly building in a very real sense symbolizes an entire generation's feeling not just about Grant, but about the Civil War and the role every foot soldier played in it."[105]

# *epilogue*

# Who's [Really] Buried in Grant's Tomb?

Casting aside the implied mockery of the famous question posed by the 1950s comedian and quiz show host Groucho Marx, what did, and what do, people see and think when they stand before the massive repository containing Grant's (and Julia's) remains? What was, and what is his legacy? Who is *really* buried in Grant's Tomb? The magnanimous warrior who saved the Union? The flawed but honest chief executive who took up Lincoln's mantle as a reconciler and as a redeemer president? An ordinary, humble man who became a democratic hero, exemplifying the aspirations of millions? A butcher general who sacrificed the lives of too many for a cause not worth the blood shed and the treasure lost? A greedy, corrupt, lazy militarist who exercised the powers of a despot against the defeated Confederacy?

In his own era there were many who did not see Grant in a positive light. Black visitors to his tomb might lament emancipationist dreams dashed on the realities of 1877. White visitors, particularly from the South, might reflect bitterly on dreams dashed by the leader of the "War of Northern Aggression." Some northern Democrats might flinch at honoring a man they viewed as one of the most dangerous and incompetent presidents ever elected. Yet, as I have argued, a majority of his contemporaries knew in their hearts that Grant, more than anyone besides Lincoln, made sure that the United States defeated the rebellion and prevailed in April 1865, preserving the country for a greater glory. At the time, and in retrospect, most approved of the Union Cause, most approved of the monument, and most also approved of and appreciated the meaning behind both. The tomb was both national in spirit (reconciliationist) and a remembrance of northern sacrifice and victory. When citizens looked at Grant's Tomb, they saw a legacy preserved. More than that, they desired and expected that legacy to be preserved for future generations as well.

It was not. Grant's legacy disappeared from popular memory with shocking rapidity. Indeed, the tomb's disrepair in the mid-twentieth century can be viewed as a metaphor for Grant's declining reputation in the 1920s and

'30s. The 1929 stock market crash (ironically, the modern-sized $50 bill with Grant's portrait was issued that year) coincided with the falling fortunes—literally and figuratively—of his Manhattan monument, still lacking most of the embellishments from the original plan. Funds for improvements were virtually nonexistent, and upkeep suffered. Covered with grime, the unprotected tomb invited vandalism and graffiti, further complicating repairs. Visitation levels were so low talk of closing the monument surfaced during the 1930s. On August 20, 1932, a letter to the *New York Times* entitled "A Plea for Beauty" advised taking a "wrecking ball" to remove the "ugliness" of the tomb from its more lovely surroundings. While Ulysses S. Grant's military reputation languished, Robert E. Lee's popularity rose even higher than it had been during the war. Statues and other images of the aristocratic, handsome General Lee adorned innumerable southern town squares and Confederate museums. Lee's admirers outnumbered Grant's in the publishing world as well. Far fewer read the *Personal Memoirs* than thumbed through the reverential four-volume Pulitzer Prize–winning *R. E. Lee: A Biography* (1934–35) by Richmond writer Douglas Southall Freeman.

The post–World War I generation feared, rather than celebrated, the endless sacrifices of the Civil War. In their minds, such sacrifice was associated with the seemingly mindless slaughter that had marked the First World War, and, memories fading, they tended to look unkindly on the kind of warfare "Butcher" Grant waged, as contrasted with the "gentlemanly" warfare of Lee. In the 1920s and '30s the history of Reconstruction was dominated by scholars who mythologized the Confederacy and demonized Reconstruction, a grip not loosened until after World War II. Somehow it was Abraham Lincoln and Robert E. Lee, not Lincoln and Grant, who emerged as the two most celebrated and representative figures of the war. Lincoln was portrayed as the saintly political hero who preserved the Union; Lee was portrayed as the saintly military hero who personified the pride, the principle, the nobility, and the courage of the Lost Cause. Both Lincoln and Lee exemplified the true spirit of sectional harmony, but while Lee was respected in the North, Lincoln was loathed in the South. Thus, in an era known for its racism and its rejection of the biracial democratic implications of both the war and Reconstruction, Grant was scorned by many.

It should not be surprising that in the 1930s his tomb was kept afloat, barely, by funds from the Works Progress Administration, plus modest sales from trinkets and other commercially inspired enterprises. The embattled Grant Monument Association planned and implemented some improvements, but needed more money. Spurred by a scandal in the making (and a desire to make sure New York was ready to host the 1939 World's Fair) two *New York Times* editorials, "Grant's Tomb," and "General Grant," published, respectively, on October 14 and 17, 1937, reminded citizens of Grant's importance and chided them for nearly forgetting. The first editorial urged New Yorkers to support the refurbishing and completion of the monument. Contrasting the care being "lavished" on Robert E. Lee's ancestral residence (even in the middle of the Depression) unfavorably with the neglect that led to the decrepitude of the Union's hero's resting place, the paper told readers (aware of the looming crisis in Europe and Asia), "It is a tomb to a great soldier, but it is also a monument to a civil peace that should never again need a war to keep it." The second editorial elaborated on the meaning of Grant's legacy. The *Times* admitted that General Grant's reputation had fallen mightily since 1885, but the newspaper asked its readers to take a mature stance toward judging him. Yes, the hero had been found to have shortcomings, mercilessly exposed by such highly regarded works as Allan Nevins's unflattering portrait in *Hamilton Fish: The Inner History of the Grant Administration* (1936). But the *Times* editorialist advised weighing Grant's shortcomings against his great achievements, as might be done for other heroic figures in history. Only then, the writer concluded, can the modern generation understand what Grant's generation instinctively knew: "The American people evidently made up its mind which chapters of it [Grant's career] were to be remembered and which forgotten. The stately tomb on Riverside commemorates their decision."

Prefiguring later ups and downs, Grant's Tomb survived intact and flourished again by the late 1930s, as tourists (200,000 a year) flocked to the memorial and its environs. Even in the darkest decade of its existence (so far) the tomb and what it represented claimed a deep part of the American psyche. The 1936 Academy Award–winning film *Mr. Deeds Goes to Town*, directed by Frank Capra, went against the grain. In it, Gary Cooper plays Longfellow Deeds, a humble poet from a small town in Ohio who inherits $20 million from a long lost uncle. Honest, idealistic, and forthright, he arrives in New York City to claim his inheritance. Once in Gotham's grip, Deeds is taken advantage of by a rascally mixture of businessmen, lawyers, and disaffected relatives who live in fear that he may donate his money to charity. The Depression-era film followed the classic Capra trademark of blending comedy, pathos, social comment, and tear-inducing patriotism. Thus, Deeds's ordinary American goodness eventually triumphs over cor-

A conversation about the meaning of America at Grant's Tomb. Jean Arthur as Louise "Babe" Bennett and Gary Cooper as Longfellow Deeds in *Mr. Deeds Goes to Town* (1936), directed by Frank Capra. (Columbia Pictures/Photofest)

ruption and the greed of selfish fat cats. Early in the film, Capra and screen-writer Robert Riskin established Deeds's genuine, humble patriotism—and by association, that of the average person—when Longfellow, asked which, among all of the amazing sights in New York City, he would like to visit the most, answers, "Grant's Tomb."

On a beautiful moonlit night, Deeds and his accomplice, a sophisticated, cynical newspaper reporter, Louise "Babe" Bennett, played by Jean Arthur, jump into a taxi, asking the driver to take them to "the tomb." Unlike today, cabbies needed no address, maps, or lengthy explanations. Walking up to the monument, the reporter takes Deeds's awestruck silence for disappoint-ment. Babe tells him not to worry about it, because *most* people feel that way. Deeds expresses surprise and says that he guesses it depends on how you see it. "What do you see?" Babe asks. Longfellow responds, while looking at the tomb: "I see a small Ohio farm boy becoming a great soldier. I see thousands of marching men. I see General Lee with a broken heart, surrendering, and I can see the beginning of a new nation, like Abraham Lincoln said. And

I can see that Ohio boy being inaugurated as President. Things like that can only happen in a country like America." The dialogue suggested both the lingering impression of Grant, and, in Bennett's sarcastic remarks, his legacy's descent. Alongside the tomb's reputation as an eyesore, rather than a meaningful memorial, on Manhattan's landscape, Grant's legacy seemed like a blot on American historical memory.

Grant's legacy rose and fell, and rose again in the succeeding years, never again approaching its previous heights. This was partly because of the Lost Cause's powerful sway and partly because the military hero and what he stood for—the Union Cause—has gone out of fashion, or is irrelevant to most Americans. As should be clear, Ulysses S. Grant never will be entirely erased from historical memory or academic examination. He's just too important for that to happen. Whenever there is an anniversary or a resurgence of interest in the Civil War for whatever reason, Grant's life and career are revisited, as they were during World War II, the Civil War Centennial, and the civil rights movement, or when Ken Burns's Civil War series was shown on public television in the early 1990s. Recently, Grant's reputation has entered another upswing, with three major biographies (as well as numerous smaller studies), publication of the final volumes of the *Papers of U. S. Grant*, novels, and a superb PBS documentary (2002) in the *American Experience* series. The renovation of Grant's Tomb in 1997 once again made it an attractive, safe place to visit, featuring interesting historical exhibits and an annual program marking his birthday.

Part of Grant's modern resurgence may be attributable to the obliteration of Lost Cause tendencies in academic monographs and textbooks, beginning in the late 1960s and reaching a crescendo in the 1990s. His reputation in popular culture, however, remains mired in the "drunken butcher" and "worst president" mode. The looming Civil War Sesquicentennial (2011–15) may, for the new century, recast (once again) interpretations of the war, and of its major figures. Perhaps now is the time for a new kind of tourist to the tomb (as well as other Grant sites), one more appreciative and knowledgeable. Never again will most citizens feel an uncomplicated pride in Grant's achievements, or in what America has become since Appomattox, but there should be a realization that Grant's goal of national reconciliation—as general and as president—included principles that are vitally important today: justice and equality for all. Ulysses S. Grant became the embodiment of the American nation in the decades after the Civil War. No living person in the postwar era symbolized both the hopes and the lost dreams of the war more fully than Grant. No living person in the postwar era more clearly articulated for posterity a powerful truth about the Civil War when he wrote, in his *Personal Memoirs* (2:489), of his feelings about Lee and the soldiers he had led and the slave republic they had defended. U. S. Grant recalled, "I felt like anything rather than rejoicing at the downfall of a foe who had fought so long and valiantly, and had suffered so much for a cause, though that cause was, I believe, one of the worst for which a people ever fought, and one for which there was the least excuse." By studying his life with a fresh perspective, visitors to Grant's Tomb may be able to see all the tangled, complicated, but ultimately inspiring dimensions of a man who truly is both an American hero and an American myth, and they just may be able to answer the question, "Who's [really] buried in Grant's Tomb?"

# Notes

## Abbreviations

GMAA    General Grant National Monument Association Archives,
        Federal Hall National Memorial, New York, N.Y.
NYT     *New York Times*
NYTrib  *New York Tribune*
PMUSG   Ulysses S. Grant, *The Personal Memoirs of Ulysses S. Grant*, 2 vols.
        (New York: Charles L. Webster, 1885).
PUSG    John Y. Simon et al., eds., *Papers of Ulysses S. Grant*, 30 vols. to date
        (Carbondale: Southern Illinois University Press, 1967–).
USG     Ulysses S. Grant
WTS     William T. Sherman

## Introduction

1. *PMUSG*, 1:49–50.

2. Joshua Chamberlain, *The Passing of the Armies: An Account of the Final Campaign of the Army of the Potomac, Based upon Personal Reminiscences of the Fifth Army Corps*, introduction by Brooks D. Simpson (Lincoln: University of Nebraska Press, 1998), 29.

3. In addition to using Grant's own words whenever possible, I have embedded my text with many quotations from contemporaries (as well as several generations of scholars) to provide the reader with a greater sense of Grant's impact on American society.

4. J. F. C. Fuller, *The Generalship of Ulysses S. Grant* (1929; reprint, New York: Da Capo Press, 1991), 414.

5. Hamlin Garland, *Ulysses S. Grant: His Life and Character* (New York: Doubleday and McClure, 1898). Garland's notes and interviews compiled during his research can be found in the Hamlin Garland Collection, Doheny Memorial Library, University of Southern California, Los Angeles. Less friendly to Grant is Owen Wister's slight volume, *Ulysses S. Grant* (Boston: Small, Maynard, 1901). See also Lloyd Lewis, *Captain Sam Grant* (Boston: Little, Brown, 1950), William S. McFeely, *Grant: A Biography* (New York: W. W. Norton, 1982); and Brooks D. Simpson, *Ulysses S. Grant: Triumph over Adversity, 1822–1865* (New York: Houghton Mifflin, 2000).

6. Marie Ellen Kelsey, comp., *Ulysses S. Grant: A Bibliography*, Bibliographies of the Presidents of the United States, Mary Ellen McElligott, series editor (Westport, Conn.: Praeger Publishers, 2005). The chapter "Iconography and Dramatic Media," addresses memory and memorialization, 399–418.

7. Eric Hobsbawm and Terence Rangers, eds., *The Invention of Tradition* (Cambridge: Cambridge University Press, 1983); Roy Rosenzweig and David P. Thelen, *The Presence of the Past: Popular Uses of History in American Life* (New York: Columbia University Press, 1998).

8. Paul Fussell, *The Great War and Modern Memory* (New York: Oxford University Press, 1975); Dominick La Capra, *History and Memory after Auschwitz* (Ithaca, N.Y.: Cornell University Press, 1998); Peter Novick, *The Holocaust in American Life* (New York: Houghton Mifflin, 1999); Edward T. Linenthal and Tom Engelhardt, eds., *History Wars: The Enola Gay and Other Battles for the American Past* (New York: Holt, 1996); Mario Gonzalez and Elizabeth Cook-Lynn, *The Politics of Hallowed Ground: Wounded Knee and the Struggle for Indian Sovereignty* (Urbana: University of Illinois Press, 1999); Jim Weeks, *Gettysburg: Memory, Market, and an American Shrine* (Princeton, N.J.: Princeton University Press, 2003).

9. Jacques Le Goff, *History and Memory*, trans. Steven Rendall and Elizabeth Calman (New York: Columbia University Press, 1992); Pierre Nora, "Between Memory and History: Les Lieux de Mémoire," *Representations* 26 (Spring 1989): 7–25; Maurice Halbwachs, *On Collective Memory*, trans. and ed. Lewis A. Coser, 1952 (Chicago: University of Chicago Press, 1992). For a thoughtful assessment of Civil War memory studies, see Stuart McConnell, "The Geography of Memory," in Alice Fahs and Joan Waugh, eds., *The Memory of the Civil War in American Culture* (Chapel Hill: University of North Carolina Press, 2004), 258–266.

10. John Bodnar, *Remaking America: Public Memory, Commemoration, and Patriotism in the Twentieth Century* (Princeton, N.J.: Princeton University Press, 1992); Michael Kammen, *Mystic Chords of Memory: The Transformation of Tradition in American Culture* (New York: Vintage Books, 1992); David W. Blight, *Race and Reunion: The Civil War in American Memory* (Cambridge: Belknap Press of Harvard University Press, 2001).

11. William Blair, *Cities of the Dead: Contesting the Memory of the Civil War in the South, 1865–1914* (Chapel Hill: University of North Carolina Press, 2004); Gaines Foster, *Ghosts of the Confederacy: Defeat, the Lost Cause, and the Emergence of the New South, 1865–1913* (New York: Oxford University Press, 1987); Gary W. Gallagher and Alan T. Nolan, eds. *The Myth of the Lost Cause and Civil War History* (Bloomington: Indiana University Press, 2000; Gary W. Gallagher, *Lee and His Generals in War and Memory* (Baton Rouge: Louisiana State University Press, 1998); Susan-Mary Grant, *North over South: Northern Nationalism and American Identity in the Antebellum Era* (Lawrence: University Press of Kansas, 2000); Melinda Lawson, *Patriot Fires: Forging a New American Nationalism in the Civil War North* (Lawrence: University Press of Kansas, 2002); John R. Neff, *Honoring the Civil War Dead: Commemoration and the Problem of Reconciliation* (Lawrence: University Press of Kansas, 2005); Nina Silber, *The Romance of Reunion: Northerners and the South, 1865–1900* (Chapel Hill: University of North Carolina Press, 1993).

12. Philip Shaw Paludan, *"A People's Contest": The Union and the Civil War, 1861–1865* (New York: Harper and Row, 1988), 316.

13. An excellent overview is found in James M. McPherson and William J. Cooper Jr., eds., *Writing the Civil War: The Quest to Understand* (Columbia: University of South Carolina Press, 1998).

14. The most notable example is James M. McPherson, the leading Civil War historian of this generation. His Pulitzer Prize–winning volume, *Battle Cry of Freedom: The Civil War Era* (New York: Oxford University Press, 1988), is the standard account of the conflict.

15. The antiwar and antimilitary sentiment that informs William S. McFeely's depiction of Grant was written after the turmoil of the second civil rights revolution and protests over the Vietnam War. While I disagree with much of McFeely's interpretative stance, his *Grant: A Biography* remains an indispensable touchstone for Grant scholars. Influenced by McFeely,

literary scholar Andrew Delbanco sees in Grant's character and career "a preview of the dead-eyed murderers one meets in fictional and factual twentieth-century texts . . . in which men kill with mundane efficiency and detachment" (Delbanco, *The Death of Satan: How Americans Have Lost the Sense of Evil* [New York: Farrar, Straus and Giroux, 1995], 139–40). Some recent publications that offer a very critical, harsher account of the war include Vernon Orville Burton, *The Age of Lincoln* (New York: Hill and Wang, 2007); Walter A. Mcdougall, *Throes of Democracy: The American Civil War Era 1820-1877* (New York: Harper, 2008); Christopher Waldrep, *Vicksburg's Long Shadow: The Civil War Legacy of Race and Remembrance* (Lanham, Md.: Rowman & Littlefield, 2005); David Williams, *A People's History of the Civil War: Struggles for the Meaning of Freedom* (New York: New Press, 2005); and Mark R. Wilson, *The Business of the Civil War: Military Mobilization and the State, 1861-1865* (Baltimore: Johns Hopkins University Press, 2006).

16. Harry S. Stout, *Upon the Altar of the Nation: A Moral History of the Civil War* (New York: Viking Press, 2006), 327. Other books exploring Civil War morality include Mark A. Noll, *The Civil War as a Theological Crisis* (Chapel Hill: University of North Carolina Press, 2006), and Randall M. Miller, Harry S. Stout, and Charles Reagan Wilson, eds., *Religion and the American Civil War* (New York: Oxford University Press, 1998).

17. Stout, *Upon the Altar of the Nation*, 461.

18. Ibid., 443.

19. *PMUSG*, 2:547; *PUSG*, 28:217.

20. *PMUSG*, 2:419.

## Chapter 1

1. "Land of Grant, Ohio-Kentucky," pamphlet, U. S. Grant Association (Georgetown, Ohio, 1999). Other recommended sites are Bethel and Ripley, Ohio; and Maysville, Kentucky. Some of the historical structures are under the auspices of the U. S. Grant Homestead Association, the Brown County Historical Society, and the Ohio Historical Society. The national military parks are Appomattox, Chickamauga and Chattanooga, Fort Donelson, Fredericksburg and Spotsylvania, Petersburg, Shiloh, and Vicksburg.

2. Herman Melville, "The Armies of the Wilderness," in *Battle-Pieces and Aspects of the War*, ed. Sidney Kaplan (Gainesville, Fla.: Scholars' Facsimiles and Reprints 1960), 99; Walt Whitman, "The Silent General," *Whitman: Poetry and Prose* (New York: Library of America, 1982), 869; Mark Twain in Matthew Arnold, *General Grant*, with a rejoinder by Mark Twain, ed., with a new introduction, by John Y. Simon (Kent, Ohio: Kent State University Press, 1995), 57; Theodore Lyman, *With Grant and Meade: From the Wilderness to Appomattox*, ed. George R. Agassiz, introduction by Brooks D. Simpson (1922; reprint, Lincoln: University of Nebraska Press, 1994), 156.

3. Two of the earliest biographies including the stories of Grant's childhood are Charles A. Dana and J. H. Wilson, *The Life of Ulysses S. Grant: General of the Armies of the United States* (Springfield, Mass.: Samuel Bowles and Company, 1868), and Benson J. Lossing, *The Life Campaigns and Battles of General Ulysses S. Grant* (New York: Ledyard Bill, 1868).

4. T. Harry Williams, *McClellan, Sherman and Grant* (New Brunswick, N.J.: Rutgers University Press, 1962), 79.

5. As quoted in William S. McFeely, *Grant: A Biography* (New York: W. W. Norton, 1982), 495.

6. Bruce Catton, Preface, in *PUSG*, 1:xiv.

7. *PMUSG*, 1:17.

8. Valuable insight into this period is found in Joyce Appleby, *Inheriting the Revolution: The First Generation of Americans* (Cambridge: Belknap Press of Harvard University Press, 2001); Daniel Walker Howe, *What Hath God Wrought: The Transformation of America, 1815–1848* (New York: Oxford University Press, 2007); and Jack Larkin, *The Reshaping of Everyday Life, 1790–1840* (New York: HarperCollins, 1989). My account of Grant's early life is based on *PMUSG*, 1:17–31; Hamlin Garland, *Ulysses S. Grant: His Life and Character* (New York: Doubleday and McClure, 1898); Lloyd Lewis, *Captain Sam Grant* (Boston: Little, Brown, 1950), McFeely, *Grant*; and Brooks D. Simpson, *Ulysses S. Grant: Triumph Over Adversity, 1822–1865* (New York: Houghton Mifflin, 2000).

9. *PMUSG*, 1:21.

10. Ibid., 20.

11. As quoted in Lewis, *Captain Sam Grant*, 14.

12. Ibid., 36.

13. *PMUSG*, 1:31.

14. As quoted in Garland, *Ulysses S. Grant*, 3.

15. Ibid., 15.

16. Hamlin Garland interview with Jesse Root Grant, undated, box 48, item 543, Hamlin Garland Collection, Doheny Memorial Library, University of Southern California, Los Angeles.

17. *PMUSG*, 1:26.

18. As quoted in Garland, *Ulysses S. Grant*, 21.

19. *PMUSG*, 1:26.

20. Ibid., 25

21. Ibid., 30.

22. Ibid., 26–27.

23. The exact phrase is used by William Ralston Balch, *Life and Public Services of General Grant* (Philadelphia: Aetna Publishing Co., 1885), 7; J. K. Larke and Prof. J. Harris Paton, *General U. S. Grant: His Early Life and Military Career* (New York: Thomas Kelly, Publisher, 1885), 5; and Lossing, *The Life Campaigns and Battles of General Ulysses S. Grant*, 5.

24. *PMUSG*, 1:30.

25. Ibid.

26. This incident has been much discussed by later scholars of Grant with the intent of psychoanalyzing the effect on Grant's self-esteem. McFeely, in *Grant*, 10–11, argued that the incident was permanently damaging to Grant's sense of self, while Simpson downplays the humiliation (*Ulysses S. Grant*, 3–4).

27. Quotations from *PMUSG*, 1:25.

28. Ibid., 32.

29. Ibid., 38.

30. Ibid., 24.

31. Ibid., 38.

32. As quoted in Lewis, *Captain Sam Grant*, 60–61.

33. Grant accepted the middle initial "S." only; he claimed it stood for nothing.

34. As quoted in Lewis, *Captain Sam Grant*, 62.

35. Ibid., 60–77; McFeely, *Grant*, 13–20; Simpson, *Ulysses S. Grant*, 11–17.

36. Lewis, *Captain Sam Grant*, 72–74.

37. *PUSG*, 1:6.

38. Ibid., 38; Paul F. Boller Jr., *Presidential Anecdotes* (New York: Oxford University Press, 1981), 161.

39. *PUSG*, 1:5.

40. *PMUSG*, 1:38–39.

41. McFeely, *Grant*, 18.

42. *PMUSG*, 1:41.

43. Lewis, *Captain Sam Grant*, 63, 82 (Longstreet quotation).

44. John Y. Simon, "A Marriage Tested by War: Ulysses and Julia Grant," in *Intimate Strategies of the Civil War: Military Commanders and Their Wives*, ed. Carol K. Bleser and Lesley J. Gordon (New York: Oxford University Press, 2001), 123–37, quotation, 124.

45. *PMUSG*, 1:50; see also Julia Dent Grant, *The Personal Memoirs of Julia Dent Grant*, ed. John Y. Simon (Carbondale: Southern Illinois University Press, 1975), 50.

46. *PUSG*, 1:44, 68.

47. *PMUSG*, 1:51.

48. *PUSG*, 1:86.

49. As quoted in Sam W. Haynes, *James K. Polk and the Expansionist Impulse* (New York: Longman's Publishers, 2002), 140. See also Robert W. Johannsen, *To the Halls of the Montezumas: The Mexican War in the American Imagination* (New York: Oxford University Press, 1985); John S. D. Eisenhower, *So Far from God: The U.S. War with Mexico* (New York: Random House, 1989); and James M. McCaffrey, *Army of Manifest Destiny: The American Soldier in the Mexican-American War* (New York: New York University Press, 1992).

50. *PMUSG*, 1:68.

51. Statistics from Hugh Bicheno, "Mexican War," in *The Oxford Companion to Military History*, ed. Richard Holmes (New York: Oxford University Press, 2001), 581–82, and Joseph G. Dawson III, "Mexican War," in *The Oxford Companion to American Military History*, ed. John Whiteclay Chambers II (New York: Oxford University Press, 1999), 433–36.

52. Catton, Preface, *PUSG*, 1:xiv.

53. *PUSG*, 1:85, 97.

54. Ibid., 144.

55. Grant's comparison of his two commanders during the Mexican War—Taylor and Scott—can be found in *PMUSG*, I:138–139; quotation from ibid., 100.

56. *PUSG*, 1:106–7.

57. *PMUSG*, 1:110–11.

58. On September 16, 1848, Grant was promoted to first lieutenant brevet rank and captain brevet rank, dated from September 8 and September 13, respectively; *PUSG*, 1:xxxviii; Lewis, *Captain Sam Grant*, 167–81.

59. *PUSG*, 1:129, 127.

60. Ibid., 146.

61. Bicheno, "Mexican War"; Dawson, "Mexican War."

62. *PMUSG*, 1:180.

63. Ibid., 56.

64. Ibid., 53.

65. The phrase is taken from Brooks D. Simpson's title, *Ulysses S. Grant: Triumph Over Adversity*.

66. As quoted in Albert D. Richardson, *Personal History of Ulysses S. Grant* (Hartford, Conn.: American Publishing, 1868), 146.

67. Lewis, *Captain Sam Grant*, 285.

68. Bruce Catton, Introduction to Julia Dent Grant, *The Personal Memoirs of Julia Dent Grant*, 7.

69. Adam Badeau, *Grant in Peace: From Appomattox to Mount McGregor* (Hartford, Conn.: S. S. Scranton, 1887), 409.

70. Ishbel Ross, *The General's Wife: The Life of Mrs. Ulysses S. Grant* (New York: Dodd, Mead, 1959), is still the standard biography of Julia Grant.

71. See John F. Marszalek, "General and Mrs. William T. Sherman, a Contentious Union," in Bleser and Gordon, *Intimate Strategies of the Civil War*, 138–56.

72. Quotes from Julia Dent Grant, *The Personal Memoirs of Julia Dent Grant*, 67; See Simon, "A Marriage Tested by War," 123–37.

73. There are too many accounts of the prewar years to cite, but two good ones are Elizabeth R. Varon, *Disunion! The Coming of the American Civil War, 1789–1859* (Chapel Hill: University of North Carolina Press, 2008), and Eric H. Walther, *The Shattering of the Union: America in the 1850s* (Wilmington, Del.: Scholarly Resources, 2004).

74. *PUSG*, 1:247.

75. *PMUSG*, 1:194–99; *PUSG*, 1:247–53.

76. *PMUSG*, 1:198.

77. Quotations from *PUSG*, 1:278, 297.

78. Ibid., 301.

79. Ibid., 257–58.

80. *PMUSG*, 1:203.

81. Quotations from *PUSG*, 1:316.

82. As quoted in Charles G. Ellington, *The Trial of U. S. Grant: The Pacific Coast Years, 1852–1854* (Glendale, Calif.: Arthur H. Clark, 1987), 17.

83. See particularly ibid., 161–83, and Simpson, *Ulysses S. Grant*, 60–61.

84. McFeely, *Grant*, 55.

85. Ellington, *The Trial of U. S. Grant*, 178.

86. Simon, "A Marriage Tested by War," 128.

87. Jean Edward Smith, *Grant* (New York: Simon and Schuster, 2001), 231. Simpson, *Ulysses S. Grant*, 44–45, 107–8, 280–81, 348–49. Simpson deftly deflects most of the drinking charges against Grant, but he apparently agrees that Grant went on a "bender" before the Vicksburg Campaign (ibid., 176–80). The details related to this so-called Yazoo River episode are discussed in *PUSG*, 8:322–25. See also Josiah Bunting III, *Ulysses S. Grant* (New York: Henry Holt, 2004), 30–32, 51; and Geoffrey Perret, *Ulysses S. Grant: Soldier and President* (New York: Random House, 1997), 202–8.

88. James M. McPherson, *Drawn with the Sword: Reflections on the American Civil War* (New York: Oxford University Press, 1996), 172.

89. *PUSG*, 5:103; James Grant Wilson, *General Grant* (New York: D. Appleton, 1897), 158–59.

90. A short list of publications that support or debunk the contention that Grant was a

drunk include Kevin Anderson, "Grant's Lifelong Struggle With Alcohol," *Columbiad* 2 (Winter 1999): 16–26; Bruce Catton, "Reading, Writing, and History," *American Heritage* 7 (August 1956): 106–9; and Brooks D. Simpson, Introduction in Benjamin P. Thomas, ed. *Three Years with Grant, As Recalled by War Correspondent Sylvanus Cadwallader* (Lincoln: University of Nebraska Press), v–xix.

91. James Thurber, "If Grant Had Been Drinking at Appomattox," in *The Thurber Carnival* (New York: Harper Perennial Modern Classics, 1999). U. S. Grant has appeared briefly in numerous movies, but as Bruce Chadwick points out in his study of film and the Civil War, "There were no biographies of generals on either side in the sound era. Explaining their stories would have meant an exploration of the reasons for the war, which studios wanted to avoid" (*The Reel Civil War: Mythmaking in American Film* [New York: Alfred A. Knopf, Publisher, 2001], quotation, 74). See also Gary W. Gallagher, *Causes Won, Lost, and Forgotten: How Hollywood and Popular Art Shape What We Know about the Civil War* (Chapel Hill: University of North Carolina Press, 2008). A listing of movies and television shows in which Grant was a character can be found on The Internet Movie Database (IMDb). One of the first was *The Battle of Shiloh* (movie, 1913) and one of the most recent is *Bury My Heart at Wounded Knee* (TV, 2007).

92. Ev Erlich, *Grant Speaks* (New York: Warner Books, 2000); Al Kaltman, *Cigars, Whiskey and Winning: Leadership Lessons from Ulysses S. Grant* (New York: Prentice Hall, 1998). Other fairly recent novels include Max Byrd, *Grant* (New York: Bantam Books, 2000), and Richard Parry, *That Fateful Lightning: A Novel of Ulysses S. Grant* (New York: Ballantine Books, 2000). Two "counter-factual" novels starring Grant have been co-authored by Newt Gingrich and William R. Forstchen (parts two and three of their so-called "Civil War trilogy"): *Grant Comes East* (New York: St. Martin's Press, 2004) and *Never Call Retreat: Lee and Grant: The Final Victory* (New York: St. Martin's Press, 2005). *Never Call Retreat* has the Union still winning; Grant is magnanimous and Lee is noble.

93. Catton, Preface, *PUSG*, 1:xv.

94. *PUSG*, 1:327.

95. Ibid., 323.

96. Grant relates his reason for leaving the army in *PMUSG*, 1:141; See also McFeely, *Grant*, 55–57, and Simpson, *Ulysses S. Grant*, 60–62.

97. As quoted in Garland, *Ulysses S. Grant*, 129.

98. As quoted in Lewis, *Captain Sam Grant*, 332.

99. Garland, *Ulysses S. Grant*, 136.

100. *PUSG*, 1:347; Simpson, *Ulysses S. Grant*, 72.

101. Richardson, *Personal History*, 176.

102. As quoted in Lewis, *Captain Sam Grant*, 341.

103. Julia Dent Grant, *The Personal Memoirs of Julia Dent Grant*, 80.

104. *PUSG*, 1:351–52.

105. As quoted in Lewis, *Captain Sam Grant*, 351; Grant's position is explained in *PMUSG*, 1:212–15.

106. As quoted in John Russell Young, *Around the World with General Grant: A Narrative of the Visit of General U. S. Grant, Ex-President of the United States, to Various Countries in Europe, Asia, and Africa, in 1877, 1878, 1879*, 2 vols. (New York: American News Company, 1897), 2:446.

107. Richardson, *Personal History*, 174–75.

108. Today, a remnant of the land (about ten acres) is managed by the National Park Service.

109. Hardscrabble is situated on a 281-acre animal preserve (a part of which was at one time owned by Grant) operated by the Anheuser-Busch Company of St. Louis. Grant's home was removed from its original site to be on view at the St. Louis World's Fair held in 1904.

110. Scott A. Sandage, *Born Losers: A History of Failure in America* (Cambridge: Harvard University Press, 2005), 2–3, 11–12.

111. William B. Hesseltine, *Ulysses S. Grant, Politician* (New York: Dodd, Mead, 1935), 1; McFeely, *Grant*, xii. A third author has a similar take on Grant's youthful failures: see Michael Korda, *Ulysses S. Grant: The Unlikely Hero* (New York: HarperCollins, 2004), 11.

112. Definition taken from *Funk and Wagnalls New Standard Dictionary of the English Language* (New York: Funk and Wagnalls, 1928), 450.

113. Allan Nevins, Preface, in *PUSG*, 1:xix; Simpson, *Ulysses S. Grant*, 462.

## Chapter 2

1. The number of military publications about Grant was reported as 1,339 in Marie Ellen Kelsey, comp., *Ulysses S. Grant: A Bibliography*, Bibliographies of the Presidents of the United States, Mary Ellen McElligott, series editor (Westport, Conn.: Praeger Publishers, 2005), 65–182. That number is already outdated, as many more books about Grant have been published since 2005.

2. Allan Nevins, *Hamilton Fish: The Inner History of the Grant Administration* (New York: Dodd, Mead, 1936), 130; T. Harry Williams, *McClellan, Sherman and Grant* (New Brunswick, N.J.: Rutgers University Press, 1962), 109–10.

3. Accounts of the unveiling in D.C., as well as the other commemorations, can be found in *NYT Book Review and Magazine*, April 23, 1922; *NYT*, Sunday Picture Section, May 2, 1922; *New York World*, April 27 and 28, 1922; *St. Louis Post-Dispatch*, May 3, 1922; and "Nation's Capital Honors General Ulysses S. Grant. Memorial Is Dedicated," *Journal of the Illinois State Historical Society* 15 (April–July 1927): 548–50.

4. The world's largest equestrian statue is that of Victor Emmanuel II in Rome. Kathryn Allamong Jacob, *Testament to Union: Civil War Monuments in Washington, D.C.* (Baltimore: Johns Hopkins University Press, 1998), 36. See also James M. Goode, *The Outdoor Sculpture of Washington, D.C.* (Washington, D.C.: Smithsonian Institution Press, 1974), 243–48.

5. *The Grant Memorial in Washington* (Washington, D.C.: Government Printing Office, 1924); Dennis R. Montagna, "Henry Merwin Shrady's Ulysses S. Grant Memorial in Washington D.C.: A Study in Iconography, Content, and Patronage" (Ph.D. dissertation, University of Delaware, 1987); and Montagna, "The Ulysses S. Grant Memorial in Washington D.C.: A Monument for the New Century," *Army* 53 (July 2003): 43–47. The Society of the Army of Tennessee, filled with veterans who fought under General Grant, urged Congress to fund the monument. It took over twenty years to build. Sculptor Henry M. Shrady was the son of Grant's doctor, George F. Shrady, during his last illness. Information on the monument's decrepit state is found in Linda Wheeler, "Controversial Proposal for Grant Memorial," *Civil War Times*, June 2008, 14.

6. USG to Jesse Root Grant, April 21, 1861, *PUSG*, 2:7.

7. *PMUSG*, 1:250.

8. *PUSG*, 2:83.

9. As quoted in Jean Edward Smith, *Grant* (New York: Simon and Schuster, 2001), 131.

10. USG, as quoted in Smith, *Grant*, 164; USG to Brig. Gen. Simon B. Buckner, *PUSG*, 4:218.

11. As quoted in Smith, *Grant*, 164; For information on how Grant handled the delicate negotiations with his friend Buckner, see Brooks D. Simpson, *Ulysses S. Grant: Triumph over Adversity* (New York: Houghton Mifflin, 2000), 117–18.

12. A. E. Watrous, "Grant As His Son Saw Him: An Interview With Colonel Frederick D. Grant About His Father," *McClure's Magazine* 2 (May 1894): 515–19, quotation, 518.

13. Quotation in Bruce Catton, *Grant Moves South* (1960; reprint, Boston: Little, Brown, 1988), 179.

14. *PMUSG*, 1:297–98.

15. Ibid., 356.

16. As quoted in Charles Bracelen Flood, *Grant and Sherman: The Friendship That Won the War* (New York: Farrar, Straus and Giroux, 2005), 114. Jean Smith wrote that Sherman's remarks were originally published in the *Washington Post* and quoted in the *Army and Navy Journal*, December 30, 1893. Smith, *Grant*, 657, n. 162.

17. A thoughtful review of Grant's generalship at Shiloh can be found in Brian Holden Reid, "Command and Leadership in the Civil War, 1861–65," ed. Susan Mary Grant and Brian Holden Reid, *The American Civil War: Exploration and Reconsiderations* (Harlow, England: Pearson Education, Ltd., 2000), 142–68.

18. USG, "General Orders No. 34," *PUSG*, 5:1–22.

19. The phrase, slightly altered, is taken from W. E. Woodward, *Meet General Grant* (New York: Garden City Publishing Company, 1928), 255.

20. Simpson, *Ulysses S. Grant*, 137; Grant, in a rare gesture, responded to Reid in a letter to the editor of the *Cincinnati Commercial* (reprinted in the *Chicago Times* of May 3, 1862). Grant's official report is found in *PUSG*, 5:32–36.

21. Simpson, *Ulysses S. Grant*, 136–37; Catton, *Grant Moves South*, 254–56, Smith, *Grant*, 204–5; *NYTrib*, April 16, 1862; see also ibid., April 17 and May 3, 1862.

22. *PMUSG*, 1:385.

23. John Keegan, "Grant and Unheroic Leadership," in *The Mask of Command* (London: Jonathan Cape, 1987), 228.

24. Joseph T. Ghatthaar, *Partners in Command: The Relationships between Leaders in the Civil War* (New York: Free Press, 1994), 161.

25. WTS to John Sherman, February 23, 1862, *The Sherman Letters: Correspondence between General and Senator Sherman from 1837 to 1891* (New York: Da Capo Press, 1969), 193; William Tecumseh Sherman, *Memoirs of General William T. Sherman*, 2 vols. (New York: Charles L. Webster, 1891), 1:400; Williams, *McClellan, Sherman and Grant*, 46. Biographies of Sherman abound. Three are John F. Marszalek, *Sherman: A Soldier's Passion for Order* (New York: Free Press, 1993); Michael Fellman, *Citizen Sherman: A Life of William Tecumseh Sherman* (New York: Random House, 1995); and Lee Kennett, *Sherman: A Soldier's Life* (New York: HarperCollins, 2001).

26. USG, "Speech," October 14, 1874, *PUSG*, 25:258; Steven E. Woodworth, *Nothing but Victory: The Army of the Tennessee, 1861–1865* (New York: Alfred A. Knopf, 2005).

27. First quotation, *NYTrib*, May 3, 1862; second quotation, "Regular," April 8 and 10, 1862,

in William B. Styple, ed., *Writing and Fighting the Civil War: Soldier Correspondence to the New York Sunday Mercury* (Kearny, N.J.: Belle Grove Publishing Company, 2004), 83–84.

28. Catton, *Grant Moves South*, 243.

29. *PMUSG*, 2:531.

30. USG, General Orders No. 60, July 3, 1862, *PUSG*, 5:190.

31. *PMUSG*, 1:368; Catton, *Grant Moves South*, 282–83.

32. WTS to John Sherman, October 1, 1862, Brooks D. Simpson and Jean V. Berlin, eds., *Sherman's Civil War: Selected Correspondence of William T. Sherman, 1860–1865* (Chapel Hill: University of North Carolina Press), 312.

33. As quoted in Mark Grimsley, *The Hard Hand of War: Union Military Policy toward Southern Civilians, 1861–1865* (New York: Cambridge University Press, 1995), 118. See also WTS to USG, November 8, 1862, Simpson and Berlin, *Sherman's Civil War*, 322–23, for more of his thoughts on waging war on civilians.

34. As quoted in Michael B. Ballard, *Vicksburg: The Campaign That Opened the Mississippi* (Chapel Hill: University of North Carolina Press, 2004), 24. Lincoln's statement came in a meeting with David Porter on November 15, 1862.

35. *Indianapolis Daily Journal*, April 5, 1863.

36. First quotation, James M. McPherson, *Battle Cry of Freedom* (New York: Oxford University Press, 1988), 588; second quotation, *New York World*, March 12, 1863.

37. Quotations in Smith, *Grant*, 231.

38. Charles A. Dana, *New York Sun*, January 28, 1887.

39. USG to WTS, May 3, 1863, *PUSG*, 8:151–52, quotation, 152.

40. As quoted in Styple, *Writing and Fighting the Civil War*, 193.

41. Gary W. Gallagher, "An Old-Fashioned Soldier in a Modern War?: Robert E. Lee as Confederate General," *Civil War History* 45, no. 4 (December 1999): 295–321.

42. *PMUSG*, 1:532.

43. "Greenback," June 24, 1863, in Styple, *Writing and Fighting the Civil War*, 201.

44. Isaac Jackson quotation in Duane Schultz, *The Most Glorious Fourth: Vicksburg and Gettysburg, July 4, 1863* (New York: W. W. Norton, 2002), cover page; "N.N.," July 31, 1863, in Styple *Writing and Fighting the Civil War*, 209; Miltmore quotation in William S. McFeely, *Grant: A Biography* (New York: W. W. Norton, 1982), 137.

45. USG to John Pemberton, July 3, 1863, *PUSG*, 8:455.

46. WTS to USG, July 4, 1863, Simpson and Berlin, *Sherman's Civil War*, 496–97. Edward Everett was a widely admired orator of the era.

47. As quoted in Catton, *Grant Moves South*, 476.

48. Jefferson Davis to Lt. Gen. E. K. Smith, July 14, 1863, in William J. Cooper Jr., ed., *Jefferson Davis: The Essential Writings* (New York: Random House, 2003), 309; see also Emory Thomas, *The Confederate Nation: 1861–1865* (New York: Harper and Row, 1979), 244.

49. *PMUSG*, 1:567–68.

50. Christopher Waldrep, *Vicksburg's Long Shadow: The Civil War Legacy of Race and Remembrance* (Lanham, Md.: Rowman & Littlefield, 2005); Herman Hattaway, *Gettysburg to Vicksburg: The Five Original Civil War Battlefield Parks* (Columbia: University of Missouri Press, 2001). Vicksburg National Military Park was established in 1899 and run by the War Department until 1933, when the National Park Service (under the Interior Department) took over. Visitation statistics are posted on <http://www.nps.gov/archive/vick/home.htm>.

51. Ballard, *Vicksburg*, 430. Other recent works on Vicksburg are William L. Shea and Terrence J. Winshel, *Vicksburg Is the Key: The Struggle or the Mississippi River* (Lincoln: University of Nebraska Press, 2003), and Schultz, *The Most Glorious Fourth*. For a sharply differing point of view on Vicksburg's importance, see Albert Castel, *Winning and Losing in the Civil War: Essays and Stories* (Columbia: University of South Carolina Press, 1996).

52. McFeely, *Grant*, 137.

53. Catton, *Grant Moves South*, 462.

54. As quoted in T. Harry Williams, *Lincoln and His Generals* (New York: Alfred A. Knopf, 1952), 272.

55. Abraham Lincoln to USG, July 13, 1863, Roy P. Basler, ed., *The Collected Works of Abraham Lincoln*, 9 vols. (New Brunswick, N.J.: Rutgers University Press 1953–55), 6:326.

56. Horace Porter, *Campaigning with Grant* (New York: The Century Co., 1897), 7.

57. Ibid., 14–16.

58. Quoted in McFeely, *Grant*, 144.

59. Quotations in Bruce Catton, *Grant Takes Command* (Boston: Little, Brown, 1968), 84–85.

60. *New York Herald*, November 28, 1863.

61. *PMUSG*, 2:97.

62. McFeely, *Grant*, 139.

63. WTS to USG, March 10, 1864, Simpson and Berlin, *Sherman's Civil War*, 603; Unidentified, November 29, 1863, in Styple, *Writing and Fighting the Civil War*, 223.

64. Abraham Lincoln to USG, December 8, 1863, Basler, *Collected Works of Lincoln*, 7:53.

65. *New York World*, November 26, 1863. Quotation from *Personal Memoirs of John H. Brinton, Major and Surgeon, U.S.V., 1861–1865* (New York: Neale Publishing Co., 1914), 239.

66. Mark E. Neely Jr. and Harold Holzer, *The Union Image: Popular Prints of the Civil War North* (Chapel Hill: University of North Carolina Press, 2000), 162.

67. The inspiration for the illustration was an official unanimous vote of thanks to Grant from the United States Congress, which also contained a provision to strike a Gold Medal to be presented to him at a later date. *Harper's Weekly*, February 6, 1864, 82. For a study of the era's most important political cartoonist, Thomas Nast, see Fiona Deans Halloran, "The Power of the Pencil: Thomas Nast and American Political Art (Ph.D. dissertation, University of California, Los Angeles, 2005).

68. Julian K. Larke, *General Grant and His Campaigns* (New York: J. C. Derby & N. C. Miller, 1864).

69. Chesley A. Mosman, *The Rough Side of War: The Civil War Journal of Chesley A. Mosman, 1st Lieutenant, Company D 59th Illinois Volunteer Infantry Regiment*, ed. Arnold Gates (Garden City, N.Y.: Basin Publishing Co., 1987), 158.

70. *NYTrib*, March 2, 1864.

71. As quoted in Simpson, *Ulysses S. Grant*, 247.

72. As quoted in David Herbert Donald, *Lincoln* (New York: Simon and Schuster, 1995), 491.

73. *PUSG*, 9:541.

74. USG to Jesse Root Grant, February 20, 1864, ibid., 10:148.

75. Basler, *Collected Works of Lincoln*, 8:332.

76. Williams, *McClellan, Sherman and Grant*, 103.

77. USG to Abraham Lincoln, June 11, 1863, *PUSG*, 8:342; see also *PMUSG*, 1:424–26. For the history of the refugee camp, see Simpson, *Ulysses S. Grant*, 162; Brooks D. Simpson, *Let Us Have Peace: Ulysses S. Grant and the Politics of War and Reconstruction, 1861–1868* (Chapel Hill: University of North Carolina Press, 1997), 31–33; and McFeely, *Grant*, 126–27;

78. Jennifer L. Weber, *Copperheads: The Rise and Fall of Lincoln's Opponents in the North* (New York: Oxford University Press, 2006); James M. McPherson, *Crossroads of Freedom: Antietam, the Battle That Changed the Course of the Civil War* (New York: Oxford University Press, 2004).

79. As quoted in Smith, *Grant*, 259–60.

80. *PUSG*, 9:196. For insightful discussions of Grant's relationship with Lincoln, see Gabor S. Boritt, ed., *Lincoln's Generals* (New York: Oxford University Press, 1994), and Glatthaar, *Partners in Command*. Grant's stance on black soldiers is explored in Brooks D. Simpson, "Quandaries of Command: Ulysses Grant and Black Soldiers," in *Union and Emancipation* ed David W. Blight and Brooks D. Simpson (Kent, Ohio: Kent State University Press, 1997), 123–50.

81. USG to Richard Taylor, June 22, 1863, *PUSG*, 8:400–401; *NYT*, November 1, 1864.

82. James Ford Rhodes, *History of the Civil War* (New York: Macmillan, 1917), 304.

83. As quoted in Smith, *Grant*, 284. Grant described the challenges that faced him in *PMUSG*, 2:116–33.

84. Quoted in Noah Andre Trudeau, "A Mere Question of Time: Robert E. Lee from the Wilderness to Appomattox Court House," in *Lee the Soldier*, ed. Gary W. Gallagher (Lincoln: University of Nebraska Press, 1996), 538.

85. *PMUSG*, 2:125.

86. Catton, *Grant Takes Command*, 124–26.

87. As quoted in Doris Kearns Goodwin, *Team of Rivals: The Political Genius of Abraham Lincoln* (New York: Simon and Schuster, 2005), 615.

88. *PUSG*, 10:195

89. *PMUSG*, 2:122.

90. As quoted in Williams, *Lincoln and His Generals*, 262.

91. USG to Charles A. Dana, August 5, 1863, *PUSG*, 9:146.

92. *PMUSG*, 2:117–18; McPherson, *Battle Cry of Freedom*, 718–50.

93. WTS to USG, March 10, 1864, *PUSG*, 10:188.

94. For a favorable assessment of Halleck, see John F. Marszalek, *Commander of All Lincoln's Armies: A Life of General Henry W. Halleck* (Cambridge: Belknap Press of Harvard University Press, 2004).

95. As quoted in Smith, *Grant*, 296.

96. *NYTrib*, March 8, 1864; *New York Herald*, March 9, 1864.

97. *Chicago Tribune*, March 13, 1864.

98. *Harper's Weekly*, April 23, 1864, 258.

99. *NYT*, March 7, 1864.

100. *Philadelphia Daily Evening Bulletin*, March 2, 1864, and March 3, 1864.

101. *NYT*, May 6, 1864.

102. USG to Julia Dent Grant, May 2, 1864, *PUSG*, 10: 394.

103. McPherson, *Battle Cry of Freedom*, 626–65; Philip Shaw Paludan, *A People's Contest: The Union and Civil War, 1861–1865* (New York: Harper and Row, 1988).

104. *PMUSG*, 2:123; USG to Julia Dent Grant, April 27, 1864, *PUSG* 10: 363.

105. USG to Maj. Gen. Henry W. Halleck, March 30, 1864, *PUSG*, 10:240.

106. USG to Maj. Gen. George G. Meade, April 9, 1864, ibid., 273.

107. *PMUSG*, 2:127–30. The three auxiliary armies were under the command of political generals: Benjamin F. Butler was a Democrat and Nathaniel P. Banks a prominent Republican from the vitally important state of Massachusetts, while Franz Sigel was a favorite of the large and politically active German American community. All three commanders caused Grant (and Lincoln) great headaches, although their armies were ready for action by April. Banks's Red River Campaign had the distinction of failing first. On April 22, Grant asked Lincoln to remove Banks from command, telling the president, "I have been satisfied for the last nine months that to keep General Banks was to neutralize a large force and to support it most expensively." Almost always, political considerations trumped military competence, however, and Lincoln did not dismiss Banks. USG to Maj. Gen. Henry W. Halleck, April 22, 1864, *PUSG*, 10:340–41.

108. Allan Nevins, ed., *A Diary of Battle: The Personal Journals of Colonel Charles S. Wainwright, 1861–1865* (New York: Harcourt, Brace & World, 1962), 329; Stephen Minot Weld, *War Diary and Letters of Stephen Minot Weld, 1861–1865* (1912; 2nd edition, Boston: Massachusetts Historical Society, 1979), 276; Harold Adams Small, ed., *The Road to Richmond: The Civil War Letters of Major Abner R. Small of the 16th Maine Volunteers* (New York: Fordham University Press, 2000), 130; Salter as quoted in Bell Irvin Wiley, *The Life of Billy Yank: The Common Soldier of the Union* (New York: Bobbs-Merrill, 1951), 323.

109. James I. Robertson, ed., *The Civil War Letters of General Robert McAllister* (1965; reprint, New Brunswick, N.J.: Rutgers University Press, 1997), 408; Theodore Lyman, *With Grant and Meade: From the Wilderness to Appomattox*, ed. George R. Agassiz, introduction by Brooks D. Simpson (1922; reprint, Lincoln: University of Nebraska Press, 1994), 80–81; as quoted in ibid., ix.

110. As quoted in Bruce Catton, *A Stillness at Appomattox* (New York: Doubleday, 1953), 39; Robert Goldthwaite Carter, *Four Brothers in Blue, or Sunshine and Shadows of the War of the Rebellion: A Story of the Great Civil War from Bull Run to Appomattox* (Austin: University of Texas Press, 1978), 390; Marcia Reid-Green, ed., *Letters Home: Henry Matrau of the Iron Brigade* (Lincoln: University of Nebraska Press, 1993), 76; Eric A. Campbell, ed., *"A Grand and Terrible Dramma": From Gettysburg to Petersburg: The Civil War Letters of Charles Wellington Reed* (New York: Fordham University Press, 200), 195–96.

111. As quoted in Wiley, *The Life of Billy Yank*, 322.

112. Larry Rogers and Keith Rogers, eds., *Their Horses Climbed Trees: A Chronicle of the California 100 and Battalion in the Civil War, from San Francisco to Appomattox* (Atglen, Pa.: Schiffer Military History, 2001), 261–62.

113. First quotation, Catton, *A Stillness at Appomattox*, 46; second quotation, Carter, *Four Brothers in Blue*, 417; third quotation, Catton, *Grant Takes Command*, 363.

114. "Ulysses Leads the Van," words and music by E. W. Locke (New York: S. T. Gordon, 1864).

115. USG to George S. Meade, April 9, 1864, *PUSG*, 10:274.

116. *PMUSG*, 2:143.

117. Abraham Lincoln to USG, April 30, 1864, and USG to Lincoln, May 1, 1864, both in *PUSG*, 10:380.

118. Gordon C. Rhea, *The Battle of the Wilderness, May 5–6, 1864* (Baton Rouge: Louisiana State University Press, 1994). For a poet's reflection on the battle, see Stephen Cushman, *Bloody Promenade: Reflections on a Civil War Battle* (Charlottesville: The University Press of Virginia, 1999).

119. "Whenever I Smoke a Cigar," in Cushman, *Bloody Promenade*, 252.

120. As quoted in Catton, *A Stillness at Appomattox*, 39.

121. K. M. Kostal, ed., *Field of Battle: The Civil War Letters of Major Thomas J. Halsey* (Washington, D.C.: National Geographic Society, 1996), 128.

122. USG to E. M. Stanton, May 11, 1864, *PUSG*, 10:422.

123. First quotation, Noah Andre Trudeau, *Bloody Roads South: The Wilderness to Cold Harbor, May–June 1864* (Boston: Little, Brown, 1989), 188–89; second quotation, Donald, *Lincoln*, 501; third quotation, *Harper's Weekly*, May 28, 1864, 338; fourth quotation, Unidentified, May 15, 1864, in Styple, *Writing and Fighting the Civil War*, 258. The story is told well in Gordon C. Rhea, *The Battles for Spotsylvania Court House and the Road to Yellow Tavern, May 7–12, 1864* (Baton Rouge: Louisiana State University Press, 1997).

124. USG to Maj. Gen. Henry W. Halleck, May 26, 1864, *PUSG*, 10:491.

125. As quoted in Porter, *Campaigning with Grant*, 179. In his memoirs, Grant wrote, "I have always regretted that the last assault at Cold Harbor was ever made. . . . At Cold Harbor no advantage whatever was gained to compensate for the heavy loss we sustained" (*PMUSG*, 2:276); a recent work highly critical of Grant's generalship at Cold Harbor and in the Overland Campaign is Ernest B. Furgurson, *Not War but Murder: Cold Harbor, 1864* (New York: Alfred A. Knopf, 2000). More favorable evaluations can be found in Rhea, *Cold Harbor*, and Edward H. Bonekemper III, *A Victor, Not a Butcher: Ulysses S. Grant's Overlooked Military Genius* (Washington, D.C.: Regnery Publishing, 2004).

126. For a discussion on battle fatigue, see James M. McPherson, *For Cause and Comrades* (New York: Oxford University Press, 1997), 43–5; 163–67.

127. As quoted in Weber, *Copperheads*, 139.

128. Mary Warner Athomas and Richard A. Sauers, eds., *The Civil War Letters of First Lieutenant James B. Thomas, Adjutant, 107th Pennsylvania Volunteers* (Baltimore: Butternut and Blue, 1995), 183

129. *Philadelphia Daily Evening Bulletin*, May 13, 1864.

130. Bruce Catton, *U. S. Grant and the American Military Tradition* (Boston: Little, Brown, 1954), 123.

131. McPherson, *Battle Cry of Freedom*, 734.

132. Smith, *Grant*, 301. This photograph is often placed at Grant's headquarters at City Point. But according to William Frassanito, one of the leading authorities on Civil War photos, Mathew Brady and his staff took the photographs of Grant and his staff, as well as other Union generals, at Cold Harbor. William A. Frassanito, *Grant and Lee: The Virginia Campaigns 1864–1865* (Gettysburg, Pa.: Thomas Publishing Co., 1983), 172–79; see also *U. S. Grant: The Man and the Image*, National Portrait Gallery exhibition catalogue (Carbondale: Southern Illinois University Press, 1985), 46.

133. Quotation in James H. Wilson, *Under the Old Flag*, 2 vols. (New York: Appleton, 1912), 1:400. Catton, *A Stillness at Appomattox*, 43.

134. Porter, *Campaigning with Grant*, 69–70.

135. USG to Edwin M. Stanton, September 13, 1864, *PUSG*, 12:158–59.

136. Abraham Lincoln to USG, August 17, 1864, *PUSG*, 11:425. Lincoln to F. A. Conkling, June 3, 1864, Basler, *Collected Works of Lincoln*, 7:374; Susan T. Puck, ed., *Sacrifice at Vicksburg: Letters from the Front* (Shippensburg, Pa.: Burd Street Press, 1997), 101; Robertson, *The Civil War Letters of General Robert McAllister*, 457.

137. Brooks D. Simpson, "Great Expectations: Ulysses S. Grant, the Northern Press, and the Opening of the Wilderness Campaign," in *The Wilderness Campaign*, ed. Gary W. Gallagher (Chapel Hill: University of North Carolina Press, 1997), 1–35, quotation, 8; Athomas and Sauers, *The Civil War Letters of First Lieutenant James B. Thomas*, 206; Rogers and Rogers, *Their Horses Climbed Trees*, 277.

138. Petersburg's travails are well described in A. Wilson Green, *Civil War Petersburg: The Confederate City in the Crucible of War* (Charlottesville: University of Virginia Press, 2006).

139. USG to Maj. Gen. Henry W. Halleck, August 1, 1864, *PUSG*, 11:361. On African American troops, see John David Smith, ed., *Black Soldiers in Blue: African American Troops in the Civil War Era* (Chapel Hill: University of North Carolina Press, 2002), and Noah Andre Trudeau, *Like Men of War: Black Troops in the Civil War, 1862-1865* (Boston: Little, Brown, 1998).

140. USG to Maj. Gen. Henry W. Halleck, August 1, 1864, *PUSG*, 11:358; USG to Maj. Gen. Philip H. Sheridan, August 5, 1854, ibid., 378. USG to Maj. Gen. Philip H. Sheridan, August 26, 1864, ibid., 12:96. Two books on the campaign are Jeffry D. Wert, *From Winchester to Cedar Creek: The Shenandoah Valley Campaign of 1864* (Mechanicsburg, Pa.: Stackpole Books, 1997), and Gary W. Gallagher, ed., *The Shenandoah Valley Campaign of 1864* (Chapel Hill: University of North Carolina Press, 2006).

141. As quoted in McPherson, *Battle Cry of Freedom*, 750; For Sherman's campaign in military perspective, see Russell F. Weigley, *A Great Civil War: A Military and Political History, 1861-1865* (Bloomington: Indiana University Press, 2000), 358–67.

142. As quoted in McPherson, *Battle Cry of Freedom*, 790.

143. *Harper's Weekly*, August 27, 1864, 546.

144. As quoted in Weber, *Copperheads*, 140.

145. As quoted in Philip Shaw Paludan, *The Presidency of Abraham Lincoln* (Lawrence: University Press of Kansas, 1994), 283.

146. USG to Elihu B. Washburne, August 16, 1864, *PUSG*, 12:16–17.

147. As quoted in Marszalek, *Sherman*, 283. USG to WTS, September 4, 1864, *PUSG*, 12:127.

148. Carter, *Four Brothers in Blue*, 484; Robertson, *The Civil War Letters of General Robert McAllister*, 502.

149. USG to Edwin M. Stanton, November 10, 1864, *PUSG*, 12:398. The politics of soldiers is discussed in Joseph Allan Frank, *With Ballot and Bayonet: The Political Socialization of American Civil War Soldiers* (Athens: University of Georgia Press, 1998), 96–97. For perspective on the 1864 election, see Michael Vorenberg, *Final Freedom: The Civil War, the Abolition of Slavery, and the Thirteenth Amendment* (New York: Cambridge University Press, 2001), and John C. Waugh, *Reelecting Lincoln: The Battle for the 1864 Presidency* (New York: Da Capo Press, 2001).

150. USG to WTS, December 18, 1864, *PUSG*, 13:129.

151. Neely and Holzer, *The Union Image*, 161–81; John Antrobus, "General Ulysses S. Grant Painted on the Battlefield of Chattanooga, 1863-1864." John Antrobus was an Englishman who

arrived in the United States in the 1850s, becoming a successful painter of portraits and land-scapes. When the war broke out, he volunteered for the Confederates, but quickly changed his mind and opened a studio in Chicago. Antrobus was the first artist to paint Ulysses S. Grant's portrait. Congress also selected him to design the Grant medal in 1863.

152. *NYT*, February 23, 1865.

153. *PUSG*, 14:361.

154. As quoted in Emory M. Thomas, *Robert E. Lee: A Biography* (New York: W. W. Norton, 1995), 362.

155. *PMUSG*, 2:485.

156. Ibid., 489.

157. Ibid., 492.

158. As quoted in Porter, *Campaigning with Grant*, 479–80; *PMUSG*, 2:492–95.

159. *PUSG*, 12:375.

160. Franklin Archibald Dick, *Troubled State: Civil War Journals of Franklin Archibald Dick*, ed. Gari Carter (Kirksville, Mo.: Truman State University Press, 2008), 190.

161. As quoted in Adam Badeau, *Military History of Ulysses S. Grant*, 3 vols. (New York: D. Appleton, 1868–82), 3:608.

162. *New York Herald*, April 14, 1865.

163. As quoted in Douglas Southall Freeman, *Lee's Lieutenants: A Study in Command*, one-volume abridgement by Stephen W. Sears (New York: Scribner, 1998), 811.

164. Accounts of the ceremony by two of Grant's aides are found in Porter, *Campaigning with Grant*, 466–84, and Badeau, *Military History of U. S. Grant*, 600–624; See also Joshua Chamberlain, *The Passing of the Armies* (New York: G. P. Putnam's Sons, 1915). The other Union officers at the ceremony were Lt. Col. Ely S. Parker, Lt. Col. Orville E. Babcock, Maj. Gen. Edward O. C. Ord, Capt. Robert T. Lincoln (Abraham Lincoln's son), Lt. Col. Theodore S. Bowers, Maj. Gen. Philip H. Sheridan, Brig. Gen. John Rawlins, Brig. Gen. Rufus Ingalls, Brig. Gen. George H. Sharpe, Brig. Gen. Michael Morgan, and Brig. Gen. Seth Williams. General Lee was accompanied by Lt. Col. Charles Marshall.

165. Information on Appomattox can be found at <http://www.nps.gov/archive/apco/index1.htm>; Grant's table is in the Smithsonian Institute, and Lee's table is owned by the Chicago Historical Society.

## Chapter 3

1. Henry Adams, *The Education of Henry Adams* (New York: Literary Classics of the United States, 1983), 960, 962, 963. "Uniquely stupid" in Brooks D. Simpson, "Henry Adams and the Age of Grant," *Hayes Historical Journal* 8 (Spring 1989): 5–23, quotation, 5. Simpson writes that "Adams's portrayal of the Grant administration and its head was shaped far more by his personal prejudices, perspectives, and disappointments than by an attempt to analyze the performance of the President" (ibid., 20). A good summation of the distain felt for Grant by contemporaries and historians is found in Frank J. Scaturro: *President Grant Reconsidered* (Lanham, Md.: Madison Books, 1999), 1–13.

2. Gideon Welles, *Diary*, ed. Howard K. Beale, 3 vols. (New York: W. W. Norton, 1960), 3:180 (August 22, 1867) and 244–45 (20 December 1867); campaign song as quoted in William S. McFeely, *Grant: A Biography* (New York: W. W. Norton, 1981), 283, and Irwin Silber, *Songs*

*America Voted By* (Harrisburg, Pa.: Stackpole Books, 1971), 101. Obviously "black" marine referred to Grant's popularity among African Americans in the South.

3. Information on the so-called "golden age" of political cartooning can be found in Allan Nevins and Frank Weitenkampf, *A Century of Political Cartoons: Caricature in the United States from 1800–1900* (New York: Charles Scribner's Sons, 1944); Wendy Rick Reaves, "Thomas Nast and the President," *American Art Journal* 19, no. 1 (Winter, 1987): 60–71; Richard Samuel West, *Satire on Stone: The Political Cartoons of Joseph Keppler* (Urbana: The University of Illinois Press, 1988). President Grant was hardly the only president (or major national politician) to be held up to partisan mocking and ridicule, then and now. Devastating caricatures were published of Senators Benjamin Butler of Massachusetts, James G. Blaine of Maine, and Roscoe Conkling of New York. Democratic politicians suffered similar treatment, no one more than New York City's Tammany Hall boss William Tweed. Tom Culbertson, "The Golden Age of American Political Cartoons," *Journal of the Gilded Age and Progressive Era* 7 (July 2008): 276–95.

4. *The Nation*, March 9, 1876.

5. *The Nation*, September 25, 1879; *NYTrib*, July 24, 1885.

6. Woodrow Wilson, *Reunion and Rationalization*, in *A History of the American People*, 5 vols. (New York: Harper & Brothers, 1912), 5:122; W. E. Woodward, *Meet General Grant* (New York: Horace Liveright, 1928), 394; Vernon Parrington, *Main Currents in American Thought*, 3 vols. (New York: Harcourt, Brace and World, 1954–58), 3:28.

7. J. G. Randall, *The Civil War and Reconstruction* (Boston: D. C. Heath, 1937), 816–17; Allan Nevins and Henry Steele Commager, *America: The Story of a Free People* (Boston: Little, Brown, 1942), 277; Samuel Eliot Morison and Henry Steele Commager, *The Growth of the American Republic*, 2 vols. (New York: Oxford University Press, 1939) 2:58

8. Robert Penn Warren, Introduction to Dixon Wecter, *The Hero in America* (1941; reprint, New York: Charles Scribner's Sons, 1971), xxi.

9. An entertaining and smart overview of the Gilded Age can be found in Mark Wahlgren Summers, *The Era of Good Stealing* (New York: Oxford University Press, 1993). See also Charles W. Calhoun, ed., *The Gilded Age: Essays on the Origins of Modern America* (Wilmington, Del.: Scholarly Resources, 1996); Rebecca Edwards, *New Spirits: Americans in the Gilded Age, 1865–1905* (New York: Oxford University Press, 2006); and Glenn Porter, *The Rise of Big Business* (Arlington Heights, Ill.: Harlan Davison, 1992).

10. Nevins and Commager, *America: The Story of a Free People*, 274.

11. William B. Hesseltine, *Ulysses S. Grant, Politician* (New York: Dodd, Mead, 1935); Allan Nevins, *Hamilton Fish: The Inner History of the Grant Administration* (New York: Dodd, Mead, 1936), quotation from Hesseltine, *Ulysses S. Grant*, viii. A friendly biography, using family papers unavailable to Hesseltine and Fish, was written by a grandson. See Maj. Gen. Ulysses S. Grant 3rd, *Ulysses S. Grant: Warrior and Statesman* (New York: William Morrow, 1969). For a comprehensive list of scholarship on Grant's presidency, see Marie Ellen Kelsey, comp., *Ulysses S. Grant: A Bibliography*, Bibliographies of the Presidents of the United States, Mary Ellen McElligott, series editor (Westport Conn.: Praeger Publishers, 2005), 183–287.

12. Hesseltine, *Ulysses S. Grant*, vii–viii.

13. Nevins and Commager, *America: The Story of a Free People*, 277. The literature on Reconstruction is vast. Noteworthy are the following: Eric Foner, *Reconstruction: America's*

*Unfinished Revolution, 1863–1867* (New York: Harper & Row, 1988); William Gillette, *Retreat from Reconstruction, 1869–1879* (Baton Rouge: Louisiana State University Press, 1979); Leon Litwack, *Been in the Storm So Long: The Aftermath of Slavery* (New York: Alfred A Knopf, 1979); James McPherson, *Ordeal by Fire: The Civil War and Reconstruction* (New York: Oxford University Press, 1982); Heather Cox Richardson, *The Greatest Nation on Earth: Republican Economic Policies during the Civil War* (Cambridge: Harvard University Press, 1997); and Brooks D. Simpson, *The Reconstruction Presidents* (Lawrence: University Press of Kansas, 1998).

14. Claude G. Bowers, *The Tragic Era* (Cambridge: Houghton Mifflin Company, 1929), 538. The most influential of this school is William A. Dunning, *Reconstruction, Political and Economic, 1865–1877* (New York: Harper and Bros., 1898). Others include E. Merton Coulter, *The South during Reconstruction, 1865–1877* (Baton Rouge: Louisiana State University Press, 1947), and Walter L. Fleming, *The Sequel of Appomattox* (New Haven: Yale University Press, 1919). Although not associated with the Dunning school, Woodward's *Meet General Grant* offers the same type of analysis, 437–42. An excellent overview of earlier historical interpretations of the era, including Reconstruction, is offered in Thomas J. Pressly, *Americans Interpret Their Civil War* (Princeton, N.J.: Princeton University Press, 1954).

15. Gillette, *Retreat from Reconstruction*; quotation from McFeely, *Grant*, xi. A recent biographer shared McFeely's negative assessment: Michael Korda, *Ulysses S. Grant: The Unlikely Hero* (New York: HarperCollins, 2004). For a refutation of McFeely, see Brooks D. Simpson, "Butcher? Racist?: An Examination of William S. McFeely's *Grant: A Biography*," *Civil War History* 33 (1987): 3–83.

16. Richard Nelson Current, "President Grant and the Continuing Civil War," in *Arguing with Historians* (Middletown, Conn.: Wesleyan University Press, 1987): 71–82, quotation, 82.

17. Simpson, *The Reconstruction Presidents*, and *Let Us Have Peace: Ulysses S. Grant and the Politics of War and Reconstruction, 1861–1868* (Chapel Hill: University of North Carolina Press, 1991); Jean Edward Smith, *Grant* (New York: Simon and Schuster, 2001); Josiah Bunting III, *Ulysses S. Grant* (New York: Henry Holt, 2004). See also Geoffrey Perret, *Ulysses S. Grant: Soldier and President* (New York: Random House, 1997).

18. For an account of the Centennial of the Civil War, see Robert J. Cook, *Troubled Commemoration: The American Civil War Centennial, 1961–1965* (Baton Rouge: Louisiana State University Press, 2007); the Grant Papers project is discussed on 212, 214, and 264. Reviews for the *PUSG* volumes have been largely favorable. See William L. Richter, "Papers of U. S. Grant: A Review Essay," *Civil War History* 36 (1990): 149–66. A legal dispute has prompted a move from Southern Illinois University to Mississippi State University; <http://news.yahoo.com/s/ap/20090128/ap_on_Re_US/grant_goessouth/print>. The project will be finished when the thirty-first volume is published.

19. Bunting, *Ulysses S. Grant*, 2.

20. Charles W. Calhoun, *Conceiving a New Republic: The Republican Party and the Southern Question, 1869–1900* (Lawrence: University Press of Kansas, 2006), 3.

21. Current, "President Grant and the Continuing Civil War," 71, 82; Simpson, *The Reconstruction Presidents*, 196; For background on how southern violence shaped Reconstruction's fate, see George C. Rable, *But There Was No Peace: The Role of Violence in the Politics of Reconstruction* (Athens: University of Georgia Press, 1984).

22. Smith, *Grant*, 18.

23. *PMUSG*, 2:509.

24. As quoted in Bruce Catton, *Grant Takes Command* (Boston: Little, Brown, 1968), 479.

25. Ishbel Ross, *The General's Wife: The Life of Mrs. Ulysses S. Grant* (New York: Dodd, Mead, 1959), 191.

26. *PUSG*, 14:428–29.

27. As quoted in Simpson, *Let Us Have Peace*, 123–24. Grant's report is in the form of a letter: U. S. Grant to Andrew Johnson, December 18, 1865, *PUSG* 15:434–37.

28. *PUSG*, 17:98.

29. As quoted in Simpson, *Let Us Have Peace*, 149.

30. *PUSG*, 16:308.

31. McFeely, *Grant*, 258–59.

32. *PMUSG*, 2:511–12.

33. USG to Bvt. Maj. Gen. Edward O. C. Ord, September 22, 1867, *PUSG*, 17:354.

34. The French intervention in Mexican affairs began during the Civil War. Johnson, jealous of Grant's growing influence, attempted to remove him by proposing he go to Mexico on a diplomatic mission, an idea Grant refused to entertain. See William E. Hardy, "South of the Border: Ulysses S. Grant and the French Intervention," *Civil War History* 54 (March, 2008): 63–86, and Simpson, *Let Us Have Peace*, 154–58.

35. Both quotations from *PUSG*, 17:251.

36. As quoted in Simpson, *Let Us Have Peace*, 191; Eric Foner provides excellent coverage of this event in *Reconstruction*, 176–227.

37. *PUSG*, 17:343.

38. USG to Andrew Johnson, February 3, 1868, ibid., 18:124–26, quotation, 126.

39. As quoted in Simpson, *Let Us Have Peace*, 244.

40. George Templeton Strong, *The Diary of George Templeton Strong, Post-War Years 1865–1875*, 4 vols., ed. Allan Nevins and Milton Halsey Thomas (New York: Macmillan, 1952) 4:172.

41. Two of these campaign biographies are William A. Crafts, *The Life of Ulysses S. Grant* (Boston: Samuel Walker, 1868), and Albert D. Richardson, *Personal History of Ulysses S. Grant* (Hartford, Conn.: American Publishing, 1868). Richardson's is of much better quality than most such publications. The genre of campaign biographies is discussed in Scott E. Casper, *Constructing American Lives: Biography and Culture in Nineteenth-Century America* (Chapel Hill: University of North Carolina Press, 1999), 195–200, 263–69.

42. The cabin was placed in Fairmont Park in Philadelphia. By 1979, it was neglected and sadly in disrepair. That year the National Park Service purchased the cabin, restored it, and returned it to its original site in City Point (now Hopewell), Virginia. The original move was discussed in a letter from Adam Badeau to George H. Stuart, July 21, 1865, *PUSG*, 15:569–70.

43. USG to WTS, June 21, 1868, *PUSG*, 18:292.

44. W. F. G. Shanks, "Recollections of General Grant," *Harper's Weekly*, June 1865, 68–76, quotation, 75–76.

45. *PUSG*, 18:xiv.

46. "The White Man's Banner," in Silber, *Songs America Voted By*, 100.

47. McFeely, *Grant*, 283.

48. As quoted in Bunting, *Ulysses S. Grant*, 84.

49. *New York Sun*, November 4, 1868.

50. As quoted in Farah Jasmine Griffin, ed., *Beloved Sisters and Loving Friends: Letters from Rebecca Primus of Royal Oak, Maryland, and Addie Brown of Hartford, Connecticut, 1854-1868* (New York: Alfred A. Knopf, 1999), 251.

51. As quoted in Ross, *The General's Wife*, 202.

52. As quoted in Horace Porter, *Campaigning with Grant* (New York: The Century Co., 1897), 385. Stephens published a textbook on the war in 1901, in which he singled out Grant for lavish praise for his magnanimity at Appomattox. *NYT*, May 5, 1901.

53. USG, "Inaugural Address," *PUSG*, 19:139-43, quotation, 140.

54. Ibid., 142.

55. *NYT*, March 5, 1869.

56. Bunting, *Ulysses S. Grant*, 86.

57. *New York Sun*, April 17, 1869.

58. *New York World*, March 23, 1869.

59. First quotation in John Russell Young, *Around the World with General Grant*, ed. Michael Fellman (Baltimore: Johns Hopkins University Press, 2002), 282 (this one-volume abridged edition of Young's work is well done, enlivened by Fellman's insightful commentary); second quotation in Eighth Annual Message, December 5, 1876, *PUSG*, 28:62.

60. Summers, *The Era of Good Stealings*, 71.

61. Julia Dent Grant, *The Personal Memoirs of Julia Dent Grant*, ed. John Y. Simon (Carbondale: Southern Illinois University Press, 1975), 171-72.

62. As quoted in Nevins, *Hamilton Fish*, 609.

63. *PUSG*: 19:xi; an informative overview of the topic can be found in ibid., 17-22. See also *PUSG*, 7: 50-56. Grant's order is discussed in Brooks D. Simpson, *Ulysses S. Grant: Triumph over Adversity, 1822-1865* (Boston: Houghton Mifflin, 2000), 163-65.

64. Mark Wahlgren Summers, *The Press Gang: Newspapers and Politics, 1865-1878* (Chapel Hill: University of North Carolina Press, 2004). See especially chapter 11, "The Silent Smoker in the Hands of the Foe"; quotation, 187.

65. The phrase is taken from the title of Alan Trachtenberg's *The Incorporation of America: Culture and Society in the Gilded Age* (New York: Hill and Wang, 1982). See also Robert Rydell, *All the World's a Fair: Visions of Empire at American International Expositions, 1876-1916* (Chicago: University of Chicago Press, 1987).

66. USG, "Annual Message," December 7, 1875, *PUSG*, 26: 385-417, quotation, 385-86.

67. Switching the focus from the South to the West: Heather Cox Richardson, *West from Appomattox: The Reconstruction of American after the Civil War* (New Haven: Yale University Press, 2007), 67; Other useful studies of the economic policy and ideology of the Republican Party are Heather Cox Richardson, *The Death of Reconstruction: Race, Labor, and Politics in the Post-Civil War North* (Cambridge: Harvard University Press, 2001); Eric Foner, *Free Soil, Free Labor, Free Men: The Ideology of the Republican Party before the Civil War* (New York: Oxford University Press 1979); and Eric Foner, *Nothing but Freedom: Emancipation and Its Legacy* (Baton Rouge: Louisiana State University Press, 1983).

68. Background on the economic and political context can be found in the following selected studies: Sean Dennis Cashman, *America in the Gilded Age: From the Death of Lincoln to the Rise of Theodore Roosevelt* (New York: New York University Press, 1984); John A. Garraty, *The New Commonwealth, 1877-1890* (New York: Harper and Row, 1968); Ray Ginger,

*The Age of Excess: The United States from 1877 to 1914* (New York: Macmillan, 1975); and Mark Wahlgren Summers, *The Gilded Age, or The Hazard of New Functions* (New York: Prentice Hall, 1998).

69. USG, "A Proclamation," October 5, 1869, *PUSG*, 19:250.

70. USG, "Inaugural Address," March 4, 1869, ibid., 139–43, quotation, 140.

71. Smith, *Grant*, 490.

72. Ibid., 488–90; McFeely, *Grant*, 319–29.

73. This sentiment is well articulated in USG, "Annual Message," December 7, 1875, *PUSG*, 26:85–417.

74. Robert H. Keller Jr., "Ulysses S. Grant: Reality and Mystique in the Far West," *Journal of the West* 31, no. 3 (July, 1992): 68–80, quotation, 69–70. See also Robert H. Keller Jr., *American Protestantism and U.S. Indian Policy, 1869–1882* (Lincoln: University of Nebraska Press, 1982).

75. USG, "Inaugural Address," March 4, 1869, *PUSG*, 19:141.

76. USG, "Draft Annual Message," December 5, 1870, ibid., 20:42.

77. Smith, *Grant*, 541. For the Lincoln administration's troubled policy, see David A. Nichols, *Lincoln and the Indians: Civil War Policy and Politics* (Urbana: University of Illinois Press, 1999).

78. Keller, "Ulysses S. Grant: Reality and Mystique in the Far West," 74.

79. USG, "Annual Message," December 6, 1869, *PUSG*, 20:39.

80. USG, "Second Inaugural Address," March 4, 1873, ibid., 24:60–64, quotation, 61.

81. Norman J. Bender, *New Hope for the Indians: The Grant Peace Policy and the Navajos in the 1870s* (Albuquerque: University of New Mexico Press, 1989); Robert L. Whitner, "Grant's Peace Policy on the Yakima Reservation, 1870–1882," *Pacific Northwest Quarterly* 50, no. 4 (1959): 135–43.

82. USG, "Annual Message," December 6, 1869, *PUSG*, 20:38. See the following on the relations between whites and Native Americans after the Civil War: Reginald Horsman, *Race and Manifest Destiny* (Cambridge: Harvard University Press, 1981); Frederick E. Hoxie, *A Final Promise: The Campaign to Assimilate the Indians, 1880–1920* (Lincoln: University of Nebraska Press, 1982); and Richard White, *The Roots of Dependency: Subsistence, Environment, and Social Change among the Choctaws, Pawnees, and Navajos* (Lincoln: University of Nebraska Press, 1983).

83. Richardson, *West from Appomattox*, 115. A sympathetic portrayal of Grant's dilemma is found in Scott L. Stabler, "Ulysses S. Grant and the 'Indian Problem,'" *Journal of Illinois History* 6 (Winter 2003): 297–316.

84. As quoted in Smith, *Grant*, 541.

85. Nevins, *Hamilton Fish*; Charles S. Campbell, *The Transformation of American Foreign Relations, 1865–1900* (New York: HarperCollins, 1976).

86. Adrian Cook, *The Alabama Claims: American Politics and Anglo-American Relations, 1865–1872* (Ithaca, N.Y.: Cornell University Press, 1975).

87. USG, "Message to the Senate," May 31, 1870, *PUSG*, 20:152.

88. James Oakes, *The Radical and the Republican: Frederick Douglass, Abraham Lincoln, and the Triumph of Antislavery Politics* (New York: W. W. Norton, 2007).

89. USG, "Annual Message," December 5, 1876, *PUSG*, 28:69.

90. As quoted in John Russell Young, *Around the World with General Grant: A Narrative*

*of the Visit of General U. S. Grant, Ex-President of the United States, to Various Countries in Europe, Asia, and Africa, in 1877, 1878, 1879*, 2 vols.(New York: The American News Company, 1879), 2:449.

91. Excellent overviews of the diplomacy of this period are R. L. Beisner, *From the Old Diplomacy to the New, 1865–1900* (New York: Thomas Y. Cowell, 1975), and Walter LaFeber, *The New Empire: An Interpretation of American Expansion, 1860–1898* (Ithaca, N.Y.: Cornell University Press, 1963).

92. As quoted in John Russell Young, *Around the World with General Grant*, ed. Michael Fellman, 335.

93. USG, "Annual Message," December 6, 1869, *PUSG*, 20:20.

94. USG, "Second Inaugural Address," March 4, 1873, *PUSG*, 24:61. The full paragraph states: "Social equality is not a subject to be legislated upon nor shall I ask that anything be done to advance the social status of the colored man except to give him a fair chance to develop what there is good in him, give him access to schools, and when he travels let him feel assured that his conduct will regulate the treatment and fare he will receive."

95. William Gillette, *The Right to Vote: Politics and the Passage of the Fifteenth Amendment* (Baltimore: Johns Hopkins University Press, 1999); Michael Les Benedict, *A Compromise of Principle: Congressional Republicans and Reconstruction 1863–1869* (New York: W. W. Norton, 1974).

96. Suffragists particularly protested against the gendered wording of the Fifteenth Amendment, preventing females from voting in national elections. Susan B. Anthony voted for Grant in 1872, but she was arrested for "illegal voting." Godfrey D. Lehman, "Susan B. Anthony Cast Her Ballot for Ulysses S. Grant," *American Heritage* 1 (December 1985): 25–31; Three books provide context: Ellen DuBois, *Feminism and Suffrage: The Emergence of an Independent Women's Movement in America, 1848–1869* (Ithaca, N.Y.: Cornell University Press, 1978); Rebecca Edwards, *Angels in the Machinery: Gender in American Party Politics from the Civil War to the Progressive Era* (New York: Oxford University Press, 1997); and Foner, *Reconstruction*, 446–49.

97. USG, "To Congress," March 30, 1870, *PUSG*, 20:130–31.

98. Foner, *Reconstruction*, 346–411.

99. The difficulties of Reconstruction are explored in Dan T. Carter, *When the War Was Over: The Failure of Self-Reconstruction in the South* (Baton Rouge: Louisiana State University Press, 1985); W. E. B. Du Bois, *Black Reconstruction: An Essay toward a History of the Part which Black Folk Played in the Attempt to Reconstruct Democracy 1860–1880* (New York: Harcourt Brace, 1935); and Michael Perman, *Reunion without Compromise: The South and Reconstruction, 1865–1868* (New York: Cambridge University Press, 1973).

100. *PUSG*, 21:258.

101. USG, "Annual Message," December 7, 1874, ibid., 25:281.

102. USG to Adam Badeau, November 19, 1871, ibid., 22:239; Simon quotation, ibid., xiii.

103. Ibid, xi.

104. Quotations from Hesseltine, *U. S. Grant*, 269–71. Nast's role in the election of 1872 is explored in Morton Keller, *The Art and Politics of Thomas Nast* (New York: Oxford University Press, 1968).

105. *NYT*, September 3, 1871.

106. Grant was a force for civil service reform. He appointed the first national commission to consider reforms, with George William Curtis as chairman. Even though opposition from Congress stymied many of the commission's recommendations, Grant persisted, and some changes were made. Most important, later administrations, such as Hayes's, built on Grant's record. John Y. Simon, "Ulysses S. Grant and Civil Service Reform," *Hayes Historical Journal* 4 (Spring 1984): 9–27.

107. USG to Henry Wilson, November 15, 1871, *PUSG*, 22:232.

108. J. Matthew Gallman, "Is the War Ended?: Anna Dickinson and the Election of 1872," in *The Memory of the Civil War in American Culture*, ed. Alice Fahs and Joan Waugh (Chapel Hill: University of North Carolina Press, 2004), 157–79, quotation, 170–71. See also, Gallman, *America's Joan of Arc: The Life of Anna Elizabeth Dickinson* (New York: Oxford University Press, 2006).

109. As quoted in Harry J. Maihafer, *The General and the Journalists: Ulysses S. Grant, Horace Greeley, and Charles Dana* (Washington, D.C.: Brassey's, 1998), 238; USG to Henry Wilson, November 15, 1871, *PUSG*, 22:232.

110. *NYTrib*, August 19, 1872; *New York Sun*, October 26, 1872.

111. James M. McPherson, "Grant or Greeley? The Abolition Dilemma in the Election of 1872," *American Historical Review* 71 (October 1965): 43–61, quotation, 46; Oakes, *The Radical and the Republican*, 265. See also Andrew L. Slap, *The Doom of Reconstruction: The Liberal Republicans in the Civil War Era* (New York: Fordham University Press, 2006).

112. *New York Sun*, November 6, 1872.

113. USG, "Second Inaugural Address, March 4, 1873, *PUSG*, 24:60–64, quotation, 64.

114. USG, "To Editor, *Cincinnati Gazette*," May 14, 1872, *PUSG*, 23:118.

115. Ross, *The General's Wife*, 335.

116. As quoted in Carl Sferrazza Anthony, *First Ladies: The Saga of the Presidents' Wives and Their Power, 1789-1961* (New York: William Morrow, 1990), 210.

117. Christopher Gordon, "A White House Wedding: The Story of Nelly Grant," *Gateway* 26 (Summer 2005): 9–19, quotation, 15.

118. Jesse published a mildly entertaining but unilluminative memoir: Jesse R. Grant, *In the Days of My Father General Grant* (New York: Harper and Brothers, 1925). See also Evelyn I. Banning, "U. S. Grant, Jr., A Builder of San Diego," *Journal of San Diego History* 27 (Winter, 1981): 1–16, and A. E. Watrous, "Grant As His Son Saw Him: An Interview with Colonel Frederick D. Grant About His Father," *McClure's Magazine* 6 (May 1894): 515–19. Depictions of the Grant family and household are taken from Ross, *The General's Wife*, and Adam Badeau, *Grant in Peace: From Appomattox to Mount McGregor* (Hartford, Conn.: S. S. Scranton, 1887), esp. 407–15. On the recent fate of the hotel, see Vallie Herman, "U. S. Grant Hotel, A Belle Epoque Beauty in San Diego," *Los Angeles Times*, March 14, 2007.

119. *PUSG*, 23:xi.

120. *New York Sun*, November 4, 1874.

121. Joe Gray Taylor, *Louisiana Reconstructed, 1863-1877* (Baton Rouge: Louisiana State University Press, 1977); see also, Foner, *Reconstruction*, 549–54, and Smith, *Grant*, 564–65.

122. Rable, *But There Was No Peace*, 190.

123. As quoted in Hesseltine, *U. S. Grant*, 377–78.

124. Perret, *Ulysses S. Grant*, 444.

125. Lewis L. Gould, *Grand Old Party: A History of the Republicans* (New York: Random House, 2003), 77.

126. John Russell Young, *Around the World with General Grant*, ed. Michael Fellman, 336–37.

127. Bunting, *Ulysses S. Grant*, 146.

128. As quoted in Simpson, *The Reconstruction Presidents*, 195.

129. Two classics on the politics of Redemption and the end of Reconstruction are Michael Perman, *The Road to Redemption: Southern Politics, 1869–1879* (Chapel Hill: University of North Carolina Press, 1984), and C. Vann Woodward, *Reunion and Reaction: The Compromise of 1877 and the End of Reconstruction* (Boston: Little, Brown, 1951). See also Brooks D. Simpson, "Ulysses S. Grant and the Electoral Crisis of 1876–77," *Hayes Historical Journal* 11 (Winter, 1992): 5–21.

130. USG, "Draft Annual Message, December 5, 1876, *PUSG*, 28:62–63; *NYTrib*, December 25, 1876.

131. As quoted in Allan Peskin, "The 'Little Man on Horseback' and the 'Literary Fellow': Garfield's Opinions of Grant," *Mid-America* 55 (October 1973), 271–82, quotation, 281. See also Hesseltine, *U. S. Grant*, 411

132. James Penny Boyd, *Military and Civil Life of Gen. Ulysses S. Grant: Leading Soldier of the Age; President of the United States; Loved and Honored American Citizen; the World's Most Distinguished Man* (Philadelphia: Garretson and Co., 1885), 496.

133. Frank A. Burr, *Life and Deeds of General U. S. Grant* (Philadelphia: National Publishing Company, 1885), 872; William O. Stoddard, *The Lives of the Presidents: Ulysses S. Grant* (New York: White, Stokes, and Allen, 1886), 324; General Charles King, *The True Ulysses S. Grant* (Philadelphia: J. B. Lippincott, 1914), 370;

134. Hamlin Garland, *Ulysses S. Grant: His Life and Character* (New York: Macmillan, 1920), 442–44; Louis A. Coolidge, *Ulysses S. Grant* (Boston: Houghton Mifflin, 1917), vii, 532.

135. James Bryce, *American Commonwealth*, 3 vols. (Chicago: Charles H. Sergel and Co., 1891), 1:1.

136. Ibid., 80.

## Interlude

1. Quotation from Mike Davis, *Late Victorian Holocausts* (New York: Verso, 2002), 2; see also Michael Korda, *Ulysses S. Grant: The Unlikely Hero* (New York: HarperCollins, 2004), 37–141. Another critical examination of American culture and ideology in this period is Matthew Frye Jacobson, *Barbarian Virtues: The U.S. Encounters Foreign Peoples at Home and Abroad, 1876–1917* (New York: Hill and Wang, 2001).

2. John Russell Young, *Chicago Tribune*, September 1, 1885.

3. John Russell Young, *Around the World with General Grant: A Narrative of the Visit of General U.S. Grant, Ex-President of the United States, to Various Countries in Europe, Asia, and Africa, in 1877, 1878, 1879.* 2 vols. (New York: American News Company, 1879). See also J. F. Packard, *Grant's Tour Around the World* (Cincinnati, Ohio: Forshee & McMakin, 1880); L. T. Remlap, editor, *General U. S. Grant's Tour Around the World* (Chicago: J. Fairbanks and Company, 1880).

4. *The Chronicle*, as quoted in J. T. Headley, *The Life and Travels of General Grant* (New

York: Hubbard Bros., 1879), 245. See also Remlap, *General U. S. Grant's Tour Around the World*. The affection of the British working class for Grant is explored in David Brewster, "Ulysses Grant and Newcastle Upon Tyne," *Durham University Journal* 61 (1969): 119–28.

5. John Russell Young, *Around the World with General Grant*, ed. Michael Fellman (Baltimore: Johns Hopkins University Press, 2002), 1–27.

6. *PUSG*, 28:237.

7. USG to George Childs, June 6, 1877, ibid., 210–11.

8. Hamlin Garland, *Ulysses S. Grant: His Life and Character* (New York: Doubleday and McClure, 1898), quotations, 456.

9. The presents kept piling up; see "General Grant's European Souvenirs," *Harper's Weekly*, March 2, 1878, 168–69.

10. Garland, *Ulysses S. Grant*, 467–68.

11. *PUSG*, 28: 08–9.

12. As quoted in Garland, *Ulysses S. Grant*, 467.

13. *PUSG*, 28:xvi.

14. Young, *Around the World with General Grant*, 2:453.

15. Adam Badeau, *Grant in Peace: From Appomattox to Mount McGregor* (Hartford, Conn.: S. S. Scranton, 1887), 318. Badeau's testimony that Grant desired a third term provided the evidence for many historians' assertions.

16. As quoted in Garland, *Ulysses S. Grant*, 465.

17. Julia Dent Grant, *The Personal Memoirs of Julia Dent Grant*, ed. John Y. Simon (Carbondale: Southern Illinois University Press, 1975), 268.

18. Young, *Around the World with General Grant*, ed. Fellman, 315.

19. Dallas Finn, "Grant in Japan," *American History Illustrated* 16 (June 1981): 36–45, quote, 40. Grant's Japanese trip is also discussed in Young, *Around the World with General Grant*, ed. Fellman, 400, and William S. McFeely, *Grant: A Biography* (New York: W. W. Norton, 1982), 474–76.

20. Julia Dent Grant, *The Personal Memoirs of Julia Dent Grant*, 295; Badeau, *Grant in Peace*, 312–13, 518–19.

21. As quoted in Spencer L. Leitman, "The Revival of an Image: Grant and the 1880 Republican Nominating Campaign, *Missouri Historical Society Bulletin* 30 (April 1974):, 196–204, quotation, 200.

22. "Gen. Grant in Florida," *Harper's Weekly*, February 21, 1880, 117. The artist Frank H. Taylor accompanied the Grants on their trip, producing a series of illustrations for *Harper's*. See Frank H. Taylor, *A Stately Picturesque Dream: Scenes of Florida, Cuba and Mexico in 1880*, Introduction by Nancy L. Gustke (Gainesville: University of Florida Press, 1984).

23. Badeau, *Grant in Peace*, 320–21. Grant later was quoted as stating that he would have accepted the nomination if it had been offered to him. One of the reason he gave was his experience in foreign countries. *NYT*, October 5, 1880.

24. Jean Edward Smith, *Grant* (New York: Simon and Schuster, 2001), 614–15; Josiah Bunting III, *Ulysses S. Grant* (New York: Henry Holt, 2004), 149; Geoffrey Perret, *Ulysses S. Grant: Soldier and President* (New York: Random House, 1997), 462–65.

25. Badeau, *Grant in Peace*, 321; see also E. L. Godkin, "General Grant's Political Education Abroad," *Nation* 30 (February 19, 1880): 130–31.

26. USG, "Speech," Jersey City, N.J., October 21, 1880, *PUSG*, 30:15.

27. Perret, *Ulysses S. Grant*, 465–66.

28. Smith, *Grant*, 618–19; McFeely, *Grant*, 489–91.

## Chapter 4

1. Two other military memoirs come close to Grant's: William T. Sherman, *Memoirs of W. T. Sherman*, 2 vols. (New York: D. Appleton, 1875), and Edward Porter Alexander, *The Personal Recollections of General Edward Porter Alexander*, ed. Gary W. Gallagher (Chapel Hill: University of North Carolina Press, 1989). The publication of Bill Clinton's memoirs, *My Life* (New York: Alfred A. Knopf, 2004), prompted reviewers to revisit all previous presidential memoirs. Many agreed that Grant's remain a gold standard that has never been met again. See Mark Perry, "All the President's Books: Why Do Their Memoirs so Rarely Say Anything Memorable?," *Washington Post*, June 13, 2004.

2. Bruce Catton, "U. S. Grant: Man of Letters," *American Heritage* 19 (June 1968): 97–100, quotation, 97.

3. *American Heritage Dictionary of the English Language*, ed. William Morris (Boston: Houghton Mifflin, 1969). Autobiography as a genre is considered in the following: Joyce Appleby, *Inheriting the Revolution* (Cambridge: Harvard University Press, 2000); Robert Folkenflick, ed., *The Culture of Autobiography: Constructions of Self-Representation* (Stanford, Calif.: Stanford University Press, 1993); Jacquelyn Dowd Hall, "'You Must Remember This': Autobiography as Social Critique," *Journal of American History* 85 (September 1998): 439–65; and Charles Taylor, *Sources of the Self: The Making of Modern Identity* (Cambridge: Harvard University Press, 1989).

4. Daniel Aaron, *The Unwritten War: American Writers and the Civil War* (Madison: University of Wisconsin Press, 1987); James M. McPherson and William J. Cooper Jr., eds. *Writing the Civil War: The Quest to Understand* (Columbia: University of South Carolina Press, 1998).

5. *NYT*, May 14, 1884.

6. *New York Sun*, May 13, 27–28, 1884.

7. In January 1885 Vanderbilt "forgave" the loan but kept the gifts on the condition that upon Grant's death they would be turned over to the U.S. government. Grant's Manhattan residence was demolished in 1936.

8. Undated, unidentified newspaper article and proposal found in "Grant Fund, misc.," box 2, George E. Jones Papers, Manuscript and Archives Division, New York Public Library, New York City; Jean Edward Smith, *Grant* (New York: Simon and Schuster, 2001), 624–25.

9. Robert Underwood Johnson, *Remembered Yesterdays* (Boston: Little, Brown, 1923), 208. See also Stephen Davis, "A Matter of Sensational Interest": The Century 'Battles and Leaders' Series," in *Civil War History* 27 (December 1981): 338–49.

10. Alan C. and Barbara A. Aimone, *A User's Guide to the Official Records of the American Civil War* (Shippensburg, Pa.: White Mane Publishing Co., 1993), 8.

11. USG to Edwin Stanton, May 29, 1865, *PUSG*, 15:106.

12. One reviewer noted approvingly that *Official Records* volumes were "fair in the treatment of Confederate as well as Federal reports and documents." However, he advised the government to drop the hated word "Rebellion" from the title, advice that was ignored. *Southern Historical Society Papers* 11 (November 1883): 11, 575–76.

13. See David W. Blight, *Race and Reunion: The Civil War in American Memory* (Cambridge: Belknap Press of Harvard University Press, 2001), for the "whitewashing" of Civil War memory, commemoration, and history.

14. Richard Watson Gilder to Roswell Smith, July 3, 1884, Robert Underwood Johnson Papers, Manuscripts and Archives Division, New York Public Library, New York City.

15. Johnson, *Remembered Yesterdays*, 210. On Grant's Shiloh submission, see ibid., 213–18.

16. Elsie Porter Mende and Henry Greenleaf Pearson, *An American Soldier and Diplomat: Horace Porter* (New York: Frederick A. Stokes, 1927), 141.

17. Julia Dent Grant, *The Personal Memoirs of Julia Dent Grant*, ed. John Y. Simon (Carbondale: Southern Illinois University Press, 1975), 328–29.

18. John Hancock Douglas Journal, quotations, 26 and 28, container 1, John Hancock Douglas Papers, Library of Congress, Washington, D.C.

19. Julia Dent Grant, *The Personal Memoirs of Julia Dent Grant*, 329.

20. Dr. Douglas worked for the U.S. Sanitary Commission during the war. He set up field hospitals in the Western Theater and had met Grant in his capacity as medical administrator. George F. Shrady was a distinguished physician who edited the New York *Medical Record*.

21. *New York World*, February 4, 1885; *NYTrib*, February 28, 1885; *NYT*, March 1, 1885.

22. Julia Dent Grant, *The Personal Memoirs of Julia Dent* Grant, 330.

23. Thomas Pitkin, *The Captain Departs: Ulysses S. Grant's Last Campaign* (Carbondale: Southern Illinois University Press, 1973), quotation, 34. Pitkin's book is the best, and most detailed, account of Grant's deathwatch. Other useful sources are Adam Badeau, *Grant in Peace: From Appomattox to Mount McGregor* (Hartford, Conn.: S. S. Scranton, 1887); Badeau, "The Last Days of General Grant," *Century Magazine* 30 (October 1885): 920–39; Richard Goldhurst, *Many Are the Hearts: The Agony and Triumph of Ulysses S. Grant* (New York: Thomas Y. Crowell, 1975); Julia Dent Grant, *The Personal Memoirs of Julia Dent Grant*; Horace Green (Dr. Douglas's grandson), *General Grant's Last Stand* (New York: Charles Scribner's Sons, 1936); William S. McFeely, *Grant: A Biography* (New York: W. W. Norton, 1982); and Ulysses S. Grant, *The Personal Memoirs of U. S. Grant*, ed. Mary Drake McFeely and William S. McFeely (New York: The Library of America, 1984), 1162–70.

24. *NYTrib*, March 2, 7, 19, April 24, May 2, June 19, 1885; quotation from ibid., March 20, 1885.

25. Ibid., March 8, 17, April 2, 14, 26, July 9, 1885; quotations from ibid., April 6, 26, 1885.

26. George F. Shrady, *General Grant's Last Days* (New York: DeVinne Press, 1908), 55. Goldhurst, *Many Are the Hearts*, 173–79, Pitkin, *The Captain Departs*, 34–35.

27. James T. Patterson, *The Dread Disease: Cancer and Modern American Culture* (Cambridge: Harvard University Press, 1987), quotation, 4. For his trenchant analysis of Grant's medical condition, see 1–11.

28. First quotation, Richard Watson Gilder to Robert U. Johnson, July 21, 1884, in box 5, Johnson Papers; second quotation, Robert U. Johnson, note in "Misc. and Undated," in ibid.; third quotation, Pitkin, *The Captain Departs*, 15.

29. As quoted in Catton, "U. S. Grant: Man of Letters," 98.

30. Johnson, *Remembered Yesterdays*, 193.

31. Horace Porter, *Campaigning with Grant* (New York: The Century Co., 1897), 7.

32. As quoted in John Keegan, "Grant and Unheroic Leadership," in *The Mask of Command* (London: Jonathan Cape, 1987), 200. See also James M. McPherson, "Grant's Final

Victory," in *Drawn with the Sword: Reflections on the American Civil War* (New York: Oxford University Press, 1996). esp. 159–73 for a superb analysis of Grant's writing style from his battlefield reports to his memoirs.

33. USG to Brig. Gen. Orlando B. Willcox, November 23, 1863, *PUSG*, 9:436–37

34. USG to Hon. E. M. Stanton, May 11, 1864, ibid., 10:422.

35. USG to Maj. Gen. Philip H. Sheridan, October 21, 1864, ibid., 12:334.

36. USG, "General Orders No. 108," *PUSG*, 15:120–21.

37. Porter, *Campaigning with Grant*, 8.

38. USG, "Report of Lieutenant-General U. S. Grant, of the United States Armies—1864-'65," *PMUSG*, ed. Mary Drake McFeely and William S. McFeely, 781–848, quotations, 781–82.

39. Ibid., 781.

40. Ibid., 794.

41. Ibid., 783.

42. Ibid., 847–48.

43. George C. Childs, "Recollections of Ulysses S. Grant," in Frank A. Burr, *The Life and Death of General U. S. Grant* (Philadelphia: Collins Printer, 1885), 22.

44. As quoted in the *Boston Post*, August 13, 1885. For more on Douglas's role as reported, see *New York Herald*, September 13, 1885, and *New York Mail and Express*, September 13, 1885.

45. Pitkin, *The Captain Departs*, 99.

46. Charles H. Gold, "Grant and Twain in Chicago: The 1879 Reunion of the Army of the Tennessee," *Chicago History* 7, no. 3 (1978): 151–60, quotation, 151.

47. *The Autobiography of Mark Twain*, ed. Charles Neider (New York: Harper and Brothers, 1959), 241–45. See also Charles H. Gold, "Grant and Twain in Chicago," 159–60, and McFeely, *Grant*, 480–81.

48. Albert Bigelow Paine, *Mark Twain, A Biography: The Personal and Literary Life of Samuel Langhorne Clemens*, 3 vols. (New York: Harper and Brothers, 1912), 2:815.

49. *The Autobiography of Mark Twain*, 236.

50. Johnson, *Remembered Yesterdays*, 219.

51. The profits from the *Personal Memoirs* were unwisely invested, leaving Webster and Company bankrupt and dashing Twain's expectations for financial security. For letters confirming Twain's excitement about profits from the memoirs, see "Grant's Memoirs and Other Schemes," in *The Love Letters of Mark Twain*, ed. Dixon Wecter (New York: Harper, 1949), 241–54.

52. *The Autobiography of Mark Twain*, 246. For a description of the hard-sell tactics employed by Webster and Company, see Gerald Carson, " 'Get the Prospect Seated . . . and Keep Talking,' " *American Heritage* 9 (August 1958): 38–41, 77–80.

53. As quoted in Patrick J. Kelly, *Creating a National Home: Building the Veterans' Welfare State, 1860-1900* (Cambridge: Harvard University Press, 1996), 52.

54. Stuart McConnell, *Glorious Contentment: The Grand Army of the Republic, 1865-1900* (Chapel Hill: University of North Carolina Press, 1992), and Mary R. Dearing, *Veterans in Politics: The Story of the GAR* (Baton Rouge: Louisiana State University Press, 1952), are the two standard works on northern veterans. See also Donald R. Shaffer, *After the Glory: The Struggles of Black Civil War Veterans* (Lawrence: University Press of Kansas, 2004), and

Barbara A. Gannon, "The Won Cause: Black and White Comradeship in the Grand Army of the Republic" (Ph.D. dissertation, Pennsylvania State University, 2005). For a thorough treatment of the development of old soldiers' homes, see Kelly, *Creating a National Home*.

55. The meetings are recorded in the calendar of *PUSG*, 24:xx–xxii.

56. Ibid., 23:289.

57. Dearing, *Veterans in Politics*, 290; *PUSG*, 28:193.

58. *Washington National Republican*, June 1, 1868; *NY Trib*, June 1, 1868.

59. *PUSG*, 24:409.

60. *Chicago Tribune*, June 11, 1880.

61. *NY Trib*, May 31, 1885.

62. Two enlightening discussions of the controversies over Grant's generalship can be found in William A. Blair, "Grant's Second Civil War: The Battle for Historical Memory," in *The Spotsylvania Campaign*, ed. Gary W. Gallagher (Chapel Hill: The University of North Carolina Press, 1998), 223–53, and Brooks D. Simpson, "Continuous Hammering and Mere Attrition: Lost Cause Critics and the Military Reputation of Ulysses S. Grant," in *The Myth of the Lost Cause and Civil War History*, ed. Gary W. Gallagher and Alan T. Nolan (Bloomington: Indiana University Press, 2000), 147–69.

63. Lee as quoted in Emory M. Thomas, *Robert E. Lee: A Biography* (New York: W. W. Norton, 1995), 367.

64. Early's postwar career is analyzed in Gary W. Gallagher, "Jubal A. Early, the Lost Cause, and Civil War History: A Persistent Legacy," in Gallagher and Nolan, *The Myth of the Lost Cause and Civil War History*, 35–59.

65. John Russell Young, *Around the World with General Grant: A Narrative of the Visit of General U. S. Grant, Ex-President of the United States, to Various Countries in Europe, Asia, and Africa, in 1877, 1878, 1879*, 2 vols. (New York: American News Company, 1897), 2:459.

66. Matthew Arnold, *General Grant*, with a rejoinder by Mark Twain, ed., with a new introduction, by John Y. Simon (Kent, Ohio: Kent State University Press, 1995), 11–12. Books on the Lost Cause include Thomas Connelly, *The Marble Man: Robert E. Lee and His Image in American Society* (New York: Alfred A. Knopf, 1977), and Gaines M. Foster, *Ghosts of the Confederacy: Defeat, the Lost Cause, and the Emergence of the New South, 1865–1913* (New York: Oxford University Press, 1987).

67. Jubal Early, "The Relative Strength of the Armies of Gen'ls Lee and Grant. Reply of Gen. Early to the Letter of Gen. Badeau to the *London Standard*" (n.p: 1870), 8; General Dabney H. Maury, *Southern Historical Society Papers* 5–6 (1878): 238.

68. As quoted in Young, *Around the World with General Grant*, 2:360.

69. As quoted in Simpson, "Continuous Hammering and Mere Attrition," 149. Two key published works that set a standard for the denigration of Grant's reputation are Jubal A. Early, "The Relative Strengths of the Armies of Generals Lee and Grant," *Southern Historical Society Papers* 2 (July 1876): 6–21, and Edward A. Pollard, *The Lost Cause* (New York: E. B. Treat, 1867). William McFeely disparaged Grant's military ability in his acclaimed biography, *Grant*, as did Ernest B. Furgurson in *Not War but Murder: Cold Harbor, 1864* (New York: Alfred A. Knopf, 2000).

70. Winston S. Churchill, *The American Civil War* (New York: Dodd, Mead, 1961), 123.

71. Grant's generalship has been debated ever since the Civil War. Three classic works portraying Grant in a highly favorable light are J. F. C. Fuller, *The Generalship of Ulysses S.*

Grant (London: J. Murray, 1929), and Bruce Catton's two volumes, *Grant Moves South* (Boston: Little, Brown, 1960) and *Grant Takes Command* (Boston: Little, Brown, 1968).

72. As quoted in Lloyd Lewis, *Sherman: Fighting Prophet* (New York: Harcourt, Brace, 1932), 643–44.

73. As quoted in Young, *Around the World with General Grant*, 2:459.

74. For example, Grant read a portion of Volume 2 of Adam Badeau's *Military History of Ulysses S. Grant*. *PUSG*, 24:166–70. See also correspondence regarding the war actions of Gen. David Hunter, ibid., 221.

75. John Y. Simon, *Ulysses S. Grant: One Hundred Years Later* (Illinois State Historical Society, Reprint Series #1, 1986), 253; see also James G. Barber and John Y. Simon, *U. S. Grant: The Man and the Image* (Washington, D.C.: National Portrait Gallery, Smithsonian; and Carbondale: Southern Illinois University Press, 1985).

76. Orville Babcock wrote to Adam Badeau, "I spoke to the President . . . about your having access to his records. . . . They are stored at the Navy Yard." Babcock to Badeau, March 5 and 8, 1877, *PUSG*, 28:190–91. See also Badeau, *Grant in Peace*, "Letters of General Grant to General Badeau," 462–565.

77. Jubal A. Early, "The Relative Strength of the Armies of Genl's Lee and Grant. Reply of Gen. Early to the Letter of Gen. Badeau to the *London Standard*" (n.p., 1870), 1–5.

78. "HFK," *Philadelphia Times*, August 5, 1881. Early histories of the war provoking controversy include Adam Badeau, *Military History of Ulysses S. Grant*, 3 vols. (New York: D. Appleton 1868–1882), and William Swinton, *Campaigns of the Army of the Potomac: A Critical History of Operations in Virginia, Maryland and Pennsylvania from the Commencement to the Close of the War, 1861–65* (1866; new ed., New York: University Publishing Company, 1871). Grant discussed Swinton in *PMUSG*: 2:143–45.

79. Gen. William F. Rosecrans, dismissed by Grant after his loss to Confederate forces at Chickamauga, was an especially impassioned enemy of his former commanding general. One example is his article, "The Mistakes of Grant," *North American Review* 140 (December, 1885): 580–99.

80. USG to Adam Badeau, November 2, 1876, *PUSG*, 28:3. Other letters and information regarding Grant's comments, criticism, and corrections of Badeau can be found in the index entry "Badeau, Adam," ibid., 522.

81. Badeau, *Grant in Peace*, 407–8.

82. Benson J. Lossing, *Pictorial History of the Civil War in the United States*, 3 vols. (Philadelphia: George W. Childs, 1866–69); John William Draper, *History of the American Civil War*, 3 vols. (Harper and Brothers, 1867–70); Henry Wilson, *History of the Rise and Fall of the Slave Power in America*, 2 vols. (Boston: J. R. Osgood, 1873–77). Other works include William A. Crafts, *The Southern Rebellion: Being a History of the united States from the Commencement of Buchanan's Administration through the War for the Suppression of the Rebellion*, 2 vols. (Boston: Samuel Walker, 1862–67); Theodore Ayrault Dodge, *A Bird's-Eye View of Our Civil War* (Boston: Houghton, Mifflin, 1897; original ed., 1883); George B. Herbert, *The Popular History of the Civil War in America* (New York: F. M. Lupton, 1884); Rossiter Johnson, *A Short History of the War of Secession, 1861–1865* (Boston: Houghton, Mifflin, 1889); Thomas P. Kettell, *History of the Great Rebellion: From Its Commencement to Its Close, Giving an Account of Its Origins, the Secession of the Southern States and the Formation of the Confederate Government* (Hartford, Conn.: L. Stebbins, 1866); and John A. Logan, *The Great Conspiracy: Its Origin and History*

(New York: A. R. Hart, 1886). Early histories of the war, from Union and Confederate perspectives, are discussed in Thomas J. Pressly, *Americans Interpret Their Civil War* (Princeton, N.J.: Princeton University Press, 1954).

83. Young, *Around the World with General Grant*, 2:459.

84. Ibid., 300, 444–45.

85. *PUSG*, 28:409–10.

86. See Gordon S. Wood, *The Purpose of the Past: Reflections on the Uses of History* (New York: Penguin, 2008), for a thoughtful discussion of the modern historical profession.

87. Young, *Around the World with General Grant*, 2:293, and *PMUSG*, 2:488.

88. *The Autobiography of Mark Twain*, 247; Julia Dent Grant, *The Personal Memoirs of Julia Dent Grant*, 330.

89. *NYTrib*, May 1, 5, 8, June 19, 1885, and *New York Herald*, July 2, 1885. Quotation from *NYTrib*, May 5, 1885.

90. Shrady, *General Grant's Last Days*, 57.

91. James Grant Wilson, *General Grant* (New York: D. Appleton, 1897), 354.

92. USG to Frederick Dent Grant, undated in an envelope marked "Small messages written by U. S. Grant Gen'l and president to his son F. D. Grant, during last illness, July 1885," in series 10, box 1, Papers of Ulysses S. Grant, Manuscript Division, Library of Congress Washington, D.C. Many letters in this collection document fully Grant's authorship of his memoirs.

93. Badeau, *Grant in Peace*, 429.

94. Paine, *Mark Twain, A Biography*, remains a good source for documenting Grant and Twain's professional and personal relationship. A more recent book likely will be the modern, definitive source: Mark Perry, *Grant and Twain: The Story of a Friendship That Changed America* (New York: Random House, 2004). Several critics of Perry have pointed out the exaggeration implied in the subtitle, but acknowledge the book's usefulness in delineating Twain's role in the memoirs.

95. USG to Dr. Douglas, July 19, 1885, "Notes of U. S. Grant to Dr. Douglas, 1885," Douglas Papers. Grant scribbled 169 small notes, plus two larger ones, to Douglas. Most of them deal with details of his physical condition; many of them are unbearably sad to read. A selection of the notes has been published as "Notes to the Doctor: written while completing the Memoirs at Mount McGregor, June–July 1885," *PMUSG*, ed. Mary Drake McFeely and William S. McFeely, 1111–20.

96. John Hancock Douglas Journal, March 23, 1885, 66, Douglas Papers.

97. Ibid., April 7, 1885; George F. Shrady, "The Last Days of Our Great General," in *The Saturday Evening Post*, September, 9, 1901, 4; *NYTrib*, March 29, April 2, 1885.

98. *NYTrib*, April 28, 1885.

99. John Hancock Douglas Journal, June 23, 1885, 166, Douglas Papers; see also Shrady, "The Last Days of Our Great General," 4–5.

100. Shrady, *General Grant's Last Days*, 49.

101. Shrady, "The Last Days of Our Great General," 4–5.

102. As quoted in Catton, "U. S. Grant: Man of Letters," 98.

103. As quoted in ibid. As the controversy developed, newspapers reported the details: *New York World*, April 29, 1885; *New York Sun*, April 30, May 1, May 6–7, 1885; *NYTrib*, April 30, May 1, 6, 1885.

104. Pitkin, *The Captain Departs*, 38–43, 114–15.

105. McFeely, *Grant*, 515.

106. Edward E. Henry, Fremont, Ohio, 23rd Regiment Ohio Volunteers, to U. S. Grant, June 22, 1885, in series 10, box 15, Papers of Ulysses S. Grant.

107. Pitkin, *The Captain Departs*, 55–57. *NYT*, June 12, 1885; *NYTrib*, June 15, 1885.

108. Pitkin, *The Captain Departs*, 57–58.

109. *NYTrib*, June 18, 1885.

110. "Notes of U. S. Grant to Dr. Douglas," June 17, 1885, Douglas Papers.

111. USG to Fred Grant, June 17, 1885, series 10, box 1, Papers of Ulysses S. Grant.

112. Julia wrote after Grant died: "For nearly thirty-seven years, I, his wife, rested and was warmed in the sunlight of his loyal love and great fame, and now, even though his beautiful life has gone out, it is as when some far-off planet disappears from the heavens; the light of his glorious fame still reaches out to me, falls upon me, and warms me" (*The Personal Memoirs of Julia Dent Grant*, 331).

113. USG to Julia Dent Grant, July 8, 1885, series 10, box 2, Papers of Ulysses S. Grant.

114. "Notes of U. S. Grant to Dr. Douglas," June 23, 1885, Douglas Papers.

115. Ibid., July 16, 1885.

116. Ibid., July 5, 1885.

117. Mount McGregor never realized the heady prospects of its boosters. See Pitkin, *The Captain Departs*, 124.

118. Johnson, *Remembered Yesterdays*, 223–224.

119. "Notes of U. S. Grant to Dr. Douglas," July [n.d.], 1885, Douglas Papers.

120. I owe a debt to three thoughtful, insightful scholarly works that have helped me understand the meaning and impact of Grant's writing: Henry M. W. Russell, "The Memoirs of Ulysses S. Grant: The Rhetoric of Judgment," in *Virginia Quarterly Review* 66 (Spring 1990): 189–209; Elizabeth D. Samet, "'Adding to My Book and to My Coffin': The Unconditional Memoirs of Ulysses S. Grant," *PMLA* 115 (October 2000): 1117–24; and Michael W. Schaefer, *Just What War Is: The Civil War Writings of De Forest and Bierce* (Knoxville: University of Tennessee Press, 1997).

121. *PMUSG*, 1:34, 38.

122. Grant covered the Mexican War in ten chapters (3–13), totaling 145 pages.

123. Ibid., 191.

124. Ibid., 56.

125. Ibid., 54–56, 216–28. Quotation from ibid., 2:542; see also, ibid., 38–40.

126. Controversies in the Overland Campaign are well covered, most recently by Blair, "Grant's Second Civil War," and Simpson, "Continuous Hammering and Mere Attrition." For Grant and the battle of Shiloh, see Brooks D. Simpson, *Ulysses S. Grant: Triumph over Adversity 1822–1865* (New York: Houghton Mifflin, 2000), 119–46.

127. Ulysses S. Grant, "The Battle of Shiloh," in *Battles and Leaders of the Civil War*, 4 vols. (New York: The Century Company, 1884–87), 1:465–87. Don Carlos Buell, "Shiloh Revisited," in ibid., 487–536. An excellent overview of the battle, and the controversies, can be found in Jay Luvaas, Stephen Bowman, and Leonard Fullenkamp, *Guide to the Battle of Shiloh* (Lawrence: University Press of Kansas, 1996).

128. *PMUSG*, 1:351–52. There are many examples of Grant reconsidering his stance when new evidence was presented. For one, see "General Ulysses S. Grant's Unpublished Correspondence in the Case of Fitz-John Porter," pamphlet, (New York: Martin B. Brown, 1884),

and Kevin Donovan, "The Court-Martial of Fitz-John Porter," *Columbiad* 2 (Winter 1999): 73–97.

129. *PMUSG*, 1:368.

130. Young, *Around the World with General Grant*, 2:307.

131. *PMUSG*, 1:574, 2:176.

132. Ibid., 2:278, 276. Scott E. Casper, *Constructing American Lives: Biography and Culture in Nineteenth-Century America* (Chapel Hill: University of North Carolina Press, 1999), 326–27.

133. Albert Bigelow Paine, ed., *Mark Twain's Letters*, 2 vols. (New York: Harper and Bros., 1917), 2:457–60.

134. *PMUSG*, 1:521.

135. Ibid., 2:375.

136. Ibid., 525.

137. Ibid., 445.

138. Ibid., 509.

139. Ibid., 553.

140. Thomas W. Higginson, "Grant," *Atlantic Monthly* 57 (March 1886): 384–88, quotation, 384.

141. Unattributed review, *Harper's New Monthly Magazine* 72 (March 1886): 649–50, quotation, 649.

142. Other favorable reviews include "Grant's Memoirs: Second Volume," *Atlantic Monthly* (September, 1886): 419–24; "Grant's Memoirs," *The Nation* 42 (February 25, 1886): 172–74; and Rossiter Johnson, "Grant's Memoirs," *The Dial* 7 (March 1886): 57–58.

143. Unidentified reviewer, *Southern Historical Society Papers* 14 (1886): 574–76, quotation, 575.

144. Arnold, *General Grant*, 49. Arnold's review was first published in an obscure English journal but then made known to an American audience when it was included in a book of essays on America, published in 1888.

145. Bruce Chadwick, *The Reel Civil War: Mythmaking in American Film* (New York: Alfred A. Knopf, 2001); Jim Cullen, *The Civil War in Popular Culture: A Reusable Past* (Washington, D.C.: Smithsonian Institution Press, 1995); and Gary W. Gallagher, *Causes Won, Lost, and Forgotten: How Hollywood and Popular Art Shape What We Know about the Civil War* (Chapel Hill: University of North Carolina Press, 2008) are three of the best books that include discussions of the impact of *Gone with the Wind* and the Lost Cause on American culture.

146. Gertrude Stein, "Grant," in *Four in America*, introduction by Thornton Wilder (New Haven: Yale University Press, 1947), 7.

147. Edmund Wilson, *Patriotic Gore: Studies in the Literature of the American Civil War* (New York: Oxford University Press, 1962), 143–44.

148. Simon, *Ulysses S. Grant: One Hundred Years Later*, 245–56, quotation, 255.

149. The *Papers* editors will work from the manuscript deposited by the Grant family in the Library of Congress. For discussion of the memoirs' importance, see Wilson, *Patriotic Gore*, 133; Bruce Catton, "Two Porches, Two Parades," *American Heritage* 19 (June 1968): 99; Alfred Kazin, "The Generals in the Labyrinth," *New Republic* 204 (February 18, 1991): 384–88); Keegan, *The Mask of Command*, 202; and McFeely, *Grant*, 495–517. In addition to the McFeely's

Library of America edition, two other recent editions are *Personal Memoirs*, with an introduction and notes by James M. McPherson (New York: Penguin Books, 1999), and *Personal
Memoirs of U. S. Grant*, with an introduction by Brooks D. Simpson (Lincoln: University of
Nebraska Press, 1996). The Library of America's January 2008 *e-Newsletter* indicated that "half
of the top ten LOA volumes are nonfiction." In order of popularity, these are *Grant: Memoirs
and Selected Letters, Walt Whitman: Poetry and Prose, Flannery O'Connor: Collected Works,
Francis Parkman: France and England in North America, H. P. Lovecraft: Tales, Mark Twain:
Mississippi Writings, Crime Novels: American Noir, Henry David Thoreau: A Week, Walden,
The Maine Woods, Cape Cod, The Debate on the Constitution 1787–88*, and *Thomas Jefferson:
Writings*.

150. *PMUSG*, 2:553.

151. Ibid., 1:170.

152. Ibid., 2:552.

153. *The Compact Edition of the Oxford English Dictionary*, 2 vols. (New York: Oxford University Press, 1971), 1:573.

154. Keegan, *The Mask of Command*, 202, 459.

## Chapter 5

1. First quotation, *Grant Memorial Services in Providence, R.I.—1885* (Providence: E. L.
Freeman and Son, Printers to the State, 1888), 16; second quotation, Peabody Education Fund,
*Tributes to Samuel Wetmore and General Grant at the Annual Meeting of the Peabody Educa-
tion Fund, New York, October 7, 1885*, (Cambridge, Mass.: Press of John Wilson and Son, 1885),
5; third quotation, undated, unattributed from Claxton Wilstach, comp., "Death of General
U. S. Grant" (Lafayette, Indiana: n.p., 1885), 58.

2. First quotation, C. L. Woodworth, D.D., "A Commemorative Discourse on the Work and
Character of Ulysses S. Grant, Delivered before the Citizens of Watertown, Massachusetts,
August 8, 1885" (Boston: Beacon Press, Thomas Todd Printer, 1885), 17; second quotation, Peabody Education Fund, *Tributes to Samuel Wetmore and General Grant*, 5; third quotation, Rev.
Bishop C. H. Fowler, D.D., L.L.D., "General Grant Memorial Address," pamphlet (San Francisco: R. R. McCabe and Co., Printers, 1885), 4. Fourth quotation, *NYTrib*, July 25, 1885. The
sources for this chapter include numerous published and unpublished accounts of memorial
services and ceremonies, printed eulogies, newspaper files and magazines. The majority of the
newspapers and journals examined come from New York, but a significant number originate
from the South, the West, and the Midwest. Only a small portion of the overall press coverage
can be cited; the articles and special "tribute editions" that were issued are too numerous to
list.

3. First quotation, Rev. Payson W. Lyman, *The Career and Character of Gen. Ulysses S.
Grant* (Belchertown, Mass.: John L. Montague, 1885), 16; second quotation, *New York Herald*,
undated, in Wilstach, "Death of General U. S. Grant," 160; third quotation, William Ralston
Balch, *Life and Public Services of General Grant* (Philadelphia: Aetna Publishing Co., 1885),
564.

4. *NYTrib*, August 4, 1885; Rev. J. O. Peck, D.D., "General Grant, Our Silent Hero, A Memorial Sermon on General U. S. Grant," pamphlet (New Haven: L. S. Panderson, 1885), 6, 16–17.

5. Nina Silber, *The Romance of Reunion: Northerners and the South, 1865–1900* (Chapel
Hill: University of North Carolina Press, 1993).

6. Background to the era is provided by Eric Foner, *Reconstruction: America's Unfinished Revolution, 1863–1877* (New York: Harper and Row, 1988); Stanley P. Hirshson, *Farewell to the Bloody Shirt: Northern Republicans and the Southern Negro, 1877–1893* (Bloomington: Indiana University Press, 1962); Joel H. Silbey, *The American Political Nation, 1838–1893* (Stanford, Calif.: Stanford University Press, 1991); Brooks D. Simpson, *Let Us Have Peace: U. S. Grant and the Politics of War and Reconstruction, 1861–1868* (Chapel Hill: University of North Carolina Press, 1991); and Mark W. Summers, *The Era of Good Stealings* (New York: Oxford University Press, 1993).

7. Stuart McConnell, *Glorious Contentment: The Grand Army of the Republic, 1865–1900* (Chapel Hill: University of North Carolina Press, 1992), and Mary P. Dearing, *Veterans in Politics* (Baton Rouge: Louisiana State University Press, 1951).

8. Works on Victorian sentiment and funeral customs include Katherine C. Grier, "The Decline of the Memory Palace: The Parlor after 1890," in *American Home Life, 1880–1930: A Social History of Spaces and Services*, ed. Jessica H. Foy and Thomas J. Schlereth (Knoxville: University of Tennessee Press, 1992), 49–74; Karen Halttunen, *Confidence Men and Painted Women: A Study of Middle-Class Culture in America, 1830–1870* (New Haven: Yale University Press, 1982); Mary Louise Kete, *Sentimental Collaborations: Mourning and Middle-Class Identity in Nineteenth-Century America* (Durham: Duke University Press, 2000); Shirley Samuels, ed., *The Culture of Sentiment: Race, Gender, and Sentimentality in Nineteenth-Century America* (Oxford: Oxford University Press, 1992); and Robert V. Wells, *Facing the "King of Terrors": Death and Society in an American Community, 1750–1990* (New York: Cambridge University Press, 2000).

9. Many books have described the rise of the Lost Cause myth, including Gary W. Gallagher, *Lee and His Army in Confederate History* (Chapel Hill: University of North Carolina Press, 2001); Rollin G. Osterweis, *The Myth of the Lost Cause, 1865–1900* (Hamden, Conn.: Shoestring Press, 1973); and Charles Reagan Wilson, *Baptized in Blood: The Religion of the Lost Cause, 1865–1920* (Athens: University of Georgia Press, 1980).

10. Nina Silber's important book, *The Romance of Reunion*, does not even mention U. S. Grant in the index; Gaines Foster's *Ghosts of the Confederacy: Defeat, the Lost Cause, and the Emergence of the New South, 1865–1913* (New York: Oxford University Press, 1987) mentions Grant only a few times and his funeral not at all; and David W. Blight, *Race and Reunion: The Civil War in American Memory* (Cambridge: Belknap Press of Harvard University Press, 2001), offers a brief but trenchant discussion of Grant's funeral (214–16). Cecilia O'Leary, writing on the rise of nationalism after the war, declared that "the occasion of Grant's funeral in 1885 testified to the increasing willingness to publicly endorse national unity" (O'Leary, *To Die For: The Paradox of American Patriotism* [Princeton, N.J.: Princeton University Press, 1999], 121). Most modern biographers of Union heroes have, understandably, ignored the funeral ceremonies in favor of the life. Early accounts of the death and funeral of U. S. Grant are Balch, *Life and Public Services of General Grant*; James Penny Boyd, *Military and Civil Life of Gen. Ulysses S. Grant: Leading Soldier of the Age; President of the United States; Loved and Honored American Citizen; the World's Most Distinguished Man* (Philadelphia: Garretson and Co., 1885); Frank A. Burr, *The Life and Death of General U. S. Grant* (Philadelphia: Collins Printer, 1885); "Memorial of U. S. Grant: Being Sermons, Addresses and Articles Collected from Various Religious and Secular Papers, 1885," Rev. William Treadway Collection, New York Public Library, New York City; Benjamin Perley Poore and Rev. O. H. Tiffany, D.D., *Life*

*of General Grant* (New York: Hubbard Brothers, 1885); George F. Shrady, *General Grant's Last Days* (New York: DeVinne Press, 1908); and Claxton Wilstach, "Death of General U. S. Grant." A more recent account is Thomas M. Pitkin, *The Captain Departs: Ulysses S. Grant's Last Campaign* (Carbondale: Southern Illinois University Press, 1973). Outstanding photographs of the funeral can be found in *The Riverside Souvenir: A Memorial Volume, Illustrating the Nation's Tribute to U. S. Grant* (New York: J. C. Derby, 1886), and U.S. Instantaneous Photographic Company, *Seven Mile Funeral Cortege of General Grant* (Boston, 1885). The latter is an elaborately designed, oversized album, which was meant to be sold, and then displayed, in the lobbies of fancy hotels throughout the East. There are only a few albums left, and two of them are in Southern California, one at the Huntington Library in San Marino, and one in the private collection of James Bultema of Thousand Oaks.

11. Some examples of works on Victorian celebrations are Len Travers, *Celebrating the Fourth: Independence Day and the Rites of Nationalism in the Early Republic* (Amherst: University of Massachusetts Press, 1997); David Waldstreicher, *In the Midst of Perpetual Fetes: The Making of American Nationalism, 1776-1820* (Chapel Hill: University of North Carolina Press, 1997); Ellen M. Litwicki, *America's Public Holidays: 1865-1920* (Washington, D.C.: Smithsonian Institution Press, 2000); and Brooks McNamara, *Day of Jubilee: The Great Age of Public Celebrations in New York, 1788-1909* (New Brunswick, N.J.: Rutgers University Press, 1997).

12. Gary Laderman, *The Sacred Remains: American Attitudes toward Death, 1700-1883* (New Haven: Yale University Press, 1996), 101. See also Drew Gilpin Faust, "The Civil War Soldier and the Art of Dying," *Journal of Southern History* 67 (February 2001): 3–38; Anne C. Rose, *Victorian America and the Civil War* (New York: Cambridge University Press, 1992); John Pettegrew, "'The Soldier's Faith': Turn-of-the-Century Memory of the Civil War and the Emergence of Modern American Nationalism," *Journal of Contemporary History* 31 (1996): 49–73; Mark S. Schantz, *Awaiting the Heavenly Country: The Civil War and America's Culture of Death* (Ithaca, N.Y.: Cornell University Press, 2008); and Gary Wills, *Lincoln at Gettysburg: The Words That Remade America* (New York: Simon and Schuster 1992), esp. chap. 2, "Gettysburg and the Culture of Death," 63–89.

13. The phrase "pageantry of woe" is taken from a prominent Philadelphia writer, Sidney George Fisher, and used in Gary Laderman, *The Sacred Remains*, 43. General studies of memory traditions include David Lowenthal, *The Past Is a Foreign Country* (Cambridge: Cambridge University Press, 1985); Michael Kammen, *Mystic Chords of Memory: The Transformation of Tradition in American Culture* (New York: Vintage books, 1991); and David Thelen, "Memory and American History," *Journal of American History* 75, no. 4 (March 1989): 1117–29. Specific studies of American memory traditions and commemorative activities include John Bodnar, *Remaking America: Public Memory, Commemoration, and Patriotism in the Twentieth Century* (Princeton, N.J.: Princeton University Press, 1992); David Glassberg, *American Historical Pageantry: The Uses of Tradition in the Early Twentieth Century* (Chapel Hill: University of North Carolina Press, 1990); and Kirk Savage, *Standing Soldiers, Kneeling Slaves: Race, War and Monuments in Nineteenth-Century America* (Princeton, N.J.: Princeton University Press, 1997).

14. The ties between mourning rituals and nationalism are explored in Peter Homans, ed., *Symbolic Loss: The Ambiguity of Mourning and Memory at Century's End* (Charlottesville: University of Virginia Press, 2000).

15. For substantial accounts of Lincoln's funeral, see Merrill D. Peterson, *Lincoln in Ameri-*

*can Memory* (New York: Oxford University Press, 1994), and John R. Neff, *Honoring the Civil War Dead: Commemoration and the Problem of Reconciliation* (Lawrence: University Press of Kansas, 2005). A psychological interpretation of Lincoln's funeral is provided by Michael Paul Rogin, "The King's Two Bodies: Lincoln, Wilson, Nixon, and Presidential Self-Sacrifice," in *Public Values and Private Power in American Politics*, ed. J. David Greenstone (Chicago: University of Chicago Press, 1984), 71–108. A complementary book to Peterson's is Barry Schwartz, *Abraham Lincoln and the Forge of National Memory* (Chicago: University of Chicago Press, 2000). See also chap. 1, "Beginning a New War," in Edward J. Blum, *Gilded Crosses: Race, Religion, and the Reforging of American Nationalism* (Lexington: University of Kentucky Press, 2003), for a thoughtful analysis of race and the consequences of emancipation in the northern reaction to Lincoln's assassination. Allan Peskin, *Garfield* (Kent, Ohio: Kent State University Press, 1979).

16. A small sampling of recent noteworthy publications on Lincoln includes Richard J. Carwardine, *Lincoln: Profiles in Power* (London: Pearson Longman, 2003); Doris Kearns Goodwin, *Team of Rivals: The Political Genius of Abraham Lincoln* (New York: Simon and Schuster, 2005); Allen C. Guelzo, *Abraham Lincoln: Redeemer President* (Grand Rapids, Mich.: William B. Eerdmans, 1999); and Ronald C. White, *A. Lincoln: A Biography* (New York: Random House, 2009).

17. Two works that explore southern reactions are Carolyn L. Harrell, *When the Bells Tolled for Lincoln: Southern Reaction to the Assassination* (Macon, Ga.: Mercer University Press, 1997), and Thomas Reed Turner, *Beware the People Weeping: Public Opinion and the Assassination of Abraham Lincoln* (Baton Rouge: Louisiana State University Press, 1982).

18. For a review of presidential polls from 1948 to 1982, see Arthur B. Murphy, "Evaluating the Presidents of the United States," *Presidential Studies Quarterly* 14 (Winter 1984): 117–26. A recent book giving Grant a low rating is Nathan Miller, *The Star-Spangled Men: America's Ten Worst Presidents* (New York: A Lisa Drew Book/Scribner, 1998); an even more recent publication offers a much higher ranking for Grant: Alvin Stephen Felzenberg, *The Leaders We Deserved (And a Few We Didn't)* (New York: Basic Books, 2008). Felzenberg gives Grant high marks for character, vision, and "preserving and extending liberty," 257. A recent presidential ranking poll conducted by the C-Span 2009 Historians Presidential Leadership Survey raised grant from thirty-third to twenty-third since the previous survey in 2000. <http://tinyurl.com/ahem49>.

19. *A Memorial of Ulysses S. Grant from the City of Boston* (Boston: Printed by Order of the City Council, 1885), 25; Companion William H. Powell, "Ulysses S. Grant: A Paper Read before the Missouri Commandery of the Military Order of the Loyal Legion of the United States, May 1, 1886" (St. Louis: James Hogan, 1886), 8; *Weekly Graphic*, August 11, 1885.

20. *New York Herald*, August 9, 1885; *New York Sun*, July 24, 1885; Peck, "General Grant, Our Silent Hero," 17.

21. General John B. Sanborn, *Oration Delivered before the Society of the Army of the Tennessee at Chicago, Illinois, September 9, 1885* (St. Paul, Minn.: H. M. Smyth., 1887), 22.

22. As quoted in Boyd, *Military and Civil Life of Gen. Ulysses S. Grant, 1885*), 675.

23. "Demand for Mourning Goods: Merchants Receiving Orders from All Over the Country," *NYT*, July 24, 1885.

24. "Mourning Grant's Death," *NYT*, July 28, 1885; "The Death of General Grant," *Frank Leslie's Illustrated Newspaper*, August 1, 1885; "The Metropolis in Mourning," *Harper's Weekly*,

August 8, 1885, 516–17; William S. McFeely, *Grant: A Biography* (New York: W. W. Norton, 1981), 517; David M. Kahn, "General Grant National Memorial Historical Resource Study," unpublished manuscript (New York: National Park Service, 1980), Manhattan Sites, 26 Wall Street, New York, N.Y., 21–22.

25. As printed in *NYTrib* and *NYT*, July 24, 1885.

26. *NYTrib*, July 24, 26, 1885, and *St. Louis Republican*, July 24, 1885.

27. *New York Herald*, July 24, 1885.

28. Sympathy messages, July/1885–August/1885, folder 2, box 13, GMAA.

29. Sympathy messages, July/1885–August/1885, folder 3, box 13, GMAA. The curator for the Grant monument described the "stupendous collection of memorial resolutions sent to the Grant family after his death. They came from organizations across the country and around the world." Kahn, "Resource Study," 27.

30. Dennis W. Bushyhead, "To the Cherokees and Other Indians," July 30, 1885, GLC03165, Gilder-Lehrman Collection, Morgan Library, New York City.

31. Frederick William Farrar, *Eulogy on Gen. Grant* (New York E. P. Dutton and Co., 1885).

32. Sympathy messages, July/1885–August/1885, folder 2, box 13, GMAA.

33. Ibid., folder 3, box 13.

34. British tributes reprinted in *NYTrib*, August 3, 1885; see also *New York Herald*, July 29, 1885. Quotation from Fred in Ishbel Ross, *The General's Wife: The Life of Mrs. Ulysses S. Grant* (New York: Dodd, Mead, 1959), 312. The exception appeared to be France, which could "see nothing in General Grant but the President who withheld his sympathy from France in her wanton attack by Germany" (*NYTrib*, July 26, 1885).

35. Quotation from "Ambitious, Vain and Weak," *NYT*, October 5, 1880. See also "Grant's Talk on Hancock," ibid., October 6, 1880. Hancock's biography is David M. Jordan, *Winfield Scott Hancock: A Soldier's Life* (Bloomington: Indiana University Press, 1988). Information on Hancock's funeral, just months after Grant's, can be found in "In Memoriam: Major-Gen. Winfield Scott Hancock, U.S.A.," John P. Nicholson, collector, 3 vols. (Philadelphia, 1886), John P. Nicholson Collection, Henry E. Huntington Library, San Marino, Calif.

36. "The Funeral Programme," *NYTrib*, July 29, 1885. Parades, processions, and similar popular demonstrations were a uniquely American cultural form. See Mary Ryan, "The American Parade: Representations of the Nineteenth-Century Social Order," in *The New Cultural History*, ed. Lynn Hunt (Berkeley: University of California Press, 1989), 131–53.

37. Sheridan's statement as quoted in Phineas Camp Headley, *Fight It Out on this Line: The Life and Deeds of Gen. U. S. Grant* (Boston: Lee and Shepard, 1885), 400–401.

38. *NYTrib*, August 1, 1885.

39. Ibid., July 27, 1885.

40. "The Great Soldier's Body," *NYT*, August 1, 1885.

41. "Order of the Procession: Funeral Plans Nearing Completion," *NYTrib*, August 3, 1885.

42. *New York World*, July 24, 1885; *NYT*, July 25, 27, 1885.

43. *New York Sun*, July 27, 28, 1885.

44. "The Dead General" and "No Autopsy to be Held," *NYTrib*, July 25, 1885; "Preparing for the Funeral," *NYT*, July 25, 1885.

45. As quoted in Stefan Lorant, "Baptism of U. S. Grant," *Life* 30 (March 26, 1951): 90–102, quotation, 102; and "The Services at Mount McGregor," *NYT*, August 5, 1885; "Farewell to Mount McGregor," *NYTrib*, August 5, 1885.

46. As quoted in Lorant, "Baptism of U. S. Grant," 94. See also "General Grant's Easter," *NYTrib*, April 6, 1885; Pitkin, *The Captain Departs*, 72–73.

47. Quotation from Samuel Clemens, *Mark Twain's Autobiography*, 2 vols. (New York: P. F. Collier and Son, 1925), 1:69.

48. As quoted in Richard Goldhurst, *Many Are the Hearts: The Agony and the Triumph of Ulysses S. Grant* (New York: Thomas Y. Crowell Company, 1975), 191. The earlier statement is from the John Hancock Douglas Journal, April 1885, 83, container 1, John Hancock Douglas Papers, Library of Congress, Washington, D.C. See also Shrady, *General Grant's Last Days*, and Adam Badeau, "The Last Days of General Grant," *Century Magazine* 30 (October 1885): 920–39. Newspaper accounts of the crisis (and Newman's role in the Grant household) can be found in *NYT*, March 29, 30, 31 and April 1, 2, 3, 1885, and *NYTrib*, March 30, April 2, 3, 4, 5, 6, 1885.

49. Grant quotation in Lorant, "Baptism of U. S. Grant," 94. *NYT*, July 24, 1885; *Pittsburg Christian Advocate*, undated clipping in "Memorial of U. S. Grant," 235, Treadway Collection. Beecher quotation in *NYT*, March 10, 1885.

50. *Christian Advocate*, August 13, 1885; *New York Evangelist*, August 27, 1885; *The Standard*, August 6, 1885.

51. Steven E. Woodworth, *While God Is Marching On: The Religious World of Civil War Soldiers* (Lawrence: University Press of Kansas, 2001), 172. For the importance of religion to the Civil War generation, see Randall M. Miller, Harry S. Stout, and Charles Reagan Wilson, eds., *Religion and the American Civil War* (New York: Oxford University Press, 1998).

52. Sydney Ahlstrom, *A Religious History of the American People* (New Haven: Yale University Press, 1972); Ronald C. White, *Liberty and Justice for All: Racial Reform and the Social Gospel, 1877–1925* (New York: HarperCollins, 1990).

53. Quotation from Andrew C. Rieser, *The Chautauqua Moment: Protestants, Progressives, and the Culture of Modern Liberalism* (New York: Columbia University Press, 2003), 140. See also Jeffrey Simpson, *Chautauqua: An American Utopia* (New York: Harry N. Abrams, 1999), 37; and Edward J. Blum, "Gilded Crosses: Postbellum Revivalism and the Reforging of American Nationalism," *Journal of Presbyterian History* 9, no. 4 (Winter 2001): 277–92.

54. As quoted in Woodworth, *While God Is Marching On*, 96. Treatments of the growth of modern American nationalism include Merle Curti, *The Roots of American Loyalty* (1946; reprint, New York: Atheneum, 1968); Gaines M. Foster, "A Christian Nation: Signs of a Covenant," in *Bonds of Affection: American Define Their Patriotism*, ed. John Bodnar (Princeton, N.J.: Princeton University Press, 1996); Melinda Lawson, Patriot *Fires: Forging a New American Nationalism in the Civil War North* (Lawrence: University Press of Kansas, 2002); Paul C. Nagel, *This Sacred Trust: American Nationality, 1798–1898* (New York: Oxford University Press, 1971); O'Leary, *To Die For*; and Harry S. Stout, *Upon the Altar of the Nation: A Moral History of the Civil War* (New York: Viking Press, 2006).

55. *Richmond Dispatch*, July 26, 1885; "The Editor's Table," in *Southern Bivouac: A Literary and Historical Magazine* 1, no. 1 (June 1885): 60–61, quotation, 60.

56. "Words of Sympathy from Many Sources," *NYTrib*, July 24, 1885.

57. *Albany Argus*, August 6, 1885; *Albany Evening Journal*, August 4, 1885.

58. "The Sad Journey to Albany" and "The Funeral Pageant at Albany," *NYT*, August 5, 1885; "The People Pay Homage," ibid., August 6, 1885.

59. "The People Pay Homage," *NYT*, August 6, 1885.

60. "Virginia Soldiers To Be Present," *NYTrib*, August 4, 1885.

61. "Fitzhugh Lee's Tribute," *New York Herald*, undated, in Wilstach, "Death of General U. S. Grant," 160.

62. As quoted in *Cincinnati Commercial Gazette*, July 28, 1885, in ibid., 57. Evidently he got the votes and more. Lee was elected governor of Virginia in 1885 and served in that capacity until 1890. He was defeated in the race for the U.S. Senate in 1893. In 1896 President Cleveland appointed Lee consul general at Havana, Cuba, where he continued to serve under President McKinley until the Spanish-American war broke out in 1898. In that conflict he served as a major general of volunteers. See Roger J. Spiller, ed., *Dictionary of American Military Biography*, 3 vols. (Westport, Conn.: Greenwood Press, 1984), 2:606–9.

63. J. A. Early to Hon. Jefferson Davis, Lynchburg, Va., April 20, 1885, Jefferson Davis Papers, Howard-Tilton Memorial Library, Tulane University, New Orleans, La. D. H. Hill to General Jubal A. Early, Hendersonville, N.C., July 29, 1885, MsslEa 765B, 46–47, Early Papers, Virginia Historical Society, Richmond.

64. Quotation from the Sparta (Ga.) *Ishmaelite*, in Wilstach, "Death of General U. S. Grant," 113.

65. Quotation from *New York Herald*, undated, in ibid., 160.

66. "Tributes from the South," reprinted in *NYTrib*, July 24, 1885.

67. Blight, *Race and Reunion*; Reid Mitchell, *The Vacant Chair: The Northern Soldier Leaves Home* (New York: Oxford University Press, 1993); Silber, *The Romance of Reunion*.

68. Quotation from Silber, The Romance of Reunion, 63

69. "The Editor's Table," in *Southern Bivouac*, 60–61, quotation, 60.

70. Adam Badeau, *Grant in Peace: From Appomattox to Mount McGregor* (Hartford, Conn.: S. S. Scranton, 1887), 456.

71. Benjamin Perley Poore and Rev. O. H. Tiffany, D.D., *Life of General Grant* (New York: Hubbard Brothers, 1885), 533; Robert B. Symon Jr., "Louisville's Lost National Holiday: Sectional Reconciliation and the Ulysses S. Grant 1885 Birthday Celebration," *Ohio Valley History* 8 (Fall 2008): 40–61, quotation, 40; *NYTrib*, April 9, 1885; "An Ex-Confederate to General Grant," ibid., July 3, 1885.

72. Badeau, *Grant in Peace*, 453–54.

73. "Buckner's Tribute to Grant," *NYT*, July 16, 1885.

74. *PMUSG*, 2:553–54.

75. Ambrose Bierce, "The Death of Grant," in *An American Anthology, 1787–1900*, ed. Edmund Clarence Stedman (Boston: Houghton Mifflin, 1900), 832. Bierce (1842–1914) served in the 9th Indiana Volunteers during the war, fighting at Shiloh and Chickamauga. His short stories depict the dark, violent, irrational side of battle. Ambrose Bierce, *Civil War Stories* (New York: Dover Press, 1994).

76. David Blight and William Blair write of reconciliation at this time. Blight, *Race and Reunion*, 338–97; William A. Blair, *Cities of the Dead: Contesting the Memory of the Civil War in the South, 1865-1914* (Chapel Hill: University of North Carolina Press, 2004), 171–207.

77. "Gath Views the Parade," in Wilstach, "Death of General U.S. Grant," 28.

78. "The Funeral Pageant," *NYTrib*, August 1, 1885.

79. New York City funeral details, and quotations, from "A Nation At A Tomb," *NYT*, August 9, 1885.

80. "Gath Views the Parade," 28.

81. Kahn, "Resource Study," 17.

82. Joshua Chamberlain to Fannie Chamberlain, August 8, 1885, in *The Grand Old Man of Maine: Selected Letters of Joshua Chamberlain, 1865–1914* (Chapel Hill: University of North Carolina Press, 2004), 124–25.

83. As quoted in Pitkin, *The Captain Departs*, 110.

84. Headlines from *NYT*, August 9, 1885.

85. Walt Whitman, *Leaves of Grass* (Boston: Small, Maynard and Company, 1904), 392; The *New York Times* received over a hundred poems shortly after Grant's death—on August 6, 1885, the paper printed a large selection of mostly very bad poetry penned by both men and women.

86. *A Memorial of Ulysses S. Grant from the City of Boston*, 67–68.

87. James Creelman, *On the Great Highway: The Wanderings and Adventures of a Special Correspondent* (Boston: Lothrop, 1901), 238.

88. *New York Evangelist*, August 6, 1885. "General Grant," July 30, 1885, *Christian Union*, in "Memorial of U. S. Grant," 239, Treadway Collection. An insightful exploration of the genre is Janice Hume, *Obituaries in American Culture* (Jackson: University Press of Mississippi, 2000).

89. A few books among many that illuminate the relationship between private loss and public roles are Stephen Cushman, *Bloody Promenade: Reflections on a Civil War Battle* (Charlottesville: University of Virginia Press, 1999); Drew Gilpin Faust, *This Republic of Suffering: Death and the American Civil War* (New York: Alfred A. Knopf, 2008); Earl J. Hess, *The Union Soldier in Battle: Enduring the Ordeal of Combat* (Lawrence: University Press of Kansas, 1997), esp. chap. 9; Mitchell, *The Vacant Chair*, esp. 115–56; John M. Coski and Amy R. Feely, "A Monument to Southern Womanhood: The Founding Generation of the Confederate Museum," in *A Woman's War: Southern Women, Civil War, and the Confederate Legacy*, ed. Edward D. C. Campbell Jr. and Kym S. Rice (Charlottesville: University Press of Virginia, 1996).

90. Sympathy messages, July/1885–August/1885, folder 2, box 13, GMAA.

91. Ibid.

92. *Memorial Services in Honor of General U. S. Grant in Pawtucket, Rhode Island* (Tower Post, No. 17, GAR, 1885), 5–6, Special Collections, Henry E. Huntington Library, San Marino, Calif.

93. Major-General Grenville M. Dodge, *Personal Recollections of President Abraham Lincoln, General Ulysses S. Grant and General William T. Sherman* (Council Bluffs, Iowa: Monarch Publishing, 1914), 111.

94. "The Voice of the Press: A United Nation in Mourning," *NYTrib*, July 25, 1885.

95. "North and South, So Lately Embattled, Mourn Alike About the Grave," *New York World*, August 9, 1885, in Wilstach, "Death of General U. S. Grant," 92.

96. *NYT*, August 9, 1885.

97. Descriptions of the services in ibid.

98. Reprinted in "The Southern Press," *NYT*, July 24, 1885.

99. Hon. John S. Wise, "Address Delivered at General Grant's Tomb," Memorial Day, 1891 (New York: Montross Y. Clarke, 1913), 9–10.

100. *Christian Worker*, August 1885, in "Memorial of U. S. Grant," 247, Treadway Collection.

101. Woodworth, "A Commemorative Discourse," 12; Charles Devens in *A Memorial of Ulysses S. Grant from the City of Boston*, 51.

102. Sympathy messages, July/1885–August/1885, folder 2, box 13, GMAA.

103. First quotation from Mrs. E. M. Rowland, "Grant the Emancipator," July 27, 1885, in "Memorial of U. S. Grant," 231, Treadway Collection. John Mercer Langston, "General Grant and the Colored American," *The National Republican*, August 8, 1885, in ibid., 200. See also "What the Colored People Owe Grant," interview with John Mercer Langston, in *New-York Daily Tribune*, July 24, 1885.

104. Kate Drumgoold, "A Slave Girl's Story: Being the Autobiography of Kate Drumgoold," in *Six Women's Slave Narratives*, with an introduction by William L. Andrews (New York: Oxford University Press, 1988), 3–62, quotation, 35. My thanks to Edward Blum for bringing this citation to my attention.

105. A picture of the unit can be found in *Seven Mile Funeral Cortege of General Grant*, no. 85. For an excellent discussion of black veterans, see Barbara A. Gannon, "Sites of Memory, Sites of Glory: African-American Grand Army of the Republic Posts in Pennsylvania," in *Making and Remaking Pennsylvania's Civil War*, ed. William Blair and William Pencak (University Park: Pennsylvania State University Press, 2001), 166–87.

106. Barbara A. Gannon, "The Won Cause: Black and White Comradeship in the Grand Army of the Republic" (Ph.D. dissertation, Pennsylvania State University, 2005); Donald R. Shaffer, *After the Glory: The Struggle of Black Civil War Veterans* (Lawrence: University Press of Kansas, 2004); John R. Neff, *Honoring the Civil War Dead: Commemoration and the Problem of Reconciliation* (Lawrence: University Press of Kansas, 2005). See also M. Keith Harris, "Slavery, Emancipation, and Veterans of the Union Cause: Commemorating Freedom in the Era of Reconciliation, 1885–1915," *Civil War History* 53, no. 3 (September 2007): 264–90.

107. Gannon, "The Won Cause," 108.

108. "The Tribute of the South: Confederates Unite with Federals in Memorial Services," *NYT*, August 9, 1885.

109. "Resolutions of Respect," *NYTrib*, August 4, 1885. Other sources on African American participation are documented in ibid., August 2 1885, and in "Memorial of U. S. Grant," 85, 200, 205, Treadway Collection.

110. The classic work on the South in this period is C. Vann Woodward, *Origins of the New South, 1877–1913* (Baton Rouge: Louisiana State University Press, 1971). See also Edward L. Ayers, *The Promise of the New South: Life after Reconstruction* (New York: Oxford University Press, 1992); Paul H. Buck, *The Road to Reunion, 1865–1900* (New York: Vintage Books, 1959), and Foster, *Ghosts of the Confederacy*.

111. Background for the election of 1884 is based on Mark Wahlgren Summers, *Rum, Romanism, and Rebellion: The Making of a President, 1884* (Chapel Hill: University of North Carolina Press) 2000; John M. Dobson, "George William Curtis and the Election of 1884: The Dilemma of the New York Mugwumps," *New York Historical Society Quarterly* 52 (1968): 215–34; and Richard E. Welch Jr. *The Presidencies of Grover Cleveland* (Lawrence: University Press of Kansas, 1988).

112. Blaine thought he was defeated in New York because of his meeting in a hotel with Protestant ministers, one of whom later denounced the Democrats as the party of "rum, Romanism and rebellion," a comment widely publicized just before the election. Summers, *Rum, Romanism, and Rebellion,* 279–85.

113. As quoted in Foster, *Ghosts of the Confederacy,* 66.

114. *NYT,* March 6, 1885. Examples of newspaper accounts of the election, and the racial tensions and anxieties it inspired, can be found in ibid., October 4, November 3, 14, 17, 19, 20, 1884.

115. *NYT,* March 8, 1885.

116. Foster, *Ghosts of the Confederacy,* 66.

117. *PMUSG,* 2:542–43.

118. *New York Herald,* "The North and South in Mourning," July 29, 1885.

*Chapter 6*

1. Both quotations from "The Grandest Sepulture," *NYT,* July 28, 1885.

2. The most helpful sources on Grant's monument are David M. Kahn, "The Grant Monument," *Journal of the Society of Architectural Historians* 41 (1982): 212–23, and David M. Kahn, "General Grant National Memorial Historical Resource Study," unpublished manuscript (New York: National Park Service, 1980), Manhattan Sites, 26 Wall Street, New York, New York, 1980. Others include Neil Harris, "The Battle for Grant's Tomb," *American Heritage* 36 (1985): 70–79; G. Kurt Piehler, "The Changing Legacy of Grant's Tomb," unpublished paper, 1995, in author's possession; Eric A. Reinert, *Grant's Tomb* (New York: Eastern National, 1997); and Donald Martin Reynolds, *Monuments and Masterpieces: Histories and Views of Public Sculpture in New York City* (1988; reprint, New York: Thames and Hudson, 1997), 214–23. A wealth of primary materials related to the monument, including correspondence, financial records, records of architectural competitions, and artifacts are contained in GMAA. Additional materials regarding the monument can be found in the Papers of Ulysses S. Grant, Manuscript Division, Library of Congress Washington, D.C.

3. First quotation from Reinert, *Grant's Tomb,* 22; second quotation from *NYT,* August 16, 1997.

4. First quotation from Reynolds, *Monuments and Masterpieces,* 214; second quotation from *NYT,* April 10, 1994. see also *St. Louis Dispatch,* March 6, 1994; *Philadelphia Inquirer,* February 16, 1995.

5. Emily M. Bernstein, "An Uncivil War over the Keeping of Grant's Tomb," *NYT,* December 19, 1993. Scaturro has subsequently graduated from law school and is currently working in Washington, D.C., where he remains active in the reestablished Grant Monument Association. The association's goal is to raise money for further improvements for the memorial, including a visitors' center (with restrooms) behind the tomb. The Grant Monument Association's website, <http://www.grantstomb.org/ind-gma.html>, offers excellent information on the history of the tomb, as well as its current status, as does the National Park Service's site, <http://www.nps.gov/gegr/>. Scaturro has published a book, *President Grant Reconsidered* (Lanham, Md.: Madison Books, 1999).

6. *NYT,* January 2, 1994.

7. Quotation from Mary B. W. Tabor, "For the Tomb of Civil War Hero, the New Battle Is in Court," *NYT,* April 27, 1994. See also Randy Kennedy, "Illinois Wants Grant's Tomb," *NYT,*

April 10, 1994; Dennis Hevesi, "No One in Grant's Tomb Unless It's Fixed, Family Warns," *NYT*, October 16, 1994; "Peace Infuses Grant's Tomb," *NYT*, April 23, 1999; and *Washington Post*, April 5, 1997.

8. Plans for a grand ceremonial road leading up to Grant's Tomb, lessening the "great congestion" caused when marches ended at the monument, were scuttled by opposition from competing real estate interests. Quotation and story from Christopher Gray, "At Curves in the Road, 2 Unusually Shaped Buildings: All That Remains of a Plan for a Ceremonial Road to Grant's Tomb," *NYT*, August 15, 1999.

9. David Quigley, *Second Founding: New York City, Reconstruction, and the Making of American Democracy* (New York: Hill and Wang, 2004), 176.

10. John Tierney, "Grant Us Peace," *NYT Magazine*, May 7, 1995.

11. Ibid. Marx's quiz show was called "You Bet Your Life." The correct answer to the question is "nobody," because President and Mrs. Grant are "entombed," not buried. On July 4, 2003, the steps of the tomb provided the venue for Macy's annual Fourth of July concert, featuring the singer Beyoncé Knowles, who sang and danced in her customary provocative style. Despite protests over the propriety of staging such a festivity so near to a tomb, National Park Service officials approved the event. "Beyoncé's Grave Dance Causes Grief," BBC News Online, July 14, 2003.

12. Modern intellectuals, scholars of memory, and historians have carefully studied the powerful emotions evoked in grand public art such as Grant's Tomb. A very small number of Civil War monuments and memorials became what Pierre Nora described as "memory sites" (*lieux de mémoire*). According to Nora, memory sites not only embody an integral part of a country's national heritage, they also summon deep emotional feelings, while at the same time educating people about a particular historical event. Pierre Nora, *Realms of Memory: Rethinking the French Past*, ed. Pierre Nora and Lawrence D. Kritzman, trans. Arthur Goldhammer, 3 vols. (New York: Columbia University Press, 1996–98), 1:xvii. André Malraux famously said that "a culture will be judged by its statues." Quotation from Gary Wills, "The Meaning of Monuments," *Washington Post*, April 27, 1997. Marvin Trachtenberg wrote, "Monuments are a way . . . [to] . . . transmit communal emotions, a medium of continuity and interaction between generations, not only in space but across time, for to be a monument is to be permanent" (*The Statue of Liberty* [New York: Viking Press, 1976], 15).

13. Two books on war monuments are Thomas J. Brown, *The Public Art of Civil War Commemoration: A Brief History with Documents* (New York and Boston: Bedford/St. Martin's Press, 2004), and Kirk Savage, *Standing Soldier, Kneeling Slaves: Race, War and Monument in Nineteenth-Century America* (Princeton, N.J.: Princeton University Press, 1997). See also G. Kurt Piehler, *Remembering War the American Way* (Washington, D.C.: Smithsonian Books, 1995).

14. David W. Blight, "Decoration Days: The Origins of Memorial Day in North and South," in *The Memory of the Civil War in American Culture*, ed. Alice Fahs and Joan Waugh (Chapel Hill: University of North Carolina Press, 2004), 94–129, 105.

15. David J. Eicher, *Mystic Chords of Memory: Civil War Battlefields and Historic Sites Recaptured* (Baton Rouge: Louisiana State University Press, 1998); Kathryn Allamong Jacob, *Testament to Union: Civil War Monuments in Washington, D.C.* (Baltimore: Johns Hopkins University Press, 1998). John Bodnar and Michael Kammen published books on the relation-

ship between memory and public art across three centuries of U.S. history, while Kurt Savage and Thomas Brown analyzed Civil War monuments exclusively. Their combined scholarship suggests that long after the excitement of the dedication ceremony fades away, national monuments were, and are, the favored places to stage patriotic events, parades, and speeches. Often monuments such as the Washington Monument and the Lincoln Memorial in D.C. became deeply embedded in popular consciousness through endlessly replicated images in postcards and paintings, as backdrops for television news reports, as settings for protests or music concerts, in books, movies, and documentaries. John Bodnar, *Remaking America: Public Memory, Commemoration and Patriotism in the Twentieth Century* (Princeton, N.J.: Princeton University Press, 1992); Michael Kammen, *Mystic Chords of Memory: The Transformation of Tradition in American Culture* (New York: Alfred A. Knopf, 1991). For Savage and Brown books, see n. 12 above.

16. Rutherford B. Hayes, *The Diary and Letters of Rutherford B. Hayes, Nineteenth President of the United States*, ed. Charles Richard Williams, 5 vols. (Columbus: Ohio State Archeological and Historical Society, 1922), quotation from July 26, 1885, 4:224; second quotation in Hayes, "Aid for the Monument," *NYT*, July 26, 1885, in which the newspaper printed a letter from R. B. Hayes written from Spiegel Grove, Fremont, Ohio.

17. Launt Thompson [New York sculptor], Calvert Vaux [architect who co-designed, with Frederick Law Olmsted, Central Park, Riverside Park, and Morningside Park], W. H. Beard [painter], Karl Gerhardt [sculptor of Grant's death mask], Henry Van Brunt [architect and author who served in the Civil War; his firm executed the commission for Harvard's Memorial Hall], Olin L. Warner [sculptor], Wilson McDonald [unable to identify], Clarence Cook [painter and author], "Grant's Memorial: What Shall It Be?," *North American Review* 141 (September 1885): 276–92. See also Horatio Seymour [ex-New York governor], John La Farge [artist and writer], Rufus Hatch [writer], Charles T. Congdon [Congregationalist minister], Dorman B. Eaton [lawyer and civil service reformer], "Notes and Comments," *North American Review* 141 (October 1885), 399–400, and C. M. Harvey, Mary A. Parker, Elizabeth A. Meriwether, Henry Forrester, F. B. Wixon, "Style and the Monument," from "No Name Essays," ibid., 443–53.

18. Thompson et al., "Grant's Memorial," 281; see also Elizabeth K. Allen, "Launt Thompson, New York Sculptor," *Magazine Antiques*, November 2002, 152–57.

19. Quotation from Cook, in Thompson et al., "Grant's Memorial," 292; quotation from La Farge, in Seymour et al., "Notes and Comments," 399.

20. Quotation from Gerhardt, in Thompson et al., "Grant's Memorial," 282; quotation from Beard, in ibid., 279; quotation from Thompson, in ibid., 276.

21. Architect Daniel H. Burnham brought the Beaux-Arts concept to its most brilliant fruition with his Union Station and Library of Congress building in Washington, D.C. See Thomas S. Hines, *Burnham of Chicago: Architect and Planner* (New York: Oxford University Press, 1974).

22. First quotation in Robert A. M. Stern, Gregory Gilmartin, and John Montague Massengale, *1900: Metropolitan Architecture and Urbanism, 1890–1915* (New York: Rizzoli International, 1983), 121; Beard quotation in Thompson et al., "Grant's Memorial," 278–79; third quotation from *NYTrib*, August 12, 1885.

23. Fred's letter appeared in the *New York World* on September 13, 1889. See also *NYT*,

July 24, September 7, 1885. Horace Porter's account in "The Tomb of General Grant," *Century Magazine* 53 (April 1897): 839–46, stressed New York as the favorite from the beginning. See also Kahn, "Resource Study," 10–12.

24. W. R. Grace to Julia Grant, July 23, 1885, Grant Family Archival Folder, GMAA; For details of the proposals, see also *NYT*, July 24, 1885, and *NYTrib*, July 26, 1885; Lt. General Hindeman to Col. Fred D. Grant, July 23 or July 24, 1885, Grant Family Archival Folder, GMAA; Fred's quotation from *New York World*, September 13, 1899.

25. Frederick Dent Grant to William R. Grace, July 23, 1885; Frederick Dent Grant to Horace Porter, March 24, 1892, Grant Family Archival Folder, GMAA.

26. Lawrence A. Clayton, "William Russell Grace," in *American National Biography*, ed. John A. Garraty and Mark C. Carnes, 24 vols.(New York: Oxford University Press, 1999), 9: 362–364). *NYT*, July 24 and 25, 1885.

27. Fred's quotation from *New York World*, September 13, 1899; headline from *NYT*, July 25, 1885.

28. *NYT*, July 24, 1885.

29. Robert A. M. Stern, Thomas Mellins, and David Fishman, *New York 1880: Architecture and Urbanism in the Gilded Age* (New York: Monacelli Press, 1999), quotations, 1027 and 16.

30. An interesting note: President Grant laid the cornerstone of the American Museum of National History in 1874 and met with the sculptor of the Statue of Liberty, Frédéric-Auguste Bartholdi in the same year. Stern, Mellins, and Fishman, *New York 1880*, 372. New York was not the only city to be remade by what architectural historians have called "The Architecture of National Power." The firm of McKim, Mead and White used a neoclassical design for the Boston Public Library, among many other buildings. See Leland M. Roth, *A Concise History of American Architecture* (New York: Harper and Row, 1979).

31. Mayor Grace's quotation in *NYT*, July 26, 1885.

32. Mayor Grace's quotation in ibid., July 29, 1885; Crimmins quotation in ibid., July 24, 1885.

33. *NYT*, July 28, 1885; following the Central Park controversy was the *NYTrib*, July 25, 1885; The *Tribune* devoted several pages to opinions on where the general should be buried, and what kind of monument should be raised, on July 28 and 29, 1885.

34. Confirmation of acceptance in letter to Col. Fred Grant from Charles Burnt, New York Department of Public Works, July 27, 1885, in Grant Family Archival Folder, GMAA; also reported in "Riverside Park Chosen," *NYT*, July 29, 1885, and "To Sleep at Riverside," *NYTrib*, July 29, 1885.

35. Earlier, Olmsted and Vaux designed Central Park. Quotation from a pamphlet by Martha J. Lamb, "The Guide for Strangers to General Grant's Tomb" (New York: J. J. Little, 1886), unpaginated, Various Collections, Rare Books and Manuscript Collections, New York Public Library, New York City.

36. As quoted in "Riverside Park Chosen," *NYT*, July 29, 1885.

37. Criticism of public transportation, *New York World*, July 30, 1885; real estate boon, quoted in Kahn, "Resource Study," 19; discussions among architects, including Olmsted and Vaux can be found in *NYT*, "An Architect on Its Position and Surroundings," August 8, 1885; "The Memorial Site," August 10, 1885; and "The Grant Memorial" August 11, 1885. The development of Riverside is discussed in Stern, Mellins, and Fishman, *New York 1880*, 741–44.

38. First quotation from *NYT*, July 24, 1885; second quotation from Kahn, "The Grant Monument," 212.

39. The meetings of the Grant Monument Association are recorded in the Minutebooks, 1885/1886, GMAA.

40. First quotation from Unsigned, "Money and Monuments: A Tract for the Times," November 8, 1885, Various Collections, Rare Books and Manuscript Collections, New York Public Library, New York City; second quotation from David M. Kahn, Curator, "Inventory of the Grant Monument Association Archives," unpublished report (New York: National Park Service), Manhattan Sites, 26 Wall Street, New York, N.Y. (June 1979, revised August, 1979), 2.

41. Information on Greener and his role in the Grant Monument Association is from Ruth Ann Stewart and David M. Kahn, "Richard T. Greener, His Life and Work: An Exhibit and Tribute Sponsored by The National Park Service and The National Park Foundation," introduction to catalog, Schomburg Center for Research in Black Culture, New York Public Library, 1–15; Allison Blakely, "Richard T. Greener and the 'Talented Tenth's' Dilemma," in *Journal of Negro History* 59 (October 1974): 305–21.

42. As quoted in Stewart and Kahn, "Richard T. Greener," 11. The New York AME Zion church was located at the corner of Bleeker and West 10 Streets. Ibid., 13.

43. Press quotations from *NYT*, July 31, 1885.

44. "Aid from the Country: The Growing Interest in The Grant Monument," ibid., September 11, 1885, and "The Givers to the Fund: Analyzing the Grant Monument Subscriptions," ibid., October 28, 1885.

45. As quoted in Kahn, "Resource Study," 33.

46. Hayes to General S. S. Burdette, August 15, 1885, in Hayes, *Diary and Letters* 4:232.

47. As quoted in Stewart and Kahn, "Richard T. Greener," 12.

48. *New York World*, July 30, 1885. George William Curtis, "Editor's Easy Chair," *Harper's New Monthly Magazine*, 71 (June–November 1885): 961.

49. "Objecting to the Choice of the Park," *NYTrib*, July 26, 1885; The *Tribune* listed the discontented. Chicago statement from *NYT*, August 23, 1885; last quotation from William Ralston Balch, *Life and Public Services of General Grant* (San Francisco: Occidental Publications, 1885), 558.

50. As quoted in Kahn, "Resource Study," 19.

51. Both quotations from *New York Herald*, July 25 and 26, 1885.

52. As quoted in *NYTrib*, August 8, July 29, 1885. See also Kahn, "Resource Study," 33.

53. As quoted in Kahn, "Resource Study," 34.

54. "The Hero's Place of Burial: A Weak Washington Protest," *NYT*, July 28, 1885. The article surveyed protests around the country. The controversy was also addressed in another section, "Mourning Grant's Death," ibid. Veterans' opposition further discussed in "Grant and the Grand Army," ibid., September 16, 1885, and "Veterans Called Upon to Contributed to the Grant Monument Fund," ibid., September 27, 1885.

55. Quoted in Balch, *Life and Public Services of General Grant*, 559.

56. Hayes, *Diary and Letters*, 4:224 (July 26, 1885). See also August 7, 1885, diary entry, in ibid., 229.

57. Hayes to Burdette, August 15, 1885 in ibid., 232 (for another letter to Burdette that em-

phasized more concerns, see ibid., 226); Hayes to James C. Reed, Secretary of the Monument Assn., May 25, 1892, in ibid. 5:84. Records show that in 1892 the GAR leadership was still being courted by the Grant Monument Association. Two good examples are Horace Porter to Frederick Phisterer, Adj. General, Grand Army of the Republic, July 7, 1892, and Horace Porter to Major A. J. Weissert, Commander-in-Chief, GAR, March 6, 1892, in Grant Monument Association Letter Book, May 5, 1892–October 14, 1896, container 1, Papers of Horace Porter, Manuscripts Division, Library of Congress, Washington, D.C.

58. As quoted in *NYT*, September 10, 1885.

59. Sherman's speech printed in ibid.

60. Letter from Julia Grant to W. R. Grace, October 29, 1885, in Grant Family Archival Folder, GMAA. Kansas City quote reprinted in *NYT*, July 30, 1885. Julia Grant did not reside in New York City after 1894. She lived in Washington with her divorced daughter and her grandchildren, seldom venturing forth in public, except to attend ceremonies honoring her husband, such as the dedication of the tomb in 1897. She died peacefully in 1902. Albert Bigelow Paine, ed., *Mark Twain's Letters*, 2 vols. (New York: Harper and Bros., 1917) 2:456–57.

61. Horace Porter to Major Weissert, March 6, 1892, Grant Monument Association Letter Book.

62. GAR information in *NYT*, September 16 and 27, 1885; information on donations in ibid., October 28, 1885; Kahn, "Resource Study," 28–32.

63. Quotation from Reinert, "Grant's Tomb," 10; Kahn, "The Grant Monument," 219–21.

64. Kahn, "The Grant Monument," 214–15; *New York Herald*, July 30, 1886.

65. *NYT*, April 25, 1897.

66. Kahn, "The Grant Monument," 222. See also *NYT*, April 1 and 2, 1890. Details of the association's concern for the second competition are found in "Report from C. O'Reilly to the Executive Committee," December 16, 1889, storage box 7, folder 9, GMAA.

67. Information on John H. Duncan in *New York Herald*, September 13, 1890; *NYT*, October 20, 1929; Reinert, "Grant's Tomb," 11; Kahn, "The Grant Monument," 222–27.

68. Reynolds, *Monuments and Masterpieces*, 216. For a thorough discussion of the competition, see *NYT*, April 25, 1897.

69. As quoted in Kahn, "The Grant Monument," 227.

70. Greener quotation in Stewart and Kahn, "Richard T. Greener," 13; Stern, Gilmartin, and Massengale, *1900*, 122; Schulyer quotation in Kahn, "Resource Study," 143.

71. Quotation from "Grant Tomb," folder 2, "G.A.R. Honor Roll, 1892–1893," box 10, GMAA.

72. Piehler, "The Changing Legacy of Grant's Tomb," 15, and *Remembering War the American Way*, 53–58; Kahn, "Resource Study," 35–36. See also John Tauranac, *Elegant New York: The Builders and the Buildings, 1885–1915* (New York: Abbeville Press, 1985).

73. Major-General Grenville M. Dodge, *Personal Recollections of President Abraham Lincoln, General Ulysses S. Grant and General William T. Sherman* (Council Bluffs, Iowa: The Monarch Publishing Co., 1914), 119.

74. Horace Porter to S. R. Van Duzer, May 10, 1892, Grant Monument Association Letter Book.

75. Joint fund-raising activities undertaken by the GAR and the Grant Monument Association are recorded in "G.A.R. Honor Roll, 1892–1893," folder 2, box 10, GMAA. See also Horace Porter to General James Fry, May 12, 1892, Grant Monument Association Letter Book.

76. Reinert, "Grant's Tomb," 13; biographical sketch titled "Horace Porter," container 5, Papers of Horace Porter.

77. Patrick J. Kelly, "The Election of 1896 and the Restructuring of Civil War Memory," in Fahs and Waugh, *The Memory of the Civil War in American Culture*, 180–212, quotation, 182.

78. Horace Porter, "Personal Traits of General Grant," *McClure's Magazine* 2 (May 1894): 507–14, quotation, 507.

79. Frederick Dent Grant to Horace Porter, March 24, 1892, Grant Family Archival Folder, GMAA. See also Frederick Dent Grant to Horace Porter, March 20, 1892, ibid.

80. Horace Porter to S. R. Van Duzer, May 10, 1892, Grant Monument Association Letter Book.

81. *NYT* Supplement, April 27, 1897, 4.

82. Horace Porter to E. H. Cook, May 14, 1892, Grant Monument Association Letter Book.

83. Quotation "became a fad" from *NYT*, April 26, 1897; Porter, "The Tomb of General Grant."

84. *Harper's Weekly*, May 7, 1892, 439.

85. Quotation from "Address Delivered by General Horace Porter, Upon the Occasion of Breaking Ground for the Erection of the Monument to General Grant at River Side [*sic*] Park, N.Y., April 27th, 1891," 14–15, container 4, Papers of Horace Porter.

86. Horace Porter to Bradley Martin, May 5, 1892, Grant Monument Association Letter Book.

87. Horace Porter to Fred. Phisterer, July 7, 1892, ibid.

88. Horace Porter to Col. S. V. R. Cruger, President, Department of Public Works, December 13, 1895, ibid.

89. Horace Porter to Hon. Hilary A. Herbert, April 6, 1893, ibid.

90. Horace Porter to C. M. Beach, March 21, 1896, ibid. The sarcophagi ended up costing $10,000.

91. Horace Porter to Editor, *New York World*, April 16, 1895, Grant Monument Association Letter Book.

92. Horace Porter to Julia Grant, June 26, 1893, Grant Monument Association Letter Book.

93. Thomas J. Brown, "The Monumental Legacy of Calhoun," in Fahs and Waugh, *The Memory of the Civil War in American Culture*, 130–56, reference to Rhind, 148–49.

94. *New York Herald*, April 24 and 25, 1897.

95. *NYT*, April 27, 1897; *San Francisco Chronicle*, April 26, 1897.

96. *Los Angeles Times*, April 27 and April 28, 1897. See also the coverage in *Century Magazine* 53 (April 1897): 821–47, 937–50.

97. *NYT*, April 28, 1897; Colonel John A. Cutchins, *Famous Command: The Richmond Light Infantry Blues* (Richmond, Va.: Garret and Massie, 1934), 199.

98. The medal is in the Museum of the City of New York; Kahn, "Resource Study," 1.

99. "Official Programme of the Exercises at the Dedication of the Monument and Tomb of General Ulysses S. Grant under the Direction of the Municipal Grant Monument Committee," Riverside, New York, April 27, 1897, Papers of Horace Porter, container 4, pp. 1–4. Extensive coverage was provided in *NYT*, April 25, 26, 27, 28, 29, 1897. Kahn, "Resource Study," 134–40.

100. One critic found the "upper portion to be out of scale with the massive square base" (quoted in Kahn, "Resource Study," 142–43); *NYT*, April 26, 1897, magazine supplement, 6.

101. *Harper's Weekly*, September 20, 1885, 562; *NYT*, July 24, 1885 (quotation).

102. Henry James, *The American Scene* (1907; reprint, London: Rupert Hart-Davis, 1968), quote, 145.

103. Schofield letter printed in *San Francisco Chronicle*, April 26, 1897; second quotation in Kahn, "Resource Study," 142.

104. *PUSG*, 28:412–13.

105. Kahn, "Resource Study," 3.

# Acknowledgments

I never visited a Civil War battlefield, or read a military account of the Civil War, until after I began teaching UCLA undergraduates the history of the conflict. Their eager desire to know more about why northern soldiers fought, and what exactly the "Union Cause" entailed, drove me to consider taking up an unfamiliar topic, but one that would prove immensely exciting and challenging. Writing a book on the top Union General, Ulysses S. Grant, combining history and memory seemed like a good idea at the time—and many years later, I owe a huge debt of thanks to my fellow Civil War historians whose expert advice and warm encouragement made this project well worth the time invested in it. The late John Y. Simon graciously answered my many questions regarding Grant and his world. Conversations with Brooks D. Simpson shaped and sharpened my ideas on how to proceed in my research. I am forever grateful for the friendship and shared expertise of Bill Blair, David Blight, Catherine Clinton, Steve Cushman, Alice Fahs, J. Matthew Gallman, Joe Glatthaar, Carrie Janney, Jim Marten, Jim McPherson, and Nina Silber.

The history department at UCLA provides a wonderful intellectual community, and I am indebted to Steve Aron, Ruth Bloch, Naomi Lamoreaux, Ron Mellor, Jan Reiff, and Teo Ruiz for their support. Graduate students Chris Bates, Ruth Behling, and Fiona Halloran, and undergraduate students Lisa Anderson, Nasreen El-Farra, Sandra Kim, and Michael Jackson provided valuable research assistance. Don Worth shared his knowledge of the Civil War and first-edition books with me, and Jackie Greenberg offered trenchant analysis on a manuscript draft.

Institutions must be acknowledged as well as individuals. Research at the Library of Congress, the New-York Historical Society, the New York Public Library, the General Grant Monument Association Archives, and the Henry E. Huntington Library was aided by courteous and knowledgeable staffs. My research was facilitated by timely financial assistance rendered by UCLA Research and Travel Grants, a Gilder Lehrman Fellowship, and fellowships at the Huntington Library, including a National Endowment for the Humanities grant for 2001–2. In 2001, with several presses expressing interest in this project, Gary W. Gallagher convinced me that the best place for it would be in his Civil War America series at the University of North Carolina Press. I agreed, and for his patience, his counsel, his intellectual generosity, and his unflagging enthusiasm for my project I offer my deepest gratitude. The skills and experience of the UNC Press staff, notably Editor-in-Chief David Perry and Managing Editor Ron Maner, show why the press is one of the finest in the country.

Last, but not least, I want to acknowledge my small family circle. The visits from Seattle to Brentwood of my brother, Michael Arboit; his wife, Julie Vance; and their son, Dexter enlivened and enriched our lives immeasurably. To my sons, Caleb Arboit Waugh and Joshua Charles Waugh, I dedicate this book.

# Index

Grant, Clara Rachel, 13

Grant, Elizabeth (née Chapman), 147

Grant, Ellen ("Nellie" Sartoris), 42, 147, 194, 198

Grant, Fannie (née Chaffe), 147, 273

Grant, Frederick Dent, 34, 75, 147, 156, 161, 162, 173, 193, 196–97, 198, 199, 223, 227–28, 230, 233, 287–88; and entombment of U. S. Grant, 270–71, 273, 295

Grant, Hannah Simpson, 14, 15

Grant, Ida M. (née Honore), 147, 162, 173, 193, 198

Grant, Jesse Root (father of U. S. Grant), 11–12, 14–15, 19, 31, 33, 41, 126, 202; business ventures of, 23

Grant, Jesse Root (son of U. S. Grant), 14, 147, 156, 193, 233, 273

Grant, Julia Dent, 112, 121, 156, 160, 162, 163, 164, 169, 171–73, 190, 192, 197, 198; relationship with U. S. Grant, 33–34, 78, 231; opinions of slavery, 34; children of, 34, 42; correspondence with U. S. Grant, 35, 37–38, 40; relationship with Dent family, 42; as first lady, 127, 146–47, 150, 185; and death, funeral, and entombment of U. S. Grant, 225, 227, 230, 233, 246, 270, 271, 281, 290, 294, 297; entombment of, 263, 273, 284, 293

Grant, Mary Frances, 13

Grant, Matthew, 11

Grant, Noah, 12

Grant, Orvil Lynch, 13, 41, 45

Grant, Peter, 12, 18

Grant, Rachel, 12

Grant, Samuel Simpson, 13, 41

Grant, Ulysses S.

—in Civil War, 1, 4, 50, 52, 123, 177–79; promotion to lieutenant general, 1, 2, 4, 71, 73, 76; magnanimity at Appomattox, 2, 4, 5, 209, 216, 211, 233, 237, 239, 252, 269; popular faith in leadership of, 7–8, 86; early campaigns of, 53–54, 55–56, 60; "Unconditional Surrender," 54; alleged drunkenness, 56, 62–63, 314 (n. 87); at Shiloh, 56–57, 58; criticism of, 57; rela-tionship with W. T. Sherman, 57–58, 207; military strategy of, 60–61, 73, 80–81, 321 (n. 107); campaign against Vicksburg, 61–64, 65; campaign against Chattanooga, 66–68; assessment of generalship of, 68–69, 98, 337 (n. 62); and party politics, 71–72; relationship with Lincoln, 75–76, 84, 101, 208; and Army of the Potomac, 76–77, 81–83; and northern press, 78; and Overland Campaign, 79, 83–95 passim, 322 (n. 125); campaign against Petersburg, 90–95; City Point meeting with Lincoln, 96–97; wartime portraiture, 96–97; and Appomattox campaign, 98–101; last meet-ing with Lincoln, 112

—after death: national myth surrounding, 1, 2, 4, 47, 264; funeral of, 2, 5, 216, 217, 220, 231, 232–37, 241–59 passim, 268, 343–44 (n. 10); memorialization of, 4, 6, 110, 221–22, 254–59; as symbol of Union Cause, 109, 202, 254; controversies surrounding, 204–5; as symbol of reconciliation, 216–17, 218, 253; popular response to death, 225–29, 248; white southern opinions of, 237–38, 250, 252, 253; concern over place of entombment, 263–64, 271–73, 288; as national icon, 269, 289, 300–301; decline in popularity of, 304–5, 307; modern resurgence of, 307–8

—early life, 4; nonmilitary employment, 1, 42; birthplace, 10; early failures, 10; name saga, 13, 19–20, 21; relationship with parents, 13–15, 16, 24; religiosity of, 14; affinity with horses, 15–17, 25; at West Point, 20–24; courtship of Julia Dent, 25–26; early army life, 25; in Mexican War, 26–32, 37; marriage of, 33–34; on Pacific Coast, 35–37; in Panama, 35–37; entre-preneurial ventures, 37–38; accusations of drunkenness, 38–40; resignation from army, 41; opinions of slavery, 42–43; life in Galena, 45–47

—postpresidency and later life: world tour, 2, 4, 156–61; writing of memoirs, 2, 5, 190–91, 192–93, 196–97, 199–201, 202; illness of, 5, 172–75, 194–97; death of, 5, 193, 201, 223–24, 268; proposed third term, 163–64; financial troubles, 168–69; publications (besides *Memoirs*) of, 175–76, 182, 192; popular support of, 181; relationship with Mark Twain, 181–82, 199; and Lost Cause, 186–87. See also *Personal Memoirs of U. S. Grant*

—postwar general-in-chief, 112–13; relationship with Johnson, 113, 116, 117–18; overseeing early Reconstruction policies, 113, 117; and presidential election of 1868, 120–21

—presidency, 1, 110; plagued by corruption, 2, 4, 126–27, 141, 143–44, 145, 148, 151; 1868 election of, 2, 122, 124; Reconstruction policies, 4, 6, 107–8, 110, 111, 122, 128, 138–42, 148; popular stereotype of, 104; caricatures of, 104, 105, 325 (n. 3); popular opinions of, 106, 119, 152; compared with Lincoln, 112, 118; Indian policy, 124, 128, 132–35; inauguration of, 124–25, 133; accusations of drunkenness, 127; accusations of anti-Semitism, 127–28, 206; and national progress, 128–30; and economic issues, 131; and conservation acts, 132; foreign policy, 135–38; nomination for second term, 142–43; and national holidays, 184. See also Reconstruction

—scholarship: centrality of in Civil War history and memory, 4, 307, 310–11 (n. 15); histories and biographies of, 5, 47, 50, 106–7, 109–12, 152–53; generalship, 188, 190, 204; controversies attributed to, 189–90

Grant, Ulysses S., Jr. ("Buck"), 37, 147, 156, 165, 193, 233, 273

Grant, Virginia Paine (Corbin), 13, 131

Grant, William, 55

*Grant: A Biography*, 109

Grant Fund, 275–76

Grant Memorial, 268, 270. *See also* Grant Monument (New York)

Grant Monument (Chicago), 278

Grant Monument (New York), 262, 264, 266, 275, 351 (n. 2); as symbol of reconciliation, 269, 296, 300; fundraising efforts for, 275–77, 289–90, 291; design of, 282–84; construction of, 285–90, 292–95; cornerstone ceremony, 290–91; dedication of, 295–99

Grant Monument (Philadelphia), 278

Grant Monument Association, 262, 274, 277, 279, 281, 282, 285–86, 288, 291, 304–5

Grant's Tomb, 5, 262, 263, 299, 303, 305, 308; neglect of, 5, 263–64, 265, 301, 304; as site of national commemoration, 264, 267, 296, renovation of, 307. *See also* Grant Monument (New York)

Great Britain, Grant administration's relations with, 136–37

Greeley, Horace, 78, 143, 145

Greener, Richard Theodore, 275, 281, 285, 286

*The Growth of the American Republic*, 106

Guillaume, Louis, 100, 101

Halleck, Henry W., 56, 57, 61, 72, 77, 78, 79, 92, 170, 177

Halsey, Thomas J., 86

Hamer, Thomas R., 17, 19

*Hamilton Fish: The Inner History of the Grant Administration*, 106, 305

Hancock, Winfield Scott, 22, 220, 227–29, 230, 235–36, 241, 242–43, 245

Harding, Warren G., 50, 222

Hardscrabble, 44, 45; mythology surrounding, 46

Harlem Heights, 273

*Harper's New Monthly Magazine*, 209

*Harper's Weekly*, 55, 69, 70, 78, 86, 94, 104, 105, 129, 142, 148, 277, 290, 299

Harrison, Benjamin, 290, 291

Harrison, William Henry, 46

Harvard University, 147

Hawkins, Albert, 242

Hayes, Rutherford B., 111, 151, 268, 276, 280, 281

Hesseltine, William B., 47, 106–7

Hill, Daniel H., 22, 237

ship with Grant, 50, 53, 62, 66, 68, 69–71, 73, 75–76, 84, 86, 90, 10, 208; memorialization of, 51, 221–22, 223, 254; Reconstruction policy of, 96–97, 113; Second Inaugural Address, 113; and Indian policy, 133; and African Americans, 137, 140; funeral of, 220; as representative figure of Civil War, 304, 306

Lincoln, Robert Todd, 258

Lincoln Memorial (Springfield, Ill.), 274, 282

Lincoln Memorial (Washington, D.C.), 51

Logan, John A., 77, 163, 242, 280

*London Standard*, 189

Long Branch, 146

Longstreet, James, 22, 25, 33, 42, 85, 126, 298

Lookout Mountain (Chattanooga), 66; Union capture of, 67

*Los Angeles Times*, 297

Lossing, Benson J., 190

Lost Cause, 6, 203–4, 219, 256, 304; influence of, 108, 186–87, 189, 257, 307; definition of, 185–86; rejection of, 191

*The Lost Cause*, 189

Lyman, Theodore, 10, 81

Maine unit: 16th Infantry Regiment, 81

Manifest Destiny, 26

Marryat, Frederick, 22

Marx, Groucho, 265–66, 303

Massachusetts units: 56th Infantry Regiment, 81; 9th Artillery, 82; 1st Infantry Regiment, 247

Matrau, Henry, 82

Maury, Dabney H., 187

Maximilian, Archduke Ferdinand (Maximilian I, emperor of Mexico), 117

McAllister, Robert, 81, 90

McClellan, George B., 21, 71, 76, 81, 83, 220; in Mexican-American War, 29; and 1864 presidential election, 94, 95

McEnery, Samuel D., 225

McFeely, Mary Drake, 211

McFeely, William, 5, 39, 47, 66, 68, 109, 121, 197, 211

McKinley, William, 287, 297–98

McLaws, Lafayette, 22

McLean, Wilmer, 98, 101

McPherson, James B., 77, 191, 206

McPherson, James M., 39, 88

McQueeny, Henry, 198

Meade, George G., 66, 74, 76, 77, 79, 80, 81, 83, 84, 177

Medill, Joseph, 57

Meiji (emperor of Japan), 161, 162

Mellins, Thomas, 272

Melville, Herman, 10, 98

Memorial Day, 255, 262, 293

Memory, national, 2, 5, 219, 220, 248–50; as analytical theme, 2, 3, 6, 205, 352 (n. 12), 352–53 (n. 15)

Memphis, capture of, 60; 1866 riots in, 115

Merritt, Stephen, 229

Metropolitan Museum of Art (New York), 272

Mexican-American War, 1, 10, 26, 46, 58, 203; battles of, 27–29; border disputes leading to, 27; Grant's descriptions of, 28; popularity of, 28; lands acquired by United States as a result of victory in, 28, 30; death from disease in, 29, 30; U.S. battlefield deaths in, 30; impact of on Grant, 31

Mexican Central Railroad, 165

Mexico City, campaign against, 29

*Military History of Ulysses S. Grant*, 189

Milliken's Bend, battle of, 73

Miltmore, Ira, 64

Missionary Ridge (Chattanooga), 66; Union attack on, 67, 71

*Mr. Deeds Goes to Town*, 305

Mitchell, Margaret, 210

Mitchell, Reid, 238

Monterrey, capture of, 28

Moody, Dwight, 232

Morgan, J. P., 274

Morgan, Matt, 104

Morningside Heights, 262

Morrill Education Act (1862), 130

Mount McGregor, 173, 197, 198, 199, 223, 227, 273; as national shrine, 200

Mugwumps, 257. *See also* Liberal Republican Party

Municipal Grant Monument Committee, 296

Napoleon III (emperor of France), 117

Nashville: capture of, 60; battle of (1864), 96

Nast, Thomas, 69, 70, 104, 123, 142, 148

Nationalism, 2, 3, 70, 218, 220, 232, 259

National Park Service, 262–63

National Portrait Gallery (Washington, D.C.), 97

National Road (Mexico), 29

Native Americans, 110, 121, 147, 226; artistic portrayals of, 22; negative impressions of, 106; U.S. policies affecting, 132–35; U.S. wars against, 135, 148

Neely, Mark E., Jr., 69

Neff, John, 255

Nevins, Allan, 47, 50, 106, 305

New Jersey unit: 11th Infantry Regiment, 86

Newman, J. P., 230–31, 243, 273, 298

New Orleans: capture of, 60; 1866 riots in, 115

New South, 256–57

New York City: Grant family's life in, 2, 164–65; Grant's funeral procession in, 2, 241, 242–46, 248; Grant's early visits to, 21; tomb site in, 272, 277, 279–80

*New York Herald*, 57, 68, 71, 78, 99, 156, 173, 222, 274, 296

New York Monument Committee, 276–77

*New York Post*, 277

*New York Sun*, 126, 148, 162, 173, 222

*New York Times*, 57, 73, 78, 79, 98, 142, 164, 173, 209, 223, 231, 246, 258, 265, 271, 273, 276, 299, 304, 305

*New York Times Magazine*, 265

*New York Tribune*, 57, 71, 104, 121, 143, 149, 152, 173, 194, 209, 233, 239, 274, 276

New York unit: 165th Infantry Regiment, 63

*New York World*, 62, 68, 92, 104, 126, 173, 197, 274, 276, 277, 294

*North American Review*, 268

North Anna River, battle of, 86

*Ohio* (steamship), 35

Ohio unit: 83rd Infantry Regiment, 64

Olmsted, Frederick Law, 273–74

Overland Campaign, 73, 76, 83–95 passim, 176, 179–80, 189, 205

Pacific Railroad Act (1862), 130

Paducah, Ky., occupation of, 53

Palo Alto, battle of, 27

Panic, financial: of 1837, 19; of 1857, 44; of 1873, 147–48

*Papers of Ulysses S. Grant*, 109, 211, 307

Parker, Ely S., 99, 134

Parrington, Vernon L., 105

*Patriotic Gore*, 210

Patterson, James, 174–75

Pedro I (Dom Pedro, emperor of Brazil), 128, 129

Pemberton, John C., 61, 63, 64

Perret, Geoffrey, 164

Pershing, John J., 235

*The Personal Memoirs of U. S. Grant*, 2, 5, 99, 168, 190–91, 192–93, 196–97, 304; evaluation of, 201–8; reviews of, 208–10, 211; sale of, 210; and theme of reconciliation, 211–13, 239–40

Petersburg: siege of, 1–2, 90, 266; operations against, 89, 90–91, 93, 95; fall of, 98

*Philadelphia Daily Evening Bulletin*, 79, 87

Pickett's Charge, 8

Piehler, G. Kurt, 285

Pierce, Franklin, 106

Pierrepont, Edwards, 158

Pitkin, Thomas, 173, 181

*Pittsburg Christian Advocate*, 231

Pittsburg Landing, 56, 57

Polk, James K., 26, 27, 30–31

Pollard, Edward A., 187, 189

Poore, Ben Perley, 239

Pope, John, 22

Porter, David Dixon, 63, 96

Porter, Elsie, 171

Porter, Horace, 67, 146, 171, 178, 190, 193, 230, 242, 273, 298, 300; and construction of Grant Monument, 285–91, 292–95

Seymour, Horatio, 120, 123, 268
Sharecropping, 140
Shenandoah Valley, 83; campaigns waged in, 2, 91, 92, 95; in Confederate strategy, 74
Sheridan, Philip H., 2, 77, 91, 92, 95, 121, 135, 149, 162, 177, 205, 206; and Grant's funeral and entombment, 228, 236, 242, 245–46, 280
Sherman, John, 60–61, 297
Sherman, William T., 2, 10, 60, 83, 95, 96, 117, 119, 121, 235, 181, 188, 200, 205, 206–7, 250, 273, 280, 281; at West Point, 21; at Shiloh, 56–57; relationship with Grant, 57–58, 77; accusations of insanity, 58; as army commander, 60–61, 66; and campaign against Vicksburg, 63; and campaign against Chattanooga, 67; and campaign against Atlanta, 68, 79, 80, 91, 92, 94–95, 207; and march through Georgia, 96; and Grant's funeral, 220, 230, 236, 242, 245–46
Shiloh, battle of, 1, 39–40, 56–57, 58, 60, 68, 171, 176, 204, 205, 266
Shrady, George, 172, 174, 180, 181, 192, 194–96, 198
Shrady, Henry Merwin, 51
Sickles, Daniel E., 181, 243, 298
Sigel, Franz, 80, 297
Silber, Nina, 218, 238
Simon, John Y., 25, 38, 109, 120, 142, 160, 189
Simpson, Brooks D., 5, 47, 91, 109, 111
Simpson, Hannah, 13; family of, 17. See also Grant, Hannah Simpson
Simpson, John, 13
Simpson, Sarah, 13
Sioux War, 135
Slavery, expansion of, 27, 30–31, 150, 203; abolition of; as cause of Civil War, 170, 180, 259; and Union Cause, 191, 212, 227, 238, 254. See also Constitution, U.S., amendments to
Small, Abner, 81
Smith, Jean Edward, 88, 109, 111, 131, 133
Smith, Roswell, 175
Smithsonian Institution, 230

Society of the Army of the Cumberland, 229, 250
Society of the Army of the Ohio, 250
Society of the Army of the Potomac, 229, 250
Society of the Army of the Tennessee, 229, 250, 280
Soldiers' and Sailors' Memorial Arch (Brooklyn), 283
Soldiers' and Sailors' Monument (Boston), 282
Soldiers' and Sailors' Monument (Philadelphia), 295
Soldiers' and Sailors' Monument (Syracuse, N.Y.), 295
Soldiers' Home Cemetery (Washington, D.C.), 279–80
Southern Bivouac, 238
Southern Historical Society Papers, 170, 186, 187, 209–10
Spain, Grant administration's relations with, 137–38
Specie Resumption Act (1875), 131
Spotsylvania, battle of, 84–86, 177, 266
The Standard, 231
Stanford, Mrs. Leland, 181
Stanton, Edwin M., 62, 66, 68, 76, 79, 86, 90, 95, 112, 117, 177, 208
Statue of Liberty, 262, 272
Stein, Gertrude, 210
Stein Manufacturing Company, 229
Stephens, Alexander H., 122, 124, 239
Stern, Robert, 272, 284
Stewart, Alexander T., 125, 126
Stoddard, William O., 152
Stonewall Brigade, 241
Stonewall Brigade Band, 297
Strong, George Templeton, 118–19
Strong, Josiah, 295–96
Stuyvesant, Rutherford, 276
Sumner, Charles, 114, 136, 143
Swinton, William, 189–90

Tammany Hall, 271
Tammany Society, 218

Tappen, Frederick D., 288

Taylor, Richard, 73

Taylor, Zachary, 27, 29, 31, 58, 203; as national hero, 28

Tenure of Office Act (1867), 117, 118

Texas, annexation of, 26

Thomas, George H., 22, 66, 91, 207

Thompson, Launt, 268–70

Thulstrup, Thure de, 290

Thurber, James, 40

Tierney, John, 265–66

Tilden, Samuel J., 111, 151

Tilton, Theodore, 144

Timber Culture Act (1873), 132

Tocqueville, Alexis de, 153

Tod, George, 12

Treaty of Guadalupe Hidalgo, 30, 35

Treaty of Washington, 137

Trollope, Anthony, 158

Twain, Mark (Samuel Langhorne Clemens), 10, 181, 192, 193, 198, 200, 206, 209, 229–30, 281

Tyrell, Harrison, 193, 196, 198–99

*Ulysses S. Grant: A Bibliography*, 5–6

Ulysses S. Grant Memorial (Washington, D.C.), 50, 51

*Ulysses S. Grant, Politician*, 47, 106–7

Union Cause, 3, 4, 92, 124, 168, 184, 188, 190, 259, 303; diminished importance of, 6, 238, 307; Grant as symbol of, 51; memory of, 185, 219; in *Personal Memoirs*, 191, 201–2, 211, 212; and reconciliation, 254, 256

*The Union Image*, 69

Union League Club, 286

Union of Locomotive Engineers, 226

Union Pacific Railroad, 144

United American Mechanics, 226

United German Singing Societies of New York, 229

United Press, 173

U.S. Army of Observation, 27

United States Christian Commission, 231

United States Colored Troops (USCT), 72; at Petersburg, 91–92

United States Corps of Cadets, 228

United States Military Academy. *See* West Point

United States units: 4th Infantry Regiment, 25, 27, 29, 33, 35, 36, 38; 22nd Infantry Regiment, 243

U. S. Grant Hotel (San Diego), 147

Van Brunt, Henry, 268

Vanderbilt, Cornelius, II, 274

Vanderbilt, William H., 198, 230

Vaux, Calvert, 273–74

Veracruz, capture of, 29

Veterans: Union, 182, 184, 229, 254–56, 299; reunions of, 184; Confederate, 253, 297. *See also* Grand Army of the Republic

Vicksburg, 1, 176, 205, 206, 223; campaign against, 60, 61–64, 71, 266; siege of, 64; significance of, 66, 68; battlefield at, 184, 268

Victoria I (queen of England), 158, 227

Vietnam War, 7

Vincent, John Heyl, 232

Virginia units: 1st Infantry Regiment, 241; Richmond Howitzers, 252; Richmond Light Infantry Blues, 297

*Virginius* affair, 137–38

*Volunteer Firemen of New York*, 229

Wade, Benjamin, 114

Wagner, Richard, 159

Wainwright, Charles S., 81

Wallace, Lew, 204, 297

Ward, Ferdinand, 165, 168

War of 1812, 24

*War of the Rebellion: A Compilation of the Official Records of the Union and Confederate Armies*, 169–70

Warren, Gouverneur K., 207–8

Warren, Robert Penn, 106

Washburn, Cadwallader C., 62

Washburne, Elihu, 46, 53, 69, 71, 124, 126, 161

Washington, D.C., as proposed site for Grant's tomb, 237, 277, 279–80, 281